THE
MARK
OF THE
NEW WORLD ORDER

TERRY L. COOK

[w] *Whitaker House*

All Scripture quotations are from the *King James Version* (KJV) of the Bible.

THE MARK OF THE NEW WORLD ORDER

Terry L. Cook
Second Coming Ministries
61535 S. Highway 97
Unit 9, Suite 288
Bend, OR 97702

ISBN: 0-88368-466-7
Printed in the United States of America
Copyright © 1996 by Terry L. Cook
Second Printing

Whitaker House
30 Hunt Valley Circle
New Kensington, PA 15068

Library of Congress Cataloging-in-Publication Data

Cook, Terry L.
    The mark of the new world order / Terry L. Cook.
        p.   cm.
    ISBN 0-88368-466-7 (trade paper : alk. paper)
    1. Bible—Prophecies—International organization. 2. Beast of the
Apocalypse—Miscellanea. 3. Six hundred and sixty-six (The number)
in the Bible—Miscellanea. 4. Identification numbers, Personal—
Miscellanea. 5. Communication—International cooperation—
Miscellanea.   I. Title.
[BS649.I56C66 1997]
323.44'8—dc21   97-108

2 3 4 5 6 7 8 9 10 11 12 / 06 05 04 03 02 01 00 99 98 97

Contents

Dedication

First and foremost, this book is dedicated to my Lord and Savior, Jesus Christ, without whose blessings, insight, and understanding of His Holy Scriptures it simply would not have been possible.

Second, this book is dedicated to my dear deceased mother, Bertha Cook, a fine fundamentalist Christian woman who walked as closely with Jesus Christ as anyone could ever hope.

Third, it is dedicated to my lovely wife, Kathy, whose support, patience, and understanding made it all possible.

And last, but certainly not least, this book would not have been possible without the help of many fine Christian friends and consultants whose technical advice, expertise in various fields, inspiration, and outright financial assistance literally made it all happen and come together. Therefore, I'd like to take this opportunity to thank ever so sincerely the following people who helped me bring this three-year project to fruition:

Annette Bradley, Peter Lalonde, Dr. Ray Brubaker, Dr. Jack Van Impe, Dr. Hal Lindsey, Don McAlvany, Charles Coppes, and many others too numerous to mention.

Thank you and God bless you for all your help and support!

About the Author

Terry L. Cook is a fundamentalist Christian researcher and retired Los Angeles Deputy Sheriff, as well as a former State of California fraud investigator/Deputy Real Estate Commissioner. He holds A.A., A.S., B.A. & B.S. degrees. He also holds California State teaching credentials in a variety of subjects and has completed some postgraduate study in Theology. He is a California-licensed real estate broker and an FAA-licensed airline transport jet pilot (commercial) and flight instructor.

For the past six years, Mr. Cook, who is an ordained minister of the gospel, has been investigating current events as they relate to the fulfillment of "last days" or "end times" Bible prophecies, with an emphasis on biometric identification technology, including smart cards and biochip transponder implants. He is accepted widely as an authority in the field. He is much in demand as a speaker in large churches and other lecture forums, including appearances and interviews on radio and television. If your organization is interested in bringing him to your area, you may contact **Second Coming Ministries at 61535 S. Highway 97, Unit 9, Ste. 288, Bend, OR 97702.**

In addition to his speaking ministry, Mr. Cook has produced several educational, informative videos and books on the subject, containing vital documentation of material which heretofore has been difficult—if not impossible—to obtain. Presently, he is making available an excellent package of information on implantable biochip technology and how it relates to the New World Order plan to enslave and control us.

Terry Cook is a man called by God for this particular mission at this particular time . . . to educate and alert the Church, so they won't be caught sleeping or unaware in these last days and overtaken as by a "thief in the night." Remember the admonition in the Word of God, "I would not have you ignorant." Mr. Cook's desire is that you would not be "ignorant" of what is going on around us and the importance of the message it foretells.

Mr. Cook hopes to convey to everyone who reads this book that Jesus is coming soon, and we need to get serious about God and get ready for what's coming!

Foreword

The prophecy of the Mark of the Beast is one of the most fascinating prophecies in the Bible. It is also one of the best known, clearest, and most easily understood. The thirteenth chapter of the Book of Revelation tells us simply that in the last days no one will be able to buy or sell anything unless they receive a mark in their right hand or forehead. That is a very easy statement to understand. It's not full of imagery, and it doesn't leave a lot of room for interpretation. Either it happens. . .or it does not.

That makes this prophecy one of the most important in the Bible because of its power to show skeptics just how amazing Bible prophecy really is. In fact, in our ministry at *This Week in Bible Prophecy,* we are convinced that it is the most powerful witnessing tool in our prophetic arsenal.

However, in their rush to emphasize the dramatic evidence we see for the potential fulfillment of this prophecy in our day, many unnecessarily have tried to over-sensationalize the prophecy. This has led to countless rumors and foolish speculations. The fact of the matter is that the prophecy is sensational enough, all by itself. What is critical is that we focus on solidly documenting how—for the first time in history—this clear and well-known prophecy potentially could be fulfilled in this generation.

That is why I have appreciated the work of Terry Cook. This book is the culmination of years of solid research into this subject and contains some of the most up-to-date and startling revelations on this topic that are available. If you sit back with this book and a highlighter, I promise that after you have completed it, you will be far more ready to share your faith than you can imagine. And if you are not yet convinced of the accuracy of the Bible and its prophecies, I am sure you will find yourself challenged as you never have been before!

Peter Lalonde
This Week in Bible Prophecy

The Mark of the New World Order:
An Overview

Clichés. . .clichés. . .clichés! Some people speak in nothing else, but sometime they seem to serve better than anything else to illustrate a point or make a difficult message more easily understood. I imagine throughout this book I'll probably use my share. . .and perhaps more. For example, there's the old "love and marriage. . .you can't have one without the other" cliché. It makes the point exactly that I wish to convey when telling you about the thrust of this book. Just substitute the words "surveillance and control" for the words "love and marriage," and you'll get the appropriate image.

The world is in the process of great shaking, and not just physically (although in fulfillment of prophecy we can expect much more of that than we presently are experiencing). We are being shaken together in order to "even out the playing field," as it were, [see, there's another of those clichés]—both socially and economically. The only way to accomplish that is if each nation surrenders its individual sovereignty to the leadership of a world governing body or leader, who in turn will see to it that all nations will capitulate, either voluntarily or by force, and follow that leader. Naturally, all of this will be "for our own good and/or convenience." What will finally "shake out" will be that about which we have heard so much lately, the *New World Order* (or some other agreed-upon name with the same goals and methods).

Many nations would benefit greatly from this "evening out" of the playing field; which, of course, would be at the expense of many others—for them it will cost *everything*—economy, military, health, education, natural resources, self-rule, in other words, all personal liberty/freedom and possessions.

However, many are not deceived by the old line that they are "doing it for our own good" and are refusing to "roll over and play dead." Now, exactly what can you do about all these rabble-rousers and troublemakers? The only way for such a turnover of power to occur successfully is if everyone complies and cooperates. Now, the "powers that be" have been planning this scenario for centuries and longer, and now that the plan is about to see fruition, they are not going to look too kindly upon dissenters or uncooperative-types. (In a speech, Rockefeller stated that there was too little time left to get the plan accomplished gradually because the fundamentalists were waking up, so they are stepping up their speed.)

The first thing they must accomplish is to remove as many as possible of our Constitutionally-protected rights and freedoms, legislatively and judicially, in effect making all dissenters "outlaws." Once they have succeeded in declaring their opposition to be the "bad guys," then they have all the power of the police, military, and judiciary behind them. You either will join the system or oppose it . . .of course, if you refuse to join, you are automatically in opposition and one of the above-described rabble-rousers and troublemakers.

Well, we've come full circle now, back to where I started above. The only way those who enforce the new regulations (for lack of a better word) will be able to achieve their goal of bringing everyone into the New World Order is through . . .no, not "love and marriage". . .through "surveillance and control." You "can't have one without the other!" They can't control you if they can't find you and keep track of your movements, activities, communications, purchases, et al. In other words, there must be a grand and global scheme for the *surveillance* of everyone before you can hope to *control* everyone.

An article by Richard Falk states, "It is evident that the new world order as conceived in Washington is about control and surveillance,....." Now, lest you be misled, do not mistake Mr. Falk for a right-wing conservative; on the contrary, he believes that their motives are anything but "pure" toward equality in the New World Order. In fact, he continues " . . .not about values or a better life for the peoples of the world." He believes the wealthy nations are using their technology as an advantage to keep the poorer nations from being a threat to them.

In this book there will be a minimum of "soapbox" tirades; and the information will be current and as up to date as I can make it . . . however, technology is expanding so fast, and news of eroding liberties is coming in on a daily basis, that it has been very difficult to find a "cutting off" place, so that I actually could begin putting the words on the paper. Normally, a book of this size and technical nature would take at least 18 to 24 months to get ready for the printer, but because information is changing so quickly, I have put a nearly impossible turnaround time on the production of this manuscript, as the material needs to get into the hands of the public with all possible haste.

Although the major thrust of *The Mark of the New World Order* is identification and tracking systems, a book such as this would be incomplete without a certain amount of foundation first being laid. Therefore, I will cover a number of subjects in addition to tracking technology (which is my personal specialty).

Some people find this subject matter to be "science fiction," some consider it fulfillment of Bible prophecy, and still others consider it the raving of some lunatic who sees a conspiracy under every rock; but the ones who study it carefully see it as the next logical step toward establishing the New World Order. Most all of the people, however, are somewhat staggered by the pervasiveness of the proposed systems, and its seeming inevitability lurking just on the horizon. In other words, they are experiencing what has come to be known as "future shock." So I will touch on future shock and its effect on the masses, as well as the individual.

I will address the New World Order. . .what is it? When is it? How will it take over? Who's in charge? Where did the idea originate and how old is this plan for a one-world government?

Other subjects will include loss of privacy and electronic bondage, the United Nations Resolution 666, the new constitution, the Illuminati, the report from Iron Mountain, computerizing people into the "super information highway" via fiber optics, biometrics (including social security), bar coding, devices to control the highway systems, the GPS (Global Positioning System), the cashless society. . . let's pause here for a minute. There are other subjects to mention, but I want to address this subject before I proceed, because we are so far down the road toward a cashless society. . . further than most of us recognize!

This is one of the first few steps that must be enacted to get us ready for biochip implants, and it is one of those "we're doing it for your own good" type of actions. Now, if studied fairly, without consideration for the prophetic implications, it really is for our own good; however, the end result of the drawbacks far outweighs any temporary convenience or good it will accomplish. Some of the good things about which you will be hearing more and more as the time draws closer and closer are: it will stop theft, robberies, and muggings; it will stop international drug dealing; it will stop income tax "cheaters;" it will stop "deadbeat dads;" it will give you access to your funds (or credits) anywhere; you won't have to carry money to shop or travel— just your identity card; your earnings could be deposited directly into your account; you could pay bills at home by PC (your personal computer); etc., etc., etc. Think of the convenience and safety!

But what are those drawbacks I mentioned? Well, to start with, everything you have, owe, or own is in a machine (including your health records, family history, religious affiliations, job history, credit history, political leanings, etc.—all this comes later, but not as much later as you might imagine), which gives everybody with the authorization all the information about your personal business. . .no more privacy —except from you; it is not intended for the holder to have access to the information on the card. The identification system (SMART Cards, MARC Cards, or whatever—again, for your own protection) must be tied unalterably to you in order to prevent theft of the card and fraudulent use thereof. The card must be used in conjunction with some other source of positive identification, such as retina scan, fingerprint match, or right hand match. Can you already see the direction this path is taking you? What if your card were lost or stolen? Well, we can fix that! Just this tiny little biochip no bigger than a grain of rice (and maybe smaller as technology progresses) can be slipped under your skin and give you lifetime access to everything the New World Order will afford its happy members.

This is the first time in history when the technology has been available to fulfill the prophecy in Revelation 13:16-18, which tells us that no one can buy or sell without the mark in their right hand or forehead. Naturally, the manufacturers of this technology try to assure us that it wasn't designed for that purpose, but even as they speak, plans are being discussed to implant the "difficult" cases, i.e. the prison population, runaway teens, the elderly who have a tendency to wander off and become lost, and even implanting babies before they leave the hospital to put an end to kidnapping and child-stealing. Now, doesn't that sound like a really GOOD thing? (Excuse me for being facetious!) Well, don't assume it never will happen. At the moment, the method is used widely in pet identification and agricultural animals; but just recently there were reports of tracking and punishing poachers of salmon with implants, and the government ruled that all surgically implanted body parts will henceforth contain a biochip (of course, that's also for your good, as it retains the information about its manufacturer, your surgeon, how and why it was implanted, etc.), and breast implants are some of the first to be manufactured with the biochip. Another recent use of radio transponder identification (biochips) was in permanently riveted vinyl bracelets applied to over 50,000 Haitian and Cuban refugees at the Guantanamo Bay U.S. military base. (Now they are investigating the possibility of producing them with a metal strip in the band, as it seems that some people resent this type of "numbering" and have been trying to remove them.) Since children's wrists are too small, they are applied to the child's ankle.

Have you noticed lately how everything on television is smart? Pay close attention to the current rash of commercials—AT&T actually is calling theirs the Smart Card, but the term smart is used in so many different advertisements that it will amaze you, once you start taking notice of the use of that one word. That's because they want you to become so acquainted with the term (read that "desensitized") it will seem like second nature to you. I'll be telling you how a SMART card is constructed, what its features are, and its intended purpose in this unstoppable chain of events. The credit card companies and banks already are offering (just this month in Bank of America) to exchange —free of charge, mind you—your old credit card with a brand new one with your digitized photo on the front. Of course, they don't tell you what else will be contained (or have the capability to be contained) on this fancy new card.

There also will be chapters in *The Mark of the New World Order* on the new ISO-9000 international labeling requirements, the MARC military identification card, and the national and/or state identification cards (with special attention to California's latest innovations).

Of course, one of the the largest chapters will discuss biochip technology—its origination, manufacture, current uses, proposed uses, and unlimited possible future uses.

Finally, I will summarize these facts, and introduce the prophetic connections as described in the Bible. I hope by reading this book you will be informed and awakened from your slumber—if, indeed, you have been blissfully, but ignorantly, slumbering along, enjoying all this new "Star Trek" technology without being cognizant of the dire consequences.

—Terry L. Cook

THE COVERT MEANING OF THIS OCCULTIC SYMBOL IS:

ANNUIT: ANNOUNCING
COEPTIS: THE BIRTH OF
NOVUS: THE NEW
SECLORUM: WORLD WITHOUT GOD
ORDO: ORDER
**Under the ALL-SEEING EYE of
the Antichrist!**

CHAPTER ONE

Future Shock is Here!

Don't reach for your wallet at the checkout counter. After your items have been priced (or "scanned"), totaled, and bagged, simply *pass your RIGHT HAND* over the scanner and the amount will be deducted from your bank account.

Impossible? The plot of a science fiction novel? Hardly! The technology to accomplish such futuristic feats is already here, and nearly every type of store is using either a stationary or hand-held laser scanner to read the bar codes and enter your purchases into the computer. Long gone are the days of the old-fashioned cash register.

"But just suggest something like an implant in human beings and the social outcry is tremendous," says Tim Willard, executive officer of the World Future Society, a Washington, D.C.-based organization that claims 27,000 members worldwide, including *Future Shock* author Alvin Toffler. "While people over the years have grown accustomed to artificial body parts, there is definitely a strong aversion to things being implanted. It's the *'BIG BROTHER is watching'* syndrome. People would be afraid that all of their thoughts and movements were being monitored. It wouldn't matter if the technology were there or not. People would still worry."

. . . But wait, we're getting a bit ahead of ourselves here. First we need to define the term *future shock* and how it came into our vocabulary. According to *Webster's New Collegiate Dictionary,* Ninth Edition, *future shock* is defined as:

> The physical and psychological distress suffered by one who is unable to cope with the rapidity of social and technological changes.

As words in the dictionary go, this one is of fairly recent origin. The dictionary tells us that it first came into common usage about 1970. I don't know if Toffler can be credited with originating the term, but using it as the title of his book certainly promulgated its wide acceptance, and the definition is one with which most people of this decade are familiar to at least some degree.

Future shock has come to be considered a negative term, and it bridges the age gap from children (who feel they are being propelled into the future before they are ready, and that adults have pretty much messed it up for them anyway) to senior citizens (who are befuddled by all this electronic/computer technology and long for the "good old days.") It also bridges all areas of life, from banking, economics, and industry to education, social sciences, art, music, communications, databases, *et al.* We are being hurled ever forward by knowledge that is expanding exponentially.

And the most distressing symptom of future shock is the dehuman-izing feeling we experience that we are all becoming nothing more than numbers. . .and in fact, that is the truth. The name of the game is surveillance and control. With the world shrinking because of travel and communication technology and the pressure by the "powers that be" to merge us all into a one-world government (spell that, New World Order), the only way to "organize" us and keep track of us (for our own good, of course), is to give us all a single identification method that can be recognized worldwide. And if you think that's not where we are headed, you're just kidding yourself.

So, future shock is real. . .it's just not very much in the *future* any-more—future shock is here. . .future shock is now! Perhaps "Big Brother" wasn't watching us by the year *1984,* as Orwell's book title speculates, but he wasn't all that far off target. The technology is here now via fiber optics, satellites, and other modern marvels for Big Brother to sit on the Internet Information Highway, right in your living room. The only difference is that during the time from 1984 to 1994, we have been brainwashed into believing that this is a wonderful thing, so Big Brother didn't have to force his way in, as Orwell postulated, but he is with us by our own invitation.

Biochip-RFID Technology

The *very IDEA* of implanting *even our pets* with identifying micro-chip transponders is a concept that for years was approached very slowly. "We wanted to make sure it's right for the animals, and that the *community is willing to accept* this new technology [emphasis added]," said Diane Allevato, director of the Novato, California, animal shelter. Now, however, such high-tech "tagging" is on "fast-forward" since people have grown accustomed—by successful *conditioning,*—to what once was considered offensive technology. For example, if people are now willing to have such devices injected into their pets, why would they not put them into their own bodies? Or, to soften the blow just a little, into old folks who wander away from home, children (to prevent kidnapping), prison inmates, and runaway teens, because all that would be for the good of society as a whole . . . it's always for your own good! Once you have edged your way into accepting these logical implant choices, it's no great leap to accept the fact that a nonremovable implant would be terribly convenient and much safer for us than carrying around cards for all our needs (economic, health, passports, travel, etc.)—cards that could be lost or stolen.

Biochip the Size of a Grain of Rice

For household pets, the transponder chip implant is about the size of a grain of rice. It is permanently imprinted with an identifying number that corresponds to the name, address, and phone number of the pet's owner. This information pops up on a viewing screen when the animal is scanned externally (up to three ± inches from the skin) by the antenna of a scanner wand.

The Novato, California, animal shelter mentioned earlier was the first shelter in the country to use the biochips. One lady phoned them to say she felt the implants were "unnatural and weird." "And there is no doubt about it, injecting an animal with such a chip is a pretty unnatural thing to do," Allevato said. "But it's also unnatural, obscene really, that about 15 million stray animals are destroyed in this country each year because their owners cannot be found," she continued.

As of the writing of this manuscript, animal implants are no longer considered "unnatural and weird." In fact, the system is in common usage worldwide, and the "service" is readily available to pet owners at many veterinarians and animal hospitals in most major cities. In addition, implant identification has gone from being *advocated* to being *mandated* by the animal control departments of most metropolitan areas.

The transponder chips being implanted into most animals today are manufactured by four major companies: American Veterinary ID (AVID) of Norco, California; Infopet Corporation of Minnesota; Hughes Aircraft in southern California, and Texas Instruments of Attleboro, Massachusetts.

Originally, Destron IDI Corporation of Boulder, Colorado, began the concept, but now they serve primarily as a research and development company for both Hughes and Texas Instruments, through various joint ventures.

RFID Implants

Many more companies now have entered the RFID manufacturing field, but few have decided to enter the implantable biochip field. As yet, this is a fairly exclusive technology. It seems, however, that RFID identification has become the wave of the future for both animate and inanimate object identification.

Biochip usage now has surpassed the "personal pet" stage and is being used in many different areas of farming, ranching, racing, and wildlife identification and monitoring. In conjunction with computer technology, RFID biochips are used to track and monitor the health histories, blood lines, etc. of various farm animals, race horses, breeding stock, and more.

In the ranching business, it eliminates the need for branding your cattle and serves as a deterrent to rustlers. It is used to identify and track the health and performance of prize breeding stock.

In the modern dairy business, good ole' Bossie can come into the barn, passing under a scanner, be directed to her own personal stall, and find her own specially prepared diet in place, just awaiting her arrival—all based upon her identification combined with the computer-stored information about what the handlers want her to eat. Her health records, milk production, and other pertinent factors are all considered, and the optimum diet assigned to her.

Wildlife has been tagged and tracked manually/visually for many years, but now it is possible to track even life as small as a honey bee by attaching RFID to its back. Of course, this is a real stroke of genius, according to the ecologists, for monitoring all types of wildlife, especially the endangered species.

According to Destron Director Jim Seiler, implantable RFID biochips are being used even to track fish. In some fishery applications, salmon are injected with these biochips, then scanned and tracked as they pass through specially equipped dam sites "to assure environmentalists that they are not being chewed up in the dam's power turbines," Seiler said.

[NOTE: At the writing of this manuscript, reports were coming out of Europe that poachers were being caught and fined because the biochip implants in the fish led the authorities to the poacher. The implications of this announcement are staggering. . . it means that the biochip no longer has to be scanned at a close distance of 3" to 12". It would indicate that technology now has been developed and actually put into service that could scan for detection of biochips at great distances, possibly even by satellite. This incident has been reported widely, and I am attempting to verify its validity as this book goes to press. Whether or not this account is factual, it is the ultimate direction biochip technology is heading, as surveillance and control of humans is of far more importance to the leaders of the New World Order than the tracking of animals.]

While there are at least "10,000 application ideas to explore when it comes to the chip's potential," Seiler insisted Destron is concerned only with animal identification and *is not considering HUMAN application*. "There is no need to apply the technology to humans because the human fingerprint is unique enough to identify them," he said. "Animals don't have such a unique identifier." All present manufacturers deny that they are considering any form of human application, however, latest info indicates to the contrary.

But Tim Willard, managing editor of the World Future Society's bimonthly magazine, *FUTURISTS,* said the technology behind such a *human microchip* is "fairly uncomplicated and with a little refinement, *could be used in a variety of human applications* . . . .Conceivably, a *number could be assigned at birth* and go with a person throughout life [emphasis added]," Willard said.

The I.D. Chip Will Be Implanted in the Hand!

"Most likely," Willard added, "it would be *implanted in the back of the right* or left *hand* for convenience, so that it would be *easy to scan* at stores. . . . It could be used as a *universal identification card* that would replace credit cards, passports, that sort of thing. . . . At the supermarket checkout stand, you would simply *pass your hand over the scanner* and your bank account would be automatically debited . . . . it could be programmed to replace a medical alert bracelet. For example, at the scene of an accident, a medic could *scan the victim's hand* to find out his recent medical history, allergies, a relative to contact, etc. This would be especially valuable if the person were unconscious [emphasis added]."

In another very logical application, such microchips could replace the need for keys to home, car, and workplace locks, since the *chip in one's hand* would serve as a *universal key* for all such locks. One simply would scan the back of his or her right hand over a high-tech microreader device designed into future locks to gain access. Security would be enhanced tremendously, since allegedly no one would be able to "pick" the locks manually. Doesn't that make you feel really safe? Not if you understand that any burglar worth his salt has always found a way around locks and security devices, no matter how complex. They steal everything from the crown jewels to nuclear missiles. It might serve as a deterrent to an inept low-life, but a serious crook would manage to get in somehow. The bigger the target, the cagier the crooks!

New Biochips of Living Proteins

Now, if you really want to go into future shock, or jump right into Star Trek, consider the probability that down the road a few years today's microchips will be outclassed by new biochips made of *living proteins.* According to Willard, "...a powerful biochip that, once surgically implanted in the brain, could make it possible to *program or upload an unlimited amount of information into the mind; without ever having cracked a book!* [emphasis added]." Compared with the microchips of today, "...it will be infinitely smaller and have the capacity to carry much more information. It will have a wide range of functions that will simply boggle our minds," Willard said.

Loss of Freedom and Privacy

Chapter 3 of this book will discuss extensively the loss of our privacy and electronic bondage, but I should at least address it briefly here, as it contributes greatly to the condition called future shock.

The capabilities described above carry with them the inherent risk of abuse by government and other organizations, particularly over the issue of privacy. How would—or could—access to such information be limited and controlled? And if (read that "when") it is passed around (usually without even our knowledge, much less our consent) to a variety of entities, both private and governmental, how will we know of errors that occur when someone is updating information? No system is foolproof...errors *always* will occur somehow—and how can we possibly get them corrected? Recipients of the error will not make any adjustments to *their* records/databases—you must determine the origination of the error and try your best to get them to correct the mistake (not likely to occur, I might warn you, since admitting such a blunder would make them financially liable for any injury you might have suffered because of their negligence). And getting them to pass such a correction on to everyone who received the erroneous data from them is practically hopeless.

Indeed, it would be very difficult to impose enforceable limitations on the availability of such information in today's sophisticated environment of internationally-linked databases. Certainly, there would be no guarantees that confidential information might not inadvertently "leak" out to someone not authorized to have it...except YOU, of course! You are not authorized. There is no plan to give you access to the information (correct or erroneous) that all the various businesses, governments, health agencies, insurance companies, credit bureaus, customs agents, etc., etc., have collected on you. Regardless of restrictions that are alleged to have been implemented, information on you *regularly* changes hands between these entities.

A Human Biochip I.D. System

A *human microchip identification system,* Willard said, "...would work best with a *highly CENTRALIZED computer system* where *only* one I.D. number would be needed to gain access to medical, credit, academic, home security, and other kinds of data. But under this arrangement, as you can imagine, *security risks are somewhat intense.*

"People tend to be *idealistic* about their independence and privacy, *but the reality is that most information pertaining to education, credit history, whatever, is readily available to just about anyone who asks.* Anyone who has ever experienced a simple credit check knows this [emphasis added]," Willard said.

Another futurist found the concept of microchip implantation in *humans* offensive. "It reminds me of tatooing concentration camp victims during World War II," said Robert Mittman of the Institute for the Future, a nonprofit research and consulting firm in California. He said there were better methods of identifying people than "violating the integrity of their skin." He continued, ". . . personally, I have problems with it . . . . people would *end up sacrificing some civil rights* [emphasis added]."

Another concerned individual is the associate director of the ACLU for Northern California, Martha Kegal. Kegal expressed concern over how private records would be kept from "inquiring minds" **if** such a system existed.

The System is Already in Place

But the question is not one of whether or not such a system exists, because we all know it does. It is already in place and obvious to all but the most naive. Rather, the question most troubling any intelligent mind would seem to be the system's final destination, as it were. Whenever we get to wherever it ultimately is taking us. . .will it have proven to be good or evil?

For an answer to this question, we must turn to our Creator's operations manual, the Bible, for only God knows how all things will end.

Only the Bible Has the Answers

According to God's Holy Word, the end result of all our present circumstances is quite clear. Our generation is apparently the one that has been appointed to be alive at the time of the conclusion of all ages, better known as the *end of the world.* For the first time in history, the technology is available (and nearly in place) to accomplish the things prophesied in a number of books of the Bible. Precisely which technology will be used is immaterial—the fact is, never prior to this generation has *any* technology been available to permit the conduct of commerce in the manner described in Revelation 13:16-17.

Such an "end-times" scenario necessarily involves the implantable biochip technology (or something comparable) around which this book has been written, for without it, the final worldwide system of satanic government, as outlined in the books of Daniel and Revelation, simply would be infeasible.

Indeed, current technological and political circumstances soon will lead to a system of universal totalitarian enslavement by means of a global economic network of computerized electronic control—an advanced system of computerized bartering. This system will be led by a global dictator whom the Bible calls the *Antichrist.* This Antichrist, Satan's personal representative on the scene—the final "Hitler"— successfully will orchestrate the affairs of the entire globe via a one-world government, the United Nations (or an organization of some other name, but similar purpose). This "man" will be the very epitome of evil. The Bible tells us about the number **666** of which Hollywood has made such a big deal in motion picture horror films. Of course, as is typical with Hollywood, the number *really is* a "big deal," even though they treat it as fiction or only a myth. Consider the following:

> . . . *or the number of his name. Here is wisdom. Let him that hath understanding count [calculate] the number of the beast: for it is the number of a man; and his number is Six hundred threescore and six [666].*
>
> Rev. 13:17-18

Now, as we are admonished to seek understanding and wisdom, for generations Bible scholars have been studying this mystery in an attempt to identify who would become this world leader. . .this Antichrist. It is not such an impossible task as it may seem, because the New Testament was written in Greek, and Greek characters not only comprise their alphabet, but each character carries a numerical value, as well. So if you were a good student of Greek and knew your scriptures well, you could become very intrigued with checking the names of world leaders who are volleying for position on the international horizon today. However, even though it seems impossible that this future dictator is not somewhere on the scene today, the Bible says that he will not be revealed for sure until about half way through the Great Tribulation. If, indeed, we are the generation who will witness the return of Jesus Christ, then he surely is born at this time and working his way up through the ranks—although whoever it is may come out of seeming obscurity and rise quickly to power because of the abilities given to him by Satan.

I have a personal theory that bears indirectly on the relevance this book. We are told in the Bible by Jesus that no one knows the exact day and hour of His return (Matt. 24:36) but we will know when it is very near, even at the door—only the Father knows when He will send

Jesus back again, although the Bible implies that it will be at the end of the age. Now consider this: if even *Jesus* does not know, it is certain that *Satan* cannot know. Therefore, in order for him to be in a position to fulfill the prophecy about the Antichrist and the "number of his name" given in Revelation, he would have had to have someone of the right age and a name that equaled "666" waiting in the wings, as it were, at all times throughout history, since Jesus' ascension. Not engraved in scripture, but interesting food for thought.

The Bible is very clear on one thing, however— that even the very elect will be deceived if they are not alert and do not exercise discernment.

The 666 "MARK" Economic System

In the Antichrist's global economic system, *no one* will be able to work, eat, own property, or "buy and sell" anything without accepting a world-government "mark" (probably a biochip) in their RIGHT hand or forehead. This New World Order biochip "mark" will be the means by which all financial transactions are consummated. Without it, no one will be able to transact any business anywhere in this forthcoming *CASHLESS, debit, computerized, bartering system.*

This sounds very sinister, doesn't it? Like science fiction? *Like your worst nightmare?!?* Well, it is, but the worst is yet to come, for if one refuses to cooperate with this global program of electronic bondage by refusing the biochip mark in his hand or forehead, *he will be killed!* (Actually, in Revelation the method is beheading, and the relevance of the method will become apparent in future chapters.) On the other hand, if one *does* accept the mark, he will burn in hell forever, according to scripture! (Rev. 14:9-11.)

Indeed, we are told in the book of Revelation that whoever resists taking the mark will be *coerced into compliance under the threat of death!* In fact, for rejecting it—as I pointed out previously—he will lose his head. How horrible! Could this be true? Yes, God tells us that this will be a classic "do or die" situation that will be the final test of all ages. Will you worship Jesus Christ or the Antichrist? There is no middle ground—either you are *for* Jesus Christ or *against* Him— if you are not *for* Him, by virtue of that decision, you automatically are *against* Him. It's that simple!

The Satanic New World Order

Such an evil scenario certainly does not sound like the "kinder, gentler, democratic New World Order of peace and safety," that George Bush, Bill Clinton, and other globalists worldwide have been selling us, does it? But according to scripture, that's exactly what's on the immediate horizon! Now you know why I have devoted all of the next chapter to the New World Order.

In any event, for now, let me just make this clear to you . . . *please do not be deceived* by all the confusing rhetoric you are hearing presently regarding how beautiful and glorious this new system of global government will be. Such propaganda and communistic disinformation is nothing more than a smoke screen—an evil satanic lie. The New World Order will be the most horrible form of totalitarian government the world has ever known. In fact, it will enslave us all.

Yes, the "Big Brother" world government system that has been dreaded for years is nearly upon us. There are many attempts being made by a myriad of "influential" people to allay our fears about "Big Brother"-style government. It is being defined and touted by many as the wonderful New World Order (as you will read later, there's nothing *new* about it—this plan has been on the drawing board in some form since Adam and Eve were kicked out of the Garden!). This diabolical global agenda finally has become public—George Bush brought it out of the occultic closet and because of the diligence of many astute, alert Christian scholars and researchers who are not afraid to stand up and put their lives on the line, this information is now available to all who will listen and learn. For the past 200 years, this plan for global unification and control has been gaining momentum . . . and gaining ground. It is a demonic "spiritual" plan that transcends generations. It would appear that this is the generation that will witness and experience the culmination of Satan's efforts in this regard. And as usual, the majority of this nation has been lulled into a stupor by the gradual desensitizing of our mental faculties about our hard-won liberties.

However, due to the efforts of the above-mentioned scholars and researchers, the "sleeping giant" is beginning to awaken (a fulfillment of prophecy, of course, as we approach the time of our Lord's return), which is exactly what Rockefeller stated as the reason for speeding up their agenda, as we conservatives and Christians are beginning to "muck up the works."

The Occultic Skull and Bones Society

Former President George Bush, a member of the highly secret cult located in New Haven, Connecticut, called the "Skull and Bones Brotherhood of Death," began conditioning America for this "New World Order of peace and security," as he involved us in the Gulf War. Remember the scripture that says when men cry peace and safety, sudden destruction will come upon them? Well, maybe I used that a little bit out of context, but it doesn't seem too far off, does it?

The C.F.R. and Trilateral Commission

In fact, Bush has vocalized this occultic, global government "New World Order" phrase *over 200 times* in public appearances since 1990. It is no mistake that he continues to advocate publicly such a United Nations-controlled world government system with this evil Masonic, Illuminist, communist, globalist terminology, for he has been associated with many socialist, occultic, globalist organizations for years. Two of the most notable of such organizations are known as the *Trilateral Commission* and *The Council on Foreign Relations* in New York.

The Secret "Bilderberger" Cult

Bush not only has been a member of the above two socialist world-government organizations for some time, but he also has served as an officer and director of the Council on Foreign Relations as recently as 1979. Additionally, Bush is a member of the very powerful secret Bilderberger club in Europe. The Bilderbergers control all the money in the world!

U.N. Resolution 666

When Bush started his New World Order Gulf War in 1990, the United Nations Security Council voted approval of it under United Nations Resolution Number 666, the biblical number of the Antichrist, the man who is called *The Beast* of the apocalypse in the book of Revelation, chapter 13! Coincidental? Hardly!

President Bill Clinton, though not a member the Skull and Bones Brotherhood of Death, also is a member of the Council on Foreign Relations, the Trilateral Commission, and the Bilderbergers. As indicated, these "clubs" are dedicated to bringing forth a satanic New World Order global government of communism/fascism whereby the national sovereignty and Constitution of the United States, as well as other nations, will be eliminated. Soon America will be subjugated to the dominion of the evil United Nations communistic system of world government. In other words, shortly the United States will cease being a sovereign, independent, free nation. But I'm sure this isn't news to most of you. Unfortunately, you can see your liberties eroding on a daily basis. . . headed toward the ultimate loss of individual and national independence.

Clinton's "New World Order" Agenda

You might ask if there is any other direct evidence that would indicate that Bill Clinton's agenda is identical to George Bush's regarding the imposition of this New World Order plan on America?

Yes, most certainly there is! The day after President Clinton's inaugura-
tion, January 21, 1993, the *Los Angeles Times* carried a front-page
article about him entitled, "Clinton Must Now Choose Big Gambles
or Safe Bets." In the first and second paragraphs of this article the
following statements were made: ". . . the Great Seal of the United
States [as seen on the back left side of every dollar bill—the pyramid
with the eye over it] and with it a motto. . . *Novus ordo seclorum* [Latin
for New World Order]—A New Age Now Begins. . . . And President
Clinton, like many of his predecessors, invoked that spirit. . . [at his]
inaugural address."

Could there be any doubt at all regarding where Clinton stands in
this regard? I'll answer my own question. . . absolutely not! Clinton
soon will slam-dunk Bush's New World Order program down our
throats in the most traumatic way possible.

A New World Order by the Year 2000

Various internationalist officials, including nearly everyone in the
Clinton Administration (in spite of the fact that a new one's dirty linen
comes flying out of the closet on nearly a daily basis, and they are
resigning with great regularity—the replacements usually are as
repugnant as the ones being replaced), continue promising us that
this wonderful New World Order system of government will have been
put firmly into place globally *by the year 2000!* In fact, their plan to
accomplish this diabolical scheme has been named appropriately,
Global 2000!

As you now can see, the proverbial "deck" has been stacked against
us. It really doesn't matter much who is voted into power. Regardless
of who is elected, he will be controlled—either willingly or unknowingly
—by the invisible, spiritual forces at work behind the scenes. . . the
unseen hand of Satan, the devil. Even if he is not a willing participant,
the time is right and this plan is moving forward—the circumstances
surrounding him will be beyond the scope of his authority to alter.
Stated simply, we are going to *get* the demonic New World Order
communistic form of global government, whether or not we want it,
irrespective of who occupies the Presidential office. That's the "Plan"!

America's Government is Controlled by
Occultists and Socialists

To the informed, astute citizen, it is quite obvious that our government has been taken over secretly and quietly from within by satanic
conspirators. Indeed, America is presently under the control of a very
powerful, elite, occultic, unseen group of people pulling the strings
like we are a bunch of puppets. And if this doesn't send you into future

shock, you already must be too numb to notice! This secret group is called the Illuminati, and they control not only our government, but all the governments of the world. The evil men who belong to this group orchestrate world affairs from their European base of operations by issuing marching orders to all the nations on earth.

What, you may ask, gives them the power and ability to do this? It sounds like science fiction again. . .just too big for our ordinary finite minds to comprehend on such a global scale. And for years there have been people who see a conspiracy "under every rock." But remember the old addage that the one who controls the purse strings rules the world? Well, *they control the purse strings*. . .in fact, they *own* the whole purse! They control all the money on this planet via international, centralized world banks, including the Federal Reserve Bank, a private banking corporation here in America ("The Fed," as it is commonly known, is a privately-owned and controlled institution, even though our government has granted them the authority to control the rise and fall of our total economy through the raising and lowering of interest, the lending/borrowing rates. . .whatever they say goes, and EVERY bank, mortgage company, savings and loan, etc. in the United States immediately capitulates to their almost daily fluctuations).

This is why the near-simultaneous occurrence of numerous earth-shaking global events is accelerating at such an unprecedented exponential rate. Such rapidly occurring global events are rushing to usher in this satanic "Global Village" international community of nations called (presently) the New World Order. *Future Shock, here we come!*

The Pope Claims He Will Control
The New World Order

Even the Pope expresses a similar New-World-Order view in Malachi Martin's book, *The Keys of This Blood,* a 700-page volume detailing "the grand design's" intricacies. According to Martin, the Pope claims that he himself will lead this New World Order world government system by the year 2000. The subtitle on the book's cover says it all: "...Pope John Paul II versus Russia and the West for Control of the New World Order."

The Cashless 666 Economic System

Before proceeding further, first we need to acquire a basic understanding of the concepts behind the coming universal cashless financial system. Such insight and knowledge will help us fully appreciate how the New World Order's system of servitude fits together. And since this is such an important issue, we are going to spend considerable time discussing it in Chapter 11, for the coming cashless society will be the financial means by which we all will be enslaved.

666 Barcode and Biochip Implants

In Chapter 8, I will discuss the **666 barcode** versus biochip transponder systems, and why biochip implants are the ultimate breakthrough in I.D. technology. In fact, we shall learn that, unlike barcodes, biochips are a foolproof, unalterable system of identification—a system of absolute certainty, if you will. As I pointed out previously, such a "Big Brother" system of positive identification is needed in the coming satanic New World Order, otherwise, it would be impossible to totally control, track, monitor, and enslave people. This is a time unlike any other time in the history of the world!

Electronic Bondage

Once this satanic, global, computerized Big-Brother financial network is fully in place, you will have lost all your privacy and freedom. You will have become enslaved to the global, electronically-controlled New World Order dictatorship!

Are you now able to visualize how all of this might materialize? And how soon? Good! Now that you all are thoroughly *future shocked,* let's move right on into Chapter 2 and get some indepth background on the New World Order.

CHAPTER TWO

The New World Order

Soros Warns of GLOBAL DISORDER
Threat of Mexican Crisis
By Michael Thurston

DAVOS, Switzerland, Jan. 27, 1995 (AFP)—*International financier George Soros* said Friday that the *globe is in need of a "New World Order"* following the collapse of the Cold War, warning of widening disintegration otherwise.

In particular, the Hungarian-born financier warned that the extension of such crises as that seen recently in Mexico could lead to *a collapse of world capital markets.*

"I am here to alert you that *we are entering a period of world disorder,*" he told the opening plenary session of the 25th World Economic Forum (WEF) annual meeting in Davos.

Addressing a session entitled "Challenges Beyond Growth: What Lies Ahead?" Soros said *the global order* in place during the Cold War "was not pleasant, but it was relatively stable."

"The failure of the western world to respond to the collapse of communism in a constructive way has set in motion *a process of disintegration* in the former Soviet states," he added.

Referring specifically to the crisis in Mexico in the last month, Soros said it had for the moment been contained but warned of *grave consequences* if it were allowed to get out of control.

"If Mexico is really allowed to go, it would have *worldwide repercussions,* it would *lead to the collapse of world capital movement* and affect world trade," he said.

His comment echoed those of US President Bill Clinton, who in an address to the opening session of the Davos forum on Thursday evening also warned of the consequences of the Mexican crisis.

"Some have said it's just foreign aid and a bale out. Well, they're not right. It's the kind of response to address a problem before it spreads that *the new world economy* demands.

"Failure to act could have grave consequences for Mexico, for
Latin America, for the entire developing world," Soros said.

Soros, speaking more generally, said the wars in ex-Yugoslavia
and Chechnya were key flare-ups which should indicate to western
leaders the need to establish *a new international order.*

"The *need for a new world order* is not generally recognized,
despite the conflicts in Bosnia, Chechnya, and Rwanda," he said.

"The western *world is in bigger trouble than people realize,* and
that trouble will only grow so long as people do not realize it,"
he added to an audience of world political and business leaders
gathered here. [Emphasis added by author.]

It doesn't take an Einstein to figure out that the above newspaper
article portends a sorry state of affairs for our future!

The New World Order! It sounds like a wonderful progressive place,
designed to benefit just everyone. Wrong! Let's see if we can figure
out just exactly what is meant by the term "New World Order."

Unfortunately, you can't just go the *Webster's Collegiate Dictionary*
and find a good definition, like we did for "future shock". . .as yet
it's not in there, although as much as the phrase has come into usage
in the past few years, I'm sure it won't be overlooked in their next
edition.

In the meantime, you can get as many different definitions as the
number of different people you ask. The liberals view it as something
beneficent—a "big brother" to look out for all of us incompetent,
uneducated masses unable to look out for ourselves. Sadly, those who
claim to be conservatives, but are engaged in politics full time, don't
view it very much differently than the liberals. After all, George Bush
was one of the biggest promoters of the New World Order, and if you
don't consider him a conservative, just ask a liberal!

The conservatives who have examined the various agendas and have
determined the New World Order to be a negative institution, generally
are fundamentalists of a variety of Judeo-Christian religious orders
who see the New World Order as a fulfillment of Bible prophecy;
something that is inevitable, but something of which we should be
thoroughly aware and for which we should be prepared to the best
of our ability. Others who recognize the dangers in a new-world-order
mentality are the conservative Americans who hold the traditional
belief that our Constitution still governs our liberties and limits government's powers to interfere in our lives, and that, to guarantee the
continuation of our freedoms, the Constitution should be protected
at all costs (liberals refer to these people as "right-wing extremists").

A Three-Pronged Agenda

The "order" of the New World Order consists of three different areas of control: (1) political; (2) economic; (3) religious. This three-fold thrust reaches into every area of our lives (we are assuming the inclusion of ecology in both areas [1] and [2]). It cleverly is designed to lead us blissfully into total global satanic bondage!

Still, exactly what is the New World Order? Well, Bill Clinton invoked it. . .George Bush promoted it. . .Mikhail Gorbachev talked about it. . .the Pope mentions it. . .the news media reports on it. . .the New Age Movement espouses it. . .the Freemasons talk about it. . .it's on the back side of the U.S. one dollar bill. . .even Hitler mentioned it during WWII!

But what is it and how will it affect you?

Stated simply, the New World Order is a soon-coming system of world communism/facism under the dictatorship of a global leader who is scheduled to achieve power in Europe in the near future. It is a global political, economic, and religious system satanically designed to enslave the earth's inhabitants by controlling all money and food electronically, via cashless debit banking. People will be informed they must take a MARK (most likely a biochip) in their right hands or foreheads, without which they'll not be able to work or buy or sell anything. And ultimately, people will be told they will either starve or be killed if they refuse to accept this MARK.

"This is impossible! It can't happen here, in the modern age in which we live, not in our free liberty-loving America," you say. Wrong again! It's nearly ready to go and it's sneaking up on us in the most subtle of ways every day. Watch out for 2000 and the New World Order! In fact, if you wait until 2000 to take action (or make preparations) on behalf of yourself, your family, and your fellow church members, it probably will be too late.

As we approach the year 2000 A.D. and the end of the second millennium, there are two major conflicting views regarding the future of mankind. On the one hand, you have a cosmic humanism declaring that we are entering the dawn of a New Age, a New World Order where mankind will enjoy world peace and a new global consciousness. On the other hand, you have those who are warning that we are facing financial collapse, nuclear catastrophe, and the final darkness before the return of Jesus Christ. Obviously, this latter view for mankind is not very popular.

Prior to leaving office, President Reagan expressed his own concern that we are living in a dangerous era and could be heading for Armageddon, as described in the Bible (Rev. 16:12-16). This statement was met with a thunderous response from the liberal media which mocked and ridiculed his doomsday prediction. (Ironically, today it is this same liberal media crying out about the inherent danger of all these nuclear weapons around the world.) Yet, despite the optimism of liberals and new agers, we are entering the twilight before the darkest period in human history—a tribulation period described in detail in the prophetic books of the Bible, particularly Daniel, Ezekiel, and Revelation. As most students of biblical prophecy are aware, Satan's final hour is at hand, the rise of the Antichrist is imminent, and somewhere along the way this world leader will be in the powerful position to dominate and control the occupants of the entire world. He will dictate that unless you receive his mark you can neither buy nor sell nor receive services. And after his power has become "absolute," he will *require the head* of those who refuse to cooperate.

Now, if it sounds farfetched and antiquated to think that the world will revert to such an outdated mode of execution, think again. You will read later in this book about a law that is already on the books which will resurrect this ancient practice. Of course, the law itself was a "harmless little thing," a sort-of proclamation designed as an acknowledgment of achievement, but with this noxious little tidbit "snuck" in so unobtrusively as to go practically unnoticed. Oh, but I'm getting ahead of myself again.

I want to tell you about an article that appeared in the San Francisco Chronicle, February 3, 1995. The whole article deals with the New World Order. . .who currently are the "movers and shakers," the heads of state, the media "giants," the world business leaders, the ecologists, the theologians, the explorers, and the futurist philosophers.

Please note the fairly recent date of the article. If you thought Gorbachev had disappeared from the world scene (or was about to), surprise! "Gorby" is the one who is heading up this big meeting. He has asked "hundreds of world leaders and thousands of business people to join him in San Francisco next autumn to discuss the state of the world." This will be a five-day conference beginning September 27, 1995 to ". . .look at fundamental priorities and values that the world should embrace. . . ." Read that "New World Order!" Notice the co-chairmen this "Gorbachev Foundation USA" has lined up for this conference: Bush, Thatcher, Havel, Tutu, Menchu, Ted Turner (how did he get in this bunch?), and Nakasone. These are current and former presidents and prime ministers, Nobel Peace Prize winner and Archbishops (except one!).

They believe that hopes for a New World Order have dimmed, so they feel compelled to get them burning brightly again. "There appears to be a great cynicism everywhere with government," said former Senator Alan Cranston, Democrat from California and chairman of the Gorbachev Foundation USA. Is there any wonder? It's not just the government about which people have grown cynical—it's the government control and interference in our lives. He concludes, "And there is a yearning for new directions." I'll say! But not the direction they have in mind for us. How about 180° in the opposite direction!

Among the things they propose to discuss at this conference is the future of the "nation state" (note that each nation will be reduced to the status of a state in the future world government [NWO]) and the rights (or the lack thereof!) of businesses and individuals.

Paragraph six gives a broad-based sampling of others who have been invited. This is not your charitable seminar; the registration fee is quite stiff. They are asking 8,000 business leaders from 75 countries to attend as paying participants . . .to the tune of $5,000.00 a person. Try the math on that five-day seminar. . .you'll arrive at something with seven zeroes behind it. It makes some of the important conferences that we attend from time to time seem like a real bargain.

Finally, Gorbachev wants to start an informal "brain trust" to continue these meetings for the next several years. Among the "projects" they want to start is a so-called Earth Charter, which they describe as an environmental bill of rights. Help us, Lord!

In the August 10, 1992, issue of *The New Republic,* p. 22, in an article titled "The Protectorate," Robert W. Tucker writes:

> . . .*The requirements of the new world order go well beyond what must now appear to be by comparison a narrow conception of interest.* In the Bush administration's new order [and carried forward by Clinton], interest demands that Israel's *former freedom of action* be severely circumscribed. This can only mean that the strongest military power in the region *relinquish the strategic independence* that until the Gulf war formed the hallmark of its policy. . . .Thus the Gulf war not only inaugurated the new world order, it foreshadowed the position Israel is likely to occupy in this order. [Emphasis added.]

This reminds me of the classic line from the musical, *The King and I:* "Might they not protect me out of all I own?!"

It's quite apparent that the Gulf War served as a most convenient means to catapult the New World Order forward with a great leap. In September, 1990, former President George Bush said, "The Persian Gulf crisis is a rare opportunity to forge new bonds with old enemies. . . .Out of these troubled times a New World Order can emerge, under a United Nations that performs as envisioned by its founders."

Then barely four months later he is quoted as saying:

This is an historic moment. . . . We have before us the opportunity to forge for ourselves and for future generations a New
World Order, a world where the rule of law, not the law of the
jungle, governs the conduct of the nations. When we are successful, *and we will be,* we have a real chance at the New World Order,
an order in which a credible United Nations can use its peacekeeping role to fulfill the promise and vision of the UN founders.

Then later in the same month, Bush says: "The world can therefore
seize the opportunity [the Gulf crisis] to fulfill the long held promise
of a New World Order where diverse nations are drawn together in
common cause to achieve the universal aspirations of mankind."

The instigators of the New World Order have taken no steps to hide
its existence or agenda. And in spite of the title, it isn't "new." H. G.
Wells talked about it in the 1930's, and Castro demanded it at the
UN in the late 1970's. But its greatest publication is credited to Bush
and Gorbachev, who mentioned it repeatedly when they were in power
(and haven't ceased to do so—in fact, I'm not so sure they actually
lost any power. . .they just switched from national power to global
power, in my opinion—bigger fish in a bigger pond). Bush and Kissinger each have referred to Operation Desert Storm as "a major stepping
stone to the New World Order."

Even though not much was done to hide the intent of the promoters
of the New World Order, still—until recently—practically no one was
aware of its presence and gradual increase in prominence. However,
the time to come out of the closet is at hand, and the plans to convert
us to a New World Order are on the front burner, as it were. Henry
Kissinger has written a book entitled *Diplomacy,* Simon and Schuster,
Inc., 1994. The section, "How to Achieve The New World Order," was
selected for the Book Excerpt section of the March 14, 1994, edition
of *Time* magazine (pp. 73-77). This book plainly lays out the plan of
the "Establishment" for moving into the New World Order. Below are
a number of quotations of interest from the excerpt in *Time.*

. . . Now more than ever, argues Henry Kissinger, the U.S. must
temper its idealism with a more pragmatic approach, especially
toward Russia, Europe, and Asia.
. . . Every "world order" expresses an aspiration to permanence;
yet the elements that make up a world order are in constant flux
and the duration of international systems has been shrinking.
[According to the Bible, this one probably will be limited to
3½ - 7 years!—Author] . . . Never before have the components of
world order, their capacity to interact, and their goals all changed
quite so rapidly, so deeply, or so globally.

Both Bill Clinton and George Bush have spoken of the new world order as if it were just around the corner. . . . In an international system characterized by perhaps five or six major powers and a multiplicity of smaller states—many of which are striving to prevail in ancient ethnic rivalries— order will have to emerge much as it did in past centuries: from a reconciliation and balancing of competing national interests.

The end of the cold war has created what some observers have called a "unipolar" or "one-superpower" world.

As the 21st century approaches, vast global forces are at work that will render the U.S. less exceptional. . . .

In the aftermath of the communist collapse, it has been assumed that Russia's adversarial intentions have disappeared. Students of geopolitics and history are uneasy about the single-mindedness of this approach. . . .

. . . Alleviating suffering and encouraging economic reform are important tools of American foreign policy, but not substitutes for a serious effort to maintain the global balance of power vis-à-vis a country with a long history of expansionism.

In the years ahead all the traditional Atlantic relationships will change. Europe will not feel the previous need for American protection and will pursue its economic self-interest much more aggressively; . . . .

. . . Poland, the Czech Republic, Hungary, and Slovakia have historically, culturally, and politically identified with West European traditions. Without ties to West European and Atlantic institutions, these will become a no-man's-land between Germany and Russia. To be economically and politically viable, they need the European Union, and for security they look to the Atlantic Alliance. Since most members of the European Union are members of NATO, and since it is inconceivable that they would ignore attacks on one of their members after European integration has reached a certain point, membership in the European Union will lead to at least de facto extension of the NATO guarantee.

In such a design, the Atlantic Alliance would establish a common political framework and provide overall security; . . . . A security umbrella would be extended over the new democracies in Eastern Europe. . . .

In the next century, China's political and military shadow will fall over Asia and will affect the calculations of the other powers, however restrained actual Chinese policy may prove to be. . . .

. . . with economic growth rates around 10% annually, a strong sense of national cohesion and an ever more muscular military, China will show the greatest increase in stature among the major powers.

The American habit of rejecting history extols the image of a universal man living by universal maxims, regardless of the past, of geography, or of other immutable circumstances. . . .

A country with this idealistic tradition cannot base its policy on the balance of power as the sole criterion for a new world order. But it must learn that equilibrium is a fundamental precondition for the pursuit of its historic goals. . . .

. . .The convictions needed to master the emerging world order are more abstract: a vision of the future that cannot be demonstrated when it is put forward and judgments about the relationship between hope and possibility that are, in their essence, conjectural. . . .

Don McAlvany, a widely respected financial advisor, is considered to be extremely knowledgeable on the subject of the New World Order. So it will help our understanding if we consider his definition of New World Order. The following is excerpted from the August, 1994, edition of his publication, *The McAlvany Intelligence Advisor.*

And what is the New World Order? It is a world government *under the United Nations* that envisions (according to its Establishment sponsors) a one-world banking system and currency, which eventually is to give way to a cashless computerized financial system; one-world (centralized) control of the global population (i.e., it would like to see the global population contract by at least 2 billion people by the year 2050. That will take a lot of wars, abortion, euthanasia, and viral plagues— but perhaps it all can be arranged).

The New World Order envisions global controls of the world's environment, economy, and of *all* world trade (both domestic and international); and a one-world, global army (i.e., a United Nations army called by the Establishment, the New World Army) which is designed to incorporate all the major armies of the world into a global police force to enforce the New World Order's will internationally and within the domestic borders of the various countries.

[ED. NOTE: A global dictatorship will require a global police force to enforce its will on recalcitrant resistors to the New World Order, just as the Third Reich required the Gestapo, and the Bolsheviks required the KGB and the Red Army to enforce their will on the people.]

The New World Order includes three major regional governments (i.e., *The European Union in Europe*—soon to include Russia and other East Bloc countries); *NACOM (the North American Common Market*—including Canada, the U.S. and Mexico); and *a regional government in the Pacific Rim* (headquartered in Tokyo). These regional governments are launched first as economic unions (i.e., the EEC in Europe, NAFTA in North America, and then "evolve" to a political union (i.e., the European Union).

Several secondary regional governments will come into being (i.e., in Latin America, in Africa—headquartered in Marxist/Leninist-dominated Pretoria, in the Middle East, and in the Southwest Pacific).

A major element of the New World Order (as articulated by Establishment leaders) is the "merger of the common interest of America and Russia" or the former Soviet Union (i.e., the so-called "convergence theory"). . . .

The New World Order has a target date for its establishment (i.e., the year 2000) and hence the tremendous speed with which it is trying to precipitate and orchestrate global events. This concurs with the target date of the year 2000 articulated by many New Age leaders for the establishment of a world government and the "dawning of the Age of Aquarius."

And it also coincides with the time frame which many students of Bible prophecy believe will see the rise of the Biblical anti-Christ; the establishment of a world government (albeit very briefly); a major military conflict in the Middle East involving Russia, the Western powers, the Islamic states, and Red China—all converging on the tiny nation of Israel; and the Second Coming of Jesus Christ (as discussed in the Biblical books of Daniel, Ezekiel, Joel, Revelation, Matthew, etc.).

The United Nations was founded in 1945 with a charter patterned after the Russian constitution. It is headquartered right in the heart of New York, and its founders viewed it as the primary "means to the end," i.e. a one-world government. One of its agreements—though traditionally kept in a very low profile—is the requirement that the UN chief military commander always would be a Russian officer, and that has been the case in every UN military intervention since World War II.

Even though the UN is dominated by our enemies and their allies, the United States always has been the chief financier of the organization. Presently, about one-third of the UN budget is supplied by the United States.

The UN has been a disappointment to its globalist founders, so far as their hope that it would lead the way to a world government. However, all that is changing now! In most recent years, the "powers that be," assisted greatly by Bush and Clinton, have brought about a resurgence of activity to the UN. New military operations are attempting to justify the existence and expansion of the New World Army, the UN's military division (think: Operation Desert Storm, Somalia, Rwanda, Bosnia, Haiti, *et al*). Massive global information campaigns have been developed to familiarize the world with the beneficent "Big Brother" and the necessity for implementing the New World Order.

McAlvany states that "there is absolutely no justification for UN/US sanctions, embargoes, or an invasion of tiny Haiti, except to advance the credibility of the UN and its New World Army. If we want to take out Caribbean dictators, why not start with Fidel Castro and communist Cuba, which has been a thorn in America's side for 36 years, instead of moving to install a new Marxist government under Jean Bertrand Aristide, a Salvador Allende-type Marxist/Leninist?"

McAlvany further informs us:

> In May '94, the Clinton Administration released its "Policy on Reforming Multilateral Peace Operations," which lays out a framework for America's participation in future UN "peacekeeping operations" [e.g., New World Army enforcement operations], and how America can move to strengthen the UN. *This policy is the beginning of a major move by the Clintonistas (and the Establishment) to move the U.S. military under the authority and command structure of the UN.* The U.S. Defense Department will begin to finance UN military operations out of its budget, while the State Department's role in peacekeeping operations will be increased."

The 1994 UN Human Development Report lays out a plan to eliminate sovereign nations and replace them with a one-world UN dictator-controlled government. The UN Secretary General has endorsed these plans which outline the establishment of "world" institutions with the unchallenged power to dictate policies to national governments, including the developing nations of the "third-world." This report calls for the replacement of "national security" with "human security," and provides for the establishment of a World Court (with the power to subpoena nations), a World Police Force (New World Army), a World Central Bank (the International Monetary Fund [IMF] would have sole power to force austerity on nations), a World Treasury, a method to demand and enforce population reduction on nations (until their population corresponds with their economic performance capabilities) [Don McAlvany believes this portion of the proposal, if implemented, would create the enforcement apparatus for massive genocide in Third World countries.], an Economic Security Council, with instructions to deal harshly with those states (formerly considered nations) that do not capitulate to UN mandates for genocide or "free trade" liberalization, and a World Trade and Production Organization (which would both regulate so-called "free" trade and prescribe production quotas to formerly independent nations).

The above described report proposes to fund all these activities by global taxation, which will include taxes on all those things that separate the wealthy nations from the poor ones. . . just another way of redistributing the wealth—the old "Robin Hood principle" of taking from the rich and giving to the poor. Some of their proposed methods for taxation include taxes on pollution (of course, the industrial nations will take the brunt of this one), taxes on savings from demilitarization (there won't be much savings here, if we have to support the global army's activities), taxes on all foreign exchange transactions (and with the new cashless society, they will have easy access to all records of any transactions of any kind), and a global income tax on nations whose people average an income above $10,000 a year (in other words, anyone who lives anywhere other than a third-world, poverty-stricken country). Remember in the previous chapter I told you they were trying to level the playing field by taking from the "haves" and giving to the "have-nots."

Of course, the topics mentioned above cover mostly the "administrative" functions of the New World Order, but their control will extend into every area of global life. They also will control population growth (or, in the case of the New World Order, population decrease), the globally "politically correct" education of the world's children, and a worldwide military service (through means of which they will disarm the developing third-world countries and dispatch the national armies of the "nation states" anywhere in the world that they choose to intervene). I will return to these particular topics later in the chapter, but at this point I want to interject some excerpts from an excellent pamphlet by Dennis L. Cuddy, Ph.D. entitled "The New World Order: A Critique and Chronology." I recommend that you order it and study it in its entirety (I will give the address below), as it is one of the best pieces of documentation to prove that there is nothing *new* about the New World Order. I suspect that the premise goes back as far as the Tower of Babel, or earlier, but this brochure begins its documentation with this century.

> To stem Saddam Hussein's aggression in the Persian Gulf, the United States in late 1990 put together an unprecedented alliance of more than 20 nations under the aegis of the United Nations. Supporters hailed it as a possible precursor to a "New World Order." In urging Congress to commit American forces to battle in Desert Storm, President Bush described the Gulf crisis as a "rare opportunity to move toward an historic period of coopera-

tion. Out of these troubled times. . .a new world order can emerge."

The term New World Order seemed to imply that the collective will of the nations of the world, exercised through the U.N., would be imposed to uphold international law—by force if necessary.

Before Americans embrace the concept of a New World Order, however, a number of questions should be asked and answered. Who would determine just how, when, and where U.N. forces would be deployed? For example, would the New World Order be invoked to liberate Croatia from Serbian-dominated Yugoslavia? What if the New World Order decreed that a Palestinian state be carved out of Israel, regardless of Israeli objections? And what if the New World Order declared that China should be attacked because of its human rights violations? Or that a preemptive strike against North Korea be ordered to destroy its emerging nuclear weapons capability?

International cooperation for peace and security is to be welcomed, of course. NATO—the North Atlantic Treaty Organization—has provided a successful example of regional cooperation without the loss of identity by any of its 16 member nations. But would a New World Order mean relinquishing U.S. sovereignty to a supra-national authority, placing at risk our universally acclaimed institutions of freedom and democratic principles?

Various ideas for a New World Order have been advanced many times before in this century and for a variety of reasons, as highlighted in the following chronology. [In many cases, I will be listing only the chronology; in other instances I will quote a portion of the text below the chronological listing.]

1910—The Carnegie Endowment for International Peace is formed. The endowment now works closely with the UN and its agencies, as well as other groups espousing world government.

1912—Edward Mandel House publishes *Philip Dru: Administrator.* Promotes "Socialism as dreamed of by Karl Marx."

1913—Woodrow Wilson in his book, *The New Freedom*, says: "Since I entered politics, I have chiefly had men's views confided to me privately. Some of the biggest men in the U.S., in the field of commerce and manufacturing, are afraid of somebody, are afraid of something. They know that there is a power somewhere so organized, so subtle, so watchful, so interlocked, so complete, so pervasive, that they had better not speak above their breath when they speak in condemnation of it."

1917—United States enters the First World War. The establishment of the League of Nations would be an integral part of [Woodrow Wilson's] plan.

1918—Russia "Points the Way." In the January 13th issue of the

New York World, William Boyce Thompson (Federal Reserve Bank director and founding member of the Council on Foreign Relations) stated: "Russia is pointing the way to great and sweeping world changes. It is not in Russia alone that the old order is passing. There is a lot of the old order in America, and that is going too. . . .I'm glad it is so."

1919—*A Social History of the American Family,* Vol. 3, by Arthur Calhoun, appears as part of a series of social service textbooks. ". . .The modern individual is a world citizen, served by the world, and *home interests can no longer be supreme* [emphasis added]. . . ."

May 30, 1919—[Col. House arranges a meeting to form the Institute of International Affairs.] Two years later, Col. House reorganized the Institute of International Affairs as the Council on Foreign Relations (CFR).

1920—Congress for the second time votes against U.S. membership in the League of Nations.

1922—CFR endorses World Government. Philip Kerr, writing for CFR's magazine *Foreign Affairs,* states: "Obviously there is going to be no peace or prosperity for mankind as long as (the earth) remains divided into 50 or 60 independent states. . . .The real problem today is that of the world government."

1923—Col. House comments on war and internationalism.

1928—*The Open Conspiracy: Blue Prints for a World Revolution* by H. G. Wells is published. A Fabian Socialist, Wells writes: "The political world of the Open Conspiracy must weaken, efface, incorporate, and supersede existing governments. . . .The Open Conspiracy is the natural inheritor of socialist and communist enthusiasms; it may be in control of Moscow before it is in control of New York. . . .The character of the Open Conspiracy will now be plainly displayed. . . .It will be a *world religion.* . . .attempting to swallow up the entire population of the world and become the *new human community* [emphasis added]. . . ."

1931—Communists predict peace movement will entrap the West. ". . .we shall start to spread the most theatrical peace movement the world has ever seen. The capitalist countries, stupid and decadent. . .will fall into the trap offered by the possibility of making new friends. . . .Our day will come in 30-40 years or so. . . .The bourgeoisie must be lulled into a feeling of security."

1932—New books urge New World Order. *The New World Order,* by F.S. Marvin, describes the League of Nations as the first attempt at a New World Order and says "nationality must rank below the claims of mankind as a whole." *Brave New World,* by Aldous Huxley, satirized the mechanical world of the future, in which technology replaces much of the everyday activities of humans.

1933—The first *Humanist Manifesto* is published. Co-author John Dewey, philosopher and one of the founding fathers of the modern American education system, calls for a synthesizing of all religions and "a socialized and cooperative economic order." Also published was *The Shape of Things to Come* by H. G. Wells, in which he predicts a Second World War will begin in or about 1940, and the plan for the "Modern World-State" would succeed on its third attempt (about 1980), coming out of something that occurs in Iraq. At this point, the book states, "Russia is ready to assimilate. It is eager to assimilate." Although the world government "had been plainly coming for some years, although it had been endlessly feared and murmured against, it found no opposition prepared anywhere."

1934—More works on the New World Order. *The Externalization of the Hierarchy,* by Alice Bailey, the occultist, states ". . .of all existing culture and civilization, the new world order must be built." The work is published by Lucis Trust, formerly Lucifer Publishing Company. *Experiment in Autobiography,* by H. G. Wells, states: ". . .a planned world-state is appearing at a thousand points. . . .When accident finally precipitates it, its coming is likely to happen very quickly. . . .Sometimes I feel that generations of propaganda . . . may have to precede it . . . .There must be a common faith and law for mankind . . . .The main battle is an educational battle." Willard Givens, later the Executive Secretary of the National Education Association, said: ". . .all of us . . . must be subjected to a large degree of social control . . . .An equitable distribution of income will be sought . . . .the major function of the school is the social orientation of the individual [as of this decade, we have seen this goal come to pass, along with the devastation in character and behavior it brings with it, but the 'three R's' are falling far behind—author] . . . .the transition to a new social order [emphasis added]."

1939—New World Order proclaimed in numerous publications. *Hitler Speaks,* by Hermann Rauschning, states: "National Socialism [Nazism] will use its own revolution for the establishing of a new world order." In an October 28th address, future Secretary of State John Foster Dulles proposed that "America lead the transition to a new order. . . ." On December 24th, Pope Pius XII outlines five points considered essential for setting up a new world order. *World Order,* by Lionel Curtis, was published. The 985-page work has been called the foundation of all thought on the design of a new order.

1940—More works popularize the concept of New World Order. *The New World Order,* by H. G. Wells, proposes a "collectivist one-world state" or "new world order" comprised of "socialist democracies." *The New World Order,* published by the Carnegie Endowment for International Peace, suggests some special plans for world order after the war. "The New World Order: A Japanese View," is published in the July edition of *Contemporary Japan.* *The Congressional Record,* on December 12th published an article entitled "A New World Order," in which John G. Alexander calls for a world federation.

1941—Still more works on the New World Order. *The City of Man: A Declaration on World Democracy,* declares: "Universal peace can be founded only on the unity of man under one law and one government . . . . All states, deflated and disciplined, must align themselves under the law of the world-state . . . the new order. . . . when the heresy of nationalism is conquered and the absurd architecture of the present world is finally dismantled. . . . there must be a common creed. . . or ethico-religious purpose." "The New World Order," an article by M. J. Bonn, states that "national planning means deliberate international anarchy. . . . with every move a step toward a new world order is taken."

1945—October 24th, UN Charter becomes effective.

1946—Alger Hiss (alleged Communist spy) elected President of the Carnegie Endowment for International Peace.

1947—New Groups call for World Federal Government. **American Education Fellowship** addresses the teachers of the nation, calling for "the establishment of a genuine world order, an order in which national sovereignty is subordinate to the world authority. . . an order in which 'world citizenship' thus assumes. . . equal status with national citizenship." **United World Federalists** coordinate efforts of like-minded organizations in promoting world federal government.

1948—Britain's Sir Harold Butler, in the July issue of *Foreign Affairs,* sees "A New World Order" taking shape. UNESCO president and Fabian Socialist, Sir Julian Huxley, calls for a radical eugenic policy "of controlled human breeding. . . . " *Preliminary Draft of a World Constitution* is published, advocating regional federation on the way toward world federation or government [Note our discussion on regionalization near the end of this chapter.]. The "Preamble" calls upon nations to surrender their arms to the world government and grants the right to this "Federal Republic of the World" to seize private property for federal use.

1949—George Orwell publishes his classic work, *1984.* In addition to the familiar "Big Brother is watching" concept, this book introduced the concept of "Newspeak" or "doublethink," which we call today, "doublespeak." The whole idea is to say one thing, while meaning something else entirely— frequently the exact opposite of what is conveyed. And on July 26th, 18 U.S. Senators sponsored Resolution 56 calling for the United Nations to be restructured as a world federation.

1950—On February 9th, a Senate Foreign Relations Subcommittee introduces Resolution 66 to consider a "separate convention, a world order." Res. 66 begins, ". . .the present Charter of the United Nations should be changed to provide a true world government constitution." Then on February 17th, CFR member James P. Warburg, tells the Subcommittee: "We shall have world government, whether or not we like it. The question is only whether world government will be achieved by consent or by conquest."

1952—On April 12th, future Secretary of State John Foster Dulles said that "treaty laws can override the Constitution." A Senate amendment that would have provided that NO treaty could supersede the Constitution failed to pass by one vote.

1954—The Bilderbergers are established.

1959—CFR calls for New International Order in "Study No. 7," issued on November 25th. *The West in Crisis,* by James Warburg, proclaims: "We are living in a perilous period of transition from the era of the fully sovereign nation-state to the era of world government. . . . American children may best be educated into . . .responsible citizens not merely of the United States but of the world."

1960—"The Technical Problems of Arms Control" is published by the Institute for International Order, and advocates an "international intelligence network" be developed which could "recruit and train competent secret agents" to find any resistance.

1961—State Department issues plan to disarm all nations and arm the U.N. ". . .The U.S. Program for General and Complete Disarmament in a Peaceful World." It details a three-stage plan to disarm all nations and arm the U.N. . . ."No state would have the military power to challenge the progressively strengthened U.N. Peace Force."

1962—New Calls for World Federalism. CFR member Lincoln Bloomfield states: ". . . if the communist dynamic was greatly abated, the West might lose whatever incentive it has for world government." In *The Future of Federalism,* author Nelson Rockefeller claims "a new world order" is needed, as the old order is crumbling, and there is "a new and free order struggling to be born. . . . led vigorously toward the true building of a new world order."

1967—Richard Nixon calls for "New World Order," and Robert Kennedy calls for a "new world society."

1968—Richard Gardner, former U.S. Deputy Assistant Secretary of State, calls for an end to national sovereignty, using terms like "The Hard Road to World Order" and "house of world order," while advocating "an end run around national sovereignty, eroding it piece by piece, likely to get us to world order faster than the old-fashioned frontal attack." The U.S. Disarmament Agency stated: ". . .the ultimate goal [is] the total elimination of all armed forces and armaments except those needed to maintain internal order within states and to furnish the United Nations with peace forces. . . .While reductions were taking place, a U.N. peace force would be established and developed, and, by the time the plan was completed, it would be so strong that no nation could challenge it." On July 26, Nelson Rockefeller pledges support of a New World Order in an Associated Press report.

1969—December 2nd, Congressman George Bush introduces the Atlantic Union Resolution, which includes: ". . .a declaration that the goal of their people is to transform their present alliance into a federal union."

1970—Education and Mass Media to promote World Order. The January issue of *War/Peace Report,* contains an article by Ian Baldwin, Jr. entitled "Thinking About A New World Order for the Decade 1990," which states: "The World Law Fund has begun a worldwide research and educational program that will introduce a new, emerging discipline—world order—into educational curricula throughout the world. . .and to concentrate some of its energies on bringing basic world order concepts into the mass media, again on a worldwide level."

1972—President Nixon visits China. Former CFR member and then President Richard Nixon expresses "the hope that each of us has to build a new world order." On May 18th, Roy M. Ash, director of the Office of Management and Budget for Nixon, declares that *within two decades* [emphasis added: that's 1992] the institutional framework for a world economic community will be in place. . .[and] aspects of individual sovereignty will be given over to a supernational authority."

1973—Trilateral Commission established. Banker David Rockefeller organizes this new private body. . .and invites Jimmy Carter to become a founding member. *Humanist Manifesto II* is published, containing text such as the following: ". . .the dawn of a new age. . .a secular society on a planetary scale. . . .we begin with humans not God, nature not deity. . . .a system of world law and a world order based upon transnational federal government. . . .The true revolution is occurring."

1974—Douglas Roche, at the World Conference of Religion for Peace (in Belgium), calls for a New World Order. In a report entitled "New International Economic Order," the U.N. General

Assembly outlines a plan to redistribute the wealth from the rich to the poor nations.

1975—New World Order recognized in diverse publications. A study titled, "A New World Order," is published by the Center of International Studies at Princeton. *The New York Times* editor, James Reston, writes that Ford and Brezhnev should "forget the past and work together for a new world order." In Congress 32 Senators and 92 Representatives sign "A Declaration of Interdependence," which states that we must "bring forth a new world order." Congresswoman Marjorie Holt refuses to sign, saying: "It calls for the surrender of our national sovereignty to international organizations. It declares that our economy should be regulated by international authorities. It proposes that we enter a 'new world order' that would redistribute the wealth created by the American people." The Rockefeller Foundation's annual report states: "We are one world and there will be one future—for better or for worse—for us all. Central to the new ethic . . . is controlled economic growth . . . . It is also necessary to control fertility. . . ." Retired Navy Admiral and former CFR member Chester Ward writes that the goal of the CFR is the "submergence of U.S. sovereignty and national independence into an all-powerful one-world government . . . . to confound and discredit, intellectually and politically, any opposition."

1977—President Carter appoints New World Order proponents to key positions. *The Third Try at World Order* is published. Author Harlan Cleveland of the Aspen Institute for Humanistic Studies, among other things, calls for "changing Americans' attitudes and institutions"; for "complete disarmament (except for international soldiers)"; for "fairer distribution of worldly goods through a new International Economic Order." *Imperial Brain Trust,* by Shoup and Minter, takes a critical look at the Council on Foreign Relations, with chapter titles, "Shaping a New World Order: The Council's Blueprint for Global Hegemony, 1939-1944" and "Toward the 1980's: The Council's Plans for a New World Order."

1979—Barry Goldwater, retiring Senator from Arizona, publishes his autobiography, *With No Apologies,* and reveals the true mission of the powerful Trilateral Commission.

1980—U.N. plans New International Economic Order.

1983—*The Hidden Dangers of the Rainbow* is published, in which author Constance Cumbey exposes the depth and breadth of the New Age Movement, and its intent to bring about a New World Order.

1984—KGB defector Anatoliy Golitsyn wrote a book entitled, *New Lies for Old,* in which he reveals information he had conveyed to the CIA as early as the 1970's. He includes "the introduction of the false liberalization in Eastern Europe and, probably, in the Soviet Union. . . .The KGB would be 'reformed'. . . .there might be an extensive display of the fictional struggle for power in the Soviet leadership."

1985—World Government called inevitable by Norman Cousins, honorary chairman of Planetary Citizens, as quoted in the Washington weekly, *Human Events*. He goes on to say, "No arguments for or against it can change that fact."

1986—International meeting in Seoul, South Korea, promotes New World Order. Finance ministers from around the world hear the New World Order praised. . . .and receive a plea for a New World Order to replace the International Monetary Fund and *assume the debt of Third World countries* [emphasis added].

1987—New World Order to replace Cold War, according to George Ball, Under Secretary of State and CFR member. In a December 7th address to the U.N., Gorbachev calls for moving "forward to a new world order." [It seems that December 7th, the "day that will live in infamy" for the sneak attack on Pearl Harbor, is still bearing bitter fruit—Author.]

1989—President Bush invites Soviets to join World Order in his address to the graduating class of Texas A&M on May 12th.

1990—Gorbachev, in an address at Stanford University, refers to a new world and says: "The Soviet Union and the United States have more than enough reasons to be partners in building it. . . .a truly global economy, indeed, and the creation of a new civilization." In the Summer/Fall edition of the World Federalist Association newsletter, Deputy Director Eric Cox faults the American press for not grasping the significance of the developments and refers to them as "slow-witted." In a September 11th address to Congress, President Bush calls the Gulf War an opportunity for New World Order . . .and a new age. On September 25th the Soviets link the Gulf Crisis to the New World Order, referring to the invasion of Kuwait as "an act of terrorism perpetrated against the emerging New World Order." November 23rd, Prime Minister Thatcher is forced to resign, in part due to her opposition to Britain's prospective economic union with Europe, because it would adversely impact on British sovereignty.

1991—New World Order praised in State of the Union message by President Bush, as "a big idea—a new world order. . .the rule of law. . . .The illumination of a thousand points of light. . . ." On February 6th, President Bush promotes the New World Order to the Economic Club of New York. February 7th, Senator Jesse Helms in a lone voice of dissent, said he hopes it would be a "long time before a 'new world order'. . . ." Bush praised in an article in the *Washington Times* for "wisely pointing America's resulting

world leadership toward the objective of a 'new world order'. . . . "
"Rethinking America's Security: Beyond Cold War to New World
Order"—In June the Council on Foreign Relations co-sponsored
a conference to explore what was called "the changing global
role of the U.S. in the 1990's." Among the topics included was
one called "The End of American History: American Security,
the National Purpose, and the New World Order." Later, there
was a closed-door meeting of the Bilderberg Society in Baden-
Baden, Germany. The Bilderbergers also exert considerable clout
in determining the foreign policies of their respective governments. On June 18th Secretary of State James Baker said our
structures need to promote "the ideals of the Enlightenment."
In July, the Southeastern World Affairs Institute discusses the
New World Order. In late July on a CNN program, CFR member
and former CIA director Stansfield Turner stated: ". . . the United
Nations is deliberately intruding into the sovereignty of a sovereign nation . . . . Now this is a marvelous precedent [to be used
in] all countries of the world. . . . "

On October 24th, the *Wall Street Journal* referred to "the
cornerstone in President Bush's oft-mentioned 'new world order'."
On October 26th, a letter published in *The New York Times,* writ-
ten by Douglas Mattern, president of the Association of World
Citizens, proposes Gorbachev be named new U.N. Secretary
General "to help bring about world unity." On October 29th,
David Funderburk, former U.S. Ambassador to Romania, tells a
North Carolina audience: "George Bush has been surrounding
himself with people who believe in one-world government. They
believe that the Soviet system and the American system are con-
verging." The vehicle to bring this about, said Funderburk, is the
United Nations, "the majority of whose 166 member states are
socialist, atheist, and anti-American." On October 30th at the
Middle East Peace Talks, Gorbachev again espouses "a new era,
a new age" and "a new world order."

While the motives of some internationalists may appear well-
meaning, there is cause for serious misgivings over the objectives
of "one-worlders." Among the skeptics is Robert Morris, the geopolitical authority and chairman of America's Future. "The term,
'new world order,' has a nice ring to it," says Morris, "but there
are caveats. Experience tells us that instead of entrusting our
foreign policy to a U.N. dominated by enemies of freedom, we
should maintain and strengthen the traditional values and principles that have made our independent nation the beacon of hope
for oppressed peoples everywhere."

May I suggest that you get the book by Dr. Dennis Cuddy entitled

Now is the Dawning of the New Age New World Order. It is published by Hearthstone Publishing, Ltd., P. O. Box 815, Oklahoma City, OK 73101. Phone 1-800-652-1144. And this pamphlet, *The New World Order: A Critique and Chronology,* is far more comprehensive than we have the space to include here. I suggest you obtain copies both for yourself and for distribution. It is available for a modest fee in small or large quantities from: America's Future, Inc., P. O. Box 1625, Milford, PA 18337-2625.

In the *Monetary & Economic Review,* Vol. IX, No. 10, October, 1993, James M. Roberts, LL.M., J.D., wrote a page-one article entitled "Educating for the New World Order: An Exposé of the Educrats' Plans to Abuse Your Children." Dr. Roberts is a Colorado State Senator, a former law professor, and a member of the Senate Education, Finance, State Affairs, and Appropriations Committees, and is eminently qualified to address this subject, therefore, I am going to quote heavily from his article.

"The continued deterioration of the American family is used as justification for more public school programs. . . . While big government has been discredited from Moscow to Washington, the education elite are pushing for an even bigger government colossus. In short, it's just socialism dressed up in modern garb.

"Yet, it is the public schools that are the cause of the deterioration of the family. Schools are used to separate children from parents—that is and has been the central goal since Horace Mann (generally known as the Father of American Public Education) announced it in 1837 as part of his effort to promote non-sectarian education. . . . Mann wanted "character" education without a higher authority.

"Today, we are well-along toward the goal of preparing the next generation for a New World Order socialism. . . through a system of global education known generally as "outcome based" (OBE) education. OBE is the development of a group of social engineers . . . . [and] not what most people think; the actual meaning of the term is the transformation of the educational system involving orientations in a process that will create a set of beliefs and values."

There's that "doublespeak" again. It sounds like one thing, but actually means another. Many people who firmly believe in the Judeo-Christian ethics system frequently complain about the public schools not teaching the students any moral values. Unfortunately, that is not true. They are thoroughly indoctrinating them in values. . . just the wrong ones! Dr. Roberts points out that "without realizing it, what the schools are doing, in 'values clarification and critical thinking,' is attacking the Hebrew-Christian values of the American Declaration of Independence, free-market economics, and educational excellence based on higher literacy. Instead, these schools are substituting the values of equality (redistribute the wealth), tolerance (for all except Christians and Jews), and secular humanism. These are the principles of socialism and tyranny."

Dr. Roberts continues, "Outcome Based Education is a total education reform designed to achieve the production of a generation of humanists 'liberated' in their behavior from the restraints of Hebrew-Christian ethics and morality. The objective (or outcome) is the creation of a humanist society. The plan of the education establishment from Horace Mann . . . through John Dewey . . . to William Spady has been not only to change society, but also to erase from human consciousness any dependence on God. What has been going on is spiritual warfare . . . a war of world views.

"It has taken years for the humanist psychologists, sociologists, and behavioral scientists to devise their OBE plan, carefully cloaked in words with hidden meanings. Outcome Based Education is a process by which traditional ethical and moral values are to be overthrown and replaced by the socialist humanist values of the New World Order."

The Futurists have long promoted the idea of a one-world government. Below are some specific quotations from an article entitled, "One World," by William E. Halal and Alexander I. Nikitin (one allegedly representing the view of the U.S. and the other the view of the U.S.S.R.), which appeared in the November/December 1990 issue of *The Futurist* magazine. These comments pretty much speak for themselves about where the Futurists stand on these issues.

> If the United States and the Soviet Union are unable to meet this challenge of redefining capitalism and socialism for a new era, Japan and Germany may emerge as major power centers governing the new world order. In this scenario, the United States would continue its economic decline to become a second-rate global power, much like Britain. . . .
>
> The most optimistic scenario would occur if the two super-powers could create a New Capitalism and a New Socialism, especially if they could work together to combine these new systems into a common framework to organize a new global order....
>
> **One World**
> . . . The next great step in social development is to synthesize these two once-great ideologies into a common conceptual framework upon which to construct a unified global order. . . .
>
> Sometime in the next decade or so, *about the turn of the century,* the coming union of a New Capitalism and a New Socialism should permit a more-active working partnership between the

superpowers, produce a vibrant global economy, reduce armaments, and *create some type of world governance.* Even now,
global enterprises from major nations are starting joint ventures
in each other's countries, thereby beginning to intermesh national
economies into one indivisible economic whole that may soon
include a common *global currency and banking system....*

...As the revolutionary force of information technology
spreads to create a central nervous system for the planet, this
trajectory should reach the next logical state of progress: a
coherent, manageable global order that works—**One World**
[italic and bold emphasis added by author].

Another article entitled, "Reflections: The Disorders of Peace," by
Richard J. Barnet, appeared in the January 20, 1992, edition of *The
New Yorker* magazine. It shed some light on the end of the Cold War
and the Gulf Crisis' ability to push forward the establishment of the
New World Order. Below are some selected quotations; however, I
recommend you see your local library for back issues and peruse the
entire article.

Ever since the Cold War ended, there has been a good deal
of talk about a new world order, but, for all the talk, the nightly
news is a kaleidoscope of disorder....The world looks more
confused than ever, and in many ways more violent than when
talk of nuclear Armageddon was in fashion.

The major international conflict of the new postwar era—Iraq's
takeover of Kuwait . . .all organized by the United States—was
hailed by President Bush last March as the event that would make
the new world order possible....

...The dominant reality of the new era in world politics is the
globalization of the world economy.....no national government
can control the huge amounts of capital that travel across the
world via computer; twenty-four hours a day, every day, more than
five hundred billion dollars flows through the world's major
foreign-exchange markets, beyond the reach of any real regulation....Similarly in this era of a global economy, every American
worker is part of a global labor pool. Even top executives are
competing with non-Americans for their jobs....

...In the aftermath of the Gulf War victory, a number of
commentators concluded that *the United States could now police
the world* on behalf of the other industrial nations....

...Administration officials are saying that it is not in the
interest of the United States to assume the role of policeman in
Asia, Africa, and Latin America; but to date the conventional
forces assigned that role have not been cut.

There are, of course, essential peacekeeping and policing tasks that will have to be performed if the world is to move in the direction of law and order. The United Nations Charter provides a framework for drawing on international military forces for this purpose. The United States has considerable expertise to contribute to a new, permament collective-security arrangement, and the political climate for such an arrangement is more favorable than it has been at any other time in this century. . . .

. . . Nations still caught in the logic of the old order face the prospect of decline and instability at home [This is disinformation in action, folks! They have to convince us that we can't get along without them and their new system of one-world government.]....

. . . To deal with the opportunities of peace as well as with its dangerous disorders, a genuinely pragmatic vision will require much bigger changes in this society than we have contemplated for fifty years. It will also require a *leap of faith*—not in the perfectibility of human nature but in the capacity of human beings to adapt their institutions to the needs of the species and of the earth itself [emphasis added].

In the "Notebook" section of the February 1993 edition of *Harper's Magazine,* Lewis H. Lapham wrote an article which he called, "God's Gunboats," which, loosely interpreted, means you can get away with anything as long as you say you're doing it for God and the greater good. Below are some excerpts of Lapham's views of the excuses used by Reagan and Bush to plunge us further toward the New World Order.

Because the American public likes to believe that its cause is either noble or just, the argument must be phrased in the language of chivalry or holy crusade, and when President George Bush sent the army to Somalia last December he borrowed the persona of a medieval pope . . . . he told the television audience that it was a mission to "ease suffering and save lives," to rescue from death "thousands of innocents.". . .

On the same day, and at almost the same time that President Bush was speaking from the White House, former President Ronald Reagan was expounding his own geopolitical doctrine to an audience in Oxford, England . . . . "Evil," he said, "still stalks the planet." As a means of conquering that evil, Reagan urged the United Nations to assemble "an army of conscience . . . nothing less than a human velvet glove backed by a steel fist of military force."

When President Bush first introduced the theory of the new world order in the autumn of 1990 as a means of promoting the war in the Persian Gulf [This shows how uninformed even the most informed are when it relates to how long the concept of the New World Order has been with us.] . . . .

If the new world order can be understood to embody a spiritual purpose, it need not bother with the worldly distractions of politics. . . . Like the decisions to send the army to Panama and the Persian Gulf, the decision to relieve Somalia was made without reference to the will of Congress or the opinion of the American people. A few of the president's counselors attended a *series of quiet meetings under the auspices of the National Security Council* and entertained the advice of a few invited guests. . . .

. . . November 21 and December 3 columnists of both the left and the right strongly advocated policies of "benign intervention" and "aggressive humanitarianism.". . .

. . . The new world order blurs the distinctions between the reasons of state and the uses of publicity, and the modern forms of gunboat diplomacy have to do with the transfer of symbols and the projection of images rather than with anything so crass as seizing the spoils of war. . . .

By redefining the balance of power as the peace of God, the new world order recasts the military establishments as quasi-religious organizations and provides them with the permanent tasks of salvation. President Harry Truman's old doctrine of containment, the one that set forth the premise of the Cold War in 1947, bound the United States to protect the world only from Communists. The doctrines of aggressive humanitarianism not only broaden and extend the mission but also guarantee the safety of the defense budget. . . .

Near the conclusion of his article Lapham makes this remarkable— but accurate—assessment of the New World Order: "Like God, the new world order reserves the right to decide which of the innumerable evils that stalk the planet deserve punishment or correction. . . ." Reading this, I'm reminded of another quotation, the one that ends "absolute power corrupts absolutely"!

In *Newsweek,* April 6, 1992, an article entitled "*This* Is the New World Order?" makes the following statements within the text:

Poor Somalia—first a battleground for the cold war, now a testing ground for the new world order. . . .

Many Somalis, starving or caught in the cross-fire, also are looking to the rejuvenated United Nations to somehow rescue what remains of their country. . . . Washington funds 30 percent of U.N. peacekeeping operations. . . .

. . . Sister Maria, a nun who has spent 16 years in Somalia [says] "The U.N. can come and see the situation, but they also have to act." *If they can't stop the chaos, then what is the new world order?* [Emphasis added.]

In the July 26, 1993, edition of *Newsweek,* in an article by Tom Post entitled, "A Despot's Survival Guide: Dictators Mocking the New World Order," the opening paragraph reads like this: " 'Clever tyrants,' Voltaire wrote, 'are never punished.' These days, even the dumber ones can get by. That wasn't supposed to happen in the new world order." No comment necessary!

U.S. News & World Report, May 18, 1992, addresses who foots the bill for all these U.N. operations in an article entitled, "The U.N. to the Rescue."

> United Nations peacekeepers are the darlings of the new world order. Since the start of 1988, the year in which the blue-berets were awarded the Nobel Peace Prize, the Security Council has authorized 12 new peacekeeping missions, as many as it had in the previous 53 years of the U.N.'s existence. . . .On the basis of these efforts, President Bush declared in January, "the United Nations has come into a very important new phase in its existence, fulfilling the dreams of some of its founding fathers."
>
> . . .The annual cost of U.N. peacekeeping operations has more than tripled, from about $750 million in 1991 to more than $2.7 billion this year, and member nations are currently behind in their peacekeeping payments to the tune of $602 million [not really very much when compared with the annual total for this year— author]. . . . [the U.S. is] responsible for 25 percent of the cost of regular U.N. operations and just over 30 percent of peacekeeping missions.
>
> . . .Still, it is unclear whether other member nations, many of whom also are facing budget problems, will take up the slack. Japan [is] everyone's favorite new world order cash cow. . . . [Emphasis added.]

In a book review in the February 21, 1994, issue of *Business Week,* Robert J. Dowling reports on a new book by Richard J. Barnet and John Cavanagh (Simon & Schuster, 480 pp.) entitled, *Global Dreams: Imperial Corporations and The New World Order.* It elaborates on the part to be played by the international giants and conglomerates in the industrial and information fields. Following are a couple of pertinent points to this publication:

> . . .Now, it's a "few hundred corporate giants. . .many bigger than most sovereign nations," becoming not just economic agents, but "the world empires of the 21st century." The authors focus on five: Bertelsmann, Philip Morris, Sony, Ford Motor, and

Citicorp. Each, they say, is a pillar of the new order, in which media and entertainment, consumer marketing, global manufacturing, and global finance are combining to form a *vast global shadow government.*

Like a lot of confused globalists, Barnet and Cavanagh are trying to redraw the post-cold-war map using an old, nationalistic template. To them, almost any form of government economic control seems better than today's unregulated, market-driven mania. . . . [Emphasis added.]

"Societies at Hyper-Speed," an article by Alvin Toffler (author of *Future Shock*) and Heidi Toffler, appeared in the Sunday, October 31, 1993, edition of *The New York Times.* The Bible tells us that in the last days knowledge will increase, and the implication is that it will increase exponentially. The Tofflers concur, although their reasons are based on observations of what is going on around them, rather than because of any biblical reference. They write: "U.S. foreign and military policy is swerving like a drunken driver without a map. . . .We need to start by understanding that the old world map is obsolete . . . .We are undergoing the deepest rearrangement of global power since the birth of industrial civilization. . . .powerful forces . . .are shaping the global system of the next century. . . .Economies rely on complex electronic infrastructures—like the data superhighway. . . .The real decision-making powers of the future. . .will be transnational companies in alliance with city-regional governments. . . .thousands of transnational organizations—Greenpeace, for example— are springing up like mushrooms to form a new 'civil society.' Add to these components of the new global system world religions like Roman Catholicism and Islam,. . . it is clear that the world system built around neatly defined nation-states is being replaced by a kind of global computer. . . .In 1930 the U.S. was a party to only 34 treaties or agreements with other countries; today, with the world's most knowledge-intensive economy, it is party to more than 1,000 treaties and tens of thousands of agreements [remember, I warned you earlier of the danger that treaties can supersede our Constitutional protections] . . . ."

Let's get down to some real specifics of how this is affecting us here at home, in America. . . right now!

In a Voice of Americanism publication by W. S. McBirnie, Ph.D., he sheds the following light on The Financial Crimes Enforcement Network (FCEN—also referred to as FINCEN):

The FCEN is an insidious agency the U.S. public knows nothing about, and through which the financial records of banks, retailers, and individuals are being made available to foreign authorities, without public announcement or the permission of the people harmed. The Mutual Legal Assistance Treaty (MLAT) [There's that "T" word again!], the main instrument of the FCEN so far, is a written agreement between the U.S. and other nations (Switzerland, Mexico, and Canada are the first ones to sign one) to cooperate in collecting information on anything each government deems a financial crime in tracking money flows between countries and within each respective banking system.

The MLAT also guarantees mutual assistance in finding people, confiscating property, and taking cases of financial crime to court. Once all significant countries have MLATs with the U.S., the global planners will establish a world headquarters for tax investigation and prosecution, assisted by Interpol (the International Criminal Police Organization).

"But," you may ask, "we've got the greatest military in the world . . . how can they take that away from us and give our armed services to the U.N.?" In the August, 1994, edition of *The McAlvany Intelligence Advisor,* Don McAlvany writes as follows:

> On 5/3/94, Bill Clinton signed an Executive Order, Presidential Decision Directive 13 (now designated PDD-25) which is a quantum leap in surrendering our sovereignty to the UN. PDD-25 provides for the:
>
> 1) Placing of U.S. troops under UN command;
> 2) Sharing classified U.S. intelligence information with the UN [**ED. NOTE:** And of course it will go straight to the Russians];
> 3) Repealing of the law that limits the amount of troops the U.S. can commit to the UN *without* Congressional approval;
> 4) Establishing of a UN peacekeeping financial account for UN military operations—again, *bypassing* Congress.
>
> PDD-25 gives the UN carte blanche to deploy U.S. troops at UN officials' whims, to deploy them to any sovereign country on the UN's target list, and to draw a check on the U.S. Treasury's account to pay for the operation. After 18 U.S. troops were slaughtered in Somalia (6 of those were beheaded, disemboweled, and mutilated) when the UN commander refused to send them aid, Senator Trent Lott (R-MS) charged:
>
> *"The Clinton Administration appears dedicated to sending the U.S. military into the dangerous seas of multinational peacekeeping in an effort to elevate the status of the United Nations into the guardian arbiter of the New World Order. Key to this new vision of the world is a vision of a New World Army whose singular purpose is to enforce the whims of the arcane United Nations Secur-*

ity Council.

"Under the new PPD-13 (now PDD-25) the U.S. becomes the trainer and bill payer of an effort to create a military command structure for the Secretary General of the United Nations."

Congressman Bill Goodling, in a strong letter to President Clinton, accused him of *"issuing a blank check by committing U.S. troops to the UN under foreign command, thereby making UN initiatives U.S. commitments, and UN conflicts U.S. conflicts, while forfeiting the leadership of U.S. troops on the ground. . . . Ordering the deployment of U.S. troops under foreign command does not properly serve U.S. interests."* Goodling and 32 other Congressmen co-signed the letter.

Pat Buchanan wrote on the issue: *". . . the Clinton Doctrine, as defined in PDD-13, is a surrender of U.S. sovereignty, a betrayal of the ideas upon which our republic was founded. It is a formula for making American soldiers Hessians of an imperial army, whose interventions could make America the most hated nation on Earth. . . . The idea of an endless spilling of American blood chasing would-be dictators and warlords around the world—to guarantee the survival, or return, of regimes such as Jean Bertrand Aristide's in Haiti—is an absurd redefinition of U.S. national interests."*

[**ED. NOTE:** Illustrative of the Clintonista attitude of subjugating the U.S. military to the UN is Al Gore's incredible remark on the day of the death of 15 Americans from "friendly fire" in Iraq. The Vice President extended *"condolences to the families of those who died in the service of the United Nations."*

Well, so far we have discussed efforts to involve U.S. forces (and finances) in "peacekeeping" operations around the world, and that would be bad enough, but the treachery doesn't stop there . . . now they want to open our own borders for military interference from outside sources. In June, 1994, Clinton's administration announced that Russian troops will soon be training and conducting joint military exercises on U.S. soil. It was planned originally for these joint activities to take place in Russia, but the Russian government and military declined in no uncertain terms.

In the June 1, 1994, edition of the *Washington Times,* Senator Sam Nunn is quoted: "I think that our American people will welcome a Russian military force for peacekeeping purposes." Yushenkov, Chairman of the Russian Defense Committee, welcomed the idea, but, according to *The New York Times* on June 4th, he wanted *us* to pay for transporting their troops and equipment over here (and word on the street is that Clinton is going to comply).

There are a number of as-yet-unsubstantiated reports indicating

Russian troops already have been training here, allegedly ground troops in Alaska, as well as joint chemical/biological warfare exercises in the southeastern United States.

Also in June, there were a number of reports of sightings of foreign combat vehicles in a myriad of locations in the U.S. Two Russian tanks were sighted on flatbed trucks near Fort Stockton, Texas. Hundreds of railroad flatcars bearing Russian military vehicles and armor, as well as UN vehicles and armor, have been spotted in Montana, Colorado, Wyoming, Pennsylvania, and South Carolina. In Mississippi, hundreds of Russian-built vehicles being refurbished for the UN are located in a large depot near Gulfport . . . allegedly, just to be "repainted." The equipment reportedly is designed to perform a variety of functions, some of the more specialized of which include: chemical and biological decontamination vehicles, urban warfare and rapid-assault offensive vehicles, armed with short-barreled 75 mm cannons and Sagger anti-tank missiles, in addition to your standard jeep-like vehicles, trucks, and personnel carriers, some of which already were painted white with UN insignia painted on them.

In an extensive report of these sightings, the August, 1994, issue of *The McAlvany Intelligence Advisor* states:

> This writer has for several years been receiving reports of Russian activity (i.e., civilian and military) in various locations in Alaska. Russian military jets fly into Alaskan air fields—some on their way to U.S. air bases in the lower 48 states. Evidence has been found of Russian Spetsnaz teams reconnoitering on Alaskan soil. It should be remembered that Zhirnovsky has said that Alaska still belongs to Russia.
>
> If a Russian *"Red Dawn"* attack on America ever took place, or a UN/New World Order "peacekeeping" action should eventuate in America, perhaps to put down the "dangerous opponents of the New World Order and radical supporters of the 'antiquated' U.S. Constitution," there is no doubt in this writer's mind that Alaska could be quickly occupied by Russian troops—probably under the UN flag.
>
> This writer believes that though Russia is an integral part of the New World Order, it will eventually doublecross its socialist "partners" in the New World Order and make a move for its own global hegemony. Remember, Russia never dismantled its KGB or massive war machine—including 45,000 warheads still targeted primarily on America.

And internal terrorist action such as the bombing of the federal building in Oklahoma City during April, 1995, is going to be just the type of catalyst they need to justify UN "peacekeeping" inside our borders. Within days following this tragic event, CNN and many other news sources reported that Clinton announced a five-feature program being instigated to inhibit further terrorist attacks. It sounds like something really needed to prevent future acts of this nature, but, basically, it just grants more and more power to the agencies that already have more than is good for us!

Just prior to all the above activity (in May, 1994), in two days of meetings in Moscow, a high-level delegation from the Clinton Administration set about systematically revealing all of our defense and security secrets, including number and types of weapons, as well as their locations and code names. In July, seven Russian defense officials actually were given a tour of the Rocky Flats (Colorado) nuclear weapons plant where most of our top secret plutonium triggers have been produced and stored for decades. Don McAlvany points out: "Four decades ago, the Rosenbergs were executed for giving such secrets to the Russians. If (or when) Russia ever turns on America, these Clinton officials should be charged with high treason!" It seems to me if we let these people get away with this, we probably owe an apology to the Rosenbergs. I'm only jesting...giving away your country's vital secrets is *always* treason—whether its currently or four decades ago.

I'm sure this is "more than you ever wanted to know" about the New World Order, but there are still a couple of subjects that I need to address before I bring this chapter to a conclusion, i.e. what the World Federalist Association thinks about our move toward a New World Order, disarming the third-world nations, the World Health Organization (specifically their activities in controlling the world's population), and the "regionalizing" of America. Then I will conclude by discussing *when* this will all take place and what we can do (within the law) to slow the progress.

In a book entitled *A New World Order: Can it Bring Security to the World's People? Essays on Restructuring the United Nations,* published September, 1991, by the World Federalist Association, in Part Four, Section 16, Gerald Biesecker-Mast quotes Richard Falk: "The rhetorical appeals to democracy and a new world order that have been heard in the Gulf War must not obscure the struggles for democratization and a just world order that so urgently remain before us.... It is evident that *the new world order as conceived in Washington is about control and surveillance,* not about values or a better life for the peoples of the world [emphasis added]."

This "same song, second verse..." of surveillance and control just keeps rearing its ugly head throughout this New World Order. Biesecker-Mast goes on to proclaim: "World law has been posited as an alternative to powerful nations pursuing unilateral aims at the expense of the weak." Both he and Falk have concluded that the Gulf War was just a case of the North exercising power over the South by maintaining a technology gap which prevents the wealthy nations from being imperiled by the poorer.

He quotes George Bush as saying to American servicemen at Maxwell Air Force Base on May 15, 1991, in which Bush describes what the New World Order *does not* mean for him. "The new world order does not mean surrendering our national sovereignty or forfeiting our interests." *Nonsense!* That's exactly what it means! Now, lest you get the impression that the World Federalists are the "good guys" and share our opinions, please stand corrected. The fault they would find with Bush's statement—even though they took it at face value, rather than an outright lie—is that it doesn't go far enough. . . *they believe him* and interpret his remarks as proving that he doesn't plan to yield our country entirely into the hands of a one-world government and level out the global playing field—which is what they seek.

Of course, they would have no problem with disarming the third-world countries, although these developing nations might want to take issue with that plan.

The 1994 UN Human Development Report (UNDP), calls for greatly expanded UN power to intervene militarily in the sovereign territory of any nation, while also ordering the concurrent dismantling of the military forces of the developing countries—stripping their national security. However, I see nothing limiting this action just to the third-world/developing nations. It just as easily could be applied to the U.S., in fact, our defense industries and military forces and bases are already in the process of being reduced and/or dismantled.

The UNDP report lists five cases in which UN Blue Helmet troops *must* be deployed into the internal conflicts in nations: (1) mass slaughter of the population of the state; (2) decimation through starvation or the withholding of health or other services; (3) forced exodus; (4) occupation and the denial of the right to self-determination; and (5) environmental destruction. The UN will have *carte blanche* to charge right in to any nation, whenever and wherever it chooses.

Further, the UNDP calls for these nations to completely disarm and demobilize their military and integrate its personnel back into civilian society, as well as promoting national arms control. The Economic Security Council could demand compliance as a condition of future loans or emergency aid. By inference, we can assume that nations who fail to comply would also be subject to UN sanctions. . .or even invasion.

The "regionalizing" of the United States may not seem so important, but in fact is basic in grabbing back the power from the local and state governments and placing it in the control of 10 regions already established by the UN.

First, let me point out that this plan is not new; it was originally conceived about 1935 with nine regions (the UN plan calls for 10). It did not pass as originally presented, but instead of taking "no" for an answer, they just did an "end run" around the naysayers and charged right ahead, using another approach. And we since have been brainwashed into accepting without question the necessity of these regions. They are used by the IRS, the postal service, and numerous other agencies—even UPS—and now they are *appearing on the back of Kix cereal boxes* (a General Mills product), although Kix used the nine-region map originally set forth in 1935. The advertising line reads: "America's Regions! Explore this great land of ours."

The following text appeared in information distributed by the Committee for Constitutional Treaties in Hanford, California:

> *The purpose is to indoctrinate families around the breakfast table into accepting the partitioning of the United States into "regions."* It is no secret! The purpose of dividing the United States into regions is explained in the article entitled, "Nine Groups Instead of the Forty-eight States." [Alaska and Hawaii were not states at the time.] These groups were also known as "departments" and they were assigned [descriptive] names [based on their area].
>
> The article, which ran in *The New York Times Magazine* on April 21, 1935, disclosed the primary reason for the new "departments" (regions), which was to make a "drastic change in our form of government . . . and *to abolish our states.*" However, the outgoing governor in the State of Colorado blew the whistle on this unlawful activity and exposed the plan which brought this 1935 effort to a temporary halt.
>
> Everyone knows that *if the states are abolished, our Constitution will be abolished* because the Constitution is a compact amongst the states (which protects the natural rights of the people). At the conclusion of the article it was admitted that there would be great resistance to this plan. Those who favored it were called "revisionists."
>
> This 1935 article concluded with this sentence: *"The revisionists may never be heard from publicly, especially if the federal courts soon experience a miraculous transformation and begin with unanimity interpreting law in the light of social change."* (This transformation was engineered by the appointment of judges: their education and placement. It also explains why the courts do not object to this illegal activity.)

...The map shows the ten region delineations under which the *United States has been operated since 1972.* These are administrative units of United Nations control over our country. All of the people of the United States were placed into one of the ten federal "regions" .... [by] *Executive Order No. 11647 and it was issued by President Richard M. Nixon.* The foreign powers who meet at the United Nations pass resolutions....the head of government *must get the resolution and its requirements enacted into law in the U.S. by any method possible....*This is the reason for the *strange changes in American government.* It is not good.
...*Bush calls the United Nations "the superior body."* It is an unconstitutional outlook....it is also working to move the people away from elected representation into a system controlled by a *self-appointed elite.* In the State of California the speaker of the Assembly, Willie Brown, has openly expressed a desire to abolish local governments (cities, counties, and special districts) which is part of the plan to abolish the states. The regional system is *unlimited* in its scope and powers....
...the Declaration of Independence...*does not allow our form of government to be changed WITHOUT THE CONSENT OF THE GOVERNED. The people have NOT given their consent* to this obvious overthrow of our lawful 1789 Constitutional government and they never will!...*The 1789 Constitution is a control on power.* It limits the power that man can exercise over his fellow man and it safeguards the natural rights given to the people by the Creator. It does not deal with economics. *It is a necessary fortress against tyranny, usurpation, and abuse....we should be objecting* to the indoctrination...of our children at the breakfast table!
The regional system is a military system. This fact will become more apparent as the federal program for General and Complete Disarmament (Public Law 87-297) advances and is *fully integrated on the regional basis....*

In his book entitled *Marxism and the National Question,* Joseph Stalin outlined the following: "Divide the world into regional groups as a transitional stage to total world government. Later, the regional groups can be brought all the way into single world dictatorship." I want to continue by quoting further from the Committee for Constitutional Treaties' publication.

Pres. Geo. Bush's New World Order is a rehash of F.D.R.'s world govt. plans. The diagram is the plan set forth by the National Resources Planning Board in the 1930's during the administration of FDR, with the *stated purpose of abolishing the states.* Read the article which accompanied the map as they ran in *The New York Times* in 1935. In the least, read the *first* paragraph and the *last* paragraph. Since the public outcry was so great, the Congress shut down the National Resources Planning Board in 1942; however the plans of the NRPB were shelved only *temporarily*.

    . . .*The dormant plans were activated in 1969 under Pres. Richard M. Nixon who partitioned the nation . . . in order* to install the regional system. In 1935 "regionalists" were called "revisionists." The plans today are the same as they were then—to disintegrate the states and the counties and to substitute *a socialist management system*. The new management system is not only geographical in change—it is a *totally different concept* of government, socially and economically. It means complete control—a *totally centralized government in Washington, D.C. It is both totalitarianism and dictatorship commanded under the United Nations system.*

    When the states are *abolished entirely* (which is very near) our palladium of freedom and liberty will *simultaneously be abolished.* The regional system is *military* in full operation. These activities being carried out by government officials are *against the law!* Protest to your state representative.

The publication concludes with the following:

    In the 1930's when people *rejected* the idea of abolishing the states, the method by which the effort was to be continued is revealed in the very last two paragraphs in this article. *Judges were selected to "begin with unanimity to interpret law in the light of the changes" desired by the designers of the new world order. Geographical, physical, economic, and social changes were then engineered to accommodate and promote the transition,* with the Congress supplying *continual legislation to advance the effort.*

    By keeping the people in utter ignorance, what was once a *theory* in the thirties, thus became an *accomplished fact. Dual governments* have been in operation since the. . .United Nations ten regions were installed. *Constitutional government hangs on a thin thread. As soon as our guns get taken away, our Constitution and individual land ownership will cease,* which is a *stated goal* of the United Nations. *Your State Legislature could stop this again as in F.D.R.'s day.*

Please remember that last statement when I get to the end of this chapter and make some suggestions as to what you can do about all this!

I mentioned earlier some of the "alphabet soup" already established on a regional working basis, but there are other agencies either already working by regions, or scheduled to do so in the near future, i.e. health

care control, federal programs (welfare), penitentiaries, law enforcement (CIA, FBI, Secret Service), etc., etc. Now, thanks to NAFTA, we
are lumped into a much bigger region—U.S., Canada, and Mexico.
GATT/WTO (World Trade Organization) is now in effect, as well.

The World Health Organization (WHO), another United Nations
invention, has been meddling in the affairs of countries around the
world for some time now. Under the guise of wanting to improve health
conditions around the world, they systematically have been moving
forward with their covert plans to reduce the world's population. A
UNDP report warns that the United Nations needs greatly enhanced
global powers to enforce population reduction, stating, ". . .the biggest threat to 'human security' is unchecked population growth." And
if you are naive enough to believe that birth control, abortion, and
euthanasia are all they have on the drawing board, guess again!

There is widespread belief in the medical community that WHO
started the AIDS epidemic nearly 20 years ago with some smallpox
inoculations in Africa—it now threatens over half the population
(250± million). Ten thousand Haitians working in the Belgian Congo
received the vaccinations and took AIDS back to Haiti, which was a
favorite vacation spot for American homosexuals, who brought it
home to America, where it spread rapidly through the gay community,
and eventually to the heterosexuals. Brazil also received the WHO
smallpox inoculations and AIDS broke out there at about the same
time as in Africa.

Don McAlvany, in *The McAlvany Intelligence Advisor,* August, 1994,
writes:

> This writer has a friend who personally knows a high official
> in the UN who once bragged to him that AIDS was a most
> "fortuitous disease" and had great potential for world population
> control. This writer heard similar sentiments expressed by several
> high officials in the former South African government.
>
> This writer also personally knows a very prominent AIDS
> researcher and a very prominent U.S. surgeon, both of whom are
> extremely knowledgeable about the virus, and both of whom
> believe that the AIDS virus, the Hanta virus, Legionnaires Disease,
> and many of the new designer viruses now emerging on the world
> scene have come straight from someone's biological warfare
> laboratories.

Robert McNamara, former Secretary of Defense, former head of the
World Bank, and a leader in the globalist movement, said that global
overpopulation is a worse problem than global nuclear war. President
Carter's Global 2000 Report called for the world population to be

reduced to two billion by the year 2000.

In his excellent *Phoenix Letter,* Dr. Antony Sutton recently wrote:

> Events in Somalia support the hypothesis that genocide is a covert United Nations policy. Two million Somalis were allowed to die of starvation before any attempt was made to send food. In Rwanda, at least 500,000 have died in tribal warfare. If the UN really believed in world peace, it could have stopped the slaughter. We see Burundi as the next locale for genocide, then possibly India and Bangladesh.
>
> What we see is a UN policy of covertly triggering genocide through social and economic policies, then standing to one side in a handwringing pose until a few more million people are removed from the earth. Next September in Cairo, the UN will hold an international conference on Population and Development. Watch this conference. We suspect it will focus on such goals as zero population growth and limited economic growth to starve populations of developing countries, along with the usual package of anti-family, abortion, sterilization proposals.
>
> The coming several decades will see the covert policy of genocide kill billions.

Well, if there were any doubt left, that should clarify the position of "Benevolent Big Brother" (read that: the United Nations/New World Order).

When, when, when will we *see* these things about which we have been warned by so many? Wake up and smell the coffee! If you don't see them now, it's because your head is in the sand and *you just don't want to see.*

Marilyn Brannan, Associate Editor of the *Montetary & Economic Review,* said in the February, 1995, issue, in an article subtitled, "When Will the New World Order Come About?":

> "What's the time table for this one world order socialist system to come about? When is all this economic and political disorder going to take place?. . ."

The answer: We read their stuff. In fact, the economic and political elite of the world have, of late, been more open in communicating their plans to their own troops. We simply listen, read what they say, and then report it to you.

In the spring of 1992, *Foreign Affairs* magazine (the primary communications medium of the elitist Council on Foreign Relations [CFR]) published an article entitled "A New Concert of Powers," by Richard Rosecrance, Professor of Political Science at UCLA, presenting a scholarly and carefully crafted argument that "a new concert of powers" is necessary to prevent the world from lapsing *very soon* into *total chaos.*

. . .Using the Professor's timetable, and we agree with his assessment that the world situation is (to use his words) "urgent and precarious," we can assume that we are accelerating rapidly toward a critical point on the continuum: 1996-1999.

Ground Zero: 2000?. . . . In his words, *"If this system is not firmly established within that period* (7 to 10 years from 1989), *the world order may again lapse into a balance of power or an unworkable multi-polar deterrence by the year 2000."*. . .and it is my guess that "we ain't seen nothin' yet."

In its broadest aspects, the new world order is the amalgamation of socialist political ideology and economic interdependence, bound together with a mix of Eastern mysticism, New Age ideas, and humanistic philosophy. . . .

Humanism and new age teachings, with their emphasis on the concept that man is basically good and that peace and harmony can be attained if we just reorder our society, are very dangerous. The gurus and prophets of a global society—the Humanists and social activists who subscribe to *The Humanist Manifesto*—will be the ones who lead society into anarchy in their process of re-ordering it. . . .What all the peace movements fail to recognize is that there are, and always have been, men who desire power above all things. They will manipulate governments, monetary systems, people—anything—to achieve their purposes.

Practically speaking, globalism might be a great idea if it were not for the problem of human nature and the reality of evil in the universe. . . .

We have yet to consider the economic implications generated by the push to the New World Order. As there are several other chapters that will elaborate on the subjects of the Illuminati, Skull & Bones Society (formerly called The Brotherhood of Death), Council on Foreign Relations, Trilateral Commission, and Bilderbergers (chapter 5), the cashless society (chapter 11), and smart cards, national I.D. cards, *et al* (chapter 14), I will try to keep my comments here as brief as possible.

From an economic standpoint, the globalists already control the U.S. That can be documented from any number of sources. Probably of more concern is, "What's on their agenda?" The answer is, they are propelling us toward a New World Order. The main players in this global game are the "Big Bankers." One of the first steps toward one-world government is placing the financial and economic power into the hands of a few. Done! Because the new interstate banking laws have allowed the big eastern banks to swallow up so many of the small banks, 85% of banking assets in a 12-state region from New England to the Carolinas are now in the control of three New York "super-banks."

In 1913 the Federal Reserve System was established. Most people mistakenly believe that this is a government institution. Wrong! It is a privately held corporation whose stockholders' names are guarded carefully. But financial newsletter publisher R. E. McMaster discovered that the FED's principal—the top eight—stockholders are: Rothschild Banks (London and Paris), Lazard Brothers Banks (Paris), Israel Moses Seif Banks (Italy), Warburg Bank (Hamburg and Amsterdam), Lehman Brothers Bank (New York), Loeb Bank (New York), Chase Manhattan Bank (New York), and Goldman, Sachs Bank (New York). Foreign banks own a significant portion of *our* Federal Reserve.

The U.S. Constitution (Art. I, Sec. 8) prohibits *private* interest from issuing money or *regulating its value* (theoretically this is a job for Congress), therefore, the Federal Reserve technically is an illegal operation. It seems like its main concern is to regulate the value of our currency, lately changing it on an almost-daily basis.

A little history is in order here. A privately owned central bank was proposed originally by the grandfather of the Rockefeller brothers. All the American stockholders are connected in some way to the Rothschilds, the dominant European banking family and financiers of many American industrialists. Their goal was to finance a global socialist government which is *perceived* to be a democracy.

In the introduction to Gary Allen's *The Rockefeller File,* late Congressman Larry McDonald wrote:

> . . . [This is] the story. . . of the Rockefellers and their allies to create a one-world government combining super-capitalism and Communism under the same tent, all under their control. . . . John D. Rockefeller, Sr., used every devious strategy he could devise to create a gigantic oil monopoly. . . to use their economic power to gain political control for first America, and then the rest of the world.

Presently, they own nearly all the U.S. oil interests, and in 1966 controlled four of the seven largest oil companies in the world. They have promoted anti-capitalist, pro-socialist, pro-global curricula in our schools by the money they funnel through the Rockefeller Foundation to the NEA (National Education Association), in hopes of preparing students for a one-world government, where the U.S. no longer enjoys sovereign control over our nation.

Speaking of foundations, have you ever heard of the Rhodes Scholars? Just another tentacle on the octopus! Cecil Rhodes—a close ally of the Rothschilds—has used his wealth to provide scholarships for higher learning. How altruistic . . . how noble. Not when your hidden agenda is to get future leaders trained in the philosophy of advancing one-world government! Successfully, I might add. Hundreds hold or have held positions in education (including dozens of college presidents), media, and government—including President Clinton, who subsequently appointed a considerable number of his Rhodes buddies to top-level positions in our government.

I'll cover more of the plans of the UN in chapter four, because they are in the process of concocting many more schemes to interfere in our private and business activities.

What can you do to slow the progress of the impending New World Order? (As it fulfills Bible prophecy, it never can be stopped entirely.)

> All that is necessary for evil to triumph is that good men do nothing.
>
> — Edmund Burke

> The people are the masters of both Congress and the courts, not to overthrow the Constitution, but to overthrow the men who pervert it.
>
> — Abraham Lincoln

As I pointed out earlier, the majority of Americans have been blissfully asleep for the last few decades, happily enjoying their abundance and comforts, while socialists, globalists, and the New World Order advocates have been busy as little ants, gradually eroding the foundations of our Constitution, our heritage, our culture, and our traditional way of life. This nefarious group also has a hidden agenda (though, not so hidden any more) to bring America to the edge of a great chasm, then push her over into the New World Order.

It's true that God does have a plan in prophecy for our future, but we are specifically instructed in Scripture to "occupy till [He] comes," and friends, over the past years, many of us have deserted our posts in the political, educational, and economic arenas. We still—though perhaps for a brief time—are in the fortunate position to change what needs changing . . . or at least delay its progress. We can make an impact while the opportunity still is available to us. Traditionalist Americans have blocked the reimposition of the so-called "Fairness Doctrine" which virtually would have eliminated all talk radio (a battle we may have to fight again after President Clinton's attack on conservative talk radio following the Oklahoma City bombing—he blames the talk show hosts for instigating this heinous act through *inflammatory rhetoric*); for the moment they have stopped the move to kill off home schooling and private Christian schools; stopped the Clinton plan to end all hunting or fishing on national forest and other government lands, and temporarily blocked the EEOC from silencing freedom of religious speech and expression in the workplace.

These were not small victories, and they were hard-fought, hard-won victories, but they show what we can do when we get angry and join forces with others who share our anger and are willing to get involved.

There are dozens of large national organizations making a major contribution toward waking up the sleeping giant and turning the tide. Some of them are: Christian Coalition, Focus on the Family, Concerned Women for America, Family Research Council, Eagle Forum, Conservative Caucus, U.S. Taxpayers Party, Summit Ministries, John Birch Society, Gun Owners of America, and others, as well as other organizations whose major thrust is protecting our Constitutional rights, such as Jay Sekulow and the American Center for Law and Justice (ACLJ).

Giving much support in the battle are the excellent Christian and conservative talk shows across America which are waking up and informing tens of millions of us daily. Listen to them and give them your support. Write letters, send faxes, and make phone calls (to them and their sponsors, if they have sponsors), letting them know of your support. This will help keep them on the air.

The wicked deeds of the "political left" can thrive only in darkness—when exposed to the light of day, opposition begins to grow exponentially. This is why the "political left" is beginning to panic and is launching a major attack against the "Christian right." The most positive aspect of the growing resistance to the New World Order is the thousands of grass roots organizations which are springing up all across the country.

The August, 1994, edition of *The McAlvany Intelligence Advisor* states:

> The state legislature in Colorado has passed a resolution invoking the Tenth Amendment—ordering the federal government to confine itself to those specific powers which were Constitutionally delegated to it, and demanding that the federal government stay within those limits. A similar resolution has been introduced in the California state legislature by State Senator Don Rogers, and other state legislatures are considering adoption of same. The Tenth Amendment is being rediscovered all across the country.

Property rights groups are now starting to surface all across America to oppose the federal government's seizures of billions of dollars of personal property, i.e. private property, businesses, cars, boats, planes, bank accounts, *et al.* We need thousands of such groups opposing the myriad of different items on the socialist/one-world agenda, and the good news is that it is beginning to happen.

Just a word of warning: Do whatever you can within the law to prevent this Clinton health care system. Does the federal government work so well now in other areas that you want them in charge of your health needs? Certainly not! They will wreck the current system, then select your doctor for you (in your own *region,* of course).

Don McAlvany said it so well in the August, 1994, *The McAlvany Intelligence Advisor,* that I couldn't say it better, so below I have excerpted from the eight steps he recommends when addressing what we should do. (He generously encourages duplication and dissemination of his newsletter.)

It is time that Christians, traditionalists, and lovers of the U.S. Constitution and freedom *get mad, get busy, and go on the offensive.* The political left, the Clintonistas, and the New World Order crowd are presently very vulnerable because of the overt, outrageous behavior of the Clintonistas, and because the accelerated speed of their socialist juggernaut (especially since 1992) is waking up millions of Americans. [**ED. NOTE:** The Establishment may have made a tactical error. As with Carter, the Clintonistas may have gone too fast—awakening the "sleeping giant." Remember, Christians and conservatives slept through the Bush years, and he was as much (or more) a New World Order socialist as Bill Clinton. But the Establishment used "patient gradualism" and the "giant" slept on. The Clintonistas may have gone too fast because the "giant" is beginning to stir!]

Some constructive things you can do, in addition to supporting and getting involved with the organizations cited above [and don't forget or underestimate the power of prayer—author], include:

1. Study (not just read, but study) the U.S. Constitution—both you and your family. The political left and the New World Order crowd are working hard to dismantle it, but it is still intact and can be used to defend and save our Republic. For American lovers of freedom, it should be what the Bible is for Christians—a blueprint for action, success, and survival. [**ED. NOTE:** For the critics, this writer knows that the Bible is superior to the U.S. Constitution, but this writer firmly believes that these two are the great documents written in history. Study them both!]

2. Study the Constitutional concept of militias—and investigate or support any which may start up in your area if they are directed by reasonable, patriotic lovers of traditional values.

3. Support Your County Sheriff—if he is pro-Constitution, pro-gun ownership, pro-traditional values, and if he opposes the current onslaught against our freedoms. If you don't have such a sheriff, run and/or elect one! The county sheriff is one of the most powerful elected officials in America, and can be a major obstacle to a federal government power grab in your county. *Your county sheriff can be one of your last defenses against federal government tyranny and the New World Order.* Support yours, or elect one who will take a stand!

4. Get involved in the upcoming Congressional elections. [Author's Note: Even though the 1994 elections are over, and the balance of power has shifted in both the House and the Senate, this is still good advice for future elections.] . . . Conservative, traditionalist candidates (Republican, Democrat, or Independent) who oppose gun control, who oppose abortion, and who support the U.S. Constitution and traditional values should be aggressively supported, and liberals (of either party) who support gun control, who support the Clintonista agenda for the destruction of America, the Constitution, the family, etc. should be aggressively opposed.

If the present liberal makeup of the U.S. Congress is dramatically altered in November, the entire Clintonista agenda—including socialized medicine, gun control, dismantling of the U.S. defenses, and the merger of the U.S. military with the UN, and the New World Order could be derailed or set back at least 5 to 10 years. The November Congressional election is *not* one to sit out. It is crucial! Get involved!

5. Start your own local newsletter. Distribute it *free* to family, friends, business associates, church leaders and members, to local leaders, or associates around the county. You are free (and encouraged) to reprint any information from *MIA* deemed useful. There are dozens of patriotic national newsletters that would encourage the same. It is getting harder and harder for the socialists to operate in the dark. Their information monopoly (via the mainline newspapers and news magazines, the television networks, and the educational system) has been blown full of holes.

Remember the part the Committees of Correspondence played in the American Revolution. Newsletters, especially small, free ones in the day of the FAX machine and computers cannot be stopped. That is a problem that Lenin, Stalin, Mao, and Hitler did not have to contend with.

6. Get your family into greater self-sufficiency. Re-read the July '94 *MIA* dealing with self-sufficiency and implement as much as possible of it in your lifestyle. The more self-sufficient you are, the harder it will be for Big Brother and the New World Order to control you. Gary North used to write about the 4 G's of survival: God, gold, guns, and groceries. The Establishment hates them all, but they are a great place to start. Adequate fire-arms to defend your family, your land, or even your county, and sufficient amounts of ammunition and firearms training are essential. Such should be acquired *immediately* and at a gun show, flea market, or from an individual if possible.

Gold (or silver) coins could mean your economic survival in the coming cashless society where the "politically incorrect" [that's us, folks—author] could have the plug pulled on their "US Card"! Stored food (i.e., dehydrated, freeze dried, or grown from your garden) will also be essential and could save your life.

7. Copy and distribute this issue of MIA as widely as possible. Occasionally readers write and tell how they have sent a copy of *MIA* to Bill or Hillary Clinton or one of their Clintonista associates. Why not instead try to educate, inform, or wake up our friends—our enemies are not doing what they do because they are dumb or uninformed. They simply have a very different agenda. Copies of this issue can be reordered from *MIA* for $5.00 each; over 25—$3.00 each; over 100—$2.00 each. [ED. NOTE: It may be cheaper to photocopy them. Either way—*just do it!]*

8. Pray for and seek a spiritual revival in the country and in your own heart. Alexander Solzhenitsyn once said that Russia lost its freedom because it forgot God. This writer wonders if the same could not be said about America today! The real Christian church may be about to be driven underground as the Clintonista/Establishment/New World Order persecution of Christian tradi-tionalists accelerates. We are in a spiritual battle (not just a political one) in America. Every reader is encouraged to spend at least an hour or two a day in studying the Bible and prayer—seeking God's wisdom as to how you should live, function, and take a stand in our day. And then get up and do something! The time for passive wimps, Christian or otherwise, is over!

THE BOTTOM LINE: There is plenty we can do to stop the socialists from destroying our freedoms, our families, our Constitu-tion, and our traditional way of life. Get mad! Get off dead center! And get involved! *It's time to draw the line in the sand!*

Well said!

CHAPTER THREE

Loss of Privacy & Electronic Bondage

Even as I write this chapter, I am reminded of the horrendous events that unfolded in Oklahoma City in April, 1995, where terrorists bombed a nine-story federal building with allegedly a single truck-bomb parked in front of the structure. Supposedly, they just parked it, drove away in another vehicle, and detonated the massive bomb from a remote location, or perhaps with a timing device. (Currently, the feasibility of this method is being challenged by some who are experts on the construction of this particular building. Their feeling is that additional internal explosives would have been required, placed on certain crucial supports, to have rendered the kind of damage that resulted.)

This terrorist act affected the federal building, which housed primarily what would be referred to as civilian activities, i.e., Social Security offices, federal assistance offices, and a sizable day-care center, as well as a few such as FBI, CIA, and Secret Service, but the devastation was not limited to that one building. The shock was felt as far away as 50 miles, and the glass in buildings as far away as four to five blocks was blown out, injuring many unsuspecting pedestrians and office workers, as well as a number of other children in the YMCA facility across the street.

The fatalities surpassed 150, with a few bodies never located. The medical personnel ran out of "body bags" and requested people to donate sheets. Dogs with high-tech extremely sensitive microphones were sent through the rubble in an attempt to locate any remaining survivors. One victim had a leg amputated on the spot in order to extricate her from the debris and permit her life to be saved.

The nine floors just "pancaked" down on top of one another and landed in a crater created by the bomb. Despite all the efforts of the engineers to shore up the wreckage, and the extreme care taken by the rescue workers, one was killed and two others injured in the heroic rescue attempts. The devastation has been compared in magnitude with the earthquake of two years earlier in Northridge, California (near Los Angeles).

However, there is a big difference . . . and the resulting effect on the population, both in Oklahoma and across our nation, is much more explosive. This act of violence was committed by some radical people with a religious or political agenda . . . some hard line fanatics who practice the principle that the end justifies the means—regardless of the innocent victims who were in no way involved in their cause, either pro or con.

Now, since by the time you read this book, all this will have been hashed and rehashed on every TV station, newspaper, magazine, talk show, and probably books, you may be asking yourself why I'm bothering to include it in this book. Well, as time passes, it will become readily apparent to most of you. When this kind of terrorism strikes the heartland of America, rather than its big cities or Washington, D.C. (where people assume such actions may occur), fear grips the hearts of everyone, and *prevention* becomes the top priority in our minds. A groundswell of cries for justice and protection starts to rise from the grassroots.

Why did this happen? *It could be for any reason in any distorted mind.* Will it happen again? *Undoubtedly!* Can we stop it? *Probably not.* What are we willing to do *to try* to stop it? *Bingo! You are willing to give up some more of your freedoms and willing to submit to more covert surveillance and more control of your lives . . . because how else can we protect the safety of all those innocent victims?*

The subject has been discussed, and the conclusion has been reached that we need to increase our surveillance techniques and strengthen our laws to aid law enforcement units in the tracking and capturing of dangerous dissidents. It already has been pointed out that the CIA, the FBI, and the Secret Service should have better information-gathering abilities, so they can know about these things *before they happen* and arrest the culprits on some kind of conspiracy charge *before a criminal act actually has been committed.*

Everything that's in me wants to shout, "Yes!" But that brings me back to the situation of how much liberty and freedom I'm willing to forego. Am I going to *invite* "Big Brother" to turn this country into an armed camp (someone on the news recently referred to it as "bunker mentality"), with all rights of privacy tossed out the window in the process? If we give them that kind of power, will it stop the terrorism? *No!* Did it stop the IRA from bombing London, *et al,* on a regular basis? Has it stopped the Islamic terrorists from bombing Israel on a regular basis? Did it protect our Marine base from a terrorist bombing? *No! to all of the above.* The very nature of terrorism means that you can't stop it . . . they don't operate by the "rules" and they are willing, if necessary, to die to deliver the explosives to the target . . . and they don't care who dies with them!

We might succeed in making them go a little further under cover, and their actions may become more covert, but if they are crazy enough and determined enough, they'll find a way.

So what will be accomplished by forfeiting our liberties? We will give the government the right to meddle even further into our businesses and lives . . . of course, for our own good, as with all the other things they are doing to us for "our benefit."

President Clinton introduced a five-point piece of legislation to the Congress that even the Senator from Oklahoma has declined to endorse in its original form because he is opposed to infringing on the Constitutional liberties of the great majority in this country in an attempt to protect us from the violent radicals. Of course, he firmly stated his willingness to cooperate fully once sufficient Constitutional safeguards for our rights to privacy were incorporated into the proposal.

In addition to adding personnel to law enforcement investigative agencies, they want to enhance the ability of these agencies in their electronic eavesdropping, via our local phones, cell phones, fax transmissions, etc., etc. Also, they want the government to help the telecommunication companies pay for the mandated purchase and installation of new software and equipment to provide access to their digital systems, which would allow government to intercept and monitor *all* telecommunications, in many cases without a warrant. Prior to the Oklahoma bombing, the government was trying to force the telecommunication companies to pay for all these expensive conversions themselves, therefore, the companies were trying to avoid cooperating. There is a particularly enlightening article titled "Privacy in the Digital Age," written by Bill Machrone. It appeared in the June 14, 1994, edition of *PC Magazine.* In it the writer points out, among other hair-raising information, that the "pending legislation provides for fines of up to $10,000 a day against telecommunications companies who don't give the Feds the access they want to the decoded data streams." It is difficult to believe what is happening. The article also contains an easy-to-understand explanation of the new "clipper chip" technology and its effect on digital "everything" systems.

Further, it would authorize this alphabet soup of agencies to infiltrate and spy on any organization *that it would deem a possible danger,* at its own discretion. Of course, that doesn't mean only Arab militants, it could mean anyone, especially anyone the government might see as radical, fanatical, right-wing extremists (I wonder why they never consider the left-wing to be extremists?). . . in other words, anyone who is vocal and who disagrees with the way things are being run.

Another option that has been suggested is bringing in the military to help us monitor and control the civilian population. The final conclusion of such an action would be devastating and would result in total loss of freedom—a police state. But when things get bad enough, even that won't suffice and those "helpful" UN troops—that are just waiting for the right opportunity—will be on your doorstep before you can wake up and smell the coffee.

The loss of our privacy and electronic bondage go hand in hand. Once you are in the system, it is impossible to extricate yourself from it. And now the various agencies, i.e., social services, health care, insurance systems, and medical groups, retail sales, credit bureaus, Social Security, IRS, vehicle/driver's license, registration, and driving record, voter registration, etc., etc., are sharing the information in their files about you.

As much as you might like to avoid it, there are plenty of places you probably already exist in Big Brother's "big brain." One of the biggest cracks in the security of your privacy is the rampant use of your Social Security number to identify you on just about everything, currently. And the fact that many, many of the people who use it to identify you freely print it in public view—or make it easily accessible to anyone who seeks it—makes it relatively easy to obtain information on your most personal activities, and even to make changes in your file.

A particularly good article by Robert S. Boyd, of the Knight-Ridder Tribune News Service, appeared in the February 25, 1994, edition of *The Phoenix Gazette.* It is titled, "Social Security privacy gap grows."

It seems a 30-year-old lawyer lost his right to vote when he refused to give the registrar his Social Security number (it was their practice to publish the number with his name as a matter of public record, and anyone could have access). He explained his reasons for refusing, to no avail. So he decided to do a test, and I quote:

> As a test, Greidinger [the attorney] had a friend dial an 800 number at the government-sponsored Student Loan Marketing Association (Sallie Mae) in Washington.
> "He entered my Social Security number into the telephone and was able to get access to my files. He found out how much I owed, and when I made my last payment. He even changed some data in my file."

Now what else would you expect an attorney to do. . . he sued the county, and a federal appeals court ruled unanimously in his favor.

"The harm that can be inflicted from the disclosure of a Social Security number to an unscrupulous individual is alarming and potentially financially ruinous," the court said.

The Greidinger case was another round in a 50-year struggle between those who want to use Social Security numbers as a personal identifier for everything from law enforcement to checking cashing—and those who view its widespread use as a serious threat to privacy.

Phil Gambino, a spokesman for the Social Security Administration, said the agency had no power to prevent the abuse of the number by private individuals or companies. [Not true, there's a lot they could do. Why, if they were so inclined, they could just call up the number of those missing "deadbeat dads" and deduct child support directly from their paychecks. They certainly have the capability, if they really wanted to.]

Rutgers University (until stopped by a lawsuit in 1992) posted the students' names and numbers on a bulletin board, along with their grades. Talk about your loss of privacy!

. . .Social Security numbers are easy to fake and hard to authenticate.

"There is no way to verify the accuracy of existing numbers or that the number holder is who he or she claims to be," the ACLU's Goldman said.

There will be more extensive discussion on the subject of Social Security in Chapter 7.

Then there's the IRS. . .we've all felt for quite some time that they knew more about us than they needed to know (certainly more than we wanted them to know!).

Well, hold on to your seats. . .it's about to get better—or worse—depending on which side of the computer you're sitting. I quote from a couple of articles.

The *Los Angeles Times* on February 12, 1995, reported: "If you have a back tax bill with the Internal Revenue Service, watch out. In the midst of a program called economic reality, the federal tax agency is going on line, searching for signs of noncompliance as well as electronic records of cars, credit and real estate it can seize from delinquent taxpayers. . .A cadre of IRS agents with computers and modems now will be searching records filed with the Department of Motor Vehicles, county tax assessor's offices, credit-reporting companies and the U.S. Bureau of the Census in an effort to find people who are underreporting their business sales, overestimating their deductions or trying to hide assets—or themselves—from federal tax collectors. IRS officials say. . . .'We will be using information from various [electronic] sources as part of our economic-reality approach'. . . .The IRS will begin compiling a host of demographic information about people in each district. . . .This information will include currency and banking reports, license information, construction contract information and census data. . . .The IRS will get current addresses for taxpayers who have apparently dropped off the rolls by buying them from credit-reporting companies. . . .it can get your full credit file to determine whether you have enough credit to pay the bill. . . .DMV records will be tapped. . .to see if you have a car to sell to pay taxes—and to help determine whether a taxpayer is lying about income or deductions. The IRS will be suspicious, for example, of a waiter who reports $20,000 in total income but drives a new Porsche. Property records will be used in the same way. . . .a few credit experts warn that it also puts a burden on individuals who are under IRS scrutiny. Why? The records are not always right. And *the tax agency does not need to inform you that it is searching these records, nor is it required to allow you to correct records that are in error.* . . .it cannot correct somebody else's database. . . .If you're under IRS scrutiny, it may behoove you to check your own records for accuracy" [emphasis added].

A helpful article appeared in *Business Week,* May 25, 1992, entitled, "Getting the Kinks Out of Your Credit Report." It gives some very good information about how to check on your records, and some suggestions for attempted correction if they contain errors. But the bottom line on this shared database situation is that if there is an error, you might correct it at that point, but you have no way of knowing how many more people have picked up that misinformation and now stored it in their own files, freely sharing it with anyone else who asks. In other words, it's an endless trail that you almost always *never win.*

Another article on the IRS appeared in the March 18, 1995, *Reno Gazette-Journal.* The thrust of this article, entitled "IRS auditors become gumshoes," is that under the new strategy, dubbed "Compliance 2000," they are training the auditors—formerly accountants, for the most part—to be detectives, using all databases at their disposal to compile a composite of YOU—what you should be driving and where you should be living (based on the income you reported), weddings of your children, your cultural background, vacations, home furnishings, etc. They want to develop a complete profile on you. And these techniques now have become standard practice for *all audits.*

"Well, aside from my W-2, this intrusion can't reach me on my job," you say. Wrong again! *U.S. News & World Report,* August 8, 1994, reports: "Employers are finding more ways to watch workers. Some use cameras. Some eavesdrop on phones. Some read E-mail. As a result, the International Labor Organization reports this week in a three-volume study, workers in industrialized nations have steadily lost privacy. American employees, the ILO concludes, are among the most closely watched. One survey indicates that perhaps 80 percent of U.S. workers in telecommunications, insurance, and banking are subject to telephone or computer-based monitoring."

An excellent article appeared in the May 18, 1994, edition of the *Los Angeles Times*. Titled, "Someone May Be Watching," it points out the surveillance scrutiny of our workplace, home, and habits. They begin: "Everywhere we go, we're increasingly under surveillance. Employers, marketers, even private detectives use high-tech tools and scan mostly unregulated databases to pry into our daily lives."

The article was accompanied by a graphic with a caption: "Always Under Watch: A Day in the Life . . .Whether by video camera or computer, surveillance techniques may threaten your privacy. Here are some of the ways: (1) The Commute: Cameras on freeways catch a driver speeding to work. (2) At Work: Parking garage video camera can note a worker's arrival time, companions in auto. (3) Workstation: Employers can monitor computer messages and other electronic work. (4) At Lunch: A diner's credit card scan shows restaurant and bill. (5) After-Work Errand: ATM camera and computer records transaction. Credit card used at store shows where consumer shopped, what was bought. (6) Drive Home: Tollbooth scanner records when auto passed."

And naturally, law enforcement will get in on the act: " . . .was to prepare for the Federal Bureau of Investigation's NCIC 2000 program. This is a forthcoming set of computer standards the FBI is mandating that will enable state and local law enforcement agencies to share information nationwide, including digitized images of fingerprints and mugshots . . . ."

And what could infringe on your privacy more than being shackled to a biochip in a vinyl bracelet. We will address this issue fully in Chapter 15 when we get into an indepth discussion on biochip technology. But just for this location, I want to tell you about all the Haitian refugees that were given RFID wristbands (anklebands for the children) for identification while interned at the naval base at Guantanamo Bay, Cuba. [Note: As of today, Clinton has recommended admitting 20,000 of these refugees—supposedly Cubans —as immigrants to the U.S. I wonder what will happen to all those ID bands.] This project is abbreviated DMPITS, so whenever you see that acronym, you'll know what they are talking about. Of course, the extended use of this technology is to keep track of prisoners who—for whatever reason—are housed at their homes, or to locate runaway teens, or to keep track of grandpa who has a tendency to wander off and get lost, or to find kidnapped kids, etc., and ultimately to keep track of you!

If you want to *help* people track you down, just apply for one of the new "500" area code numbers. Rather than your standard area code that gives the location of your base set, the new 500 codes will usher in the "one person/one number era." They claim that individuals can be reached on any communication device anywhere, at a number they keep throughout their lives. The article tells how it works and explains how the calls find you.

Then there's the high-tech matters affecting your automobile (and its driver). A lot of different things are being combined on your driver's license, which we will address in detail in a later chapter. According to one article there will be a 2-D bar code on your driver's license, title, and car registration. Another article (*The Advocate,* Baton Rouge, LA, Aug. 3, 1994) tells about the "Auto Arrester" which targets high-speed evaders and electronically overloads the ignition systems, disabling fleeing cars. The activator switches are kept by law enforcement personnel. The device itself can be used three different ways. It can be embedded in the road permanently and activated by police when needed; it can be set on a road ahead of a fleeing vehicle (in other words, a patrol car from another area could intercept the escape route before the fleeing vehicle arrives at that point); if the vehicle had been pulled over for some reason, then tries to race off, the officer actually could throw the device on top of the car and then activate it.

From the October 17, 1994, issue of *Forbes 400,* Editor's column, "Fact and Comment," here are a few of the comments by Malcolm S. Forbes, Jr., Editor-in-Chief: "A cry for a national identification card is rising again . . . .We should resist the temptation. Such a card will rapidly be used for far more than employment. The loss of privacy outweighs any gains . . . .Assurances that laws would protect our privacy rightly ring hollow. With a national I.D. card your whole life could end up on a government central computer file . . . .Do we as a nation of individualists really want that?"

A comprehensive discussion of I.D. cards will be given in Chapter 14.

Below are some crucial excerpts from an article that appeared on page 16 of *Spotlight* magazine, June 13, 1994. It's in the section called Technology & Liberty and is titled: "Danger in the Mail . . . Now that I have free access to your bank records . . . Your House is Next! Nibbling away your freedom bit by bit."

Don't look now, but Uncle Sam has some shiny new shackles

with your name on them. Indeed, sources in the U.S. Postal Service recently revealed that they're all set to deliver your very own personalized federal ball and chain directly to your mailbox.

. . .the Postal Service: They told several people that they were prepared to mail 100 million of the cards in a matter of months.

. . .The Clinton administration, which says it's determined to "break the cycle of dependency" among welfare recipients, is preparing to reduce every American to total dependence—and near-total surveillance—through these infamous cards.

. . .The Postal Service's proposal (which was echoed by the IRS—what a coincidence!) calls for the card to "mediate" the information about you in every government database. It will be like a magic key, which opens every government database with information about you.

And here's another troubling fact. If federal computer systems are already integrated to this extent—where one card can "unlock" every piece of information about you—then what makes you think you have the only key?

Of course you won't have the only key. And potentially everything you own and all your assets, benefits and entitlements can be "withheld" from you with the push of a few buttons at the Treasury Department, IRS, or who-knows-where.

. . .the databases are ready to be integrated under the card.

To me, that means the databases are integrated now. It can take well over a year to integrate a couple of big databases. If the Postal Service is ready to start mailing 100 million of these cards within months, then the databases are integrated now. They work together—for Big Brother—now. They are being used now.

. . .people at the conference expressed reservations about the U.S. Card. Not technical reservations, mind you. They know the U.S. Card will work as advertised.

They expressed political reservations.

Those people buy and sell folks' privacy for a living. I guess it's one thing to sell branding irons, but quite another thing to accept a brand yourself. It's up to you.

Let's conclude this chapter with some information from one of my most reliable sources, *The McAlvany Intelligence Advisor* (any quotations below are from the August, 1994, edition).

We're under constant observation; everything goes on a permanent record; much of what we say, do, and feel may be recorded by others we don't know.

—Gary Marx

The only way Big Brother (in George Orwell's *1984)* was able to successfully maintain control over the lives of the people was to abolish all personal privacy. They were under total surveillance, stripped not only of their privacy, but of their freedom, worth, and dignity, as well. Orwell describes the scene this way:

> The telescreen received and transmitted simultaneously [Author's Note: check out the capabilities of today's fiber optics systems coming into your homes via television, computer, modem, cable, telephone, fax, *et al*]. Any sound that Winston made, above the level of a very low whisper would be picked up by it; moreover, as long as he remained within the field of vision which the metal plaque commanded, he could be seen as well as heard. There was, of course, no way of knowing whether you were being watched at any given moment.
>
> How often, or on what system, the Thought Police plugged in on any individual was just guesswork. It was even conceivable that they watched everybody all the time. But, at any rate, they could plug in your wire whenever they wanted to. You had to live—did live, from habit that became instinct, with the assumption that every sound you made was heard, and except in darkness, every move was scrutinized.

McAlvany says: "This is happening in America today as we are rapidly becoming a total surveillance society, and privacy, as we have known it since the founding of our country is now being abolished."

Within the past year the Clinton administration has been pushing consistently for a number of new high-tech systems to enhance their "people control and monitoring" activities. Among their favorites are the National I.D. card (discussed in Chapter 14), the Information Superhighway (covered in Chapter 7), and installation of a "clipper chip" in our telephones, computers/modems, fax machines, and other electronic devices, to allow the government easy access for the purpose of tapping and monitoring *all* of our communications via those systems.

McAlvany informs us that even though the clipper chip project is being pushed hard by Clinton, Reno, and FBI Director Louis Freeh, it actually was launched by George Bush in 1991 and developed by the National Security Agency (NSA), a supersecret organization.

The August, 1994, issue of *The McAlvany Intelligence Advisor* reports as follows:

> Reno and Freeh are presently pushing Congress to enact requirements that telecommunications providers (i.e., local telephone services, cellular phone companies, wireless services, long distance networks, etc.) be mandated to develop and install soft-

ware and equipment that allows the government to intercept and monitor *all* telecommunications in America. Freeh and Reno argue that *"to stop terrorism and organized crime, the American people must give up some of their personal freedom and privacy."* [Author's Note: You can see from the date of this newsletter that this plan was on their agenda long before the Oklahoma City bombing occurred. This just gave them the excuse they needed to push such legislation through the Congress. Kind of makes you wonder whose "plans" benefited most from that act of terrorism.]

The FBI has reintroduced its 1992 proposal to require that communications service providers redesign their equipment to facilitate electronic surveillance. The Digital Telephony and Communications Privacy Improvement Act of 1994 [**ED. NOTE:** That title is Orwellian "doublespeak," because the act will *destroy all privacy.*] mandates that phones, cable, and computer network companies modify their switches and computers *to ensure that surveillance can be conducted concurrently from a remote government facility. All transactions and phone calls (in and out) will be monitored and recorded. Companies who refuse to comply will be fined $10,000 per day.*

The Electronic Frontier Foundation has warned: *"The FBI scheme would turn the data superhighway into a national surveillance network of staggering proportions."*

The Clintonistas have said that within a few years they plan to link every home, business, lab, classroom, and library via their high-tech computerized information superhighway. The *Wall Street Journal* warned in an editorial (7-10-94) that even if the Congress blocked the government-backed installation of the "Clipper Chip" that the bureaucracy would make an end run and install it anyway.

The *Wall Street Journal* pointed out that *sophisticated terrorists and organized crime syndicates could easily evade the "Clipper Chip" surveillance, but that it would enable the Big Brother bureaucracy to monitor every phone call, every credit card purchase, every bank transaction, and every telecommunication of every private citizen in America.* The *Wall Street Journal* concluded that: *"The potential for government manipulation and intimidation of the citizenry is enormous."*

USA Today (7-20-94) carried a front-page story entitled: "Privacy Abuse Confirms the Worst Fear," which discussed how IRS officials had admitted at a Senate hearing that more than 1,300 IRS agents have been investigated over the past five years on suspicion of improperly snooping through taxpayers' files. About 56,000 IRS employees (nearly half of the agency's 115,000 work force) have access to the Integrated Data Retrieval System (IDRS), the computer system that handles collection and storage of taxpayer information.

Evidence of IRS privacy abuses was revealed by the Senate Governmental Affairs Committee in August '93. Committee member Senator David Pryor (D-AR) said: "The IRS' disregard of taxpayer (privacy) rights confirms the worst fears that the American people have about the IRS. This illegal and offensive activity must stop and it's clear that Congress must act." *But the major problem with the IRS violation of taxpayer privacy rights is not just IRS snooping of taxpayer returns. It is the sharing of that information with dozens of other government agencies—a practice which until recently was strictly forbidden.*

The most ominous part of the *USA Today* article was the revelation that "the IRS is in the middle of an **$8 billion** computer systems upgrade. Eventually, optical character readers will be used to scan and direct tax returns into three main computers hooked together in a national network that links the 10 IRS service centers, eight regional offices, and 65 district offices." [Author's Note: Not to beat a dead horse, but I just want to point out again that these correspond to those same U.N. "regions" which I pointed out to you previously in this book.]

Because of grass roots pressure and their success in enlightening the populace as to the true meaning and end results of some of these measures, many of the "control" elements of the New World Order will not be passed by the Congress. But that doesn't seem to be hindering the progress of the Clinton group as they move us ever forward toward the New World Order.

No problem! They'll just enact what they want via an "Executive Order." Executive Orders give a president the ability to declare a state of emergency, martial law, and a suspension of all Constitutional rights, in essence converting our democractic form of government into a total dictatorship with merely the stroke of a pen. Congress subsequently can accept these Executive Orders, publish them in the Federal Register, and establish them as laws of the land. These can be implemented at the whim of the current President on a moment's notice just by declaring a state of emergency.

Clinton used this method to move U.S. troops under UN command (PDD-25 signed May 5, 1994). Whether allowing foreign (Russian and UN) troops onto U.S. soil, implementing the National ID card, or a host of other measures, if they can't get it through Congress, they simply write an Executive Order and use unconstitutional, dictatorial powers to accomplish their goals.

Executive Orders date back as far as Franklin Delano Roosevelt. President Carter signed No. 12148 delegating the power to run the entire country to FEMA, then for no "apparent" reason, on June 3, 1994, Clinton signed a new Executive Order transferring control of the country in an emergency from FEMA to the National Security Council and the National Security Advisor.

Some of the Executive Orders which subsequently have made their way into the Federal Register (and now are laws) are reported by McAlvany as follows:

10995—All communications media seized by the Federal Government. **10997**—Seizure of all electrical power, fuels, including gasoline and minerals. **10998**—Seizure of all food resources, farms and farm equipment. **10999**—Seizure of all kinds of transportation, including your personal car, and control of all highways and seaports. **11000**—Seizure of all civilians for work under Federal supervision. **11001**—Federal takeover of all health, education and welfare.

11002—Postmaster General empowered to register every man, woman and child in the U.S.A. **11003**—Seizure of all aircraft and airports by the Federal Government. **11004**—Housing and Finance authority may shift population from one locality to another. Complete integration. **11005**—Seizure of railroads, inland waterways, and storage facilities. **11051**—The Director of the Office of Emergency Planning authorized to put Executive Orders into effect in "times of increased international tension or financial crisis." He is also to perform such additional functions as the President may direct.

In short, if there should be nationwide riots (ala Los Angeles in '92) for any reason [**ED. NOTE:** i.e., perhaps upon conviction of O.J. Simpson]; a national financial crisis; massive social upheaval (i.e., a huge quantum jump in crime); major resistance to national gun confiscation or to the installation of the New World Order or other socialist/police state measures; etc., *Bill Clinton and his "comrades" have the power and machinery to instantly suspend the Constitution and declare a total dictatorship.*

As recently as April 19, 1995, an article appeared in the Clifton, New Jersey, *Herald & News.* Writer Rich Calder titled the article: "Clifton group OKs listing of residents; City council urged to register everyone." This city is calling for a computer database with which it can *track all residents.* "A 26-member committee . . . recommended last night that the city council approve an ordinance requiring all residents to register with the city. This proposal would obligate all renters and homeowners to fill out a dwelling certificate . . . listing all occupants in their household. The certificate would require residents to list their names and ages, along with the names and ages of their children. This measure . . . may raise constitutional issues. Members of the ACLU have said that this procedure will threaten residents' privacy. Committee members who support the proposal said that people with nothing to hide shouldn't have anything to worry about. . . . Mayor James Anzaldi hailed the plan at last night's meeting, saying the council should implement an ordinance right away. . . . The dwelling certificate would be supplied to several city agencies. . . . The proposal also calls for a centralized computer database to be created that would help track . . . violations."

Finally, I recommend that you acquire a copy of the June, 1986 edition of *The Gospel Truth,* a publication of Southwest Radio Church. (For reprints write to: Southwest Radio Church, P. O. Box 1144, Oklahoma City, OK 73101.) Written by Noah Hutchings, it is titled, "Liberty or Electronic Bondage: How Near the Choice?" Even though he was a few years ahead of much of the commentary on this situation, he was seeing the "handwriting on the wall" where this subject was concerned. It is an excellent piece with much research reported.

Have we lost our privacy?—for sure! But as one lady put it earlier, "You ain't seen nothin' yet!" Are we in electronic bondage? You bet! And probably already too far into the system ever to get out. All we can do is sound the warning and get prepared for the battle cry, because for most of us, it's too late to pull a "disappearing act" from the system, unless it's the disappearing act described in the Bible when the Lord returns to snatch us away. However, we don't know exactly when that will be, so we *must be prepared* to survive (victoriously, I hope) in the troubled times that lie ahead, as scripture is emphatic about one thing: in the end times (and we're there, folks), things are going to get *worse* before they get better.

But we are not to despair—we have a blessed hope and lots of promises in the Word from our heavenly Father, such as He "will never leave us nor forsake us," His "strength is made perfect in our weakness," "I've never seen the righteous forsaken, or their seed out begging for bread," and finally His instruction to "comfort one another with these words": "when you see these things begin to come to pass, look up for your redemption draweth nigh."

CHAPTER FOUR

The 666 System

The United Nations & U.N. Resolution 666
Congressional Bill HR 666 / The New U.S.
Constitution / The New World Constitution

When I refer to the "666 System," I will be discussing a number of different foundational items for the establishment of the New World Order. The United Nations already has been discussed somewhat, but will be investigated further in this chapter. I will give you some information on an occultic organization called Lucis Trust, which has close ties to the United Nations.

The United Nations, which already is accepted widely, is the agency chosen to move us toward world government, however, the UN charter is not a constitution. Further, the UN is still a collection of sovereign nations (at least for the time being), which is unthinkable to true globalists. Therefore, a world constitution has been drafted and is presently being circulated for ratification by nations around the world. It is called, "A Constitution for the Federation of Earth."

Now, lest you misunderstand, the UN is not a toothless beast, but a fearsome tool being used to push us directly into the New World Order, wherein our presently sovereign nations will become nothing more than "nation states."

I will quote briefly from Publication No. 1083, A Voice of Americanism Publication, in my comments below. "In December 1992, the U.N. General Assembly president declared that the General Assembly must 'truly become a functional world parliament'. . . . Boutros-Ghali said the U.N. should have its own intelligence service and declared 'the time of absolute and exclusive [national] sovereignty' has passed."

Remember, I warned you earlier about Treaties, and the fact that they take precedence over our own Constitutional laws and liberties. Those politicians engaged in promoting the New World Order and one-world government have interpreted our Constitution to declare that treaties become the supreme law of the land. "Tragically, the U.S. is rushing headlong into a number of U.N. treaties that will override our constitutional freedoms and open up U.S. citizens to horrible intrusions. [This is in addition to the several trade agreements/treaties into which the U.S. recently has entered.] The Senate already has passed and President Reagan signed the Genocide Treaty, which is a first-class fraud: The Soviet Union, Red China, and communist Cambodia signed it, along with other bloodthirsty regimes.

"Genocide and 'hate crimes' go hand in hand. U.S. gay activists have asked the U.N. to defend gay and lesbian human rights. Protection of gays' 'human rights' could mean that Christians could be hauled before world courts for the 'genocide' of homosexuals by simply *speaking* out against homosexuality. It is conceivable that U.S. gay activists may soon petition the U.N. to directly intervene against the few American communities (state and local governments) that defend Judeo-Christian values. This is an outrage—U.N. interference with local governments in the U.S.! Does this seem farfetched? It isn't— the U.N. has already been asked to investigate Tasmania's anti-homosexuality statute."

The Clinton administration is striving to further increase these international treaties. Consider: The Convention on the Elimination of All Forms of Discrimination Against Women (barring any distinction, exclusion, or restriction, made on the basis of sex); The International Convention on the Elimination of All Forms of Racism (prohibiting any distinction, exclusion, restriction, or preference based on color, descent, or national ethnic origin); The Covenant on Economic, Social, and Cultural Rights (which would guarantee employment—as in the old Soviet Union—social security, an adequate standard of living, and the highest attainable standard of physical and mental health); The American Declaration of the Rights and Duties of Man (a list of 27 human rights and 10 duties).

"Don't be deceived by this high-sounding 'rights' rhetoric. The U.N.'s definition of 'rights' excludes the rights of those who would impede the progress toward globalism.

"Moreover, in June 1993, the Senate Foreign Relations Committee endorsed an international criminal tribunal (which essentially **nullifies** our 4th, 5th, 6th, and 7th amendments!), thus scrapping fundamental protections against arbitrary arrest, imprisonment, conviction, or punishment. Under this scheme, individual Americans could be tried, convicted, and punished according to *international* rules which could be open to all sorts of evil, capricious interpretations. Under most U.N. laws, *governments* are protected, not *individuals*. The U.N.

Covenant on Economic, Social, and Cultural Rights and the Covenant on Civil and Political Rights will likely become 'law' under Clinton.

"The U.N. Conference on Human Rights met in 1993 to fortify the U.N.'s human rights enforcement authority. In doing so, the U.N. would receive dominion over every aspect of the life of every human being. . . .Clinton supports Ibrahim Fall for a proposed position of High Commissioner for Human Rights. This is an absurd choice. Fall served as foreign minister for the socialist government of Senegal. Fall wants to empower a global court to watch over the human rights of all nations and punish rights abusers. Incidentally, the only rights a person will have are those the planetary government chooses to give him— and they can be withdrawn at the whim of the government."

Sometime it seems that the UN has a treaty for just about every-thing, and that they are making more on a daily basis. Unfortunately, they are totally hypocritical in the enforcement of these treaties. For example, on the one hand they support and promote equality for women in every respect. . .then stand by *monitoring* female infanticide commited regularly in Red China *with the help of UN subsidies!* Boutros-Ghali, head of the UN, has openly criticized what he refers to as "cultural obstacles experienced in the context of family, com-munity, and religious institutions." I suppose, in the light of scripture, that Christians probably would stand accused of denying the rights of both women and children.

Of course, the cause about which the UN is most vocal, and probably receives the greatest support worldwide (along with their "scare-tactics" strategies on ecology), is children's rights. That's because it sounds so lofty, and who can see the pictures of the starving, dying children in the war-torn countries and lands of famine without experiencing a guilt-wrenching feeling in your heart? Even the poorest of us have so much by comparison, and we seem so wasteful. Who of us wasn't told sometime in their childhood by their mother to "finish your dinner, the children in China are starving." Of course, we never could figure out how to get our dinner to them, which we would have done gladly to get out of eating our vegetables!

Now, don't misunderstand me. . .I firmly believe those of us who have been so blessed have an obligation to help feed and clothe the poor—Christ told us to do so. However, he also taught us to be good stewards of the finances entrusted to us, so investigate thoroughly any organization before you "join up," as there are many fraudulent groups in the business of parting generous people from their money. Conversely, there are many fine organizations who keep their admin-istrative overhead to a bare minimum and the greater portion of your contributions actually reach the needy families for the feeding, clothing, health, and education of the recipients.

Trying to accomplish these goals through the efforts of the UN, however, can lead to a *loss* of children's rights, rather than guaranteeing them rights, as purported.

"Under the children's rights convention, children would be brought up in the 'spirit of the ideals proclaimed in the Charter of the United Nations.' Christianity doesn't fit in here at all. Would teaching children Christianity be a violation of children's supposed rights? Note this: In a city in Maine, government officials visited a classroom and asked the children which ones had parents who spanked them. Several raised their hands. Their names were taken down—and the parents subsequently arrested for child abuse! The children didn't suffer from broken bones, burns, bruises, or other signs of true abuse. U.N. interpretations of 'rights' can get horribly ridiculous—and frightening."

For those of you who think it couldn't happen here, consider what occurred in France in 1993. French authorities exercised their commitment to the United Nations Convention on the Rights of the Child. According to a report in the September, 1993, edition of *Monetary & Economic Review,* "Police forcibly took seven children from their parents and placed them in the care of the French Directional Department of Health and Social Actions. One mother, Sylvia Bahjejram, was hospitalized with injuries sustained during the raids. Other families were quietly taken in for questioning when the police used phony search warrants. All the children and families involved were members of the now disbanded Church Eglise Christienne La Citadel (Christian Citadel Church), which is a non-denominational Bible-believing Protestant congregation.

"Elizabeth Farrell of *News Network International* reports that police authorities allege the parents have indoctrinated their children with biblical teaching, home schooled them, 'sequestered' them, disciplined them by spanking, held them in confinement, and encouraged them to fast for religious reasons."

The children were contacted by persons hostile to the church, while their own parents were denied visitation privileges. One of the youngsters avoided surveillance long enough to contact a friend, saying that she was being imprisoned and wanted to return to her home.

The judge assigned to the case gave the following findings and decisions: "Whereas the conditions. . .are likely to seriously endanger the evolution, the psychological equilibrium, and the full development of the minds. . .for these motives we order the placement of the children at the DDASS."

Church members claimed this to be the final blow in the persecution which began six years earlier when they were labeled a "cult" by ADFI.

Their church is in good company among the list of 200 organizations branded as cults. . .a list which includes the Assemblies of God, Full Gospel Businessmen's Fellowship, Int'l., and any "church believing in the efficacy of the blood of Jesus and the power of the Holy Spirit."

"[This] case is just an example of the United Nations Rights of a Child put into action. Parents were violating their children's UN given rights. Judge Croissant seems to be applying Article 17, which protects children from material injurious to the child, because it is now international judicial thought that the Bible is dangerous to children. She might use Article 14 to assure these French children's freedom of thought, conscience, and religion. In short, French authorities have determined that Biblical based parenting is not in the 'best interest' of the child."

How close are we to experiencing such interference in our country? Well, since the Clinton(s) were elected, we have witnessed mandatory child immunization, education for police service programs, and children divorcing their parents.

Patriotic Americans must object to these UN "rights." The future of your family and society at large, as we presently know it, is at risk from the ever-increasing encroachment of New World Order control. Write your Congressmen and Senators about proposed UN resolutions and treaties. Many of our representatives honestly do not recognize the serious repercussions built into such resolutions and treaties, and in an effort to do something truly humane, they ignorantly are signing away our rights.

I'm sure you realize that all these things can't come to pass at once —a foundation must be established upon which other pieces of the building can be raised before we can reach the completed structure of the New World Order. Some of these bills and resolutions are discussed below, and ironically, the number "six" (the biblical number related to man) appears in the great majority of them.

The trail begins much earlier, but for purposes of this study, we will begin with the "Laws of the 102nd Congress, First Session." The "short title" for Public Law 102-1, dated January 14, 1991, is "Authorization for Use of Military Force Against Iraq Resolution." It is subtitled a: "Joint Resolution to authorize the use of United States Armed Forces pursuant to United Nations Security Council Resolution 678 ." In Sec. 2-a, we find where UN Resolution 666 (among others in that numerical sequence) was used as the basis for the President to send U.S. military troops to the middle east and start the Gulf War.

In the March, 1995, edition of *Flashpoint,* the newsletter of Living Truth Ministries, Texe Marrs addresses a number of the "6"-labeled bills and resolutions. "Is God now revealing to end-time Christians important clues about the evil agenda of high officials in government? That would seem to be what's happening. In fact, our Lord may just be providing His people prophetic warnings by exposing *occult numbers.*

"Case in point: the Persian Gulf conflict. When Iraq's Saddam Hussein invaded Kuwait, President George Bush sent U.S. troops off to war under the authority of the United Nations. This was to be a conflict, said Bush, that would usher in the New World Order. The UN's Security Council quickly voted its approval of UN Resolutions 660 and 666, designed to carry out the world body's goals in the Gulf."

Marrs goes on to call to our attention HR-66. A bill was introduced in the Senate in 1991, designed ultimately to force all U.S. citizens to come under the authority of a UN-created International Criminal Court. For this, Senator Arlen Specter, sponsor of the bill, was highly praised by the World Federalist Association, long recognized as an organization pushing for a one-world government. Jim Leach introduced the corresponding bill in the House of Representatives (as HR-66). Marrs also points out that the sponsors "are both members in good standing of the U.S.A. sovereignty-hating *Council on Foreign Relations.*"

Then there was Bill HR-6, a time bomb looking for a place to go off. . . fortunately, the grass roots rose up and caused it to fail. A liberal Democrat from California introduced it in the last [1993-94] session of Congress. The bill would have been effective in outlawing all home schooling efforts in this country, both by Christians and any other freedom-loving Americans who are convinced that they can do a better job of educating their children than the hopeless public school system. Of course, this little "nugget" was well hidden amidst other pieces of legislation, and it almost sneaked through. However, just days before the vote, some concerned Christians discovered it and began a concerted effort to notify everyone so they could bombard their legislators, telling them not to pass the bill. They called conservative talk shows and other grass roots organizations and got the word out. Congressmen received a blitz of phone calls and faxes. Once feeling the heat, as it were, the Congressmen promptly defeated this legislation, but prior to the Christian protest, HR-6 had been expected to pass with ease.

Even earlier than this we find a Resolution 66 with a powerful ability to affect our lives, including our finances, and which promotes the concept of a one-world order. The following quotation is from the same publication quoted earlier in this book giving the chronological sequence for events leading to the New World Order.

1950—Senate Foreign Relations Subcommittee considers World

Government. **February 9:** A Foreign Relations Subcommittee introduces Senate Concurrent Resolution 66 which begins: "Whereas, in order to achieve universal peace and justice, the present Charter of the United Nations should be changed to provide a true world government constitution." The document was prepared by Hutchins, Adler, Tugwell [who authored the later version], and others, and the resolution was first introduced in the Senate on September 13, 1949, by Senator Glen Taylor (D-Idaho). Senator Alexander Wiley (R-Wisconsin) called it "a consummation devoutly to be wished for," and said, "I understand your proposition is either change the United Nations, or change or create, by a separate convention, *a world order.*" Senator Taylor later stated, *"We would have to sacrifice considerable sovereignty to the world organization to enable them to levy taxes in their own right to support themselves* [emphasis added]."

Marrs calls the current HR-666 "An Unconstitutional Gestapo Measure." I agree! In an effort to better protect us (of course, my tongue is planted firmly in my cheek), our legislators have, for all intents and purposes, stripped us of our Fourth Amendment protections. Here is what Marrs has to say on this measure: "More recently, the same network of anti-American legislators slam-dunked through the House of Representatives HR-666. It is advertised by its sponsor, Representative Bill McCollum (D-Florida), as a bill 'to control crime.' But what it *really* does is control people! If passed by the Senate [and it was subsequent to this article] and signed into law by President Clinton, the Orwellian HR-666 will suspend the constitutional rights of Americans. This monstrous, new law allows federal and local law enforcement agencies—including the Gestapo-like DEA, FBI, FINCEN, etc.— *to search and ransack people's homes and property without a search warrant.*"

Speaking of foreign influence, did you know that August 11, 1993, a native of Russia and Poland was named to succeed retiring General Colin Powell as Chairman of the Joint Chiefs of Staff of our military? It has been reported that his grandfather was a Russian General and his father a member of Hitler's SS Troops. Some observers say it looks like we are truly moving fast toward a one-world government with foreign commanders for our own military.

Texe Marrs has written an insightful investigative exposé entitled, "New Age Politicians and the End of American Sovereignty." I encourage you to obtain and read it.

Just how close are we to having a police state, with a national police force? As you might expect, closer than you think! A UPI wire story appeared on September 7, 1993, which received very little mention, until the recent bombing in Oklahoma City, then it was widely published as part of the plan to better enable the "good guys" to go after the "bad guys," with Janet Reno announcing the proposed changes on nationwide television news. Below is the content of the news release from 1993 which was all but ignored by the media at the time.

> Washington (September 7) UPI—The Clinton Administration's plan announced Tuesday to streamline federal government would merge the law enforcement functions of the Drug Enforcement Administration and the Bureau of Alcohol, Tobacco and Firearms into the FBI.
>
> The move would go a long way toward creating a national police force.
>
> The plan's recommendations would also designate Attorney General Janet Reno as director of law enforcement.
>
> At present, the FBI and DEA are part of the Justice Department. The ATF is part of the Treasury Department.

I am sure there are perfectly valid economic reasons for eliminating overlap and redundancy in law enforcement, but there is also great danger in concentrating too much power in the hands of so few. However, I'm also sure that we can expect a major push in this direction, as this is a main part of the people-control plan, which was made to seem incidental to the Clinton administration's "reinventing of government" plan.

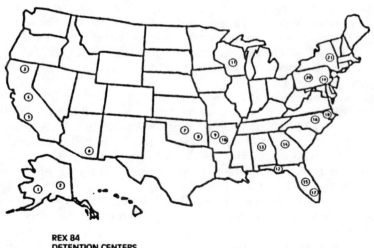

REX 84
DETENTION CENTERS

A military police state here within our own borders? An article appeared in the March 19, 1993, edition of *The Orange County Register,* with the headlines, "Urban Combat Training" and "Marines hit the rooftops," appearing above the text and photos. Just above the byline of writer Jonathan Volzke, the subtitle appears: "Camp Pendleton [a southern California Marine Base] adds $8.4 million facility to train for city warfare." This article is truly hair-raising. If it weren't true, you would swear it was the script for a bad "B-Movie."

Another thing that's hair-raising is the close relationship between the occultic Lucis Trust (formerly Lucifer's Trust) and the United Nations. The articles in their newsletter, *World Goodwill,* are so United Nations-specific that one would just assume it was written and distributed by the UN. Not so! And no where in the newsletter does it tell you that it is published by Lucis Trust. The brochure telling about Lucis Trust proudly displays a label reading as follows: "LUCIS TRUST is on the Roster of the United Nations Economic and Social Council."

Now if you think this is some benign little New Age group, guess again! In their roots lie the occultic proponents Alice Bailey and Elisabeth Kubler-Ross, and their production division still boldly features Bailey's and Ross' teachings in their literature, audio, and video programs. One program, "Twelve Spiritual Festivals," is "designed for the purpose of group meditation at the time of the full moon. Each program is a talk on the impact of energies radiating from one of the signs of the zodiac." "Each human being on the planet should consider himself or herself as a member of the United Nations. . . .We need to have one human family well coordinated, working together, and in harmony with the planet [—Robert Muller]." Their brochure further states: "Lucis Productions produces radio and video programs based on the principles of the Ageless Wisdom. Radio programs include such topics as meditation, the new world order, spiritual values, and death and dying."

Enough said! That's all the space I care to give that satanic organization in this book. Just be warned. . . Lucis Trust is not something with which you want to be involved, either purposely or inadvertently.

When it comes to starting a New World Order, it seems that everybody wants to get into the act. The *Kansas City Star* (February 16, 1994) carries a story entitled, "Ex-senator backs world government—Missouri chosen as site for drive to pass a new constitution." Actually former senator and project founder Mike Gravel began this action in California in 1993.

However, Mr. Gravel is a "Johnny-come-lately" where such matters are concerned. Back in 1948, a *Preliminary Draft of a World Constitution* was published by U.S. educators Robert Hutchins, Mortimer Adler,

Rexford Tugwell, and others, advocating regional federation on the way toward world federation or government. Their Constitution provides for a "World Council," along with a "Chamber of Guardians," to enforce world law. Also included is a Preamble calling upon nations to surrender their arms to the world government, and it includes the right of this "Federal Republic of the World" to seize private property for federal use.

The most recent World Constitution, currently being circulated among nations for ratification, is the product of the World Constitution and Parliament Association of Lakewood, Colorado. Their time table projects all to be completed by 1999.

That brings us to the draft of a New Constitution for the United States. First the World Constitution will have to be in place, then we are ready to ditch "old faithful" for something that allegedly meets our current needs better than our old Constitution.

Rexford Guy Tugwell, at the request of Mr. Robert Hutchins of the Center of the Study of Democratic Institutions, drafted this proposed New Constitution to replace our existing Constitution. Tugwell was an instructor at the University of Chicago and the London School of Economics (a socialist school in England). He has been described as "fully committed to Socialism on a national and international scale." He was affiliated with a series of organizations, at least five of which have been described as "Communist fronts" by various committees of the Senate and House of Representatives.

The Center of the Study of Democratic Institutions was created in 1959 by the Fund for the Republic. . .which was created in 1953 by the Ford Foundation, the financier of the "most extreme leftwingers all over the world."

In his front section titled "ADOPTION," Tugwell admits that the President (or whoever) will have to sneak this through "in unorthodox fashion," and acknowledges that "There is the expected uproar from those who fear the loss of privileges." When you obtain a copy and read it, you will understand why. Don't just "surface" read; on the surface it sounds pretty reasonable. But read between the lines; extrapolate some of those proposals to their ultimate conclusions, and you will know how devastating this will be to freedom as we know it.

Well, it seems this chapter isn't ending up as brief as I expected, but there is still one important subject to address, and I don't know of another chapter where it could be more appropriately placed. . . that is the subject of FEMA (Federal Emergency Management Agency).

Much has been said about FEMA and the high-sounding purpose for which it was created, but as with other federal instututions, it "grew like Topsy," and now far exceeds the limits originally established for it. Did you notice the prominent place they were given in the control of things following the Oklahoma City bombing? To get us started, I am reprinting (below) a startling article by Mark Weston which appeared in the Spring 1994 edition of the magazine, *Paranoia*. It is titled: "FEMA: Fascist Entity Manipulating America." I believe this article documents the accusation that money budgeted for FEMA is being siphoned off for use in any number of covert activities.

Few Americans realize that agents of the New World Order have infiltrated a government agency which was originally chartered to protect and serve them. This agency was initially set up to coordinate communication and rescue efforts during times of man-made or natural disasters.

Nixon started the ball rolling by signing Executive Order 11490 [Author's note: Remember, I told you earlier about the havoc that could be wreaked with these Executive Orders.] which allowed federal departments and agencies to draft plans for emergency preparedness functions. By 1979, the avalanche of paperwork that this executive order created caused the birth of a new government agency known as the Federal Emergency Management Agency (FEMA).

The new agency plodded along in typical bureaucratic fashion until the newly elected President, Ronald Reagan, decided to use it in the furtherance of the agenda proposed by such groups as The Trilateral Commission and the Council on Foreign Relations. Thus in 1982 he signed National Security Directive 58. This directive allowed the National Security Council, under the auspices of Robert "Bud" McFarlane and Oliver North, to infiltrate FEMA and carry out the objectives of Directive 58. As was the case with Iran/Contra, McFarlane and North carried out their mission with zealous disregard of that pesky old rag, the U.S. Constitution.

Taking one-third of FEMA's employees into their secret program, they managed to divert massive amounts of taxpayers' money. They did this by simply submitting a yearly budget request to Congress for disaster relief and other items "submitted under a separate package." These separate packages of itemized expenses were never presented to Congress. At any rate, Congress never seemed to notice. Neither did anyone in Congress ever question the fact that *these "separate packages" amounted to more than twelve times the legitimate requests* [emphasis added].
Where did the money go?
For the ten years between 1982 and 1992, Congress gave FEMA $243 million for disaster relief. During the same period, McFarlane and North's "separate packages" amounted to $2.9 billion. As you will see, these funds were used to turn FEMA into

a very useful tool for those who view the Bill of Rights as an impediment to their plans.

Much of the secret funding went into a program known as Mobile Emergency Response Support (MERS). This program supplies 300 specially equipped and nuclear-hardened vehicles designed to shuffle the President and his cabinet around the country so they can maintain control after a nuclear holocaust. These expensive toys are kept in the states of Texas, Georgia, Colorado, Washington, and Massachusetts. Thus they are within immediate striking distance to anywhere in the continental United States.

Make no mistake, dear reader. Although ostensibly a disaster relief agency, FEMA is in actuality a highly sophisticated organization which has been set up to take over the government of the United States. Everything is in place for the crackdown. FEMA computers gather information. Specially equipped "doomsday vehicles" are on "alert" status. Representatives of the Shadow Government are poised in top secret underground bunkers waiting for the green light.

Special Facility

Not far from the nation's capital there is a large natural feature known as Mount Weather, located on Highway 601, just outside the bucolic town of Berryville, Virginia. This mountain sits in mute testimony to the human propensity toward the exercise of total control. Deep inside the mountain the Shadow Government develops its devious plans, collecting information on the citizenry while comfortably ensconced in what FEMA euphemistically calls the "Special Facility." This facility appears to be very special indeed. It comes equipped with all the computer power and satellite uplinks necessary to control all the communications systems in our country and beyond. The security measures are so stringent at Mount Weather that anyone entering is subject to being searched for such proscribed contraband as cameras, sketch pads, or any other item capable of recording the interior layout.

Although only a handful of insiders know exactly how big the facility is, those who have gotten a glimpse inside Mount Weather describe a huge underground city. It is known that contained within the mountain are all the supplies necessary to keep FEMA running for months without contact with the outside world.

Why would our government feel the need to hide in a cave now that the threat of nuclear annihilation [allegedly, but I doubt it— Author] no longer hangs over our heads? To answer this question, one need look no further than the agency's own writings, in which FEMA allows itself to bypass our Constitutional guarantees during "peacetime or wartime national security emergencies...accidental, natural, and man-made occurrences." Please take note that FEMA does not need an all-out war as an excuse to trample on the Constitution. Any "peacetime emergency" will do. Such as a repeat of the L.A. riots.

As we go to press, President Clinton is calling for the passage of his Omnibus Crime Bill. This piece of legislation will restrict gun purchases while at the same time putting 100,000 new police on the streets. [The Bill subsequently passed.] Meanwhile, the press reports that prisons are the new growth industry of the nineties.

El Generalismo

To get a grasp on how an aberration such as FEMA could have been spawned, a short history lesson is in order. The agency's policies became official after the appointment of Louis O. Giuffreda as director of FEMA by his old buddy President Ron Reagan. As the commanding general of the California National Guard, Giuffreda was instrumental in developing "Operation Cable Splicer." This program was developed for the sole purpose of spying on citizens that Reagan and his paranoid counterpart Ed Meese considered politically incorrect. Expanding on this program, Giuffreda (who prefers the title General) had the agency's powerful computers across the country tied into a vast network capable of gathering information on dissidents and potential troublemakers via records obtained through local police departments. Therefore, the agency is engaged in a constant data-gathering frenzy via the FBI, Department of Energy, National Military Command Center, CIA, National Security Agency, and the Defense Intelligence Agency.

At huge FEMA campuses located in Emmitsburg, Maryland, and Carson City, Nevada, agents attend seminars in "continuity of government" and workshops on "nuclear weapons accidents." These colleges are also used to inculcate officials from towns and cities across America in "counter-terrorism tactics." For good measure, foreign police and military officials are trained in FEMA techniques. Thus, in Giuffreda's own words, "We have made joint military/civil planning far more effective both here and overseas."

At this point you might ask yourself just what all this espionage training has to do with disaster relief? The answer is simple. Nothing. In fact, when winds reaching 160 m.p.h. devastated Homestead, Florida, in August of 1992, the city manager requested 100 hand-held phones. FEMA responded by sending one of the high-tech nuclear-hardened MERS vehicles. Although capable of communicating with an aircraft on the other side of the globe, it could not place a simple phone call to Miami. More recently, FEMA failed its relief mission after the earthquake in Los Angeles. The official excuse was "we didn't expect so many victims." The above incidents are just two examples demonstrative of this evil agency's true agenda. Far from being established as an aid to America's citizenry, FEMA has been created as an agent of repression, working solely for the elite hidden government.

Justified by Law

A short listing of just some of the policies ready to be implemented by this agency of repression is well worth reading. The following is taken directly from a FEMA document called "The Defense Resources Act."

• Section 1001—"Whenever the President shall deem that the public safety demands it, he may cause to be censored, under such rules and regulations as he may from time to time establish, communications by mail, cable, radio, television, or other means of transmission crossing the borders of the United States."

• Section 903 empowers the President to "limit employment opportunities to activities essential to the national health, safety, or interest."

• Sections 201 and 501 give the President authority to requisition, condemn, or seize property for the "national defense." The government is required to compensate property owners, but those "unwilling to accept" the price determined by the President will get "75%" of such amount; they can go to court to recover the rest.

• Section 1213 regulates the personnel practices of government and federal contractors. They are prohibited from employing "any person who engages in a strike against the government of the United States, or who is a member of an organization of government employees that asserts the right to strike against the government of the United States, or who advocates, or who is a member of an organization that advocates, the overthrow of the government of the United States by force or violence." Loyalty oaths are authorized; federal workers who have illegal affiliations "shall be fined not more than $1,000 or imprisoned for not more than one year, or both."

The agency also has another trick up its sleeve called "Plan D." This 364-page document refers directly to the takeover of the media by ensuring that "all telecommunications resources of radio and television licensees are available for use and responsive to a war situation." FEMA is also involved in planning exercises with the Pentagon such as "Operation Night Train" which establishes prison camps along the Mexican border to be used in case there is a sudden and unacceptable influx of immigration by our southern neighbors. This is a program close to the agency's black heart. While still an army student in 1970, Giuffreda wrote a paper detailing just how these prison camps could be set up. It should be noted here that Clinton's crime bill calls for "boot camps" for youthful offenders.

FEMA also worked closely with the Pentagon in trying to determine ways in which to bypass Constitutional rules, such as the Posse Comitatus Act. This is the law stating that no military equipment or personnel may be used against civilians. Anyone who watched army tanks equipped with flame-throwers torching "cultists" in Waco [Texas] has to figure that their efforts must have borne fruit.

Just what kind of man is General Guiffreda? What kind of person would be so ready to roll a tank over the Constitution? The legacy left by this one man should give pause to all lovers of freedom. Is our democracy headed for history's scrap heap? Will the New World Order determine our future from the bowels of some nuclear-hardened sanctuary reminiscent of the movie *Doctor Strangelove?*

For an indication of what might be if we drop our vigilance, simply let Giuffreda speak in his own words: "Legitimate violence is integral to our form of government, for it is from this source that we can continue to purge our weaknesses."

In addition to the article reprinted above, I want to refer you to a "Special Supplement" edition to *The SPOTLIGHT,* May, 1992. The 12-page special supplement is dedicated entirely to the subject of FEMA and is entitled: "FEMA vs. Your Constitutional Rights." Some articles in the supplement include: "Constitutional Rights Could Disappear," "Americans Computerized by FEMA," "FEMA Order Reprinted," "Disarming People First Step in NWO," "Carter's True Legacy," "Blueprint for U.S. Dictatorship," and "Dictatorship Possible Here." It is available in reprints, and even though it is three years old, it is replete with pertinent information that you really must read. Request reprints or subscription information from: *The SPOTLIGHT,* 300 Independence Ave. SE, Washington, DC 20003, or phone 1-800-522-6292.

Now it is time to move on to chapter five and examine the many organizations promoting the New World Order. . . really just a continuation of the "666 Systems."

ANNOUNCING THE BIRTH OF THE NEW WORLD ORDER

Back of U.S. One Dollar Bill (Enlarged)

N.W.O. Organizations:

The Illuminati / Skull & Bones / Freemasonry
Council on Foreign Relations
Trilateral Commission / Bilderbergers

This is going to be a difficult chapter to write because it addresses so many different topics of importance. Many writers have covered these subjects in depth, therefore, it is not my intent to duplicate their efforts. On the contrary, I only want to give you a brief background and call your attention to any new information that may have come to light recently. I will suggest some "recommended reading" from other sources. And I want to forewarn you that as you study these groups and their activities, be especially alert for the recurring presence of the Rockefellers and the Rothschilds throughout this integrated maze of secret organizations (even though said organizations vehemently deny that they are doing things in secret—and have enlisted the aid of the media to announce their meetings and meeting places, just to prove they're not trying to hide their activities—don't you believe it!).

The Council on Foreign Relations, Trilateral Commission, and Bilderbergers (with covert assistance from others) run the world through manipulation of the banking systems. In the United States it is the Federal Reserve, a private organization which most Americans *incorrectly assume* is owned, run, and/or controlled by our government. In other countries the World Bank is in control of international finance.

The Illuminati

Webster's Illustrated Encyclopedic Dictionary gives the following definition under the word *illuminati,* and it couldn't be more accurate if it had been written by your traditional right-wing conservative.

Il·lu·mi·na·ti (I-loo'mə-nä'tĕ) *pl.n.* **1.** Persons claiming to be unusually enlightened with regard to some subject. **2. Illuminati. a.** The members of a secret society of freethinkers and republicans that flourished in Germany during the late 18th century. Also called "Illuminaten." **b.** Persons regarded as atheists, libertines, or radical republicans during the 18th century (such as the French Encyclopedists, the Freemasons, or the freethinkers). **3. Illuminati.** The members of a heretical sect of 16th-century Spain, who claimed special religious enlightenment. [Latin *illūmināti*, "enlightened ones," plural of *illūmināti*, past participle of *illūmināre*, ILLUMINATE.]

Consider the **first** definition: "Persons *claiming* to be unusually enlightened with regard to some subject [emphasis added]." The Illuminati consider themselves the only ones qualified and sufficiently enlightened to run the world, and they are power-hungry enough to scheme until they actually control it. . .and us! The **second** definition (part "**a**") refers to a "secret society" going back to Germany as far as the 18th century; part "**b**" says they were regarded as atheists, libertines, and radicals, and further adds a reference to the Freemasons; the **third** brings in the religious aspect of the Illuminati, calling them a heretical sect claiming special religious enlightenment. They're enlightened, alright! But exactly what is the source of their light? Reminds me of the scriptures telling about Satan coming as an "angel of light," for the express purpose of deceiving us.

Where the CFR, Trilateral Commission, and Bilderbergers emphasize control of the world through control of world finances, the Illuminati/Freemasons, Skull & Bones, and similar secret societies found on university campuses around the world focus on education, or the control of the minds of our future leaders. Of course, they all adhere heavily to the "old boy" network, where anyone who belongs to the organization is assured successful placement in a position of power and prominence. In personnel or other selection, priority is always given to candidates who are brothers of this elite group over applicants or candidates who are not.

Antony Sutton, former research Fellow at the Hoover Institution, Stanford University, as well as professor at California State University, Los Angeles, has authored a book entitled *America's Secret Establishment: An Introduction to the Order of Skull & Bones*. It is on my recommended reading list for you. It details as much as you will ever find on the Order of the Skull & Bones (without becoming an initiate), gives a brief background on the origin of the Illuminati, and makes the case for a plausible link between the two groups, though the author is careful to point out that his documentation is still inconclusive as yet; but he is convinced his further research will provide sufficient evidence to prove a definite connection between the two.

The Illuminati was a group of Bavarian conspirators dedicated to the overthrow of government. The society was founded on May 1, 1776 [Note: while in America we were busy drafting the Declaration of Independence], by Adam Weishaupt of the University of Ingolstadt. It was a secret society, but the Order of the Illuminati presumably ceased to exist when it was raided by the Bavarian police in 1786. The Order was dissolved and its papers seized and published. Because the Bavarian state ordered the papers to be published, we have authentic information about the organization and its methods of operation. Subsequent investigation of those documents determined that the aim of the Illuminati was world domination, using any methods to advance the objective, i.e., the end always justifies the means. It was anti-Christian, although clergymen were found in the organization, and each member had a pseudonym to disguise his identity. . .a truly secret society in every sense of the term.

The Illuminati's concept of education can be traced to the influence of early 19th century German philosophers. These concepts were introduced in the United States by postgraduate students studying in Europe, bringing their ideas back home with them, then instigating the Illuminati plan to educate our youngsters according to their goals and philosophies.

Sutton states (quoting John Robinson, in *Proofs of a Conspiracy*):

> So far as education is concerned, the Illuminati objective was as follows:
> "We must win the common people in every corner. This will be obtained chiefly by means of the schools, and by open, hearty behaviour, show, condescension, popularity, and toleration of their prejudices *which we shall at leisure root out and dispel* [emphasis added]."

Johann Friedrich Herbart was a major German philosopher when the Yale postgraduate students were studying there. Herbart adhered to the Hegelian philosophy (the State is superior to the individual) and thoroughly indoctrinated his protegés in this teaching. Therefore, for Herbart, education had to be presented in a scientifically correct manner, and the chief purpose of education, in his opinion, was to prepare the child to live properly in the social order of which he is an integral part. The individual is not important. The mere development of individual talent, of individual fitness, mental power, and knowledge is *not* the purpose of education. The purpose is to develop personal character and social morality, and the most important task of the educator is to analyze the activities and duties of men within society.

The function of instruction, according to Herbart, is to fulfill these aims and impart to the individual *socially desirable ideas.* In today's vernacular, we would call this being "PC" (politically correct!). All these ideas in today's American educational philosophy can be recognized as originating and being transmitted by members (knights and patriarchs) of the Order of Skull and Bones, having been learned at the feet of Illuminati educators. This link may not have been proven beyond doubt at this point, but it looks pretty obvious to me.

GRAND ARCHITECT OF THE UNIVERSE

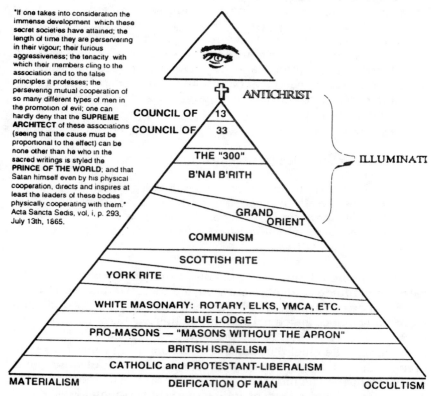

"If one takes into consideration the immense development which these secret societies have attained; the length of time they are perservering in their vigour; their furious aggressiveness; the tenacity with which their members cling to the association and to the false principles it professes; the persevering mutual cooperation of so many different types of men in the promotion of evil; one can hardly deny that the **SUPREME ARCHITECT** of these associations (seeing that the cause must be proportional to the effect) can be none other than he who in the sacred writings is styled the **PRINCE OF THE WORLD**; and that Satan himself even by his physical cooperation, directs and inspires at least the leaders of these bodies physically cooperating with them." Acta Sancta Sedis, vol, i, p. 293, July 13th, 1865.

ANTICHRIST

COUNCIL OF 13
COUNCIL OF 33
THE "300"
B'NAI B'RITH
GRAND ORIENT

ILLUMINATI

COMMUNISM
SCOTTISH RITE
YORK RITE
WHITE MASONARY: ROTARY, ELKS, YMCA, ETC.
BLUE LODGE
PRO-MASONS — "MASONS WITHOUT THE APRON"
BRITISH ISRAELISM
CATHOLIC and PROTESTANT-LIBERALISM

MATERIALISM   DEIFICATION OF MAN   OCCULTISM

THE MASONIC PYRAMID
ILLUMINISM AND FREE MASONRY — FATHER OF LIES

The Illuminati has long been connected to Freemasonry (as described in Webster's definition above) and comprises the top portion of the Masonic Pyramid. Although I won't be pursuing the Freemasonry connection any further, I am reprinting The Masonic Pyramid herein. There is an abundant proliferation of pyramids appearing in the last decade in every walk of life, from the money we spend to the architecture of the mint in which it is printed, not to mention San Francisco hotels, Las Vegas casinos, banks, cigarette ads, gyms, office buildings, theaters, convention centers, *et al.*

Before we get away from this brief look at Freemasonry, I want to quote a couple of paragraphs from Texe Marrs' excellent book, *Millennium*. In the chapter on Secret Societies and Other Conspiracies, he introduces the Vatican into the mix, as follows:

Intrigue at the Vatican

That the Vatican and the Pope might be involved in the dark labyrinth of the secret societies may shock some readers. But those who have studied carefully the history of the Vatican and its dealings with secret societies over the centuries are not at all surprised. For many years the Vatican has maintained links with the various brotherhoods, orders, and secret societies that have flourished throughout Europe and the Middle East.

Some of the Catholic orders—for instance, the Jesuits—have themselves carried out secret operations and missions. A number of popes promoted the Great Crusades, and during that era, the Knights Templar literally became a functionary of the Vatican— its designated agent in a holy war against the Moslems. In addition, mountainous evidence can be marshalled to demonstrate that today the Vatican is heavily infiltrated and influenced by Masonic interests.

As we progress further into this chapter, you will become increasingly aware of the difficulty I am experiencing trying to keep these organizations separated for study purposes, as many people are members of two or more. For example, President George Bush is a member of the Order of Skull & Bones (as was his father before him), as well as a member of both the CFR (Council on Foreign Relations) and the TLC (Trilateral Commission). Other prominent contemporary members of Skull & Bones include Winston Lord, former ambassador to China, U.S. Senators David Boren of Oklahoma and John Chaffe of Rhode Island, as well as William F. Buckley (allegedly conservative publisher of the *National Review*), among others.

Another good book written on the bizarre cultic society of Skull & Bones is by researchers Walter Isacsson and Evan Thomas, entitled *The Wise Men.*

But I'm getting ahead of myself again! Let's discuss the questions, "What is the Order of Skull & Bones and how did it begin?" According to Sutton, those on the "inside" know it simply as "The Order." Others have known it for more than 150 years as "Chapter 322" of a German secret society. For legal purposes it was incorporated in 1956 as The Russell Trust. It was also once known as the "Brotherhood of Death." The casual name (or sometimes used derogatorily) is "Skull & Bones," or just plain "Bones."

Believe me. . .The Order is not just another Greek letter campus fraternity, with passwords and secret handshakes. It is far more insidious. Chapter 322 is a *secret* society whose members are sworn to silence (they are supposed to actually leave the room if someone outside The Order even mentions the name Skull & Bones). So far as we can determine, it exists only on the campus of Yale University, though rumors are beginning to surface indicating there may be a select number of other locations and possible links to a couple of other secret societies on the Yale campus, the Scroll & Key and Wolf's Head, both founded in the mid-19th century. Allegedly, these are competitive societies, however, Sutton believes them to be part of the same network. It has rules and rituals. . .ceremonial rites which I will mention briefly a little later.

Sutton states that its members always deny membership, and in checking hundreds of autobiographical listings for members, he found only half a dozen who cited an affiliation with Skull & Bones. He is concerned about whether the many members of the various Administrations (either elected or appointed) have declared their membership in the biographical data supplied to the FBI for their obligatory "background checks," implying that it is not likely.

Further, Sutton asserts, then documents, that The Order is unbelievably powerful.

Skull & Bones is an organization of only senior students at Yale University. Each year, only 15 initiates are selected in their junior year (all males prior to 1995, when they proposed inducting women into the formerly all-male group—at present Buckley has an injunction in place to stop this). Therefore, the organization is oriented primarily to the post-graduate outside world. The Patriarchs only meet annually on Deer Island in the St. Lawrence River.

Admission into Skull & Bones is by invitation only, therefore, there is no lobbying, electioneering, or applying for membership. During commencement week, the juniors are privately "tapped." The Junior simply is given an option: "Skull & Bones. Accept or reject?" This method has not changed since The Order's inception in 1832. Those who accept (presumably the greater number) are invited to attend the Bones Temple on campus to undergo an initiation ceremony (described briefly below). For the ambitious, "tapping" is the magic password to a future success-guaranteed career. Potential candidates apparently are selected based on their school and extracurricular activities, their support of Yale, and particularly sports ability. . .team-work is held in very high esteem. The most unlikely choice would be a loner, an iconoclast, or an individualist—a person who goes their own way in the world. They want people who put The Order first, with-out question, and who will abide by the rules at all costs. Sutton states:

> The most likely potential member is from a Bones family, is energetic, resourceful, political, and probably an amoral team player. A man who understands that to get along you have to go along. A man who will sacrifice himself for the good of the team. A moment's reflection illustrates why this is so. In real life, the thrust of The Order is to bring about certain objectives. Honors and financial rewards are guaranteed by the power of The Order. But the price of these honors and rewards is sacrifice to the common goal, the goal of The Order. Some, perhaps many, have not been willing to pay this price.

Initiates undergo bizarre rituals and initiation ceremonies with sexual overtones, conducted on the order of brainwashing techniques, designed to strip the initiate of all pride and sense of self, then being "reprogrammed" to embrace only the philosophies and goals of The Order. (Sutton describes these rituals in great detail in his book.)

At any given time about 500-600 are alive and active. Roughly about one-quarter of these take an active role in furthering the objec-tives of The Order—the others either change their minds or just lose interest and become silent dropouts.

Before I tell a little about some of the past members, I will present a couple of ideas that have been postulated concerning the number "322" under the skull and crossed bones of The Order's logo or official emblem. Since the organization was imported from Germany in 1832 as the second chapter of a German order, it has been specu-lated that the "32" denotes the year of origination and the next "2" indicates that it is the second chapter of the organization. A much more likely theory is that this order descended from a fraternal society dating back to Demosthenes in 322 B.C., as Bones records are dated by adding 322 years to the current year, i.e. records originating in 1950 are dated Anno-Demostheni 2272.

Inside The Order there are many other numbers and symbols which appear beside the names of the members in the "Catalogue" (or mem-bership list, later called "Addresses"). Although we don't know for sure, Sutton makes some interesting speculations regarding their possible meaning. The Catalogue contains the birth names of the members, but Sutton tells us:

> Entry into The Order is accompanied by an elaborate ritual and no doubt psychological conditioning. For example:
> "Immediately on entering Bones the neophyte's name is changed. He is no longer known by his name as it appears in the college catalogue but like a monk or Knight of Malta or St. John, becomes Knight so and so. The old Knights are then known as Patriarch so and so. The outside world are known as Gentiles and vandals."

In discussing the original member list, the class of 1833, Sutton points out that the name which should appear at position eleven has been replaced by two lines. "This supports the argument that the society has German origins and this is the listing of the anonymous German connection."

In the 150 years since The Order was founded, active membership has evolved into a core group of perhaps 20-30 families, according to Sutton. ". . . it seems that active members have enough influence to push their sons and relatives into The Order, and there is significant inter-marriage among the families. These families fall into two major groups.

"First we find the old line American families who arrived on the East coast in the 1600's, e.g., Whitney, Lord, Phelps, Wadsworth, Allen, Bundy, Adams, and so on.

"Second, we find families who acquired wealth in the last 100 years, sent their sons to Yale, and in time became almost old line families, e.g., Harriman, Rockefeller, Payne, Davison. . . . In the last 150 years a few families in The Order have gained enormous influence in society and the world."

Although the "old line" families used to look down their blueblood noses at the *nouveau riche,* that is not so much the case any more. They have discovered it takes money to maintain the power—not just the name—so if they couldn't make it on their own, they "married" it into the family. But whatever it takes, you maintain the power at all costs.

The Order has penetrated every segment of American society, e.g. the White House, executive branch, legislatures, political parties, foundations (charitable and otherwise), "think tanks," policy groups, education, media, publishing, banking, Federal Reserve System, business, industry, commerce, and even churches. In many cases The Order is the founder of these organizations. . .they determine the goals and objectives, as well as the methods for achieving them, then usually installs the first President, Chairman, or CEO and/or CFO. This explains why so many such organizations are based on the premise of secular humanism. Their roots can be traced back directly to active members of The Order.

Since it seems the most unlikely, let's first take a look at the connection of The Order to the Church. Although the percentage has declined in recent years, about 2% of the Order is in the Church—all Protestant denominations. Again quoting Sutton:

> A key penetration is the Union Theological Seminary, affiliated with Columbia University in New York. This Seminary, a past subject of investigation for Communist infiltration, has close links to The Order. Henry Sloane Coffin (1897) was Professor of Practical Theology at Union from 1904 to 1926 and President of Union Theological Seminary, also known as the "Red Seminary," from 1926 to 1945. Union has such a wide interpretation of religious activity that it has, or used to have, an Atheists Club for its students.
>
> Henry Sloane Coffin, Jr. (1949) was one of the Boston Five indicted on federal conspiracy charges.
>
> And this is only **part** of The Order's penetration into the Church.

I will let Mr. Sutton expand on the connection between The Order and the other areas, i.e. the law, communications, industry, the Federal Reserve/banking, and the White House/politics/government.

The Law

The major establishment law firms in New York are saturated with The Order.

In particular, Lord, Day, and Lord, dominated by the Lord family already discussed; also Simpson, Thacher, and Bartlett, especially the Thacher family; David, Polk, Wardwell, and Debevoise, Plimpton, the Rockefeller family law firm.

Communications

There has been a significant penetration into communications. Some examples:

- Henry Luce of *Time-Life* is in The Order.
- So is William Buckley ('50) of *National Review,*
- And Alfred Cowles ('13), President of Cowles Communications, *Des Moine Register, Minneapolis Star,*
- And Emmert Bates ('32) of Litton Educational Systems, plus
- Richard Ely Danielson ('07) of *Atlantic Monthly,*
- Russell Wheeler Davenport ('23), *Fortune,*
- John Chipman Farrar ('18) of Farrar, Strauss, the publishers.

The most prestigious award in journalism is a Nieman Fellowship at Harvard University. Over 300 were granted from 1937-68. The FIRST Director of the Nieman Fund was member Archibald McLeash.

Industry

The oil companies have their links to The Order. Members Percy, Rockefeller, the Paynes, the Pratts, all link to Standard Oil. Shell Oil, Creole Petroleum, and Socony Vacuum also link. A wide variety of manufacturing firms have members in The Order, from the Donnelley family in Chicago (printers of the *Official Airline Guide* and other references); lumber companies like Weyerhaeuser, who is also a Trilateralist; Dresser Industries, and so on.

The Federal Reserve System

A dozen members can be linked to the Federal Reserve, but one appointment is noteworthy, Pierre Jay ('92), whose only claim to fame in 1913 was to run a private school and be an obscure Vice President of Manhattan Bank, yet he became FIRST Chairman of the New York Federal Reserve, the really significant Reserve Bank.

The White House, Politics, and Government

This is the area where The Order has made headway, with names like Taft, Bush, Stimson, Chafee, Lovett, Whitney, Bundy, and so on.

I have done my best to give you "skeletal" information (no pun intended) on the Illuminati and The Order of Skull & Bones. Before I move on, I want to address the matter of the extreme secrecy in both movements (which Sutton believes is further evidence of a link between the two). I already have mentioned the fact that Bonesmen are supposed to refuse any comment regarding The Order or their membership therein. The same unquestionably applied to the Illuminati (if, indeed, you can relegate the Illuminati to the past tense). Secrecy can be used to conceal illegal activities, among other things. *Obviously, secrecy is needed only if there is something to conceal.* Secrecy is superfluous if you have nothing to hide. A private letter between members of the Illuminati which was published by the Elector of Bavaria, contained the following statement: "The great strength of our Order lies in its concealment; let it never appear in any place in its own name, but always covered by another name and another occupation." And just as The Order works, so does/did the Illuminati, as this excerpt from an Illuminati letter reveals: "The power of the Order must surely be turned to the advantage of its members. All must be assisted. They must be preferred to all persons otherwise of equal merit."

Although we are not yet to our discussion of the CFR and TLC, I briefly will address them here, as they relate to Skull & Bones Chapter 322.

CFR and TLC, though not looking for a spotlight on their discussions and activities, are not secret organizations in the sense that the Illuminati and Skull & Bones are secret. Their membership rosters are available to anyone who asks, and they are making the dates and locations of their meetings available to the media, though the media is not permitted inside to witness the activities, nor are their members permitted to give interviews revealing what has occurred at their meetings (as spelled out in their bylaws).

The Order is represented in these organizations, but does not always dominate. David Rockefeller, former chairman of the CFR, is not a member of The Order, but the family was represented in The Order by Percy Rockefeller; however, a later CFR chairman, Winston Lord, is a member of Bones.

Visualize three concentric circles, consisting of the inner core, the inner circle, and the outer circle. The outer circle is made up of large, open organizations (e.g., CFR or TLC) some of whose membership is made up of Bones members. The inner circle is made up of one or more secret societies, such as Chapter 322 (even though it is suspected that there is at least one other, it cannot be proven beyond doubt at this time). The inner core is believed to be a secret society within The Order, a decision-making core. As yet the existence of this inner core cannot be documented, but evidence points to its existence. Sutton even believes that he could identify the Chairman.

The CFR is the largest organization in the outer circle, with about 2,900 members at any one time (as many as The Order in its entire history). The TLC has 325 members world wide, but only about 80 in the United States. Other groups in the outer circle include the Pilgrim Society, the Atlantic Council, the Bilderbergers, and the Bohemian Club (of San Francisco). As an example of the number of Bones members who are also members of the CFR, following are just the Bones members whose last names begin with the letter "B": Jonathan Bingham (Congressman); William F. Buckley (Editor, *National Review* and The Order's house conservative); McGeorge Bundy (Foundation executive); William Bundy (CIA); George Bush (former President of the United States).

The Trilateral Commission was founded in 1973 by David Rockefeller, who was not a member of The Order. The same appears to be true of many TLC members; however, if you investigate the family tree, you will find members of The Order sometimes as close as one generation removed, and in other cases in the family line in great numbers, though not the current TLC member. Sutton points out that the TLC is not a conspiracy, it just doesn't publish its activities too widely, as the general populace probably wouldn't appreciate what they are planning for us behind closed doors.

Sutton reports that he "has openly debated with George Franklin, Jr., Coordinator of the Trilateral Commission on the radio. Mr. Franklin did show a rather ill-concealed dislike for the assault on his pet global New World Order—and made the mistake of attempting to disguise this objective. . . ." Where the TLC connection is concerned, even though David Rockefeller is not a Bones member, keep these facts in mind: J. Richardson Dilworth, chief financial and administrative officer for the Rockefeller Family Associates, is a member of The Order, as was Percy Rockefeller (1900). And TLC purposes, as portrayed in their own literature, are almost identical to those of The Order.

So far as Sutton can determine, William F. Buckley is the only member of both The Order and the Bilderbergers. The Pilgrim Society has no current Bones members, but the family names of past members are found, i.e., Aldrich and Pratt.

I have discussed the guarantees of success for Bones members, as well as the intermarriages to consolidate the power, wealth, and influence of the families. Now, we will look at the chain of influence.

A chain of influence that is spread over many years guarantees continuity and must be extraordinarily impressive to any new initiate who doubts the power of The Order. In a horizontal chain (there is also a vertical chain which I will not address), members of The Order are to be found in every segment of our existence: education, foundations, politics, government, industry, law, and finance. Consequently, *at any time The Order can tap influence in any area of society.* The major occupations, however, are in law, education, business, finance, and industry. Percentage of Bones members in each area follows: 18%—Law, 16%—Education, 16%—Business, 15%—Finance, 12%—Industry. The remaining 23% are scattered among all remaining occupations.

Sutton makes a good case for the interference of The Order in promoting wars and conflict in order to maintain and increase their world control.

> If we can show that The Order has artificially encouraged and developed **both** revolutionary Marxism **and** national socialism while retaining some control over the nature and degree of the conflict, then it follows *The Order will be able to determine the evolution and nature of the New World Order* [italic emphasis added].

He makes the above statement while documenting a link between the Union Bank and support for the Nazis during World War II. He traced the flow of the money through a long trail that attempted to hide its ultimate destination, and proved the involvement of at least eight men, four of whom were members of The Order (including Prescott Bush, father of President George Bush) and two of whom were Nazis.

As I conclude this section on The Skull & Bones, Brotherhood of Death, I want to discuss the spiritual aspects of The Order. Sutton tells us:

> What happens in the initiation process is essentially a variation of brainwashing or encounter group processes. Knights, through heavy peer pressure, become Patriarchs prepared for a life of the exercise of power and continuation of this process into future generations.
>
> In brief, the ritual is designed to mold establishment zombies, to ensure continuation of power in the hands of a small select group from one generation to another. But beyond this ritual are aspects notably satanic.

We can make at least three definite statements about links between The Order and satanic beliefs. First, photographic evidence documents the satanic device (as well as the name) of the skull and crossed bones. Second, there is a link to satanic symbolism. Third, the link between The Order and the New World Order is well documented in the book, *The Hidden Dangers of the Rainbow,* by Constance Cumbey.

The skull and crossed bones is not just a logo or printed artwork; photographs exist that show the use of actual skulls and bones in the ceremonies of The Order. According to other evidence, at least three sets of skulls and other assorted human bones are kept within the Bones Temple on the Yale campus. At best, that makes the members grave robbers. But using these bones for ceremonial purposes shows absolutely no respect for the dead, and is a blatantly satanic activity.

Another ceremony includes the presentation of a grandfather clock to each Knight upon initiation. It stays with him throughout his life as a memento of what is called "the Bones experience." I have not discovered the hidden significance of this gift, but I think it's a safe bet that there is one.

Author Constance Cumbey identified and linked several organizations to The Order and its objectives. She identified Benjamin Creme and the Tara Center as a New Age phenomenon, then linked Creme to the Unity and Unitarian Churches. Sutton continued the chain by pointing out The Order's longstanding and significant link to these churches. Former President William Taft, whose father co-founded

The Order, was President of the Unitarian Association in his time.

Cumbey identifies the link between Hitler and the New Age move-ment and previous research by Sutton linked The Order to the founding and growth of Naziism. Cumbey states that the New Age movement plans to bring about a New World Order "which will be a synthesis between the USSR, Great Britain, and the United States." Later infor-mation indicates that it will come closer to encompassing the entire world, i.e., both industrialized nations and third-world countries.

Finally, Cumbey points out that the anti-Christ and satanic aspects are woven into the cult of the New Age movement. I don't think there is any doubt about it! The goals and activities of the Skull & Bones and their leaders' plans for our future are undoubtedly satanically inspired.

As we move on to investigate the groups who endeavor to control world governments, wars, *et al,* through control of finances, I am going to discuss our money and its emblems. That means going back into the discussion of the Illuminati and Freemasonry, as they are at the root of most of these satanic symbols.

Earlier in this chapter I printed the Pyramid of Freemasonry. On page 88 herein, you will find the pyramid that is shown on the back of our money. Note that the Latin translates: Announcing the birth of the New Order World.

Although the pyramid on the American dollar with its 13 levels ties in with the 13 colonies, the original association was with ancient Egyptian and Babylonian mysticism. Note also that the cornerstone or capstone is missing from the top of the pyramid. In its place is the All-Seeing-Eye. The Illuminati's mutual spying system was an integral part of the program to keep its associates in line. The eye symbolized the "Big Brother" concept for controlling its domain. Some dismiss this idea, claiming the eye in the illustration is the "all-seeing" eye of God. However, the literal translation of the Latin, *Annuit Coeptis* and *Novus Ordo Seclorum,* indicates quite the contrary, i.e., "Announcing the Birth of a New Secular Order," commonly known today as the New World Order.

Another book to add to your "recommended reading" list is *The Cosmic Conspiracy* by Stan Deyo, which exposes the plans of the Illuminati and the New World Order.

Before we progress (if you can call that progress) to a cashless society, many changes will take place in our currency. . . in fact, some already have taken place (under the guise of inhibiting counterfeiting, of course). There are a lot of speculations and a lot of opinions about the significance and symbolism of the new money. Below I will quote several commentaries of interest. In the March, 1995, issue of *Flash-*

point, Texe Marrs had this to say:

New Money or Beast "666"Currency?

Significant changes in U.S. currency are about to occur. This is the conclusion I have come to after reviewing convincing intelligence reports from reliable sources. These sources tell me that the *New Money* is on the way. I have so far been able to piece together these amazing facts:

Crane & Co., a paper manufacturer from New England, will supply the specialty paper on which the new currency will be printed. The paper is designed to permit the embedding of metallic threads which can be electronically "read."

Now consider this: On March 15, 1991, the U.S. Bureau of Engraving and Printing awarded Crane & Co. a **$66** million contract to supply this paper to the U.S. Mint in Ft. Worth, Texas. What's more, according to the *Berkshire Eagle* newspaper (Pittsfield, MA, March 16, 1991), to accommodate orders from the U.S. government for the new paper, Crane & Co. has built a **66,000** square foot addition to its mill and is spending **$6** million to upgrade its equipment.

A $66 million contract. . .a 66,000 square foot addition to existing facilities. . .a $6 million upgrade of equipment! Pardon me, but does anyone out there recall what the Bible has to say about that very peculiar number 6?

As far back as January 9, 1988, the cover of *The Economist* magazine (published in London and New York) was warning us to "Get ready for a world currency."

In a Special Report from Texe Marrs, Living Truth Ministries, he states that the New Money is not coming. . .it's here now and soon will be issued. [Author's Note: At this writing, much of it is already in circulation.] Marrs states in his Special Report:

. . .This is the conclusion I have come to after carefully analyzing the growing body of evidence. Its introduction, I am convinced, was plotted in Colorado two years ago. There, our Secretary of State, James Baker, who formerly was U.S. Secretary of the Treasury, met with David Rockefeller, founder of the Trilateral Commission and Chairman of Chase Manhattan Bank; Edmond de Rothschild, British financial tycoon; Maurice Strong, New Age environmentalist; and other world financial figures. The formal occasion was a meeting of the elitist World Wilderness Congress to discuss their plan for a World Conservation Bank.

The plan to give us the New Money has also been mapped out and honed at high level meetings in Paris [France], Houston

[Texas], Jackson Hole, Wyoming, and elsewhere. President Bush has participated in some of these meetings.

As I revealed in *Flashpoint* (April/May, '91), the new U.S. currency will have metallic threads. These threads can be "read" by laser scanners and computer optical recognition devices. Eventually, all transactions can be recorded and an individual's buying and selling tracked and monitored. Imagine what a horrible invasion of privacy this will entail. Also know how it fits in with Rev. 13—"That no man might buy or sell, save he that had the mark, or the name of the beast, or the number of his name."

[Refer to the photos included in Marrs' Special Report.] Below is a picture of the new U.S. Mint in Ft. Worth, Texas, that was built complete with high tech presses, to print and produce the New Money. Observe its "sacred architecture:" the occultic Pyramid within the Satanic Circle. In New Age esoterism and occultic symbology, this conveys a profound message—namely, that the Plan for the success of the Mystery Babylon religious system (symbolized by the pyramid) is protected and guarded by Satan himself, its Great Architect (the circle, indicating the eternal unbroken nature of Lucifer).

The New Money **is** here now. But we must always remember **who** is on the throne. The conspirators, the plotters, the evil lords can only work while it is night, but we who have Christ know that the day is coming soon when the darkness will forever be banished. The Lord Himself will see to it! In that alone is our Blessed Hope!

Former Congressman Ron Paul has this to say about the new facility (note particularly his comments about the pyramid shape of the building):

> The government is crowing, the greenback will be produced on U.S.-made presses for the first time in more than a century. Only it won't be green.
>
> The Stevens Graphics Corporation is producing an ominously named Alexander Hamilton press for the Bureau of Engraving and Printing. (Hamilton was—appropriately enough—a proponent of fiat-paper money, big deficits, and big government.)
>
> The new press is twice as fast as the previous presses, it prints the bills on both sides at once. At present, only one side is printed at a time, and left to dry for 24 hours before having the other side printed....
>
> The new press can embed plastic or other strips in the bills, do the microprinting the Treasury has talked about, and—oh, yes—print in three colors.
>
> The feds say not to worry. The greenback will remain green.

But why then pay for this extra capacity? It can only be to print the New Money.

In an effort to find out more about where the New Money will be printed, I went on an investigative visit to Fort Worth, Texas, to survey a new BEP currency plant. This is no normal federal building. It is one of several places in the country where the New Money is in preparation.

The new BEP building is a monstrosity that perfectly symbolizes unconstitutional abuse of power. A giant windowless block-house [circular], it sits on an enormous piece of land, surrounded by a prison-style cyclone fence topped with barbed wire.

The appropriately evil-looking New Money plant went up fast. On my last visit, I noted a new addition to the administrative end of the building: a pyramid. Two interpretations are possible: one, that it copies the Masonic-Illuminatist symbol that also, unfortunately, made it on the back of our one dollar bill; or two, that it symbolizes the kind of society the politicians and bankers have in mind for us: they're the pharaohs and we're the enslaved workers. Or maybe it's both.

Paul pointed out also that former House Speaker Jim Wright and H. Ross Perot were instrumental in the selection of Fort Worth, with the enthusiastic backing of Senator Phil Gramm. He also calls it "a 'public-private partnership,' not unlike the Federal Reserve itself."

Probably the most comprehensive report on the New Money and its intended uses is in a brochure from Voice of Americanism. It is entitled, "You're Already Using the New Money and May Not Know It!" by news analyst W. S. McBirnie, Ph.D., and Lona Ann White, Research Director/Writer. I strongly urge you to write to P.O. Box 90, Glendale, CA 91209, and request a copy of Voice of Americanism Publication No. 1082. It is full of informative material, as well as some sound advice about getting your own financial affairs in order, as it relates to this subject.

McBirnie points out that the Treasury Department has finally issued the "new" money we have been expecting, with little fanfare. This is not the radically revised money most have anticipated; rather it looks very much like our old, familiar currency. But don't let its appearance fool you . . . it is *very much* different in its construction. In fact, it could be referred to more appropriately as *interim money,* rather than *new money,* as it seems that more changes are on the horizon. McBirnie thinks this may be a psychological ploy to "condition" Americans who might reject a more radical design, such as colored currency with watermarks, chemical coating, diffraction gratings, and even holograms.

Allegedly to protect us from high-tech counterfeiters, this is the first physical change in the U.S. currency in over 30 years. The new color copiers, laser scanners, graphic computers, *et al,* can produce "funny money" nearly indistinguishable from the genuine article. In addition to inhibiting counterfeiting, the new money is supposed to help officials catch money launderers and drug dealers. However, I suspect that other more covert and sinister reasons are behind the issuance of the revised currency.

There are two changes in the new bills which are obvious to the naked eye. The first is a security thread on the left end of the bill (visible when viewing the money in the light and which cannot be duplicated by copying machines, no matter how high-tech); the second (visible without a light) is an additional border printed around the photo on the bill—it is merely a minuscule line of continuous type which reads THE UNITED STATES OF AMERICA, so tiny that it appears to be just a fuzzy line until viewed under a magnifying glass or otherwise enlarged.

The third major "enhancement" has not been publicized at all . . . since many people know about its existence I don't suppose I can refer to it as "secret," however, it is far from common knowledge—in fact, I dare say that the public at large is not aware of its presence in the new currency. A half-inch band of magnetic ink (much like on the bottom of your checks) has been placed, in microscopic size, along the bottom of the face of the bill, cleverly hidden within the bill's design.

Enlarged, it resembles the bar codes appearing on most products today, and the bills can be "read" by ordinary banking equipment. The $100 denominations already have the magnetic ink, and I suspect lower denominations will soon be impregnated with the special ink— if, in fact, they have not already been so printed. All large banks in cities with a population exceeding 50,000 have magnetic-ink-reading equipment, according to McBirnie, which enables officials to trace the bills, allowing financial "snooping" on all cash transactions! Although magnetic printing is not new to the banking industry, it is new to the printing of money.

McBirnie points out that even with all these changes, the U.S. still lags behind the rest of the world in currency design. Many European and Asian currencies already share a number of common character-istics, which the U.S. will probably adopt later in this decade—pastel colors, watermarks, holograms, and interference filters, the latter two of which change color or image when tilted. McBirnie is particularly concerned about the "blank" area on most foreign currency:

A particularly ominous feature of most foreign currencies is the watermark, which appears as a blank area on the bills of such Economic Community nations as France, Belgium, the Netherlands, England, Spain, Germany, and Italy, but also on money in Japan, Brazil, Argentina, and other countries. The watermark contains a faint image that is difficult, though not impossible, to counterfeit. Is there a secondary purpose for this blank area? Possibly it will be used for a *world currency* overprint in the future! The overprint could be an international symbol and an international monetary value.

I would agree that McBirnie's concern is justified.

Of course, McBirnie is also concerned about the secrecy and security measures concerning the printing facility located near Haslet, Texas, a small community north of Fort Worth. It is designed like a "maximum security prison with barbed wire fences, wide-open fields on three or four sides, guard boxes, and barricades. Full of three-color printing presses and spy device embedders, it belongs in Beijing, not Texas!" Visitors are not allowed, even though public tours are available through other facilities such as the FBI, the Pentagon, and the Washington, DC, office of the BEP. McBirnie states that there is no *sensible* explanation for all this secrecy and security, unless there is a cover-up going on . . . something being planned which might be endangered by the public finding out about it. Of course, the pyramids in the design do not slip by McBirnie, who appropriately makes the connection with the New World Order and the pyramid on the back of our dollar bill.

"Cashless" is the wave of the future . . . that is agreed upon by both conservative and liberal economists, those opposed to and those in favor of the New World Order. (We will get into that in more detail in Chapter 11.) According to financial advisor Lawrence Patterson, the number of these new bills ($20, $50, and $100) being issued is extremely limited and may at some point be rationed, perhaps distributed in minimal amounts each month, upon presentation of your Social Security Card and/or other national I.D. card. This would force you to use checks, debit cards, and/or credit cards . . . in other words, you will be compelled to go cashless.

The ability to track and tabulate amounts of cash in transit would be a practically foolproof way of keeping tabs on a person's transactions.

McBirnie asks, "Can we expect a currency call-in?"—then answers his own question:

Without telling the public, the Federal Reserve gradually began calling in the old 100-dollar notes on November 1, 1992. Only the 1990 magnetic ink bar-coded bills are to be distributed. Please take note: This is a **secret recall!** The public has not been notified. This proves malintent on the part of the government. The old cash notes will gradually disappear as a result of this call-in. Then, all denominations of the old money will be cancelled.

Eventually, however, we feel a major recall will occur (perhaps coming in stages, so as to avoid panicking the public): The absence of a watermark on our "interim" new money suggests that an entirely new currency will have to be issued—and all the old money recalled—so that U.S. currency will match the EC's, including having a blank area for a world monetary unit overprint (which can be stamped on by your local bank). [Author's note: This could explain the purchase of those three-color presses.]

McBirnie concludes that the real purpose for the new currency is to eliminate financial privacy and usher in the cashless society, where every transaction is recorded and the amount of resources you have is strictly controlled (don't forget Revelation 13). He suggests that those with substantial cash to turn in at the time of a recall (perhaps $1,000 or more) automatically will be suspect of any number of crimes—not the least of which is money laundering and tax evasion—and flagged in the master computer for special attention and future surveillance. One financial advisor suggests that you hold a substantial portion of your liquid assets in U.S. gold or silver coins. However, other experts disagree. Real estate is no longer a good investment. In fact, what you need is something to help you and your family through the forthcoming planned financial collapse. What I strongly suggest is a substantial food supply, packaged in a form with an indefinite shelf life, and many silver dollars. . . in other words, don't invest in anything that must be liquidated in order for you to survive. At the time you need it most, it may be impossible to liquidate it. "A prudent man foreseeth the evil, and hideth himself; but the simple pass on, and are punished (Proverbs 27:12). The Living Bible states it this way: "A sensible man watches for problems ahead and prepares to meet them. The simpleton never looks, and suffers the consequences."

Discuss with your own financial advisor the investment possibilities that will survive best in a time of financial instability. . .which we surely will encounter on the road from trackable cash to a totally cashless society.

The Council on Foreign Relations (hereafter referred to as CFR) is undoubtedly tied in to all this monetary control through the Federal

Reserve and the World Bank, as well as through government influence and other sources of control. Let's go back to our "time line" and learn a bit about the history of the CFR as it relates to the promotion of the New World Order.

May 30, 1919—Originally founded by prominent British and Americans as two separate organizations: the Royal Institute of International Affairs (in England) and the Institute of International Affairs (in the U.S.). Two years later, Col. House reorganized the Institute of International Affairs as the CFR.

December 15, 1922—CFR endorses World Government. Philip Kerr, writing for CFR's magazine *Foreign Affairs,* states: "Obviously there is going to be no peace or prosperity for mankind as long as [the earth] remains divided into 50 or 60 independent states. . . . until some kind of international system is created which will put an end to the diplomatic struggles incident to the attempt of every nation to make itself secure. . . . The real problem today is that of the world government."

February 17, 1950—CFR member James P. Warburg, co-founder of the United World Federalists and son of Federal Reserve Banker Paul Warburg, tells the [Senate Foreign Relations] Subcommittee that, ". . . studies led me, ten years ago, to the conclusion that the great question of our time is not whether or not one world can be achieved, but whether or not one world can be achieved by peaceful means. We shall have world government, whether or not we like it. The question is only whether world government will be achieved by consent or by conquest."

November 25, 1959—CFR calls for New International Order. "Study Number 7," advocated "a new international order (which) must be responsive to world aspirations for peace, for social and economic change. . . an international order. . . including states labeling themselves as 'socialist' (communist)."

1975—In *The New York Times,* CFR member and *Times* editor James Reston writes that President Ford and Soviet leader Leonid Brezhnev should "forget the past and work together for a new world order."

1975—Retired Navy Admiral Chester Ward, former Judge Advocate General of the U.S. Navy and former CFR member, in a critique writes that the goal of the CFR is the "submergence of U.S. sovereignty and national independence into an all-powerful one-world government. . . . Once the ruling members of the CFR have decided that the U.S. Government should adopt a particular policy, the very substantial research facilities of the CFR are put to work to develop arguments, intellectual and emotional, to support the new policy, and to confound and discredit, intellectually and politically, any opposition."

1977—*Imperial Brain Trust* by Laurence Shoup and William Minter is published. The book takes a critical look at the CFR with chapter titles, "Shaping a New World Order: The Council's Blueprint for Global Hegemony, 1939-1944" and "Toward the 1980's: The Council's Plans for a New World Order."

When writing for the brochure about your money, I am recommending you also obtain a copy of Voice of Americanism Publication No. 1083 (refer to ordering information given earlier in this chapter), entitled "How the Globalists Already Control the U.S. and What Their Chilling Agenda Is," from which I will be quoting below.

We are going to "back our way" into this discussion by telling about the CFR, then getting into the Federal Reserve and world financial control . . . and who controls it! The current membership list for the CFR reads like a *Who's Who* of American leaders in every walk of life, i.e., government, private industry, education, the media, military, and high finance.

In 1921, Edward Mandell House founded the CFR (from an organization begun two years earlier called Institute of International Affairs). He was a close friend and advisor of President Woodrow Wilson and persuaded him to support and sign the Federal Reserve Act and to support the League of Nations, forerunner of the UN and other globalist groups. Finances to found the CFR came from the same crowd who formed the Federal Reserve, namely J. P. Morgan, Bernard Baruch, Otto Kahn, Paul Warburg, and John D. Rockefeller, among others.

The CFR shares a close cross-membership with other globalist organizations, which we shall disclose in the course of this section. At the time of the publication of this brochure, the Council had 2,670 members (presently there are over 2,900 members), 2,021 of whom resided in just three cities: New York, Boston, and Washington, DC. The CFR had 38 affiliated organizations located in major U.S. cities.

As I reported earlier, Rear Admiral Ward said they planned to bring about the surrender of the sovereignty and national independence of the U.S., and in 1950 member James Warburg testified before the Senate Foreign Relations Subcommittee that "We shall have world government whether or not you like it—by conquest or consent." Presently, their plan is to erode national sovereignty piece by piece. The New World Order came "out of the closet" at the time of the Gulf War when former CFR director George Bush publicly used the term.

Now, pay careful attention to the next paragraph:

> At the start of World War II, the CFR, with the help of Franklin
> Roosevelt, gained control of the U.S. State Department and our

foreign policy, and after the war, helped establish the U.N. *The U.S. delegation for the U.N.'s founding conference in 1945 contained 47 CFR members,* including **John Foster Dulles, Adlai Stevenson, Nelson Rockefeller,** and Soviet spy **Alger Hiss,** who was the secretary general of the founding conference. Former U.N. Secretary General U Thant praised Lenin as a man whose ideology was "in line with the aims of the U.N. Charter."

Many prominent people have served as director of the CFR, including Walter Lippmann, Adlai Stevenson, Cyrus Vance, Zbigniew Brzezinski, Paul Volcker, Lane Kirkland, George Bush, Henry Kissinger, David Rockefeller, George Shultz, Alan Greenspan, Brent Scowcroft, Jeane Kirkpatrick and Dick Cheney.

I told you it reads like *Who's Who!* And you "ain't seen nothin' yet."

Private industry financially supported and/or controlled by the CFR includes (because of space I have abbreviated the company names): ARCO, BP, Mercedes-Benz, Seagram, *Newsweek, Reader's Digest, Washington Post,* American Express, Carnegie Corp., Ford Fdn., GE Fdn., General Motors, Mellon Fdn., Sloan Fdn., Xerox Fdn., IBM, AT&T, Ford, Chrysler, Macy, Federated Dept. Stores, Gimbels, Sears, JC Penney, May Dept. Stores, Allied Stores, and various Rockefeller concerns.

The CFR shares many cross-memberships with The Bilderbergers, which we will address last in this study. I will share some of their names with you at that time.

The Club of Rome draws many members from the CFR. It was founded in 1968 and consists of scientists, educators, economists, humanists, industrialists, and government officials who see it as this organization's task to oversee the regionalization and unification of the entire world. It has divided the world into ten political/economic regions or "kingdoms." McBirnie says:

> Here, we glimpse the dark, spiritual side of the globalist movement: The Club's founder, Aurelio Peccei, revealed in his book *Mankind at the Turning Point* his pantheist/New Age beliefs, writing about man's communion with nature, the need for a "world consciousness" and "a new and enlightened humanism." He was a student of Pierre Teilhard de Chardin, one of the New Age occultists' most frequently quoted writers.
>
> Club members include the late **Norman Cousins** (former honorary chairman of Planetary Citizens), **John Naisbitt** (author of *Megatrends*), **Betty Freidan** (founding president of the National Organization for Women), **Robert Anderson, Harlan Cleveland,** and many New Age speakers and authors. Four U.S. congressmen are members, as well as Planned Parenthood representatives, U.N.

officials, and Carnegie and Rockefeller foundation people.

McBirnie refers to the founding of the Trilateral Commission (TLC) at this point, but I wish to address it more fully at the conclusion of our discussion on the CFR. McBirnie is convinced—and I wholeheartedly concur—that the CFR has a stranglehold on America. The CFR effectively controls the four most powerful positions (after the Presidency) in our government, i.e., secretaries of state, treasury, and defense, and the national security advisor.

> Since 1920, 15 of the 21 treasury secretaries have been CFR members; plus 12 of our last 14 secretaries of state (since 1944); 10 of 13 national security advisors (since Eisenhower); and 11 of 12 defense secretaries (since Eisenhower). Of the 60 people who have held these strategic positions during the years specified, 48 have been CFR members—that's 80%!
>
> By the Nixon administration, 115 CFR members held positions in the executive branch. Carter appointed scores of TLC and/or CFR members. All of his National Security Council were or had been members: Mondale, Brzezinski, Vance, Brown, Jones, and Turner.
>
> Even Ronald Reagan appointed 76 CFR and TLC members to key posts, but George Bush broke all records with 354 [recognizable names in highest levels of government] . . . .The State Dept. is saturated with CFR/TLC members. Almost every ambassador or diplomat whose name you read in the paper is a globalist.
>
> As for the Treasury Dept., Brady and Regan are members, and Federal Reserve Chairmen Greenspan, Anderson, Vance, and Volcker are all insiders.
>
> Every U.S. secretary of defense for the past 35 years, except Clark Clifford, belonged to either [the CFR or the TLC]. Every Supreme Allied Commander in Europe and every U.S. ambassador to NATO have been insiders, as well as 9 of 13 CIA directors.
>
> Almost every U.S. president, except John F. Kennedy and Ronald Reagan, was either a CFR or TLC member. One interesting sidelight here: JFK may have been a member of the Boston affiliate of the CFR. Ted Kennedy is definitely a member of the affiliate, though his name is not listed in the general CFR membership.
>
> The bottom line is: **The same one-world agenda moves forward, despite who wins our elections!**

The media is well represented in the membership of the CFR, including such familiar names as Paley, Rather, Moyers, Tisch, Brokaw, Chancellor, Kalb, Levine, Brinkley, Scali, Walters, Schorr, McNeil, Lehrer, and Carter III. Not surprisingly, Rockefellers' Chase Manhattan

Bank has minority control of all three major networks (CBS, ABC, and NBC).

AP, UPI, and Reuters wire services all have CFR members in major positions. Other CFR members in the media include, William F. Buckley (also a Bones member), Diane Sawyer, Rowland Evans, and David Gergen.

Most major newspapers today have strong CFR influence, including *The New York Times, Washington Post, Wall Street Journal, Boston Globe, Baltimore Sun, Chicago Sun Times, L.A. Times, Houston Post, Minneapolis Star/Tribune, Arkansas Gazette, Des Moines Register & Tribune,* the Gannett Co. (which publishes *USA Today* and newspapers in more than 40 cities), *Denver Post,* and *Louisville Courier.* This is just a partial listing of papers staffed by CFR affiliates.

Magazines with CFR connections include *Fortune, Time, Life, Money, People, Sports Illustrated, Newsweek, Business Week, U.S. News & World Report, Saturday Review, Reader's Digest, Atlantic Monthly, McCall's,* and *Harper's Magazine.*

Book Publishers include MacMillan, Random House, Simon & Schuster, McGraw-Hill, Harper, IBM, Xerox, Yale Univ. Press, Little Brown, Viking, Cowles Publishing, and Harper and Row. Many of these publish school textbooks, which brings us to just how far the tentacles of CFR influence reach into the education of our children.

McBirnie informs us that CFR foundations, primarily Carnegie and Rockefeller, provided two-thirds of the gifts to all American universities during the first third of this century. And the man who is considered the "father of progressive education," John Dewey, was an atheist who taught four of the five Rockefeller brothers. He spent most of his life educating teachers, including those in the USSR. This man's influence extends not just through years, but throughout generations. Today, 20% of all American school superintendents and 40% of all education department heads have advanced degrees from Columbia where Dewey headed the education department for many years.

The National Education Association (NEA) adopted his philosophy of humanism, socialism, and globalism, then put them into our classrooms. CFR members head the teaching departments at Columbia, Cornell, NYU, Sarah Lawrence College, Stanford, Yale, U of Chicago, Johns Hopkins U, Brown U, U of Wisconsin, Washington U, and Lee U. At the time this brochure was written there were 69 CFR members on the faculty at the U of Chicago, 58 at Princeton, and 30 at Harvard.

As I have emphasized since the beginning of this book, this New World Order plan has it roots in the spiritual, rather than a material or physical basis, as its proponents would have you believe. McBirnie agrees, tying the CFR leaders and members directly to the New Age movement, which ultimately includes the radical ecology groups, Lucis Trust, nominal churches, the UN, and others. He puts it this way:

> How does the New Age fit into the one-world movement? The New Age is pantheism—the belief that God is the sum total of all that exists. No personal God exists, but rather "God" is a god-force or life-force which flows through all living things—and which supposedly makes humans "gods." The New Age believes that since global unity is essential to the proper flow of the god-force, that when unity occurs in a one-world government, all humans will suddenly receive mystical powers and a new age of enlightenment will emerge. Occult practices (and eastern mysticism) accompany pantheism.

The Theosophical Society (TS) is at the forefront of New Age globalism. TS leader Alice Baily established the Lucis Press (offspring of the Lucis Trust, which, until recently, was headquartered at the UN). It believes in the preeminence of Satan (Lucifer) and is well connected with the one-world political societies and the World Constitution and Parliament Association. [Author's note: Refer to Chapter 4 of this book for information on the new World Constitution.] Past and present members include TLC and CFR people [cross-memberships]: **Robert McNamara, Donald Regan, Henry Kissinger, David Rockefeller, Paul Volcker,** and **George Shultz**.

The World Constitution and Parliament Association (WCPA) has already written a world constitution, the Constitution for the Federation of Earth, and has submitted it to world leaders for ratification. Dominated by environmentalists, US personnel, Nobel Laureates, leftist churches (i.e., the WCC), educators, financial leaders, and eastern mystics (pantheists), it calls for an international monetary system; administration of the oceans, seabeds, and atmosphere as the common heritage of all humanity; elimination of fossil fuels; redistribution of the world's wealth; complete and rapid disarmament (including confiscation of privately owned weapons); an end to national sovereignty; a global environmental organization; world justice system; and world tax agency.

Many of its members embrace eastern mysticism. US members include **Jesse Jackson** (also CFR) and former Attorney General **Ramsey Clark**. Its director, Philip Iseley, belongs to Amnesty International, the ACLU, Global Education Associates, Friends of the Earth, Sierra Club, Audubon Society, American Humanist Association, SANE (nuclear freeze group), Planetary Citizens, and the Global Futures Network, among many other organizations.

The UN, which is already widely accepted, is the chosen agency that is moving us toward world government; but the UN charter is not a *constitution*. Plus, it is an organization of *sovereign* nations, which is anathema to globalists. So the WCPA's world constitution is ready for acceptance at the proper time.

In the November 2, 1994, edition of *The Los Angeles Times,* Doyle McManus writes, "U.S. Leadership Is More Diverse, Less Influential."

> Almost half a century ago, when Harry S. Truman needed help running the foreign policy of the United States at the dawn of the Cold War, the remedy was simple: "Whenever we needed a man," one of his aides recalled, "we thumbed through the roll of Council [on Foreign Relations] members and put in a call to New York."

He tells about the expanding of the so-called "elite" to include every area of influence, from academics, scientists, and religious leaders to rock stars and others. Leslie H. Gelb, new president of the CFR, says, "This is the largest foreign policy elite this country has ever enjoyed," and adds that he plans to expand and diversify the "august" organization's membership to embrace new areas such as sports and the arts. Ironically, says McManus, just as the elite is growing in size and diversity, it may also be diminishing in power.

> Recent surveys, including the *Times Mirror* polls, suggest that the general public is less willing than in the past to accept the advice of the foreign policy elite—at least on issues that come close to home, like free trade with Mexico or the use of American troops in peacekeeping missions overseas.
>
> "There's more information going straight to the general public now," said Brent Scowcroft [CFR and TLC member], who served as national security adviser to President George Bush. "That tends to reduce the influence [of the elite]. It makes it more difficult to get support for a potentially unpopular policy."

Gelb says that today there are 2,905 CFR members (you'll be amazed at some of the names you find there).

Now for the Federal Reserve, a.k.a. the FED! This entity is closely tied to the policies and policymakers of the CFR. As I told you earlier, it is not a federal agency, just because the word appears in its name. It's just another profit-making banking corporation, which has been given unconstitutional control over US finances and the printing/re-calling of currency, as well as determining the interest we pay. . .all of which duties were constitutionally assigned to Congress. We all are familiar with the term "prime rate." That is the lowest interest rate set by the FED (the rate paid by large banks who borrow from them and then increase the interest rate as they lend the money to you, i.e. "prime-plus"). The prime rate fluctuates frequently and regularly, with interest rates determined by the FED in an attempt to manipulate inflation or recession, followed by immediate reaction by the stock market in response to whichever direction the variable interest takes. In a brochure by Thomas D. Schauf, a CPA, the FED is exposed totally. He encourages reprinting his brochure freely, so I have quoted some of his information below:

> The Federal Reserve Bank (FED) can write a check for an unlimited amount of money to buy government bonds and the U.S. Treasury prints the money to back up the check. UNBELIEV-ABLE. . . IT'S TRUE! Read *National Geographic,* January, 1993, pg. 84. Go to the library and read the books exposing this SCAM! The FED is a private bank for profit. . . just like any business! Check the *Encyclopaedia Britannica* or, easier yet, look in the *1992 Yellow Pages.* The FED is listed under COMMERCIAL BANKS, not GOVERNMENT. The FED is no more a *Federal* agency than *Federal* Express.

Schauf goes on to explain some of the intricacies of how the FED prints currency, then sells it to the government in exchange for government bonds, on which we pay interest, and which becomes part of the national debt which we, the taxpayers, are obligated to repay. Then the FED sells these instruments to others, including foreign agencies, spreading around, as it were, our debtors. It seems they don't want to keep all their eggs in one basket, or to put it another way, if they spread around the debt, they also spread around the risks. Just remember, as they sell off all this debt and receive funds or obligations for funds in exchange, they haven't yet done anything to earn this money, but authorize the printing of the currency. A pretty good scam, isn't it? For a more detailed account of how all this works, I recommend reading Patman's book, *A Primer on Money.*

This system can be bypassed; we can print our own money, as the Constitution requires. On June 4, 1963, President John F. Kennedy issued Executive Order No. 11110 (one of the rare instances where this executive power was used for something worthwhile) and printed *real* US dollars with no debt or interest attached, because he bypassed the FED bank! However, upon his death the printing ceased and the currency was withdrawn. For proof, ask any coin dealer to show you a 1963 Kennedy dollar. You'll find that it says "United States Note," NOT "Federal Reserve Note"!

> Today the government prints dollars and forwards the cash interest free to the FED. The FED exchanges this cash to buy

newly issued Federal Bonds and collects the interest. Much of the government debt is owned by the FED banking system.

If Kennedy had lived and continued to print U.S. dollars, interest free, debt free, there would be no $4 Trillion of debt! Why give the FED dollars interest free and allow the FED to use these dollars to buy new government bonds paying them interest? Kennedy's solution (Exec. Order. No. 11110) made this seem ridiculous. Why didn't the media tell the truth. We need to force Congress to make the change. [Schauf tells below why the media is silent.]

Article I, Section 8, of the Constitution states that only Congress can coin (create) money. In 1935, the Supreme Court ruled that Congress cannot constitutionally delegate its power to another group and the FED illegally controls the printing of money through its 12 banks. Rockefeller and Rothschild are two of the original 300 owners of the FED!

Rothschild, a London banker who dreamed up the FED, wrote a letter saying: "It (Central Bank [FED]) gives the National Bank almost complete control of national finance. The few who understand the system will either be so interested in its profits, or so dependent on its favors, that there will be no opposition from that class. . . .The great body of the people, mentally incapable of comprehending, will bear its burden without complaint, and perhaps without even suspecting that the system is inimical [harmful] to their interests." The FED profits from our stupidity and apathy! OUR FOREFATHERS TRIED TO PREVENT THIS!!! . . .

Congressmen McFadden and Patman, Chairmen of a Banking Committee, plus others, attempted to abolish the FED. The problem was that the media remained silent, so citizens remained ignorant. . . .

Why has the media remained silent? [Author's note: At the lower levels of writing and reporting, I'm sure that the people don't understand the situation any better than most of us. Let's face it, they have concocted a very complex system that even the would-be experts have difficulty comprehending. However, in the upper eschelons of management, it's a different story. They understand, alright, but to them it's a matter of personal and business financial interest. . . read on!] Rockefeller is one of the original 300 shareholders of the FED. In July 1968, the House Banking Subcommittee reported that Rockefeller, through Chase Manhattan Bank, controlled 5.9% of the stock in CBS, and the bank had gained interlocking directorates with ABC. In 1974, Congress issued a report stating that the Chase Manhattan Bank's stake in CBS rose to 14.1% and in NBC to 4.5% (through RCA, the parent company of NBC). The same report said that the Chase

Manhattan Bank held stock in 28 broadcasting firms. After this report, the Chase Manhattan Bank obtained 6.7% of ABC, and today the percentage could be much greater. It only required 5% ownership to significantly influence the media. The FED knows if people become informed, they will demand change. . . .The FED can control the media by withdrawing loans! Ask any C.P.A.!

Rockefeller also controls the Council on Foreign Relations (CFR). Nearly every major newscaster belongs to this Council. The CFR controls many major newspapers and magazines. Additionally, major corporations owned by FED shareholders are the source of huge advertising revenues that surely would influence the media. By controling the media, you control the population, the elections, and public opinion....

How did [FED control] happen? In 1913, Senator Nelson Aldrich, maternal grandfather to the Rockefellers, pushed a bill through Congress just before Christmas when many of its members were on vacation. Private bankers funded and staffed President Wilson's campaign. When elected, Wilson passed the FED. Later Wilson remorsefully replied (referring to the FED), "I have unwittingly ruined my country." The media misled the public, and sponsors of the FED made 10 promises, none of which were kept. Now the banks fund both Democratic and Republican candidates. The bankers employ members of Congress on weekends (nickname T&T Club) as consultants with lucrative salaries (supporting documentation can be provided). Within months of starting the FED, income tax was created to pay for this new interest expense. The same 1913 law said the FED will pay no IRS tax! Our taxes pay interest on all new currency issued! Note: The bankers created this new legislation (Law), not Congress! Now the FED wants the New World Order (NWO) and Cashless Society (CS)! People, oppose it! The FED's CS would absolutely control you!

. . .Thomas Jefferson said this about a FED-type banking system: "If the American people ever allow private banks to control the issue of their currency, first by inflation then by deflation, the banks and the corporations will grow up around them, will deprive the people of all property until their children wake up homeless on the continent their fathers conquered." Experts believe the FED created the Great Depression and inflation, and profits from people's misfortune. Before Congress, FED Chairman Eccles admitted the FED creates new money from thin air (printing press) and loans it back to us at interest. Before the U.S. had huge deficits, we printed new money interest-free, without paying bankers interest. Today, the FED profits from huge deficits. . .and they're getting BIGGER every day!

Schauf adds that the US Government can **buy back** the FED at any time for $450 million, according to the Congressional Record, and tells some of the ramifications of doing so. If you are interested in more information on the Federal Reserve and efforts to end it, I recommend you write to Thomas D. Schauf, CPA, at P. O. Box 681164, Schaumburg, IL 60108-1164. I'm sure by now you are beginning to see how the tentacles of these various occultic organizations are all intertwined.

Another major faction involved in world control through economics and trade is the Trilateral Commission. It was founded in 1973 by banker David Rockefeller to promote world government by encouraging economic interdependence among the three superpowers: North America, Japan, and Europe. Rockefeller selected Zbigniew Brzezinski (later to become Carter's National Security Advisor) as the Commission's first director and invited President Jimmy Carter to become a founding member. In his book *Between Two Ages,* Brzezinski calls for a new international monetary system and a global taxation system. He praised Marxism as a "creative stage in the maturing of man's universal vision" and quoted New Ager de Chardin.

By 1979, just six years after the TLC was founded, its activities already were known well enough to be addressed by retiring Arizona Senator Barry Goldwater in his autobiography, *With No Apologies.* Goldwater writes:

> In my view The Trilateral Commission represents a skillful, coordinated effort to seize control and consolidate the four centers of power—political, monetary, intellectual, and ecclesiastical. All this is to be done in the interest of creating a more peaceful, more productive world community. What the Trilateralists truly intend is the creation of a worldwide economic power superior to the political governments of the nation-states involved. They believe the abundant materialism they propose to create will overwhelm existing differences. As managers and creators of the system, they will rule the future.

The European Community, North America (US and Canada), and Japan—the three main democratic industrialized areas of the world— are the three sides of the Trilateral Commission. The Commission's members are about 330 prominent figures with a variety of leadership responsibilities from the three regions.

When the first triennium of the Trilateral Commission was launched in 1973, the most immediate purpose allegedly was to draw together —at a time of considerable friction among governments—the highest level unofficial group possible, supposedly for the purpose of examining the common problems facing the three areas.

At a deeper level, there was a sense that the United States was no longer in such a singular international leadership position, and founders of the TLC felt that a more shared form of leadership—including Europe and Japan, in particular—would be needed for the international system to successfully navigate the major challenges of the coming years. They still purport to have these needs as their goal.

The rise of Japan and the emergence of the European Community (EC) dramatizes the importance of such shared leadership, in the eyes of TLC members. And instead of seeing the break up of the Soviet Union as beneficial, the TLC viewed it as "the receding Soviet threat dissolving the 'glue' holding the regions together" as it began its 1991-94 triennium. They claim that "handling economic tensions among our countries and maintaining the benefits of a global economy will require even more effort than in the past."

From the 330± membership, an executive committee is selected, including the Chairmen (one from each side of the triangle), Deputy Chairmen, and 35 others. Once each year the full Commission gathers in one of the regions; recent meeting locations have included Paris, Washington, DC, and Tokyo. They insist these are not secret meetings, and as I mentioned earlier, Henry Kissinger was interviewed by the media when entering a hotel conference room at a recent meeting, where he pointed out that they were not a secret organization; their meeting times and locations were in plain view for all to see. Of course, he failed to mention that the media representatives were not welcome at the meeting, nor would information discussed behind closed doors be made available for public consumption.

According to the TLC Organization and Policy Program publication, a substantial portion of each annual meeting is devoted to consideration of draft task force reports to the Commission. These reports are generally the joint products of authors from each of the three regions who draw on a range of consultants in the course of their work. Publication follows discussion in the Commission's annual meeting. Although a number of changes usually are made after some discussion, the authors are solely responsible for their final text.

In addition to task force reports, the Commission considers other issues in seminars or topical sessions at its meetings. A wide range of subjects have been covered, including the social and political implications of inflation, prospects for peace in the Middle East, macroeconomic policy coordination, nuclear weapons proliferation, China and the international community, employment/unemployment trends and their implications, and the uses of space. Relations with developing countries have been a particular concern of the Commission, and speakers from developing countries have addressed each annual meeting since 1980.

Task force reports are distributed only "to interested persons inside and outside government." The same is true for the publication issued on each annual meeting.

Finally, the Bilderbergs! "Last, but not least" is a phrase that definitely fits this group. They are power brokers of the world, and that is no exaggeration!

The Bilderbergers were established in 1954 by Prince Bernhard of The Netherlands, husband of Queen Juliana. She was among the first endorsers of "Planetary Citizens" in the 1970's. Numerous leading Americans have been "Bilderbergers," including Dean Acheson, Christian Herter, Dean Rusk, Robert McNamara, George Ball, Henry Kissinger, and Gerald Ford (be observant for cross-membership names with CFR, TLC, Skull & Bones, etc.).

The Bilderbergers, funded by major one-world institutions, was created to regionalize Europe. The Treaty of Rome which established the Common Market—today's European Community (EC)—was produced at Bilderberger secret meetings. Cross-membership with the CFR includes David Rockefeller, Winston Lord (State Dept. official and Bones family tree), Henry Kissinger, Zbigniew Brzezinski, Cyrus Vance, Robert McNamara (former World Bank president), George Ball (State Dept. and director of Lehman Brothers), Robert Anderson (ARCO president), Gerald Ford, Henry Grunwald (managing editor, *Time*), Henry J. Heinz II, Theodore Hesburgh (former Notre Dame president), and others.

Some reliable unnamed sources have provided a pipeline into the secret organization's meetings and furnished copies of the "not for circulation" agenda and roster of attendees to reporters from the *SPOTLIGHT*. Again, the names read like a *Who's Who* from around the world. In a report on the Bilderberg meeting at Baden-Baden, Germany, June 6-9, 1991, reporter James P. Tucker, Jr., writes in the September, 1991, reprint of *SPOTLIGHT,* an article titled "World Shadow Government Planning for Another War":

> The Bilderberg group plans another war within five years.
>
> This grim news came from a "main pipeline"—a high-ranking Bilderberg staffer who secretly cooperated with our investigation —behind the guarded walls of the Badischer Hof, who was operating from inside with colleagues serving as "connecting pipelines.". . .
>
> While war plans were being outlined in "Bilderbergese," the

air traffic controller at Baden-Baden's private airport reported numerous incoming flights from Brussels, where NATO headquarters are based. . . .

Aboard one of those planes, *en route* to the Bilderberg meeting, was Manfred Woerner, NATO's general secretary.

It was repeatedly stated at the Bilderberg meeting that there will be "other Saddams" in the years ahead who must be dealt with swiftly and efficiently.

What the Bilderberg group intends is a global army at the disposal of the United Nations, which is to become the world government to which all nations will be subservient by the year 2000.

Crucial to making the UN a strong world government. . . is to bestow it with "enforcement powers."

"A UN army must be able to act immediately, anywhere in the world, without the delays involved in each country making its own decision whether to participate, based on parochial considerations," said Henry Kissinger. . . . [who] expressed pleasure over the conduct of the Persian Gulf war, stressing that it had been sanctioned by the UN, at the request of President George Bush, himself a Trilateral luminary, before the issue was laid before the U.S. Congress.

The fact that the president would make his case to the UN first, when the Constitution empowers only Congress to declare war, was viewed as a significant step in "leading Americans away from nationalism.". . .

It was "good psychology" for Bush to allow congressional and other leaders to express their fear of losing 20,000 to 40,000 American lives [in the Gulf War]. . .when Bush knew the loss of life would be much lower.

When the allied casualty toll reached "only 378" and Americans read and heard of "only four" Americans dying in a week of ground war, it "was like nobody had died at all," one said, "and Americans enjoyed it like an international sporting match."

Such an adventure was essential to getting Americans into "the right frame of mind for the years ahead," said another. . . .they promised each other, there will be "more incidents" for the UN to deal with in the years ahead. The Bilderberg group and its little brother, the Trilateral Commission, can set up "incidents" on schedule, they said, but in less direct words. The words "within five years" were heard repeatedly.

Another important step toward a strong, recognized, and accepted world government is taxing power. . . .

At its April meeting in Tokyo, the Trilateralists called for a UN levy of 10 cents per barrel of oil coming from the Persian Gulf.

It would be sold as "temporary," lasting only long enough to rebuild Kuwait and feed the Kurds until they are back on their feet.

The Bilderbergers approved of the move by their brother group, in which Rockefeller and Kissinger. . . serve as leaders. Once people get used to a tax, it never is repealed. . . it could be extended worldwide "with appropriate increases" in the years ahead.

From the sum total of all things said, the Bilderberg strategy emerged: Start the tax by imposing it on a newly established "bad guy" who must suffer, and use the revenue for such humanitarian purposes as feeding the Kurds. Keep the initial tax so low that the public is unaware that it is levied. Then kick it up.

Also discussed was the dividing of the world into major regions, eliminating individual countries' borders, "for convenience of administration." Yeah, right! Then they were to apply pressure to the US to pass the free trade treaty with Mexico, another step toward establishing the Western Hemisphere as another region—first free trade with Canada, then Mexico, followed by all other Latin American nations.

Their plan is to have a single currency for all of Europe by 1996, with a one-currency movement for the Western Hemisphere to follow, and ultimately a world government with world currency. They expressed their pleasure with the progress of the trade agreements/treaties which were under way.

How can I close a chapter containing as much information about so many as does this chapter? I only can point out that, according to Scripture, we don't wrestle against "flesh and blood." Our warfare is spiritual, and given the roots of these ungodly organizations, I strongly suggest that you yield your soul to the Lord Jesus Christ, submit yourself to God, and put on the whole armor which Paul describes to us in Ephesians. . . not just to protect yourself from our enemy and adversary, Satan, but so we can go on the spiritual offensive and drive him out of our lives, our government, and our land. You will notice in the description of the armor that there is nothing provided to protect your backside—from which I think we safely may assume that God intended us to go forward in His victory, rather than let the devil put us on the run.

Finally, my brethren, be strong in the Lord, and in the power of his might. Put on the whole armour of God, that ye may be able to stand against the wiles of the devil. For we wrestle not against flesh and blood, but against principalities, against powers, against the rulers of the darkness of this world, against spiritual wickedness in high places. Wherefore take unto you the whole armour of God, that ye may be able to withstand in the evil day, and having done all, to stand. Stand therefore, having your loins girt with truth, and having on the breastplate of righteousness; And your feet shod with the preparation of the gospel of peace; Above all, taking the shield of faith wherewith ye shall be able to quench all the fiery darts of the wicked. And take the helmet of salvation, and the sword of the Spirit, which is the word of God: Praying always with all prayer and supplication in the Spirit, ...

Ephesians 6:10-18

CHAPTER SIX

Report from Iron Mountain

In this chapter you will find that I have used liberally the term "allegedly," as there is very limited documentation available. Although this may seem incongruous with the rest of this book—where the major thrust is either to confirm or refute popular speculation—I felt it necessary to address the subject of the Iron Mountain Report because of its influence on the actions of many, regardless of its accuracy.

First, what is Iron Mountain? Though not listed in the index of the Rand McNally map book, nor was I able to locate it on the actual map, Iron Mountain (according to the Report) is located near the town of Hudson, New York, and "is something out of Ian Fleming or E. Phillips Oppenheim. It is an underground nuclear hideout for hundreds of large American corporations. Most of them use it as an emergency storage vault for important documents. But a number of them maintain substitute corporate headquarters, as well, where essential personnel could presumably survive and continue to work after an attack. This latter group includes such firms as Standard Oil of New Jersey, Manufacturers Hanover Trust, and Shell."

A book was published in late 1967—this is the full title: *Report from IRON MOUNTAIN on the Possibility and Desirability of Peace.* The subtitle is: Is Our Government Secretly Operating on the Theoretical Principle that Lasting Peace is NOT Desirable? If So, WHY? With introductory material by Leonard C. Lewin, The Dial Press, Inc., 1967, New York.

The book was written as factual/nonfiction, allegedly by John Doe as reported to Leonard C. Lewin, who assumed the role of editor and publisher. Its contents were so controversial that it sparked an uproar immediately. After the pressure and criticism rose to the boiling point, Lewin reversed his position with an announcement that none of it really happened...he had written the whole thing himself, and it was intended purely as satire all along. By this time, the book had gained such momentum with its followers (who secretly believed such things as described in this book were being planned by conspiracy, anyway), no one could determine whether Lewin was telling the truth the first time—or the last time, when he "admitted" that he was the author of *all* the content, not just the introductory portion.

In the same way that any rumor gets started and spreads, it was too late to undo or stop all that had been set in motion. So, whether or not it is true (and I have no proof either way), I'm going to tell you about it briefly, as its contents are the basis of many grass roots movements (i.e., militias, etc.) who have accepted it as fact and taken steps to protect themselves against its recommendations. . .which, by the way, nearly 30 years later are well on the way to being carried out, whether or not they may have been written originally as satire/fiction.

After ending its last chapter with this quotation from Thomas Jefferson, one readily can understand how a book of this nature could incite men to a radical response, as it makes it seem as though the "powers that be," a.k.a. the "Braintrust," are conspiring to relegate us all to universal bondage.

> I hold it, that a little rebellion, now and then, is a good thing.
> . . .The tree of liberty must be refreshed from time to time with the blood of patriots and tyrants.

I am not alone in addressing an issue that—one would think—after 30 years should have disappeared peacefully from the scene. As recently as May 9, 1995, a front-page article appeared in *The Wall Street Journal,* still debating the validity of the *Iron Mountain Report.* Of course, the recent attention directed to the armed militia groups in this nation, subsequent to the Oklahoma City bombing, is what resurrected this subject, as the Report is seen to be something that "fuels the fire" of these militia groups. Here are some of the headlines and subtitles used by writer Robert Tomsho, staff reporter of *The Wall Street Journal:* "A Cause for Fear; Though Called a Hoax, 'Iron Mountain' Report Guides Some Militias; Work From 1960s Suggests Federal Raids on Citizens; Armed Groups See a Plot; Writer Says Book Was Satire; A Cause for Fear: Though a Hoax, 1960s Document Still Guides Some Armed Militias, Who See a Plot." Without even reading the article, you know immediately where this writer stands; however, he still gives some good history on the subject, so I am quoting below from the article. I suggest that you read it completely and form your own opinion, based on Mr. Tomsho's facts, but without his bias.

The article begins. . .

Scores of Americans believe the government is secretly plotting against them. They think the feds—using helicopters and Russian tanks—are planning to attack and conquer their own people, then turn the whole country over to United Nations rule. They even are convinced that the federal government blew up its own building in Oklahoma City [a theory to which Texe Marrs alludes in his latest newsletter], then arrested a man with possible ties to citizen militias to justify a crackdown on the paramilitary groups.

Do these people know something the rest of the country doesn't? A slim volume called "Report From Iron Mountain" offers a bit of insight into the source of at least some of their beliefs.

Tomsho goes on to suggest that many militia members believe the Report was written by a group of eminent scholars clandestinely assembled by the Kennedy administration to determine how the US would deal with peace—totally free of the Cold War and other conflicts —should such a condition ever be attained. He describes the Report as being written in "clipped, dispassionate tones," and arriving at the conclusion that "lasting peace might trigger upheaval in a society focused upon war. In the absence of real enemies, it suggests that the government turn on its own people—initiating ritual 'blood games,' renewing slavery, and creating an 'omnipotent' international police force."

Tomsho links the Report with other works, such as William Pierce's *The Turner Diaries* and Pat Robertson's *New World Order,* which he claims the militia groups regard as a sort of "bible." He further alleges that militia-oriented publications are "salted with references to *Iron Mountain*" and that "dog-eared copies circulate among antigovernment groups." Note the automatic assumption that these groups are "antigovernment." If they are "anti" anything, they are against the overthrow or disregard of our *legal constitutional government,* or the replacement of it with a global constitution and world government. Of course, he labels as "far-right radicals" those who accept the Report as authentic, and he quotes a number of militiamen from assorted groups who firmly believe the Report and make statements such as: "This is the plan for the destruction of the U.S."

Tomsho gives a reasonable history of the *Iron Mountain Report,* dating it back to a time when everyone was still trying to find a conspiracy behind the Kennedy assassination, there were bloody race riots and burning in Newark and Detroit, and the Vietnam war raged on, in spite of promised victories from military spokesmen. It was amid all this chaos and uncertainty that galleys of the manuscript began circulating among politicians, journalists, and others in Washington, DC, and New York.

. . . it was said to have been written anonymously by a prominent Midwest social-science professor. He was identified only as
"John Doe." After much soul-searching, he had purportedly
asked his friend, editor Leonard C. Lewin, for help in getting the
suppressed document published.

According to an introduction that Mr. Lewin wrote under his
own name, John Doe and 14 other scholars were part of a top-
secret "Special Study Group" summoned to a huge underground
bomb shelter near Hudson, N.Y., in summer 1963. For more than
two years, Mr. Lewin wrote, they worked "to determine, accurately
and realistically, the nature of the problems that would confront
the United States if and when a condition of 'permanent peace'
should arrive, and to draft a program for dealing with this con-
tingency."

Theoretically, the Report was supposed to be a critical assessment
of what might occur—prepared empirically/scientifically and totally
without regard to any moral, religious, or cultural values. Supposedly,
the Report concluded that war was a necessary part of our society,
until something better could replace it, and to suppose that it could
be resolved by a "beat their swords into plowshares" approach was
simplistic in the extreme. . .and for all practical purposes, such a view
was totally naive and couldn't possibly work. He quotes Lewin:

"War fills certain functions essential to the stability of our
society," Mr. Lewin wrote. "Until other ways of filling them are
developed, the war system must be maintained—and improved
in effectiveness."

Now, that's where the real trouble begins! Tomsho points out that
there was a "dark menu of possible war substitutes, laid out in cold
think-tank jargon. . . . " It is the substitutes that are suggested that
got everybody into an uproar. I will spell those out for you at the end
of the commentary in this chapter, but Tomsho gives this accurate
synopsis:

. . . As part of a search for "alternate enemies," the government
might instigate massive environmental pollution or create a
fictional extraterrestrial threat. A national-service program
[Author's note: Clinton has proposed this already and instigated
service programs for college students in exchange for student
loans, et al.] might be used as the first step toward a more palatable
form of servitude.

Meanwhile, birth-control drugs could be added to food and
water supplies for population control, and "individual aggressive
impulses" might be tamped down by creating organized blood

sports modeled after witch hunts.

"What they asked us to do, and what I think we did, was to give the same kind of treatment to the hypothetical problems of peace as they [the think tanks, such as Rand, et al] give to a hypothetical nuclear war," Mr. Lewin quoted John Doe as saying. "We may have gone further than they expected, but once you establish your premise and your logic, you can't turn back."

Given the tumultuous times when the document surfaced and the air of respectability surrounding those involved with it, few readers were willing to dismiss the mysterious headline-grabbing book as a hoax.

Dial Press was a well-regarded publisher, and its president vouched for the work's authenticity on the front page of *The New York Times* in November, 1967. Then in December, *Esquire* magazine published a condensed version, lending even more credibility to the Report. Even book reviewers who doubted its "nonfiction" status still acknowledged it as an important piece of political satire.

Naturally, since it was getting so much attention and allegedly was written by "John Doe," anybody and everybody was speculating about the identity of John Doe and the other unnamed members of the "Special Study Group." Even *Time* magazine and *The Wall Street Journal* were seeking John Doe. Many prominent names were suggested, and other prominent folks (and organizations) were stepping forward to officially deny any involvement. Both the White House and the State Department denied any knowledge of such a group. Of course, that's not unusual . . . they are notorious for denying knowledge of anything with which they don't want to be connected—recent history has proven that beyond doubt!

"Everyone was accusing everyone else of authoring it," recalls Irving Lewis Horowitz, a Rutgers University sociologist and longtime editor of *Trans-action,* then a widely read sociology bimonthly that devoted a 1968 issue to the work. "The real thing was its plausibility factor," he adds. "The whole Vietnam pathology was in full swing, creating an aura of conspiracy."

Some claimed to recognize it as a hoax immediately, but by early 1968, the Report had made it to *The New York Times'* list of nonfiction bestsellers. For the next several years it was debated by uppercrust academia in university seminars and scholarly journals, and subsequently was translated into 15 languages. Now do you understand why 30 years later many people still believe in it? Once something has attained this amount of public recognition (or notoriety), it is practically impossible to retract it, or change your claims concerning it. It seems to take on a life of its own. But that is exactly what Lewin did—he had had enough of all the suppositions concerning the book's authorship and finally "confessed" in an essay in the Time Book Review in 1972: "I wrote the 'Report,' " he confessed. "All of it." Lewin said he simply had wanted to "pose the issues of war and peace in a provocative way." No one can accuse him of not achieving that goal! This book is nothing, if not provocative. But the question of authenticity refused to go away. An organization got hold of his book and published it without his knowledge and/or consent. When he obtained a copy, he found they had changed the cover. The back cover did acknowledge his reversal about having written the book, but also added this question: "Does editor Leonard Lewin's claim of authorship represent the truth? Or was it just another move in the deception game being played with exceptional cunning and skill?" This is a no-win question, rather similar to the old "when did you stop beating your wife?" question . . .there is no acceptable answer for the one at whom the charge is being directed.

In 1992, Mr. Lewin filed a copyright-infringement suit, claiming full authorship. Subsequently, Mark Lane, attorney for Liberty Lobby, decided that Mr. Lewin was indeed telling the truth about having written the document. "There is no doubt in my mind that it is not a government report," Mr. Lane says [emphasis added]."

This is a good place to remind you of our original reason for including this chapter: regardless of the validity (or lack thereof) of the Report from Iron Mountain, if a large part of the populace still believes it to be true [and they do], without a doubt it will influence their actions. So we must consider the content and conclusion of this "Report" and its recommendations.

Section 2 of the Book is called, "Disarmament and the Economy." In this section the author(s?) points out that whether disarmament is the byproduct of peace or a precondition of peace, the greatest effect of said peace will be to the national economy.

> General agreement prevails in respect to the more important economic problems that general disarmament would raise. A short survey of these problems, rather than a detailed critique of their comparative significance, is sufficient for our purposes in this Report.
> The first factor is that of size. The "world war industry," as one writer has aptly called it, accounts for approximately a tenth of the output of the world's economy. . . .The United States, the world's richest nation, not only accounts for the largest single share of this expense, currently upward of $60 billion a year

[Note: this was in 1967], but also " . . . has devoted a higher proportion of its gross national product to its military establishment
than any other major free world nation. This was true even before
our increased expenditures in Southeast Asia."

The Report points out that conversion of military expenditures to
other (peaceful) purposes entails many difficulties. One problem is
the degree of rigid specialization involved in nuclear and missile technology, trades and skills not easily converted to peacetime use.
Another problem is posed by the geographic location of all these wartime and cold war military installations, personnel, and equipment.
For the moment considering only our own country, since our military
establishment is scattered around the world, "closing up shop" and
retreating back within our own borders would create monumental
problems, both logistically and economically, and the economic
impact of our withdrawal would seriously affect the countries from
which we would withdraw, as well as our own economic quandries
encountered. Just ask the mayors and governor of California (or any
other state—I just mention California because of so many recent scale-
downs or closures of military bases in that state), for example, what
happens to their economy when a major military facility is closed
down or relocated to another region.

In addition to geographical and occupational problems, there is the
industrial problem . . . to what kind of industry can you convert factories that specialize in missiles, tanks, ships, submarines, bombers
and fighter planes, stealth technology, etc.? Over a long period of
time, perhaps *some* of it might be "converted" to peacetime industry,
but not the majority of it . . . and at what cost?

And the success of retraining personnel for peacetime trades is
highly questionable. Do they have the right skills? Do they have sufficient education? Are they retrainable? Are they willing to start over
from scratch after achieving a career in the war industry? And perhaps
the most important consideration, how many placements actually
could be made by retraining, considering the "automation" factor that
is already taking its toll on employment numbers in our present industries. Even now, they are not able to compensate for automation simply
by attrition, but in many cases are downsizing with massive layoffs
of workers . . . especially in the blue collar positions. And the information industries are feeling the crunch, as well. In their cases, the downsizing usually affects middle-management personnel and older
employees who are nearing retirement age, whose pensions and total
retirement are negatively affected by layoffs at this late stage in their
lives. There are many, many such applicants out there searching for

a position to serve the last 10 to 15 of their working years; most can't find anything comparable with the position they left, with its many years of seniorty, and have to settle for much less income and status than their former position.

Considering all this, what will happen when we flood the job market with all these "converted" job applicants?

The Report continues to tell us that to handle these economic transitions will require "unprecedented government assistance (and concomitant government control). . .to solve the 'structural' problems of transition." One group of economists sees the "arms budget being returned, under careful control, to the consumer, in the form of tax cuts." The theory of returning taxes assumes a comparable increase in consumption, i.e., consumer spending, but they feel it is incorrect to make this inference; it is their opinion that the "consumption" will be made by the government on behalf of the public sector, not by the individual on consumer goods of their choice. ". . .consumption in what is generally considered the public sector of the economy, stresses vastly increased government spending in such areas of national concern as health, education, mass transportation, low-cost housing, water supply, control of the physical environment, and, stated generally, 'poverty'."

This section concludes with five reasons why any plans put forth to date to resolve this economic transition are inadequate to do the job and most certainly will fail.

Regarding the substitutions, transitions, or conversions from the functions of war to peace proposed by the book, it makes this statement:

> . . .Such a plan can be developed only from the premise of full understanding of the nature of the war system it proposes to abolish, which in turn presupposes detailed comprehension of the functions the war system performs for society. It will require the construction of a detailed and feasible system of substitutes for those functions that are necessary to the stability and survival of human societies.

Below I have quoted from the summarized "Functions of War" section at the end of the book. These will be followed by the summary, "Substitutes for the Functions of War," interspersing quotations from the earlier expanded commentary where I feel they are pertinent, and interjecting some examples of suggested substitutes from the section called "Models."

The Functions of War

The visible, military function of war requires no elucidation; it is not only obvious but also irrelevant to a transition to the condition of peace, in which it will by definition be superfluous. It is also subsidiary in social significance to the implied, nonmilitary functions of war; those critical to transition can be summarized in five principal groupings. . . . It is a premise of this study that the transition to peace implies absolutely that [the functions of war] will no longer exist in any relevant sense.

1. Economic

War has provided both ancient and modern societies with a dependable system for stabilizing and controlling national economies. No alternate method of control has yet been tested in a complex modern economy that has shown itself remotely comparable in scope or effectiveness.

2. Political

The permanent possibility of war is the foundation for stable government; it supplies the basis for general acceptance of political authority. It has enabled societies to maintain necessary class distinctions, and it has ensured the subordination of the citizen to the state, by virtue of the residual war powers inherent in the concept of nationhood. No modern political ruling group has successfully controlled its constituency after failing to sustain the continuing credibility of an external threat of war.

The war system makes the stable government of societies possible. It does this essentially by providing an external necessity for a society to accept political rule. . . . an effective political substitute for war would require "alternate enemies," some of which might seem equally farfetched in the context of the current war system. . . . What other institution or combination of programs might serve these functions in its place?

3. Sociological

War, through the medium of military institutions, has uniquely served societies, throughout the course of known history, as an indispensable controller of dangerous social dissidence and destructive antisocial tendencies. As the most formidable of threats to life itself, and as the only one susceptible to mitigation by social organization alone, it has played another equally fundamental role: the war system has provided the machinery through which the motivational forces governing human behavior have been translated into binding social allegiance. It has thus ensured the degree of social cohesion necessary to the viability of nations. No other institution, or groups of institutions, in modern societies, has successfully served these functions.

In a world of peace, the continuing stability of society will require: (1) an effective substitute for military institutions that can neutralize destabilizing social elements and (2) a credible motivational surrogate for war that can ensure social cohesiveness.

4. Ecological

War has been the principal evolutionary device for maintaining a satisfactory ecological balance between gross human population and supplies available for its survival. It is unique to the human species.

5. Cultural and Scientific

War-orientation has determined the basic standards of value in the creative arts and has provided the fundamental motivational source of scientific and technological progress. The concepts that the arts express values independent of their own forms and that the successful pursuit of knowledge has intrinsic social value have long been accepted in modern societies; the development of the arts and sciences during this period has been corollary to the parallel development of weaponry.

Substitutes for the Functions of War

1. Economic

An acceptable economic surrogate [their preferred term for "substitute"] for the war system will require the expenditure of resources for completely nonproductive purposes at a level comparable to that of the military expenditures otherwise demanded by the size and complexity of each society [worldwide]. Such a substitute system of apparent "waste" must be of a nature that will permit it to remain independent of the normal supply-demand economy; it must be subject to arbitrary political control....

[Models proposed as economic surrogates.] (a) A comprehensive social-welfare program, directed toward maximum improvement of general conditions of human life. (b) A giant open-end space research program, aimed at **unreachable targets**. (c) A permanent, ritualized, ultra-elaborate disarmament inspection system, and variants of such a system.

[Let's] assume that so-called social-welfare expenditures will fill the vacuum created by the disappearance of military spending....the assumption seems plausible....

Health—Drastic expansion of medical research, education, and training facilities; hospital and clinic construction; the general objective of **complete government guaranteed health care for all**, at a level consistent with current developments in medical technology.

Education—The equivalent of the foregoing in teacher training; schools and libraries; the **drastic upgrading of standards, with the general objective of making available for all an attainable educational goal equivalent to what is now considered a professional degree.**

Housing—Clean, comfortable, safe, and spacious living space for all, at the level now enjoyed by about 15 percent of the population in this country (less in most others).

Transportation—The establishment of a system of mass public transportation making it possible for all to travel to and from areas of work and recreation quickly, comfortably, and conveniently, and to travel privately for pleasure rather than necessity.

Physical environment—The development and protection of water supplies, forests, parks, and other natural resources, and the elimination of chemical and bacterial contaminants from air, water, and soil.

Poverty—The genuine elimination of poverty, defined by a standard consistent with current economic productivity, by means of a guaranteed annual income or whatever system of distribution will best assure its achievement.

. . .In the past, such a vague and ambitious-sounding "program" would have been. . .*prima facie,* far too costly. . . .Our objection to it. . .could hardly be more contradictory. **As an economic substitute for war, it is inadequate because it would be far too cheap** [bold emphasis added].

[The space-research surrogate proposes] the development of a long range sequence of space-research projects with largely unattainable goals. This kind of program offers several advantages lacking in the social welfare model. First, it is unlikely to phase itself out, regardless of the predictable "surprises" science has in store for us: the universe is too big. . . .Second, it need be no more dependent on the general supply-demand economy than its military prototype. Third, it lends itself extraordinarily well to arbitrary control. . . .current programs are absurdly and obviously disproportionate, in the relationship of the knowledge sought to the expenditures committed. . . .As a purely economic substitute for war, therefore, extension of the space program warrants serious consideration.

The "elaborate inspection" surrogate is fundamentally fallacious. . . .it might be economically useful, as well as politically necessary, during the disarmament transition, [however] it would fail as a substitute for the economic function of war for one simple reason. *Peacekeeping inspection is part of a war system, not of a peace system.* It implies the possibility of weapons maintenance or manufacture, which could not exist in a world at peace as herein defined.

2. Political

A viable political substitute for war must posit a general menace to each society of a nature and degree sufficient to require the organization and acceptance of political authority.

[Models proposed as political surrogates.] (a) An omnipresent, international police force. (b) An established and recognized extraterrestrial menace. (c) Massive global environmental pollution. (d) Fictitious alternate enemies.

. . . the end of war means the end of national sovereignty, and thus the end of nationhood as we know it today. . . .

A number of proposals have been made governing the relations between nations after total disarmament; . . . institutions more or less like a World Court, or a United Nations, but vested with real authority. . . . [However] none would offer effective external pressure on a peace-world nation to organize itself politically.

It might be argued that a well-armed international police force, operating under the authority of such a supranational "court" could well serve the function of external enemy. This, however, would constitute a military operation, ...

. . . [Regarding extraterrestrials] such a menace would offer the "last, best hope of peace," etc., by uniting mankind against the danger of destruction by "creatures" from other planets or from outer space. Experiments have been proposed to test . . . the invasion threat; it is possible that a few of the more difficult-to-explain "flying saucer" incidents of recent years were in fact early experiments of this kind. If so, they could hardly have been judged encouraging.

. . . [Regarding global environmental pollution] poisoning of the air, and of the principal sources of food and water supply, is already well advanced . . . it constitutes a threat that can be dealt with only through social organization and political power. . . . It seems highly improbable that a program of deliberate environmental poisoning could be implemented in a **politically acceptable** manner.

However unlikely some of the possible alternate enemies we have mentioned may seem, we must emphasize that one must be found, of credible quality and magnitude, if a transition to peace is ever to come about without social disintegration. **It is more probable, in our judgment, that such a threat will have to be invented** [bold emphasis added].

3. Sociological

First, in the permanent absence of war, new institutions must be developed that effectively control the socially destructive segments of societies. Second, for purposes of adapting the physical and psychological dynamics of human behavior to the needs of social organization, a credible substitute for war must generate an omnipresent and readily understood fear of personal destruction. This fear must be of a nature and degree sufficient to ensure adherence to societal values to the full extent that **they are acknowledged to transcend the value of individual human life** [bold emphasis added].

[Models proposed as sociological surrogates.] Control function: (a) Programs generally derived from the Peace Corps model. (b) A modern, sophisticated form of **slavery**. Motivational function: (a) Intensified environmental pollution. (b) New religions or other mythologies. (c) Socially oriented blood games. (d) Combination of forms.

Most proposals that address themselves, explicitly or otherwise, to the postwar problem of controlling the **socially alienated** turn to some variant of the Peace Corps or the so-called Job Corps for solutions. The **socially disaffected, the economically unprepared, the psychologically unconformable, the hardcore "delinquents," the "incorrigible subversives," and the rest of the unemployable** are seen as somehow transformed by the disciplines of a service modeled on military precedent into more or less dedicated social service workers.

The problem has been addressed in the language of popular sociology, by Secretary McNamara . . . ."It seems to me that we could move toward remedying that inequity [of the Selective Service System] by asking every young person in the United States to give two years of service to his country—whether in one of the military services, in the Peace Corps, or in some other volunteer developmental work at home or abroad."

Another possible surrogate for the control of potential enemies of society is the reintroduction, in some form consistent with modern technology and political processes, of **slavery**. Up to now, this has been suggested only in fiction . . . .The traditional association of slavery with ancient pre-industrial cultures should not blind us to its adaptability to advanced forms of social organization, nor should its equally traditional incompatibility with Western moral and economic values. **It is entirely possible that the development of a sophisticated form of slavery may be an absolute prerequisite for social control in a world at peace** [bold emphasis added].

. . . the motivational function of war requires the existence of a genuinely menacing social enemy. . . . the "alternate enemy" must imply a more immediate, tangible, and directly felt threat of destruction. It must justify the need for taking and paying a "blood price" in wide areas of human concern. . . . the possible substitute enemies noted earlier would be insufficient. One exception might be the environmental-pollution model, if the danger to society it posed was genuinely imminent. The fictive models would have to carry the weight of extraordinary conviction, **underscored with a not inconsiderable actual sacrifice of life**;. . . .

Games theorists have suggested. . . the development of "blood games" for the effective control of individual aggressive impulses. . . . such a ritual might be socialized, in the manner of the Spanish Inquisition and the less formal witch trials of other periods, purposes of "social purification," "state security," other rationale both accountable and credible to postwar societies. . . . It is also possible that. . . . the antisocial, for whom a control institution is needed, [could be considered] as the "alternate enemy" needed to hold society together. The relentless and irreversible advance of unemployability at all levels of society, and the similar extension of generalized alienation from accepted values may make some such program necessary even as an adjunct to the war system.

4. Ecological

A substitute for war in its function as the uniquely human system of population control must ensure the survival, if not necessarily the improvement, of the species, in terms of its relation to environmental supply.

[Models proposed as ecological surrogates.] A comprehensive program of applied eugenics [genetic engineering and other such methods of selecting who is born].

There is no question but that a universal requirement that procreation be limited to the products of artificial insemination would provide a fully adequate substitute control for population levels. Such a reproductive system would, of course, have the added advantage of being susceptible of direct eugenic [relating to good offspring] management. Its predictable further development—conception and embryonic growth taking place wholly under laboratory conditions—would extend these controls to their logical conclusion. The ecological function of war under these circumstances would not only be superseded but surpassed in effectiveness.

The indicated intermediate step—total control of conception with a variant of the ubiquitous "pill," **[pill for total human sterilization]** via water supplies or certain essential foodstuffs, offset by a controlled "antidote"—**is already under development** [bold emphasis added].

5. Cultural and Scientific

A surrogate for the function of war as the determinant of cultural values must establish a basis of sociomoral conflict of equally compelling force and scope. A substitute motivational basis for the quest for scientific knowledge must be similarly informed by a comparable sense of internal necessity.

Strictly speaking, the function of war as the determinant of cultural values and as the prime mover of scientific progress may not be critical in a world without war. . . .The absolute need. . .is not established. . . .A cult has developed around a new kind of cultural determinism,. . . .Its clear implication is that there is no "good" or "bad" art. . . .it provides a working model of one kind of **value-free culture we might reasonably anticipate in a world of peace** [bold emphasis added].

[Models proposed as cultural and scientific surrogates.] Cultural: No replacement institution is offered. Scientific: The secondary requirements of the space research, social welfare, and/or eugenics programs.

The book arrives at the following conclusions, with great accuracy, I might add. "Such solutions, if indeed they exist, will not be arrived at without a revolutionary revision of the modes of thought heretofore considered appropriate to peace research. . . .Some observers, in fact, believe that it cannot be overcome at all in our time, that the price of peace is, simply, too high."

As it would appear that some of these seemingly farfetched suggestions are at least on the horizon, if, indeed, not imminent, it is easy to understand why this book won't just "go away." And whether or not we do away with war, it would seem that some of these "solutions" are being put into practice anyway, i.e., eugenics, worldwide birth control practices, a global government with its own court and policing agency, etc., etc.—all prominent parts of the rapidly approaching New World Order.

I suggest that you visit your library and read the entire article by Robert Tomsho. It appeared in *The Wall Street Journal*, Western Edition, Palo Alto, CA, May 9, 1995.

UPDATE

Iron Mountain is a subject that seemingly refuses to die or go away. Recently, I was brousing in the airport gift shop for something to read while flying to a speaking engagement. You can imagine my total amazement to find a brand new copy of the *Iron Mountain Report* on the bookshelf. This 1960's report—convinced by so many to be a complete hoax—is once again in print. Simon and Schuster, Inc., under their Free Press division, have published it, with a fresh (1996) copyright by Leonard C. Lewin, who now claims authorship of this work. It is denounced as total satire by Victor Navasky in a scathing introduction (which he has copyrighted independently from the remainder of the work). Of course, it is an overt attack on "right wing extremists," *et al.* This new publication was undoubtedly spawned by the incidents at Waco (Texas), Ruby Ridge (Idaho), and Freeman (Montana), as well as the Oklahoma City bombing.

It even received a full column in the book review section of the May 6, 1996, edition of *Business Week* magazine. Book Reviewer Hardy Green's opening words declare it to be "True satire, ... Concocted in the 1960s by a band of leftists. . . ." But in the same paragraph he refers to "right-wing militias" and "rightists" as the groups who perpetuate the book. Then he uses the rest of his review to ridicule the *Report From Iron Mountain.* Of course, he mentions the raging debate over its authenticity that made front-page news in *The New York Times* some 30 years ago, but authoritatively settles that question for us by stating: "Henry Kissinger declared it a hoax." Well, that should end all debate, right? If Henry said it, it must be so!

Whether or not it was, in fact, originally true or merely intended as fictional satire, its contents become more relevant with each passing day, which is why it is viewed with such importance by so many. And I predict it won't go away any time in the near future.

CHAPTER SEVEN

Computerizing People On the Super Information Highway

Fiber Optics / Social Security / And More

Information Warfare is about the control of information. As a society we maintain less and less control as Cyberspace expands and electronic anarchy reigns.
—Winn Schwartau

The computerization of people demands a "mega-sized" infrastructure. Just consider the number of people in our country alone, then try to imagine the total number of people in the world—we are but a drop in the bucket by comparison. The databanks to handle such a phenomenal task would have to be enormous. Yet, with the shrinking size of the hardware and the great advances in software technology, it is within sight in the foreseeable future . . . and getting closer with each passing day.

One dictionary defines infrastructure as:

1. An underlying base or supporting structure. 2. The basic facilities, equipment, services, and installations needed for the growth and functioning of a country, community, operation, or organization.

Another dictionary defines it almost identically:

1: the underlying foundation or basic framework (as of a system or organization) 2: the permanent installations required for military purposes.

I believe that by now, we all are aware of the partial extent to which Big Brother has his tentacles reaching into every aspect of our lives—

even though what we know barely scratches the surface of what is *really* going on in this regard.

We are hearing about the Super Information Highway regularly, to such a degree that the term barely catches our attention anymore. There have been so many "on line" programs added for the convenience of the masses, and to which a multitude of patrons have subscribed, that it has become common terminology. If you haven't "signed up" yet, you probably will sooner or later; if you aren't "interactive" yet, you probably will be sooner or later; if Big Brother doesn't have access to your private lives via phone, fax, modem, cable TV, etc., yet, he probably will sooner or later—I'm guessing sooner than you expect!

There is such an array of information (as yet uncensored) available on this "highway" that Congress is now feeling the need to step in and regulate what is available because of the rapidly expanding amount of pornography being displayed and its easy access by children and teens. However, they still are trying to figure out how that can be done from both a hardware standpoint and a "First Amendment" standpoint. What they need is something comparable to the "V-Chip" they found to enable parents to control what comes into their homes via their television sets. Unfortunately, the network doesn't operate that way.

Falcon Cable, one of this nation's largest cable networks, is in the process of converting all their cable lines to fiber optic cables. This is being done to enable their customers to become "interactive" by way of their television sets. *The advantage* of this is that you can exchange information from your living room; *the disadvantage* of this is that you can exchange information from your living room. Get the point? If you can reach out, they can reach in!

As usual, all of this great technology is for our convenience and to make our lives easier. It's getting easy, all right. We're already better than half way down the slippery slope to electronic bondage. Consider all the areas of your life that are in somebody's computer. . . now consider how you would get that information out of their computer, or correct it if it were incorrect. Now consider how convenient it would be if it all were in the same big computer database (infrastructure) and *everybody* (but you, of course) had access to it. Most of us are far past the half-way point; in fact, about all that remains before total electronic enslavement is the banking/economic conversion—and we are so close to the cashless society right now that you probably wouldn't believe it if I told you.

In Chapter 14, I will be telling you in detail about the national identity program, and in Chapter 15, I will be discussing the biochip and radiofrequency technology currently available to implement the final aspects of the worldwide bondage, as described in the book of Revelation. Some of the smaller chapters in between will be brief, dealing with some specific aspects of global control of commerce, travel, manufacturing, etc.

Touted as "everything you need to know to join the communications revolution" in their December, 1994, edition, *Reader's Digest* published an article condensed from the May, 1994, edition of *Popular Science.* The title was: "The Information Superhighway: What's In It for You?" It is an excellent article, and if you missed it, I suggest you go back and locate it. Read it in its entirety. I'm furnishing brief quotations below of some of the most pertinent information.

> So what's all this to-do about the information superhighway? What is it? What will it do for you? How will it change your life?
>
> The vision is simple: *an unprecedented nationwide—and eventually worldwide*—electronic communications network that connects everyone to everyone else and provides just about any sort of electronic communication imaginable [emphasis added].

The goal can't be expressed much clearer than that! They ask, "What's the purpose?" Then they proceed to tell you it will provide remote electronic banking, schooling, taxpaying (I know you just can't wait to grant the IRS unlimited automatic access to your funds!), video-conferencing, medical diagnosing, *et al.* "The list goes on and on."

Of course, they address the innocuous questions of video-on-demand, video games, and home shopping opportunities, as well as the potential new hardware required, but then they get to the bombshell question which probably will be of the greatest interest to most of us:

How will it affect my privacy?

> The information superhighway will carry all kinds of personal matters, from your tastes in movies to your political affiliations to your buying habits. *How this information will be protected is one of the great unknowns.*
>
> Computer hackers—those potential terrorists of cyberspace—represent another threat. [Author's Note: Check your newspaper—you'll find that this type of threat is long past being "potential."] Last February, high-tech marauders were able to pilfer thousands of passwords from Internet; this would allow them to read hundreds of personal files, including e-mail. Such a break-in could result in anything from a minor inconvenience to a loss of privacy [not to mention the looting of your bank accounts and maxing out your credit cards].

On the other hand, computerized systems give financial institutions much better tools for tracking transactions and spotting
patterns of criminal behavior. [Emphasis added.]

One such bank already is slipping this information into their TV
commercials, i.e., they called a customer to see if he really was buying
a tuxedo, when such a purchase fell out of the range of the *norm* for
his usual purchases—again, for his protection, to be sure someone
hadn't stolen his credit card.

Then comes the *hard sell.* They ask: "Will it be good for U.S. businesses?" and respond, "Absolutely." "When it's finally here, will
society benefit?" To which they respond by giving you all the wonderful benefits, such as unlimited access to all the world's knowledge,
telemedicine from great distances, and others. And they close with
these statements:

> Social Security and Medicare forms could be administered
> electronically [already happening!], just as income-tax returns
> are beginning to be processed—with similar advantages [not to
> mention the similar disadvantages!].
>
> So the outlook is for Americans to become better educated,
> healthier, more productive, and more informed than ever before
> in history.

Oh, but what you're going to sacrifice to take advantage of these
tremendous opportunities(?).

Do you think I'm alone, or perhaps overly concerned with this
mounting technology? Not so! In fact, I'm in some very prominent
company. The July 25, 1994, edition of *The New American,* carried
an article by William F. Jasper entitled, "High-Tech Nightmare: Traveling Big Brother's Information Superhighway." Jasper begins by
reminding us of the events in George Orwell's book, *1984.* The pro-
tagonist, Winston Smith, could scarcely look in any direction without
coming under the wary scrutiny of the ever-present Big Brother. In
Smith's world, we see the individual stripped of all freedom, worth,
dignity, and privacy—even in his own apartment, since the "telescreen"
received and transmitted simultaneously. Jasper says:

> Our technological capabilities today are more than adequate
> to implement this same kind of Orwellian nightmare, and politi-
> cally we are headed in that direction. In the past year the Clinton
> Administration has been aggressively pushing a number of statist,
> privacy-invading initiatives that have groups and individuals all
> across the political spectrum screaming "Big Brother." Clinton
> proposals for a national identification card, a national "informa-

tion super highway," and installation of a federal "Clipper Chip" in our telephones, computers, fax machines, and other electronic devices to allow government monitoring certainly justify the concern that we have embarked on the "slippery slope."

He goes on to tell us it is apropos that the Clinton programs be introduced with the same kind of "doublespeak" that Orwell called "Newspeak," in which words often mean the opposite of what we normally assume they mean. "With the Clipper chip proposal, Team Clinton is saying, in effect: 'In order to protect your privacy, Fedgov has to have the ability to invade your privacy—but you can trust us not to.' "

Jasper points out that Clinton's pitch is aimed at a legitimate concern. In this information age in which we live, our lives are transparent.

> Our employment history, credit rating, banking transactions, school and medical records, shopping habits, travel, telephone and electronic communications, and many other intimate details of our personal lives are floating in the ether of cyberspace, available for abuse by government, commercial interests, hackers, personal enemies, or other interested parties. In order to protect against unauthorized use of this information, many individuals, companies, and institutions are making use of data and voice [see chapter 13 on biometrics] encryption devices and software.

But the government is vehemently opposed to such encryption (unless they are the only ones doing the encrypting), as it prevents them from eavesdropping on private conversations, as they were able to do with the old wire-tapping systems. Therefore, they have given the communications industry an ultimatum—come up with methods and technologies of tracking and listening in on any message . . .within three years. At first, they were trying to make the respective communications companies pay for the R & D to meet the deadline; however, after running into much resistance, it has been decided that the taxpayers should foot the bill. FBI Director Louis Freeh says that the American people must be willing to give up a degree of personal privacy in exchange for safety and security. Apparently, they also must kick in up to *half a billion dollars* to cover the cost of equipping the government to spy on them.

The Electronic Frontier Foundation, an industry lobbying group warned on its computer bulletin board:

> Do not be fooled, the FBI scheme would turn the data superhighway into a national surveillance network of staggering proportions.

John Perry Barlow of the Foundation said, "Relying on the government to protect your privacy is like asking a Peeping Tom to install your window blinds."

Now, lest we mistakenly apply all the heat to Clinton, I should point out that the Clipper chip project originated with George Bush (surprise, surprise!), and a bill similar to the one presently in the works was included in the 1991 crime bill.

The Clipper chip is the device the government proposes to use in unscrambling the scrambled (encrypted) communications, and subsequently make illegal the use of any encryption that couldn't be unscrambled by the Clipper chip. However, after examination and testing, flaws have been discovered in the function of the Clipper chip. Jasper's article states:

> (1) with sufficient knowledge, resources, and motivation, criminals could evade Clipper via the Blaze technique; and (2) there are ways to evade Clipper's surveillance requiring even less knowledge, resources, and motivation than the Blaze method. Either way, it is the ostensible targets of Clipper—criminals and terrorists—who are most likely to have the knowledge, resources, and motivation to evade the technology.
>
> That leaves the average, law-abiding citizen as the logical primary target of the Clipper. There is a parallel here, of course, with the Clinton drive for more gun control laws, which (as always) are ignored by the criminal element and serve only to penalize and criminalize the responsible gun owner.

You probably have noticed a certain amount of overlap from chapter to chapter throughout this book, and this section is no exception. Because Jasper's article was so powerfully organized, condensed, and comprehensive, I'm going to share more of it with you in this chapter—even though the content deals with smart cards and biochips, which I will repeat in chapters 14 and 15 as I deal with those specific topics.

Jasper points out that Big Brother is not stopping with surveillance of telecommunications and Clipper is just the beginning, and he offers the following quotations from *PC Week* magazine:

> The Clinton administration is working on creating an identification card that every American will need to interact with any federal government agency.
>
> Sources close to the administration said President Clinton is also considering signing a pair of *executive orders* that would facilitate the connection of individuals' bank accounts and federal records to a government identification card [emphasis added].

Remember, several chapters earlier I explained to you all the havoc that could be generated by the creation of the "executive order" system—literally, a way to bypass Congress and place any whim of a sitting president directly into law.

PC Week said the national ID proposal was presented by the US Postal Service as a general purpose US services smart card. It would be for both individuals and companies to send or receive any electronic transaction, i.e., E-mail, funds transfer, or interacting with government agencies.

Postal Service representative Chuck Chamberlain outlined how an individual's US Card would be connected automatically with the Health and Human Services department, the US Treasury, the IRS, the banking system, and *a central database* of digital signatures for authenticating electronic transactions. While the US Card is still only a proposal, according to Chamberlain the Postal Service is prepared to put more than 100 million of the cards in citizens' pockets within months of administration approval, which—according to him—could come at any time.

William Murray, security consultant to accounting firm Deloitte and Touche, charges, "There won't be anything you do in business that won't be collected and analyzed by the government....This is a better surveillance mechanism than Orwell or the government could have imagined."

Do you think it's a giant leap from a smart card to an implantable biochip? Think again—by these one-world pundits it is viewed as the next logical step, and perhaps even something to which we should go directly, eliminating all the wasteful and time-consuming steps in between. Jasper continues:

> The "smart card" is also a central feature of the Clinton "health care reform" program. However, some "Friends of Hillary" have even grander visions. Mary Jane England, MD, a member of the executive committee of the White House Health Project...is especially excited about the potential for implanting smart chips in your body....Dr. England said: "The Smart Card is a wonderful idea, but even better would be capacity not to have a card, and I call it 'a chip in your ear,' that would actually access your medical records....We need to go beyond the narrow conceptualization of the Smart Card and really use some of the technology that's out there. *The worst thing we could do is put in place a technology that's already outdated....* Now is the time to really think ahead....I don't think...access through a chip in your ear is so far off and I think we need to think of these things [emphasis added]."

Jasper concludes by accusing (and rightfully so!) the Clinton regime of having an Orwellian mindset. He says that under these circumstances ". . .the Administration's fervent campaign for creating a national (federally funded and controlled) 'information network' that will 'link every home, business, lab, classroom, and library by the year 2015' becomes positively frightening."

Then he admonishes us not to forget that this is the same administration that is advocating a huge new National Police Corps, implementing warrantless searches for firearms, advocating severe restrictions on firearms ownership by law-abiding citizens, usurping control of state jurisdiction over law enforcement and criminal justice, and attempting to purge all religious expressions and symbols from the workplace.

I say a hearty "Amen!" to Jasper's final paragraph:

> With due respect to Electronic Frontier's Mr. Barlow, trusting *this* government to protect your privacy and your rights is more like asking Jack the Ripper to install the locks on your home.

In the March, 1995, editorial in *Automatic I.D. News,* Editor-in-Chief Mark David stated: "We've entered into an unprecedented period of social upheaval—and are the vanguard of a new era based on information exchange. The transition has meant upheaval for our social, economic, and religious institutions. . . . " And we get this admission from a man who is on the "Front Line" (the title of his editorial column) of I.D. technology, and who vigorously is pushing us further and deeper into electronic enslavement.

Some of these subjects overlap to the extent that it is difficult to decide the proper chapter where I should place them. I already have recommended that you subscribe to Don McAlvany's excellent newsletter, but allow me to reiterate that again at this point before I quote from the July, 1991, edition. You may write for information to: *The McAlvany Intelligence Advisor,* P. O. Box 84904, Phoenix, AZ 85071. As you read, it will become evident why I have included this information in this particular chapter.

> *The computerization of the American people* will enable the government to watch and control you from the cradle to the grave. . . .The New World Order/New Age government of the future will be able to watch and control its subjects more completely and efficiently than any totalitarian power in the past.
>
> Since 1985, the IRS has been computerizing all Americans and that project is now virtually complete. A computer profile now exists on virtually every American family or individual, which will enable the government by computers to monitor virtually

all of your activities, trace, track, and watch your financial, business or personal dealings, locate you in very short order, and perhaps eventually directly assess your taxes based on your computerized financial profile—electronically debiting your bank account for the taxes due.

As a sample of the kind of people-tracking information which is now being amassed on computers by the US government, the following government memo was sent to employees of one large government agency charged with tracking and monitoring Americans and their finances:

"We now have available to us a new source of background information called METRONET which provides information on over 111 million people in 80 million households across the country. Not only does it eliminate the need for ATLAS, since ATLAS was originally purchased from METRONET by the credit bureau, but it also allows for the following variety of searches:

"PHONE SEARCH—provides a complete name and address report which is provided in accordance with US Postal Service standards. As mentioned above, it is the same as ATLAS except that the record search can continue further once the name and address of the subject has been determined.

"ADDRESS SEARCH—requires that the zip code, street address, and last name be entered in order to verify an address and receive the subject's current phone number. If it is a single family dwelling and your subject has moved, METRONET lists the current resident.

"HOUSEHOLD PROFILES—provides the time at current residence, type of dwelling, the subject's age and year of birth. It also provides the names, ages, and years of birth of up to four additional family members.

"NEIGHBOR SEARCH—requires only the address to obtain details on up to thirty neighbors at new or old addresses. These details include names, addresses, phone numbers, dwelling types, and length of residence. It also provides the current resident at the subject's last-known address.

"CHANGE OF ADDRESS ALERT—automatically searches the US Postal Services's National Change of Address files which is updated every two weeks. With 20% of the population moving to a new residence annually and the fact that 30% of these people never notify the postal service of their new address, METRONET also checks for any change of address that a subject has provided to a publisher or marketing company to make sure that their magazines or other products will be forwarded.

"STREET NAME SCANNING—helps obtain the correct street name abbreviations by checking an alphabetical table of all street names in any given zip code that begins with a specified letter.

"SURNAME SEARCH—allows the investigator to search an entire geographic region (i.e., state, county, city, zip code, etc.) when the only information known is the last name of the subject."

If this sounds like something out of a detective movie, where the private eye can just pick up the phone and find out anything . . . that's pretty close to the truth. Be sure to read the information supplied in "The Bottom Line," my conclusion, from Winn Schwartau's new book, *Information Warfare.* He gives the latest on the extent of the capability of people to gather and share information about the formerly most private aspects of your lives, and the dangers inherent therein.

In *The McAlvany Intelligence Advisor* referenced above, McAlvany reports briefly how we got to this point.

We live in the day of the computer. Computer knowledge, speed of processing, and technology is now doubling every two years. This tremendous explosion in computer technology and gathering of information has set the stage where all sensitive personal and financial information about you will be centralized and available for review.

For years, the government collected vast amounts of sensitive information about you but was not able to make full use of the information because managing and correlating this material was impossible. All that has changed with the computerization of virtually all government files. This process happened at a rapid speed in all levels of government and in the private sector over the past 10 years. The banks, credit agencies, insurance companies, all types of stores and businesses, and general employers now have access to these records, which within seconds can give massive quantities of sensitive information about you.

Part and parcel of this total computerization of all information is the cashless society, whereby computers will electronically transfer credits and debits. As credits and debits are electronically transferred to and from your different financial accounts, no "real money" will change hands—there will be no need for cash because computers will electronically conduct the transactions. The need for cash and checks will evaporate. Today, upwards to three-fourths of all banking is done electronically. The US government electronically deposits most payroll, welfare, and social security checks, as do many businesses.

Each American has dozens (if not hundreds) of computer data files on him—with the government now maintaining between two and three dozen separate files on each American. The key for the government's managing, merging, integrating, and using all of this miscellaneous computerized data is a single, universal number—to tie all the various data bases together. Your Social Security number has become that universal key to merging and releasing all that computerized information.

It is virtually impossible to live in America without your Social Security number. If you have any contact with the government, you must have the number. It is required for federal, state, and local tax forms; for all medical plans; for passports; to receive welfare, unemployment benefits, medicare payments, food stamps, or any government check for any purpose; to open a bank account or a securities account, etc. Most businesses and retail stores have begun asking for Social Security numbers on transactions, as do most doctors, dentists, and medical practitioners. (No one is legally bound to give the number to these latter groups, and it seems unwise to this writer to do so.)

Out of this explosion in computer technology and tying together of dozens (or hundreds) of data bases via the Social Security number has come a national computer network where government agencies can almost instantaneously call up any or all information on you or your family, covering your life, finances, and activities literally from the cradle to the grave.

And how does the secular world view all this? They call us bees in an electronic hive. *Harper's Magazine,* May, 1994, carried two essays (pro and con) on the subject, titled "The Electronic Hive: Two Views." The first writer, Sven Birkerts, took the argument, "Refuse It." The opposing argument, entitled "Embrace It," was presented by Kevin Kelly. The first excerpts below are from "Refuse It."

The digital future is upon us. From our President on down, people are smitten, more than they have been with anything in a very long time. I can't open a newspaper without reading another story about the Internet, the information highway. . . .The dollar is smart. It is betting that the trend will be a juggernaut, unstoppable; that we are collectively ready to round the corner into a new age. We are not about to turn from this millennial remaking of the world; indeed, we are all excited to see just how much power and ingenuity we command. By degrees—it is happening year by year, appliance by appliance—we are wiring ourselves into a gigantic hive.

. . .we trade for ease. And ease is what quickly swallows up the initial strangeness of a new medium or tool. Moreover, each accommodation paves the way for the next. . . .the inventions coming gradually, one by one, allowing the society to adapt. . . .

. . .formerly the body had time to accept the [new technology], whereas now we are hurtling forward willy-nilly, assuming that if a technology is connected with communications or information processing it must be good, we must need it . . . . Since the early 1970s we have seen the arrival of—we have accepted, deemed all but indispensable—personal computers, laptops, telephone-answering machines, calling cards, fax machines, cellular phones, VCRs, modems, Nintendo games, E-mail, voice mail, camcorders, and CD players. Very quickly, with almost no pause between increments, these circuit-driven tools and entertainments have moved into our lives. . . .They don't seem to challenge our power so much as add to it.

I am startled, though, by how little we are debating the deeper philosophical ramifications. . . .why do we hear so few people asking whether we might not *ourselves* be changing, and whether the changes are necessarily for the good?

. . .The ultimate point of the ever-expanding electronic web is to bridge once and for all the individual solitude that has hither-to always set the terms of existence . . . .Telephone, fax, computer networks, E-mail, interactive television—these are the components out of which the hive is being built. . . .

My core fear is that we are, as a culture, as a species, becoming shallower; that we have turned from depth—from the Judeo-Christian premise of unfathomable mystery—and are adapting ourselves to the ersatz security of a vast lateral connectedness. That we are giving up on wisdom, the struggle for which has for millennia been central to the very idea of culture, and that we are pledging instead to a faith in the web. . . .

. . .This may be the awakening, but it feels curiously like the fantasies that circulate through our sleep. From deep in the heart I hear the voice that says, "Refuse it."

Kevin Kelly, former editor of the *Whole Earth Review,* defends the position, "Embrace It."

. . .The symbol of science for the next century is the dynamic Net. . . .The Net is the archetype displayed to represent all cir-cuits, all intelligence, all interdependence, all things economic and social and ecological, all communications, all democracy, all groups, all large systems. This icon is slippery, ensnaring the unwary in its paradox of no beginning, no end, no center.

. . .the Net, also known as the Internet—links several million personal computers around the world. No one knows exactly how many millions are connected, or even how many intermediate nodes there are. The Internet Society made an educated guess last year that the Net was made up of 1.7 million host computers and 17 million users. Like the beehive, the Net is controlled by no one; no one is in charge. The Net is, as its users are proud to boast, the largest functioning anarchy in the world....

. . .the Net stimulates another way of thinking: telegraphic, modular, non-linear, malleable, cooperative.

. . .The Net (and its future progeny) is another one of those disrupting machines and may yet surpass the scope of all the others together in altering how we live.

The Net is an organism/machine whose exact size and boundaries are unknown. All we do know is that new portions and new uses are being added to it at such an accelerating rate that it may be more of an explosion than a thing. So vast is this embryonic Net, and so fast is it developing into something else, that no single human can fathom it deeply enough to claim expertise on the whole.

The tiny bees in a hive are more or less unaware of their colony, but their collective hive mind transcends their small bee minds. As we wire ourselves up into a hivish network, many things will emerge that we, as mere neurons in the network, don't expect, don't understand, can't control, or don't even perceive. That's the price for any emergent hive mind.

. . .An aggregation of fragments is the only kind of whole we now have. The fragmentation of business markets, of social mores, of spiritual beliefs, of ethnicity, and of truth itself into tinier and tinier shards is the hallmark of this era. Our society is a working pandemonium of fragments—much like the Internet itself.

Well, how about that! It looks like even if the government didn't do it to us, we are in the process of doing it to ourselves.

The October, 1993, issue of *Monetary & Economic Review,* addressed the subject of the electronic superhighway as follows:

The Clinton administration linked up with some of the captains of industry and began an effort to build a data super highway that would link schools, businesses, government, and private citizens nationwide. "We are going to push as hard as we possibly can to put this national infrastructure in place," Vice President Al Gore said in Washington in unveiling the plan to coordinate private industry and government efforts to promote the flow of information nationwide.

As we've reported on these pages many times, the goal of the the New World Order crowd is to control the economic and social behavior of everybody. This electronic superhighway is a vital link in their plans to control and censor the flow of data and information to the masses, as well as monitor your activities.

Was Kevin Kelly right? Is it going to be impossible to control what goes on over the superhighway? Not if the government has anything to say about it. *Newsweek* magazine reported in the January 24, 1994, edition, that while in Los Angeles, Vice President Al Gore gave a speech on the future of telecommunications. They stated:

> With new technologies like satellite and microwave battling cable and telephone for control of the Information Highway, Gore has set himself up as a high-tech traffic cop.

[I won't be addressing the use and purpose of satellites in this book, as it is much too complex. It is sufficient to say they are linked with digitized communications and connect with fiber optics to complete the information superhighway. They also are tied in with global positioning systems (GPS), which I discuss in chapter 10.]

U.S. News & World Report of the same date reported on Gore's speech, but accused him of ducking many of the issues.

Infomart Magazine, Second Quarter, 1994, carries an article entitled, "On the Fast Track with ATM." It's time to change some common acronyms which have come to be accepted in daily usage—for example, ATM no longer exclusively means *automated teller machine.* As the subtitle on the article elaborates: "Asynchronous Transfer Mode: Will It Pave the Fast Lane to the Information Highway?" The article begins:

> For lack of one good name, it goes by many: the digital superhighway, the information superhighway, the electronic superhighway, the Al Gore Causeway, the National Information Infrastructure.
>
> Sooner or later, that "superhighway" may pass by your house or business, jammed lane to lane with digital traffic. And all you may need to merge with the fast-track flow is a single, thin cable.
>
> That one small conduit will carry your telephone calls and data to and from your computer, plus hundreds of high-definition television (HDTV) channels and other electronic services.
>
> Exactly how the proposed National Information Infrastructure will work, how you will hook up to it, and what you can do with it are all still subjects of intense debate between telephone companies, cable TV providers, and various industries and agencies. No firm roadmaps have been drawn up.
>
> But many components already exist or are being put into place to create the pavement that will support the massive movement

of electronic signals nationwide. The major components include fiber optic cable networks, special switching devices, and a technique for packaging and sending voice, data, and video signals together over one circuit at very high speed: asynchronous transfer mode (ATM).

In the Book Review section of *Business Week,* December 20, 1993, you will find a report on Howard Rheingold's book, *The Virtual Community: Homesteading on the Electronic Frontier.* After reading this book, Jeffrey M. Laderman titled his review, "Is the Info Superhighway Headed the Wrong Way?"

In *Business Week* of June 7, 1993, you will find an article titled "Boob Tube No More." The article begins, "The computer industry has seen the future, and it's sitting in your living room. Today your television brings you *The Simpsons* and *Murphy Brown.* But in a few years, it will bring you on-line shopping, electronic banking, and electronic video mail." Nathan P. Myhrvold, Microsoft's vice-president for advanced technology, says interactive TV will profoundly change our lives.

> . . .One prototype is under construction in Orlando by Time Warner. When service begins later this year, the system is expected to provide the first true two-way capabilities:. . . .
> . . .And as cable and phone companies spend billions this decade to build information highways, nobody wants to be stalled on a side road.

Time Magazine, May 23, 1994, states: "The interactive-TV pilot projects play a critical role in the race to build the communications networks of the future."

Business Week, October 24, 1994, ran an article titled "An Express Lane for the Infobahn," which carried the following statement: "There's another part of the Net, the World Wide Web, that gives you a hint of what the multimedia Information Superhighway of the future may look like." If you think this business isn't going worldwide, you're not correctly interpreting the input you are being given. *Business Week,* May 30, 1994, ran an article asking the question: "An Information Superhighway Snaking Across Asia?" in which they tell us about Japan's and South Korea's efforts to jump on the highway. Japan plans to connect every home in the country with optic fiber by 2010. South Korea, Japan, and one other country plan to create a pan-Asian Info Highway by the early 21st century for their mutual benefit (which in this case seems primarily economic).

An excellent article appeared in the March 14, 1994, edition of *Newsweek.* The title was "Keeping the Cybercops Out of Cyberspace:

Why techies have a Big Brother complex." Even the photo caption gets your attention: "The brave new world, like the old, will be plagued by techno-bandits. How should we safeguard ourselves against them?" If you didn't get this edition, I strongly recommend you borrow it from your local library and read all of it. I am quoting a portion below:

> His instructions were clear. Be careful what you put on your computer, and encrypt everything. But Aldrich Hazen Ames didn't heed the advice of his alleged KGB handlers, offered in a secret letter written during the summer of 1989. That was a mistake. Federal investigators later tapped into his home computer, over a phone line, for evidence that would be used against him.
>
> Thank God for stumblebum spies. Ames could easily have encrypted his CIA secrets, foiling our best high-tech sleuths. That fact goes to the heart of a debate roiling the Clinton administration: the proper balance between privacy and public security in the dawning Digital Age. The problem is that the explosion of electronic information and instant communication creates enormous opportunities for abuse. A new generation of sophisticated techno-bandits will soon be prowling the Information Highway, armed with technologies that will increasingly help them elude detection. To ferret out the bad guys—be they financial defrauders, spies, or would-be terrorists—the good guys say they need help. The White House is determined to give it—and backs controversial legislation that would, in effect, turn the nation's telephone system and electronic byways into a vast eavesdropping net. To critics, that smacks of Big Brother.
>
> The battle promises to be a donnybrook. It also points up an unsettling development, at least for the cybercops. For years, government has monitored citizens' private conversations and transactions. FBI wiretaps and electronic "bugs," implanted with court permission, have sniffed out crooks. The National Security Agency's satellites—eyes and ears in the sky—alert us to espionage and terrorist plots. But those listening capabilities are eroding. One problem is that the nation's digital phone networks are getting so fast and complicated that communications often can't be tracked. To remedy that, the Justice Department proposes new laws requiring telephone companies to accommodate FBI wiretapping gear in their digital switching systems.
>
> At the same time, commercial encryption programs have grown so sophisticated that cops can't break the codes. The White House aims to fix that, too, by persuading businesses to install a standard encoding device, or "scrambler," into every computer and telephone made in America. This so-called "Clipper chip," a micro-

processor designed by the National Security Agency, offers all the privacy you could wish—with one catch. It also comes with a built-in "back door," to which the Feds have a "key." Think of the arrangement as a sort of hotel. Every guest has his own room and doorlock; but management keeps a master key in some safe place, where no one but trusted hotel employees can get to it.

Sounds sensible, but the plan has civil-liberties folk in an uproar. Critics don't buy government claims that it's merely preserving the degree of surveillance it has always had. Instead, they foresee vastly more invasive eavesdropping. With the Clipper chip, writes New York Times columnist William Safire, echoing a common fear, federal snoopers can overhear "everything we say on a phone, everything we write on a computer, every order we give to a shopping network or bank or 800 or 900 number, every electronic note we leave our spouses or dictate to our personal-digital-assistant genies." From the keepers of the secrets, there would be no secrets, no privacy.

The concern is understandable . . . . Business people are especially worried about giving the government a key to the corporate castle. "What if it's lost?" asks Thomas Lipscomb of Infosafe Systems in New York. What if a hacker breaks into a government computer and gets the codes for Chase Manhattan Bank, or someone bribes an official for advance word of a competitor's bid in a billion-dollar takeover war? The Feds are saying, "Trust us. This won't happen," says Lipscomb. "We don't believe it."

Much is being said about sex on the super highways and how parents can censor it out.

ATTENTION PARENTS:
CYBERSPACE SAFETY

Like any thoroughfare, the information superhighway has its own hazards. Computer bulletin boards are the on-line equivalent of a public park—open to all. "You wouldn't leave your child alone in a mall," says Carol Wallace, spokeswoman for Prodigy, an on-line service. "Allowing him to wander around in on-line public areas is the same thing." Parents should warn kids never to give out personal info (phone numbers, passwords, etc.) when chatting (computer real-time conversation), sending E-mail, posting on a message board or doing a user profile. According to Wallace, Prodigy is "improving its membership verification methods." Still, the bottom line on on-line services is that it's difficult to control who gets

> connected. So if you join a service, make sure it has a
> "lock out" feature designed to block kids' access to cer-
> tain public areas. And if you or your child receive inap-
> propriate correspondence, alert the on-line service.

Of course, whenever the subject of censorship comes up (in any form), there are always those who point out our rights preserved under the First Amendment. Even though our founding fathers never intended the First Amendment to be used to protect the distribution of pornography, they are correct in pointing out that we must not permit our fundamental rights under that amendment to be abridged simply because the mode of our speech now embraces new forms of technology.

The government isn't dragging its heels when it comes to making use of the new technology. . .and I don't mean to investigate alleged spies or potential terrorists. Read the following article reprinted from *The McAlvany Intelligence Advisor* of April, 1995.

FTC ATTEMPTS TO STRANGLE TELEMARKETING

In 1994 the Congress passed legislation authorizing the Federal Trade Commission to write regulations to combat "telemarketing fraud." It has now done so. The FTC is now moving to regulate businesses who sell or take orders for products by telephone—especially catalogue companies and precious metals/coin dealers. Using the excuse that there are fraudulent practices done via telephone (i.e., via so-called "telemarketing")—and of course there are—the FTC has formulated Draconian regulations which will, if enacted as proposed, strangle tens of thousands of small businesses who rely on telephones to solicit and receive orders for business.

Expanding the definition of "crimes" to catch almost everyone in a vast government net and treating honest law-abiding citizens as if they were criminals is a major element of the strategy of the socialists. "Telemarketing fraud" is to be given a broad definition which includes the violation of any of the vast new myriad of regulations being pushed by the FTC. If a business using the telephones to solicit or receive orders does not precisely follow the complex, detailed, laborious, time-consuming paperwork, written and verbal warning to customers, etc., *they can be deemed to be guilty of "telemarketing fraud" and can be heavily fined, shut down, or their owners or managers jailed.*

So, as with hate "crimes," child abuse "crimes," money laundering/structuring "crimes," financial privacy "crimes," gun ownership "crimes," environmental "crimes," etc., a whole new category of crimes, criminals, and penalties is about to be born—courtesy of the FTC bureaucrats (who were given the authority by Congress to do so). And if the government can regulate everything businesses can and cannot say on the telephone, next will come censorship and control of e-mail, computer bulletin boards, interactive computer links, faxes, and virtually all communications on the so-called information highway.

The FTC regulations define almost everyone in business as a "telemarketer." For example, the FTC states that if a business is involved in 10 telephone sales calls per year, it is a "telemarketer." And those don't have to be outgoing calls initiated by the business. They can be solicited or unsolicited incoming calls initiated by the customer or potential customer.

If a sale is made by a business through a combination of face-to-face encounters and a few phone contacts between the business and customer, it is still considered to be "telemarketing" under the new regulations and covered by the regulations. If a person reponds to a *"Yellow Pages ad, to a post card, brochure, catalogue, advertisement, or any other printed, audio, video, cinematic, or electronic communications on behalf of the seller, and places an order by phone, the seller is deemed to be a telemarketer"* under the new regulations.

[**ED. NOTE:** These new telemarketing regulations could ultimately give the government control over almost every business in America—since all businesses use telephones and are involved in some kind of sales of their product or service. The socialists have found another back door way to control and strangle business—just as they have done with their insane people/property controlling environmental laws over the past decade or so. And once they have erected the regulatory machinery (as the EPA has done), it is almost impossible to dismantle it.]

This gives a whole new meaning to "let your fingers do the walking!" Think of all the inconvenience you will experience . . . and the time, energy, gasoline, *et al* you will waste collecting the information you currently can obtain by the push of a few buttons on your telephone. Remember, what affects business ultimately affects the consumer—you and me! Furthermore, that surveillance works both directions—whenever they monitor how and what the business is selling, they also are tracking what you are purchasing.

The *Tribune Democrat* of Johnstown, Pennsylvania, reported on July 9, 1993, that Pennsylvania is mandating the installation of fiber optics by the 40 telephone companies in that state.

By this time I've probably told you more than you ever wanted to know about fiber optics, *et al,* so I won't make further reference to it.

In earlier chapters, I've already thoroughly covered how the IRS ties in, so that information will be omitted from this chapter, for the most part.

SOCIAL SECURITY AND EBT
(Electronic Benefits Transfer)

Everything in our lives now revolves around our Social Security number. The origination of the Social Security system was the basis that permitted our present I.D. infrastructure, and it now has insinuated itself into every avenue of our daily activities—you can't even call your bank without it! On the original page 1360 dated August 10, 1939, the Senate and House enacted certain Social Security legislation. By an amazing coincidence it is labeled "Chapter 666."

The National Employment Screening Services has produced a booklet explaining a bit about the history of the Social Security Administration, as well as supplying information on how the numbers are assigned and how to detect—on the spot—many falsified numbers. Since the first number was issued in the 1930's, they have issued approximately 300 million, and this leaves nearly two-thirds as yet unassigned, which they assure us will suffice for many decades—"even many generations"—to come. But consider what they plan for the future of the SSN:

> However, the SSN has also come to play a far bigger role than its creators could have ever envisioned. From job applications, to tax returns, to driver's licenses, to educational records, the SSN has become the standard identifier used on a wide variety of records. The decision of so many offices to adopt the SSN for their own purposes is understandable. There is no more widely held number in the country. Most individuals acquire an SSN at a fairly early age [now required by age one if claimed as an exemption on your tax return], generally no later than the time they enter the work force. And, unlike names and addresses, a person's SSN cannot be duplicated or changed. An SSN, once issued, is ours to keep. It never changes. The SSN is truly the "universal identifier."

The SSN consists of nine numerals, separated into three basic groups of three/two/four. The first three digits determine the location or area. The two digits in the middle identify the portion of the state in which the card was issued. The last four digits are called the "serial number." There are many complex rules regarding which sequence of numbers can be valid, including the even/odd test. Personnel directors and others who have a need to make an on-the-spot verification of the truth/accuracy of an applicant's SSN would find this booklet most helpful. It won't tell you if a number is false if the person has selected the proper sequences, but it can eliminate imposters if they are just picking numbers at random. You can write to National Employment Screening Services, 8801 South Yale Avenue, Tulsa, OK 74137.

As predicted in the above-mentioned brochure, the SSN is now being used for everything . . . sometimes with perilous consequences, including fraud, theft, impersonation, etc. Beginning in 1993, newspaper articles were starting to appear challenging the privacy issue relating to your SSN. Even the ACLU jumped on the bandwagon because of the potential for abuse. I won't even hazard a guess as to why it took the media from 1991 to 1994 to report the following precedent-setting event.

At least two articles report the experience of Marc Greidinger, a 29-year-old staff lawyer with the U.S. Court of Appeals for the Fourth Circuit in Richmond, Virginia. He sued the State of Virginia—and won— after it refused to permit him to register to vote unless he provided his SSN. "By using your number, clever crooks can dip into your bank account, take out a credit card in your name, get hold of your government benefits, or browse through your college records or financial investments."

That's why Greidinger refused to supply his SSN when he tried to register to vote. Greidinger says he began to fear for his privacy two years ago [the early 1990's] when he moved to a small town in Virginia and found it nearly impossible to obtain a driver's license, open accounts with local utilities, or even rent a video without encountering demands for his SSN. He explained to the registrar of voters that it had been his practice not to give out his SSN without a good reason, stating, "It can be used to rip me off or violate my privacy."

When he was denied his voting rights, he started investigating the abuses of the SSN and did a few simple tests with the help of a friend. As he suspected, the abuses were widespread. He found out that by dialing an 800 number and punching in the SSN, his friend not only could access his academic files, but obtain information on his student loans, including how much he owed and when he made his last payment. "He even *changed some data* in my file." Until 1992, students' names and SSN's were posted openly on bulletin boards, along with their grades, at Rutgers University.

The ACLU says if the SSN is used as an identifier for recipients of health services, the privacy and security of personal health information will be compromised. In addition, the ACLU states: "There is no way to verify the accuracy of existing numbers or that the number holder is who he or she claims to be." This is confirmed by Phil Gambino, a spokesman for the SSA, who also admitted that the agency had no power to prevent the abuse of the number by private individuals or companies.

There is a small note of encouragement to this story. Greidinger won his lawsuit with the State of Virginia, and in the summer of 1993 a federal appeals court unanimously ruled in his favor, stating with their verdict: "The harm that can be inflicted from the disclosure of a Social Security number to an unscrupulous individual is alarming and potentially financially ruinous." Virginia still collects the SSN as a check against voter fraud, but no longer makes them available to the public, as it did formerly.

In April, 1995, the SSA announced that it was "streamlining" its operation and "downsizing" by eliminating a number of regional offices. Now, I'm all in favor of downsizing bureaucracy, but they had other efficiency measures in mind, as well.

> Officials also said they would seek to move all retirees with bank accounts into a direct deposit program, and may allow banks to issue a single debit card that would add Social Security benefits to other federal payments, such as welfare or food stamps, that are now paid via "smart cards." About half of Social Security's 44 million beneficiaries receive their monthly checks through electronic deposit.

Now they propose to have the bank issue you a debit card to spend your funds (just like the smart cards used for other benefits), attempting to eliminate altogether the need for you to have any cash. Successfully, I might add!

The privacy "seismograph" jolted strongly that April, as other parts of the SSA's plans were revealed. To help states catch illegal immigrants, fugitives, and dead-beat dads (or moms), "the federal government will soon offer to scour motor vehicle records for drivers with phony Social Security numbers."

Criminals and others seeking to establish new identities frequently use false SSN's to get a driver's license or other form of approved identification. Of course, the illegal alien seeking an SSN to obtain employment is of great concern to many states. However, in addition to illegally gained employment, the subsequent phony documents then can be used to obtain fraudulent welfare, health care, and other public benefits. The SSA was scheduled to begin May 8, 1995, comparing its records with motor vehicle records from states that request the service, looking for fake numbers. Then they will notify the states who will have the task of catching the violators.

Critics point out the potential hazards to privacy, since states could give the lists to police or other agencies, or sell them to credit bureaus (selling motor vehicle information to insurance companies and other businesses seems to be a common practice for virtually all states, according to the *Privacy Journal*). Phil Gambino (mentioned in the last article) said the SSA shares those concerns, but doesn't plan to let that slow them down, since Congress authorized the states to collect SSN's in the mid-1980's. The data collected and maintained by the SSA is highly coveted by collection agencies and private investigators.

One of the best reasons to decry this action is that it violates the initial promise made by the SSA. Hendricks, editor and publisher of the *Privacy Times* said the decision to screen state records "betrays the notion that the Social Security number is not supposed to be used for identification." He also criticized the SSA for burying the announcement of its plan in the *Federal Register.*

Is there any way at all to avoid having an SSN? The answer is, "Yes, but it's not easy." And this in no way relieves you of the obligation to pay your FICA (social security taxes). You will have to have an identification number of some kind in place of it, in order to file your tax returns. Many people also are objecting to the IRS requirement that their children must have an SSN by the age of one in order to claim them as exemptions on their tax returns. A superb three-part article entitled "Social Security Numbers and Minor Children" was written by Daniel J. Pilla, tax editor for *Monetary & Economic Review.* It appeared in their November and December, 1993, and January, 1994, editions. I am including some important excerpts below, but if you are affected in any way by this subject, I strongly advise you to write or call them and request these back issues: *Monetary & Economic Review,* 3500 JFK Parkway, Fort Collins, CO 80525, phone 1-800-325-0919.

What Does the Law Really Say?

The Tax Reform Act of 1986 was the most sweeping tax legislation in history. The act modified or added more than 2,700 provisions of the tax code and more than 2,000 new forms and procedures. Among them was a requirement that minor children have an "identifying number" if they are to be claimed on their parents' tax return. The common belief is such number must be a social security number.

When the law passed, the requirement was for a number attached if the child reached the age of five years during the year he was claimed as an exemption. Subsequently, the threshold dropped. In 1988, it was reduced to two years. Current law demands a number if the child has reached "the age of one year before the close of (the) taxable year." See Code section 6109(e). This trend indicates the requirement may soon be mandated "at birth."

. . .Without a particular number assigned to each citizen (who then uses it in all areas of his life), the government's ability to electronically spy on that person is virtually nonexistent. An Orwellian-style government is upon us and the SSN is at the apex of that system.

Social Security Numbers and Religious Objectors

Objections to obtaining and using SSNs, especially for minor children, go well beyond the privacy issue. For many, the desire to avoid use of such a number is a matter of religious principle.

. . . many conservative Christian leaders and church members . . . are wary of the number's conspicuous tie to *all financial transactions* and the trend toward eliminating cash or replacing it with traceable currency. . . . tens of thousands of conservative Christians believe in their hearts the SSN poses a serious threat to their spiritual security.

Social Security Numbers and the Tax Law

The IRS' public declarations regarding the SSN leave most with the impression there is no alternative but to apply for a number. Not surprisingly, IRS' statements make no mention of any right to avoid using or obtaining a number on religious grounds. True to form, misinformation and disinformation circulate regarding the matter. . . .

. . . to avoid confusion, I wish to distinguish between payment of the social security *tax* and participation in a retirement program which offers a *package of benefits.* When I say participation is not mandatory, I refer to the latter situation. . . . Whether you participate in the benefits program or not, the social security tax remains non-optional.

. . . the regulation makes it plain that a number is to be assigned to a newborn *only* "where a parent has requested" such assignment.

. . . By letter dated May 24, 1988, Senator Lloyd Bentsen responded by saying, "There is no law requiring every citizen of the United States to obtain a social security number. There are a limited number of circumstances in which an individual would be able to meet his or her legal obligations without obtaining one."

. . . It is true that for most people, a TIN, or taxpayer identification number, is also their social security number. However, for those religiously opposed to the use of an SSN or participation in the social security retirement benefits program, no SSN is

required. [In these cases, the IRS will issue the necessary TIN.]
. . . there are alternatives to an SSN which, in my opinion, allow one to meet his tax obligations without infringing his religious liberty.

The Penalty for Failure to Provide a TIN

Despite the clear language of the law, the IRS continues to insist all children *must* have a social security number to be claimed as dependents. In fact, the IRS has been generous in administering the penalty for failure to supply a number.

Code section 6723 provides a penalty of $50 for failure to supply the TIN of any dependent when claimed as an exemption on the return.

. . . it can be said there are two elements which must exist in order to cancel a penalty for failure to provide a TIN. First, the citizen must show the existence of "significant mitigating factors" which led to the failure. Next, he must show he acted in a responsible manner with regard to his legal obligation.

Surely a person's deep-seated, sincerely held religious beliefs are a significant mitigating factor. This is particularly true when you consider Congress *expressly stated* it never intended to force those with religious objections to apply for a number or to use one. Moreover, an entire body of federal court rulings has supported the proposition that one religiously opposed to the use of a number cannot be forced by government to do so [at least for now]. We study some major cases below. The conclusion is, when you are a bona fide religious objector, that fact constitutes mitigating circumstances sufficient to eliminate the penalty.

Given this fact, we explore alternatives to the SSN which allow the IRS to meet its needs, while at the same time, allow one the continued enjoyment of his sacred First Amendment rights.

Alternatives to the SSN

The compelling state interest asserted by the IRS is the need to combat "exemption fraud." The IRS claims millions of dependent exemptions are falsified each year. Without the means of a "universal identifier" assigned to each person, the IRS believes it is without the capacity to abate the alleged fraud.

The question now is, how do we preserve religious objections while allowing the IRS to further its interest in combating exemption fraud? I believe there are two very specific methods of accomplishing this. . . . (1) The Internal Revenue Service Number, and (2) Affidavit Proving the Dependent Exemption.

Congress expressly stated those opposed to the number on religious grounds *could continue* to use alternative means of providing a taxpayer identification number (TIN) to the IRS. Specifically, the committee explained the IRS is to continue its practice of assigning TINs to religious objectors.

For years, the IRS has been quietly assigning TINs to those religiously opposed to SSNs. . . . It is referred to as an Internal Revenue Service Number, or IRSN. It is not and cannot be used by the Social Security Administration for benefits purposes!

". . .The identifying numbers issued by the IRS are similar in appearance to social security numbers, but begin with the number 9 (9xx-xx-xxxx)."

The ruling concludes by saying such numbers may be used "for any federal tax-related purpose for which an identification number is required."

You may be asking how the IRSN is, in practical effect, any different from the SSN issued by the SSA. The answer is simple . . . . the IRSN does not operate to entitle one to benefits under the social security program.

Affidavit Proving the Dependent Exemption

The IRSN serves well for those adults required to file an annual tax return, but who are opposed to using an SSN. The question remains, however, why brand a young child with a number, regardless of its nature or origin, if that child earns no income or otherwise has no independent obligation to file returns? That answer for some may well be that *no* number of any kind is appropriate. The next question is whether minor children can be claimed on an income tax return, even without an IRSN. I believe the answer is yes. . . .The issue, then, is not one of a number *per se*. The issue is whether you can prove the children exist and that they are not claimed on any other tax return.

The article continues in great detail (including a sample form you can adapt for your use) about how to accomplish this, then goes on to instruct you in the recovery of previously lost exemptions, without compromising your sincerely held religious convictions. Pilla concludes:

. . .As long as government adheres to the principles of religious liberty expressed in the plain language of the First Amendment, no Christian can be required to surrender his beliefs regarding social security numbers.

And therein lies the rub. . .it's really a matter of how much longer we can rely upon the government to support our freedoms under the First Amendment. The very same issue carries a short article with the headline, "It's Coming," which would indicate it won't be much longer. If they can't get permission to number our children one way, they already are in hot pursuit of another!

Not even waiting for the Clinton Health Care Plan to pass, his allies in Congress are already proposing laws to compel parents to submit their families to "SmartCarding" or risk losing their children. The Childhood Immunization Bill S-732, introduced by Senator Ted Kennedy (D-MA), calls for a national computerized registry of all children under six, together with at least one parent. The Senator's legislation mandates children to be "SmartCarded" at birth and inoculated later. Kennedy's Chief Legislative Aide, Keith Powell, said the card system "will create a national registry with the capacity to do tracking and surveillance of all U.S. children."

Just to bring us back into focus, let us remember that the subject of this chapter is computerizing people. And none are more at the mercy of the Big Brother computers than those receiving some kind of welfare or government benefits.

Many states now are converted totally to EBT (Electronic Benefits Transfer), and the federal government has established the Federal Electronic Benefits Transfer Task Force to incorporate this new technology into federal programs. This isn't like the automatic deposit of your social security check into your bank account (although that certainly qualifies as an EBT transfer). This is like establishing an account for you into which the designated agency (welfare, food stamps, etc.) will place the same amount you've been receiving, then they will furnish you a card to use in an ATM-style machine. Approved purchases will be deducted from your account, via your card, until the account is depleted . . . then more will appear there automatically at the next appointed time. Below is a sample of the proposed federal EBT card.

The computer trail will let them know what you buy, where you buy, and when you buy. And with enough of that information on file, the computer even will be able to figure out *why* you buy. Now, why would they need to know all that? To catch the cheaters, of course. It goes without saying that to catch the bad guys, the good guys have to surrender some more of their privacy.

In the January, 1994, issue of *Government Technology,* the following recommendation appeared, supposedly to improve federal systems and management:

Launch Electronic Benefits Transfer

Build a consortium with agencies experienced in EBT, sharing insight and reducing the costs of the technology. The logical progression from credit cards to smart cards also involves integrated electronic revenue collection. Use tools consistent with your mission to efficiently disburse benefits; direct deposit, for example, will suffice where smart cards have yet to tread.

Caveat: Security issues, as always, are paramount concerns. The financial community, following years of actual and attempted computer crime, is all too aware of this fact. Government efforts carry the additional burden of Privacy Act requirements and watchful privacy advocates. Careful attention to these two EBT aspects up front will deter abuses in years to come.

An article by Sheila Sanchez appeared June 13, 1995, in *The Daily Herald,* which read, in part:

Utah County welfare recipients will begin receiving cash grants and food stamps with a new electronic card beginning Oct. 1.

That means more than 5,000 welfare clients in Provo, American Fork, and Payson will no longer receive an Aid to Families with Dependent Children check or food stamp coupons in the mail. The amount of their cash grants and food-stamp benefits will not be reduced or changed.

The Utah Department of Human Services and the Office of Family Support have awarded Zions First National Bank a contract to operate the Utah Horizon Electronic Benefits Transfer program.

Their system will operate the food assistance program, AFDC program, general assistance program, and child support enforcement program.

The system will allow welfare recipients to withdraw money from a Zions Bank Reddi-Access Automatic Teller Machine. Food stamp benefits will be accessed through point-of-sale terminals at retail outlets.

With the great number of people who receive at least some form of benefit from one or more agencies, you can see that Big Brother has us in his system, whether or not we like it.

Even if you don't receive welfare or food stamps, most companies offer you automatic deposit of your payroll check through your choice of banks, and the funds just show up one day in the bank's computers under your account number (if nothing goes wrong—for which there is no guarantee!). Once the funds are in your account, if you still do things the old fashioned way, you sit down and write out the checks to pay your bills and seldom see any cash. If you are "state-of-the-art," you just transfer the funds around from your home computer or laptop to the designated recipients; and if you are even more modern (and trusting), you just let the bank tap your account directly for payment of your mortgage, phone bill, utilities, etc., etc.

When you go shopping you just whip out your bank debit card (unless the computer says your account is depleted, then you whip out your credit card), pass it through the point-of-sale machine at the checkout counter, and go your merry way without ever having seen any actual cash, unless you happened to request some with your purchase—the stores are now serving as surrogate banks to dispense cash on request.

Getting Us All in a Big Database . . . Preferably Only One

Currently, the major databases are maintained by the credit bureaus, which are able to accumulate an amazing amount of sensitive information on people, however, law enforcement is now networking in an effort to close the loop, and insurance/medical agencies won't be left behind. Our total electronic bondage is almost complete!

Here is another of those "recommendations for improvement" that appeared in *Government Technology*, referenced above:

Build a National Law-Enforcement/Public Safety Network

Security and privacy will be the key issues. Integrate and standardize all available law-enforcement networks under the aegis of the Justice Department. Use existing telecommunications technologies to distribute and exchange information relevant to law-enforcement professionals at all levels. Provide utility to public safety officials through less strenuous means [interpret that to mean "no warrant necessary"]; electronic bulletin boards and Internet connections are used today.

Caveat: For obvious reasons, this effort should represent the pinnacle of secure communications. [Talk about your "double-speak"! In just the previous sentence they were advising "less strenuous" access.]

Build an Information Infrastructure

Eliminate redundancy in information services and facilities

[interpret that as "put it all in one place"]. Adhere to applicable standards and emphasize interoperability. Agencies can capitalize on this trend by actively pursuing strategic information systems objectives in concert with other agencies.

Like I said, as soon as they can have their way, Big Brother will have it all in one big computer! Another article in the same issue says, "They will have full access to information databases—including fingerprint, mug shot, vehicle location, photo, and document systems—from an MDT or laptop computer. . . . this hasn't been integrated into one commercial system yet, *but it will be* [emphasis added]."

Remembering our subject matter in this chapter, computerizing people, you will find the next article of interest. The title is "Computer Heaven or Techno-Hell?"

Depending upon your perspective, the future of state [California] service could be computer heaven or techno-hell.

In its exalted ideal, the system the state has in mind would *make you part of an information team,* interconnected by voice and electronic mail, optical document processing, and video conferencing, all linked to vast mines of instantly accessible data on all phases of state operations.

HUMAN BIO-CHIP

At its most demonic, the technology can become a sort of Orwellian "big brother" monitoring your every move, and making you no more than a human bio-chip in a data network over which you have no control [emphasis added].

I vote for "techno-hell!" And I'm nearly ready to rest my case.

By the time you've read this far, and cover the material at the close of the book in the section I call the "Bottom Line," you will be familiar with the extent to which credit agencies will go to obtain information— any and all information—about you, even if it has absolutely nothing to do with you seeking to obtain credit somewhere. Michael Precker of the *Dallas Morning News* wrote an article that ran in the *San Diego Union-Tribune* on November 7, 1994, concerning the inaccuracies in these reports, the damage that can do, and the nearly impossible task of getting errors corrected:

Big Brother has a file on you

Need a loan? Seeking a job? It may be up to a credit agency. To hear critics and cynics tell it, Big Brother lives a little north of Dallas, right alongside the North Central Expressway, just one exit past Plano.

Amid security and technology befitting the Pentagon, the super-computers of TRW hold 4 trillion bits of information.

Every day, stacks of computer tapes arrive from across the country from stores, financial institutions, and companies that scour public records. They are fed into the system, updating files on 180 million Americans—how they spend their money, and how much they owe.

And more than 2 million times a day, businesses throughout the country tap into the network to check on someone's credit history. . . .TRW's national database, which was consolidated in Allen, Texas, a year ago, usually shoots an answer back down the electronic superhighway in a couple of seconds.

But Precker asks, "Is it right?" Obviously, the answer depends upon whom you ask. TRW, Equifax, and Trans Union (the three largest nationally) report an exceedingly low error factor, from under 1% to less than 2%. However, consumer advocate groups' reactions to those figures range anywhere from "skepticism to contempt." Edmund Mierzwinski, consumer program director for the U.S. Public Interest Research Group, says: "Based on what I've seen, up to one out of three reports has mistakes." Based on my calculation, that would be about 33%.

Three years ago, *Consumer Reports* magazine randomly surveyed 161 credit reports and found that almost half contained errors. Other publications and critics of credit bureaus toss around figures ranging from 20 percent to 80 percent.

Whatever the percentage, says consumer advocate Benjamin Dover, "the problem is that we're all *guilty until proven innocent.* The American consumer doesn't know how powerful those companies are and how much they influence our quality of life [emphasis added]."

The May, 1992, issue of *SPOTLIGHT,* featured an article by Warren Hough and Martin Mann entitled, "Americans 'Computerized' by FEMA."

Fort Meade, Maryland, is the government's most tightly guarded installation (it houses, among others, the secret National Security Agency). In an unmarked, windowless office building on the grounds of Fort Meade, hundreds of thousands of American citizens are being "computerized" by technicians on the payroll of the Federal Emergency Management Agency (FEMA).

"Administratively, this place is the equivalent of an unlisted telephone," explained a former senior official of FEMA, who agreed to an interview on condition that his identity be protected. "It has no official existence. There is no listing for it, no traceable designation. But it's there, idling quietly, like a doomsday bomb waiting for its moment in history."

The task of FEMA's secret data control annex at Fort Meade is to develop so-called CAPs—the term stands for "crisis action programs"—to be implemented in national emergencies. The term was originally used to denote disaster relief plans at the Federal Preparedness Agency, once a department of the General Services Administration, now merged into FEMA.

But the computerized action plans instrumented at Fort Meade have nothing to do with aiding victims of hurricanes or other natural disasters. They are blueprints for taking over the U.S. government and converting it into a command system under the "emergency management" of federal bureaucrats.

Privately, congressional investigators, intelligence analysts and veteran Washington newsmen familiar with the inner machinery of the vast federal bureaucracy have long expressed concern and anxiety about FEMA. An "umbrella administration" born in 1978 when President Jimmy Carter combined the disaster and emergency response functions of nearly a dozen scattered federal outposts into a single agency, FEMA has always been known as an "activist" and secretive fraternity.

Under Louis Giuffrida, appointed FEMA director by President Ronald Reagan in 1981, the agency developed a top-secret project for arresting tens of thousands of "suspect aliens" along with troublesome critics and dissenters whom the White House found annoying enough to be labeled "potentially subversive."

Tagged Operation Rex 84, these un-Constitutional plans were first discovered and revealed by this populist newspaper in a series of exclusive investigative reports in the April 23 and May 14, 1984 issues.

But although The SPOTLIGHT's exposé wrecked FEMA's plans for setting up mass "emergency detention centers"—and cost Giuffrida his post as director—secret preparations for "[ensuring] the continuity of the federal government" in ill-defined "emergencies" remained the major concern of FEMA's senior officials.

"Those words, enunciated by President Gerald Ford in Executive Order 11921, were understood by FEMA to mean that one day they would be in charge of the country," explained Dr. Henry Kliemann, a political scientist at Boston University. "As these bureaucrats saw it, FEMA's real mission was to wait, prepare, and then take over when some 'situation' seemed serious enough to turn the United States into a police state."

To illustrate FEMA's conspiratorial core, knowledgeable Washington intelligence sources cited the instance of the 1989 visit by President George Bush to Cartagena, Colombia, to attend a so-called regional drug summit with three Latin American presidents.

"There were rumors of a terrorist threat against Bush by Colombian drug hit squads," recounted Monroe H. Brown, a former federal security officer with long years of service in Miami. "Teams of Secret Service, FBI, and CIA agents were mobilized to find out how serious the threat was, while back in Washington FEMA went to work on an emergency program in case the presidential plane was hit by a Stinger missile somewhere over Colombia."

FEMA's emergency measures included preparations to round up more than 10,000 Americans "red-lined" in the agency's computers as "activists, supporters, or sympathizers of terrorism in the United States," explained Brown.

In August 1990, after Iraq invaded Kuwait, FEMA got ready to deal with "terrorist emergencies" in the United States by churning up the same old discredited computer compilation of "terrorist supporters and sympathizers," adding thousands of names to it and alerting the U.S. Army to set up detention camps to hold these innocent victims of its bureaucratic brutality.

National Security Agency: 10 Acres of the Most Powerful Computers on Earth

The NSA possesses one of the largest, most sophisticated computer systems in the world, with an unimaginably comprehensive database. Whereas most organizations measure their computers in square feet, NSA's are measured in *acres*—about 10 acres! In 1983, NSA established global links, networking 52 separate databases under the codename PLATFORM. Today, FEMA and all other government agencies (and possibly others) can tap into this Big Brother system, all located in the subterranean area beneath their headquarters facility in Ft. Meade, MD.

It's always for our own good, isn't it? Now they are "digitizing" our kids, the next logical step before implanting that chip behind the ear that Dr. England suggested earlier in this chapter. The April, 1994, issue of *Government Technology,* carried an article entitled "KIDS Protects Children." The article begins with the scenario of a parent's worst nightmare . . . they blinked for just a second and their child disappeared, inciting everyone to the justifiable question, "What can we do to protect our kids?"

Naturally, the answer is to enroll your kid in the "system"—digitized information technology.

   . . .This is the rationale behind the Kid Identification Digital Systems (KIDS).
   After the digital images are taken, each is combined with data listing height, weight, hair color, special medical alerts, and other pertinent information.

Sounds kind of like what they want to put on your national I.D. smart card, doesn't it? Only it's on children. Officials believe that "school districts can integrate KIDS into the annual school picture-taking sessions...during the photographer's usual routine...." That means that the picture and information will be updated on an annual basis. But what are they going to do with this information once the child is grown and no longer in school? Dump it? Hit the delete/erase button? Not a chance!

> ...This could also be used to quickly identify criminals—a police officer would instantly have a mug shot so when he or she goes to a strange house they know who they're looking for...."I can see a real value in having this type of information available," said [police] Captain Rick Sayre...."It's on the cutting edge of how we get and use information to solve crimes...."

Smile, kid! You're about to get your first mug shot!

CONCLUSION

The evidence leads us irrefutably to the purposes for which they are accumulating all this data on us...*surveillance and control.* The methods to carry it out will be biometrics (see chapter 13), identification techniques (smart cards, digital, *et al,* see chapter 14), and eventually biochip/RFID technology (already in use in bracelets for Cuban refugees and proposed for use in the military [to replace dog tags], prisoners, the elderly, runaway teens, abducted children, etc.—see chapter 15).

In case you are one of the few who trust the government agencies and credit bureaus to "get it right, keep it right, and not abuse the privilege," don't get too comfortable, because now the experts are writing "do-it-yourself" books on how *anyone* can access this information and find out virtually anything they want to know about nearly anyone...and that includes *you!*

Dennis King has written just such a book—and very well, I might add. It is well organized and includes enough detail to allow the reader to find out much information on their own, and tells them how and where to get help if they reach the end of their own resources. The title is *Get the Facts on Anyone: How you can use public sources to check the background of any person or organization,* 224 pp., Prentice Hall, NY. ISBN 0-671-86470-X.

I think it's safe to say that this author and I do not agree philosophically, e.g. his Appendix A, Investigating Cults and Political Extremist Organizations. But he certainly knows how to do the job.

Now let's move on to a brief study on how bar codes work.

CHAPTER EIGHT

Barcodes

Because of its technical nature, this easily could become one of those "You're telling me more than I want to know!" chapters. I'll try not to bore you, but it is an important part of the control and surveillance going on globally, and I must give the details so you will recognize what it is when you look at some of the variations of the standard barcode.

I think by now you are convinced that the time is rapidly approaching when *everything* on this planet will be marked, controlled, tracked, or monitored. If it *moves,* it will have a transponder (biochip/RFID— see chapter 15); if it doesn't move, it will have a UPC number in the form of a barcode of some variety. (UPC stands for Universal Product Code.)

You will laugh at the following report, which is fine because it is funny, but it just illustrates how far barcodes have progressed, and how commonplace they have become. Cathy Smith of Houston, Texas, submitted these two paragraphs, which were printed by *Reader's Digest* in their August, 1994, edition, "Life in These United States" section.

> I take my husband's shirts to a laundry that has recently instituted a new identification system. Inside the collar of each shirt, they place labels bearing a bar code and the customer's name. Since I started our account, the words "Smith, Cathy" have appeared on my husband's collars.
>
> Because he did not want a woman's name on his shirts, he made a special trip to the cleaners to have the account changed to Marshall Smith. Unfortunately, only the first six letters of each name are used. Now his collars read: "Smith, Marsha."

Such limitations are quickly disappearing with the newer technology, and I'm sure that before long "Marsha" will once again be "Marshall."

The Global 666 Barcode

In and of itself, there is nothing inherently evil about a barcode— it is just another, more efficient way of keeping track of your inventory and movement of freight, laundry, etc.—chores formerly accomplished with painstaking manual labor. The problem lies in placing this technology at the disposal of a New World Order-minded government(s) who not only wants to meddle in our affairs. . .they want to control them (and us!).

The barcode is simply a mathematically arranged symbol of vertical lines. It is a parallel arrangement of varying width BARS and SPACES. The structural arrangement or spacing of these lines, relative to a given set of parameters, can be made to represent a product's identification number. The Universal Product Code (UPC), better known simply as "barcode," has been put to this use since 1973, having been adopted by the retail industry in 1972. The UPC barcode is considered to be the "mother" of all microchip transponder technology.

The code is not really as complicated as it may first seem. A typical UPC *Version A* barcode symbol contains 30 black vertical lines (called "bars"). A *pair* of these lines equals only *one digit* or number. In other words, this coding system *requires two lines to equal one number.*

Details of the UPC Version A Code Construction

As depicted herein, the actual UPC code is a 10-digit code: the first five digits represent the manufacturer of the labeled item, and the next five digits are a unique product identifier code. This 10-digit code is then preceded with a "number system digit" and followed by a "transpositional check digit" (TCD), to verify if any of the preceding 11 digits have been transposed.

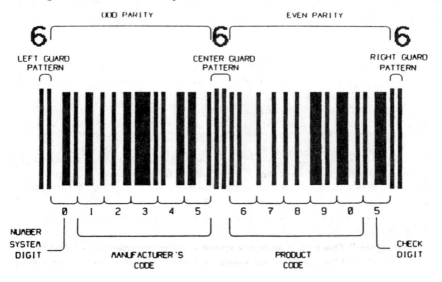

On each side and in the center of this series of carefully spaced lines are three pairs of longer lines that extend slightly below the others. These longer pairs of lines are special—they are called "guard bars."

Guard bars provide reference points for store computer scanners (barcode reading machines) by segregating the left half of the code lines from the right half. This is needed because the left lines have a different message on them than the right lines and must, therefore, be read by the scanner differently. The center pair of guard bars in the UPC barcode are used to both divide the code in half and tell the scanner/computer what it needs to know in order to readjust its program to interpret the remaining half of the code. Note again the diagram—the left half represents the manufacturer's code and the right half represents the product code. The following chart defines the numerical values:

UPC VERSION A NUMBER SYSTEMS ASSIGNMENTS

Number System Digit	Application
0	92,000 manufacturer identification numbers 8,000 locally assigned numbers
1	Reserved
2	Random weight consumer packages
3	Drug products
4	In-store marking without format
5	UPC coupons
6	100,000 manufacturer identification numbers
7	100,000 manufacturer identification numbers
8	Reserved
9	Reserved

In summation, a typical UPC *Version A* barcode symbol consists of two halves, representing a total of 12 numeric digits. These two six-digit halves are surrounded by left, center, and right guard bar patterns.

Together, the black and white lines produce series of electronic "dits" and "dahs," similar to the old Morse code telegraph key "dots and dashes." The scanner reads these electronic messages as a series of "zeros" and "ones." These zeros and ones represent what are called *binary numbers,* in computer language.

Binary numbers are a "machine language" which is the basic internal language of modern computers. In other words, this is how the computer thinks and gives itself orders. All computers operate on the basis of this two-digit mathematical binary system.

The barcode industry informs us that the UPC system is a binary system. Can we believe that? Is the UPC code, indeed, a true binary configuration as the barcode industry suggests? No, not really. As you can see, the entire system is very deceptively designed around an infamous numerical configuration, Biblically known as **666**, the **mark** of the Antichrist or devil (Revelation 13:16-18).

Now, please do not jump to hasty conclusions—it is not likely that the barcode will be the actual technology used to *mark* a person, but in all likelihood, it is the forerunner of that technology.

The 666 Barcode Configuration

Time and space do not permit a thorough examination and discussion of this "666" UPC configuration. However, somehow it was surreptitiously designed around this satanic number described in the Bible. And these "coincidences" just keep adding up. It's kind of like circumstantial evidence . . . if you collect enough of it, you can convict someone. Doesn't it seem just a little strange that out of over 121 million billions of possible mathematical combinations of code numbers, someone would have just randomly arrived at this very unique, evil numerical configuration? I don't believe this is something consciously planned by the developers of barcode technology; I'm convinced that the spiritual powers have contrived with the circumstances to make it work out that way. I think we can rule out coincidence. Fulfillment of Biblical prophecy? Possibly. What do you think?

Before we get into some of the more technical aspects of the many variations of barcodes, let's review this coding system a final time to ensure clarity. The code's designers inform us in their books that the code was designed as a "coding system," as well as "a symbology." They tell us that the UPC is a fixed-length, numeric, continuous symbology design employing four element widths. In addition, they tell us that there are three different versions of the UPC symbol: (1) Version A—encodes 12 digits (6+6); (2) Version E—encodes 6 digits; (3) Version D—encodes various lengths of digits, but is seldom used.

Of these three codes, however, the primary one in use today in the retail industry is Version A. As we have explained above, it was designed and configured primarily around the satanic number 666, no matter how inadvertently it may have occurred.

The actual data in this coding system is encoded as two bars and two spaces within seven modules. The UPC Version A system is also called a "7,2" code that has 20 unique patterns.

I am not going to spend much more time on this subject in this book, as having more than a superficial knowledge of barcodes is really not necessary in our study here, since these applications do not specifically relate to "buying or selling" as indicated in Revelation. However, let me briefly familiarize you with the existence of a few other barcode systems currently in use globally, as they indirectly are a part of the comprehensive global system that will track, trace, monitor, and electronically control and enslave all of us by means of computers (remember, don't personify a computer as evil—it is just a machine/tool, no more or less evil than the individual operating it). Such encoding systems include but are not limited to the following:

EAN System—European Article Number System (similar to the UPC)

Interleaved "2 of 5" Code	The "Code 93" Code
The Codabar Code	The "Code 49" Code
The "Code 39" Code	The "Code 16K" Code
The "Code 128" Code	

Most present-day general applications make use of the UPC, EAN, Code 39, Codabar, Interleaved 2 of 5, Code 128, Code 93, Code 49, and Code 16K barcode systems. They are the established industry standards. However, several additional symbologies exist and need to be mentioned for the sake of completeness in this overview of global barcoding systems. I'm sure you all will recognize the familiar postal barcode shown here which is now being printed across the bottom of your mail.

The "2 of 5" Code	The Vericode Code
The "Code 11" Code	The Data Code
The Postnet/Postal Code	The UPS Code
The Codablock Code	The PDF-417 Code
The USD-5 Code	

2-D Barcodes

I could not in good conscience close this chapter without including one of the latest innovations in barcode technology. It is referred to as 2-D technology (and with the use of holograms, etc., 3-D barcodes currently are in development). Once you switch to 2-D barcodes, you have greatly expanded your capacity to retain information. In an April, 1995, edition of *Traffic Management* magazine, an article titled "2-D or not 2-D?" carried a subtitle: "2-D bar codes could revolutionize distribution and warehousing, but is now the time to jump on the bandwagon?" Their article began:

> Imagine fitting all the information found in a shipping document into a space the size of a postage stamp. Two-dimensional or "2-D" bar codes promise to do just that.
>
> Unlike conventional linear bar codes—the familiar black and white stripes found on grocery-store packages—which essentially string data along a horizontal axis, 2-D codes use both the vertical and the horizontal axes to encode data, hence the name two-dimensional. As a result, hundreds of characters can fit into the space occupied by 30 characters on a linear bar code.

Two-dimensional barcodes were featured in the August, 1994, edition of *Automatic I.D. News,* in the sections "Case Study of the Month" and "Industry Focus."

Since 2-D barcodes bring this technology much closer to home from an I.D. standpoint (of both objects, i.e. cars and buildings, and people, i.e. firefighters in this article), I briefly have quoted portions from both articles below.

In the Line of Fire: 2-D bar codes track whose [sic] battling fires and provide rescue workers with firefighter's medical history. State accountability OSHA requirements met with 2-D coded Velcro ID tags; eventually, firemen will know a building's layout, gas main shut-offs, and contents by scanning a 2-D code.

Every fire department at one time or another has wrestled with the problem of accounting for its personnel on the fireground. This includes the problem of *having an accurate and readily accessible medical history for any personnel* that are injured and need to be transported to a hospital. And every firefighter, at some time in his/her career, has said, "I sure wish we knew what was in that building BEFORE we arrived on scene and went in." These are the same problems that the Grand Traverse Fire Department has been facing, until now [emphasis added].

Automotive industry recommends 2-D standards

One of the more amazing technical innovations in Auto. ID to evolve during the latter 1980s and early 1990s is the creation of a whole new generation of high-tech bar codes called two-dimensional bar codes or 2-D symbols. 2-D symbols are designed to hold enough information within the symbol itself to be a small database.

These very unfamiliar-looking bar codes can contain a whole lot more data than a regular bar code. In fact, many 2-D symbols can carry 2,000 characters of data in a single symbol, as compared with a regular or linear bar code capacity of 15 to 22 characters. 2-D symbols can also carry binary data, which can be made to run a computer program or generate photographs and drawings. In addition to carrying a lot of information, 2-D symbols can be made very tiny and shaped in unusual ways.

Probably the most fascinating thing about these symbologies is that, in some cases, you can actually destroy or damage 50% or more of the label and still get 100% of the data contained in the symbol when it is read or scanned! Most 2-D symbol types have "error correction"; that is, there are mathematical formulas embedded in the code that will "reconstruct" any missing portion of the symbol and recreate the missing data.

As you can see this new technology has enormous possibilities. However, the problem occurs when they start applying it to us. Again, let me warn against a premature conclusion that the barcode is the "mark" of the beast, especially in light of the photograph I have included below. Recently, these "Feel like a number?" billboards appeared in the Los Angeles area; we are being conditioned, or de-sensitized, for the time when someone will want to put a mark on our head.

Hopefully by now, you are getting the picture that it is a very sinister plan. In fact, it should be apparent to anyone at this point that very soon nearly everything in the world — both animate and inanimate — will be marked, tagged, coded, numbered, implanted, and identified with some type of ID system that will allow the dictatorial New World Order global government to label, trace, track, monitor, and control everything and everybody on earth! Indeed, the coming New World **Dis**order will be the most evil system the world has ever known.

I have long warned people that RFID biochip implants—and *not* barcodes—will be the technology the New World Order Antichrist will use to mark and control humans globally, but some insist otherwise. Even after all my warnings, there are still Christians who vehemently insist that the barcode is going to be the mark to which we find reference in Revelation 13. Please consider all the facts. There is no doubt that this system is conditioning us for more advanced technologies which, in fact, do have the capability to fulfill the Biblical prophecies of Revelation, but my scholarly research of both the technology and the scriptures has convinced me that the barcode likely *will not* be used for the mark of the Beast.

Now, let's move on to another aspect of this demonic, global system of deception and enslavement. . .tracking our movement via the highway systems.

CHAPTER NINE

Automated Highway Systems

Where to start?!? There is so much happening so fast on this subject that I could write a whole book just on the automating and computerizing of highways and vehicles alone. So what I'm going to do is touch on a few things briefly and I won't even *consider* other modes of transportation. I'm sure you can extrapolate this information and see where all the rest are headed, as well.

In the editorial column of the June, 1994, issue of *Roads & Bridges* magazine, Tom Kuennen titled his article, "IVHS: The next revolution." This is a publication targeting engineers, contractors, construction companies, city/county/state/federal road departments, and others interested and/or involved in the infrastructure of streets, roads, highways, and bridges across this nation. Kuennen writes:

> There is a revolution in transportation services and consumer products fast coming on us, and America's national, state, and local road systems are its focus and its heart. Those not intimately connected with this revolution have little idea it is almost upon us. And while it will revolutionize the way we use our road system, it ultimately will become a revolution in electronic consumer products.
>
> Welcome to the world of **Intelligent Vehicle/Highway Systems**, or IVHS for short. And while the IVHS "buzz word" has been bandied about by many people in this industry, those not in the know have only the barest outlines of what to expect from that "hot button" we call IVHS.
>
> . . .What we learned [at a recent regional forum] was astonishing.
>
> **So what's it all about?** IVHS is a coming, red-hot growth industry of mobile computers, screens, receivers, and transmitters mounted in the nation's trucks, buses, and cars, with supporting infrastructure. **Driven by government subsidies and mandates**, IVHS may become a $200 billion industry. . . .The IVHS

industry as envisioned by the U.S. DOT would encompass

- Travel and traffic management. . .
- Public transportation management...
- Electronic payment. . .
- Commercial vehicle operations. . .
- Emergency management. . .
- Advanced vehicle safety systems, including collision avoidance systems and even automated vehicle operation.

Licking their chops are four high-tech consortia vying to be the successful 1996 finalist selected to provide the *basic nationwide "architecture"* into which these systems will be "plugged." Not all drivers will be able to afford a system with all the "bells and whistles". . . . (Because the U.S. is starting the system from the top down, with a *prescribed national architecture,* it can avoid the problems of Japan and Europe, where a bewildering variety of incompatible intelligent vehicle systems confound drivers.)

But there are unanswered questions, as well. **IVHS will provide a truly Orwellian national system which could monitor and record private citizen movements, as well as that of over-the-road trucks.** Who'd want that? To keep IVHS from becoming an "elitist" system, should subsidies be provided to enable low-income drivers to install systems in their cars? And how will road agencies administer these systems, when many can barely keep their signs repaired and bridges inspected?

. . .look over your shoulder: **IVHS is coming** [emphasis added].

Kuennen hit the nail on the head with his conclusion; this is the infrastructure required to effectively track everything that moves on the nation's highways. Planning is in the advanced stages, and testing is actually going on in a number of areas of the country, with construction of IVHS highways already in progress in some areas. Kuennen touched on many areas involved in the IVHS system, and I will elaborate on a few of them.

When driving across the open country in the midwest or southwest, you may have taken notice of some strange-looking contraptions with a high-tech appearance that seemed remarkably out of context sitting beside the road out in the middle of no where. It is very possible you unknowingly were participating in some of the early testing for the automated highway system, later to be known as IVHS. On a freeway going across Oklahoma, they actually put up a warning sign that all vehicles were going to be scanned a few miles down the road. The sign implied that it was a test for large trucks with RFID transponders. I guess they felt a warning sign was necessary so you could exit and use another road if you didn't want to be scanned. Such evasive options may not be available to you in the future, as IVHS becomes a comprehensive system throughout the nation.

There will be mobile computers, screens, receivers, and transmitters mounted in vehicles, and the other end of that two-way system will be incorporated into the infrastructure of the IVHS. The U.S. DOT (Department of Transportation) envisions many computers or transponders in the same vehicle to serve the many different purposes it has on its agenda. Hughes tracking systems can pick out and access the proper transponder from a car with as many as eight different RFID's in it.

Now, you may ask why a car would need eight chips in it. . .well, to provide all those things the U.S. DOT envisions, namely: travel and traffic management (which includes anything from pre-trip travel plans, accurate radio traffic reports, enroute information, and route guidance assistance to actual control of the traffic itself—rerouting for an accident or limiting access during peak times to enhance traffic flow); public transportation management (busses, *et al*); electronic payment (automatically deducted from your prepaid account for toll roads and bridges, via RFID transponder affixed somewhere on your vehicle—being built in to all new model vehicles beginning in 1997, if they remain on schedule); commercial vehicle operations (to improve management and monitoring of commercial trucks and semis); emergency management (among other things, permits you to send out a police "mayday" call or summon road service/tow truck); advanced vehicle safety systems (this one is the "star trek" system of the bunch—it includes collision avoidance systems and automated vehicle operation devices).

Notice the progression of these systems—help in planning a trip and getting radio traffic reports all the way up to "just jump in the vehicle and trust us to get you there." Not only will Big Brother be able to track your movements and know your whereabouts, he will be able to determine whether or not you get there. Kuennen rightly calls it "a truly Orwellian national system."

Now that you have an idea what's coming, let's see what some others have to say about it and how it will be accomplished.

New "SMART" roads (there's that word again) will be operational in Atlanta, Georgia, for the 1996 Olympics. The April 25, 1994, issue of *ENR* ran an article entitled "SMART HIGHWAYS: Atlanta shows traffic system." The photo caption reads: "Intelligent vehicle highway system will enable Atlanta to manage traffic during the 1996 Olympics. Below are some excerpts from the article, into which I have inserted some author comments in brackets.

[New technologies] will advance Atlanta's state-of-the-art automated traffic management system beyond the original plan. Last week, the Georgia Dept. of Transportation got a preview of the $80-million system it commissioned under a $13.2 million design contract with TRW Corp. [TRW is a member of the Council on Foreign Relations.]

Georgia DOT and officials of the San Diego-based firm claim the system, due to be finished in time for Atlanta's 1996 Olympic Games, will be the most sophisticated intelligent vehicle highway system (IVHS) in the world. It will be the first to integrate highway and arterial street control and will emphasize continuous upgrading as new technologies emerge.

. . . [TRW] demonstrated the integration of information from highway sensors, video cameras, television and radio stations, and phone-in traffic reports to allow a regional overview of traffic conditions.

When operational, Atlanta's system will control traffic lights, send information to digital traffic signs, and allow *centralized monitoring and control from networked command centers*. [Next they call this model a national prototype.]

The prototype will serve as a Transportation Modeling Center for U.S. and overseas officials to experiment with different system configurations, says Frank Herrin director of Transportation and Support Systems for TRW's Avionics and *Surveillance Group*.

A new type of durable roadside sensor that sends information by radio frequency. . .will be used. . . . [That would be RFID transponders, of course.]

Atlanta's system is. . . shared 80%-20% between the Federal Highway Administration and the state. . . .Total spending prior to the Olympics could exceed $120 million [emphasis added].

80%!! Those are your tax dollars at work. . . in Atlanta.

Hughes (Aircraft Company) designs these systems and Texas Instruments produces the devices to make them function (primarily). In 1993, Texas Instruments issued the following press release.

TEXAS INSTRUMENTS EXPANDS RADIO FREQUENCY PRODUCT LINE FOR INTELLIGENT VEHICLE HIGHWAY SYSTEMS (IVHS)

TIRIS™ Transponders Designed for Automatic Vehicle ID (AVI)

A new pocket-sized radio frequency transponder being developed by Texas Instruments will soon help motorists get to work faster, speed freight and commerce, and reduce pollution at congested highway toll booths. These benefits come in part from a Radio Frequency Identification (RFID) system designed by Texas Instruments for Intelligent Vehicle Highway Systems (IVHS) now being constructed across the country.

The new RFID transponder and reader system, part of the company's TIRIS™ (Texas Instruments Registration and Identification System) technology, electronically identifies vehicles at speeds up to 100 miles per hour. Through the identification of vehicles and automatic assessment of toll charges via a computerized collection and enforcement system, traditional toll booths can be eliminated—along with congestion, traffic delays, and miles of idling cars spewing pollution and wasting fuel.

This effort, part of a cooperative agreement with MFS Network Technologies, Inc. of Omaha, a subsidiary of MFS Communications Company, Inc., will create an RFID system exceeding present CALTRANS (California Department of Transportation) standards for all Automatic Vehicle Identification (AVI) systems. The current standard calls for a technology that can process a minimum of 2,500 vehicles per lane per hour, four times faster than any current coin-operated express lane. In this system, overhead readers communicate via high-frequency radio waves with RFID tags placed on the dashboard. Through each tag's unique code, the reader can distinguish vehicles traveling in separate lanes within 30 centimeters of each other and can even identify individual motorcycles riding side-by-side in a single lane.

The CALTRANS standard also calls for what is known as "read/write" capability, which allows data in the tag to be both read and updated. This enables the transponder to carry a prepaid toll balance, from which tolls are directly and automatically deducted.

MFS Network Technologies recently announced the first large-scale implementation of this technology on State Route 91 (SR-91) in California, the first private and all-AVI tollway to be built in America. The new expressway is scheduled to be operational by December 1995. MFS Network Technologies is also proposing the use of this TIRIS-based system for existing toll roads and bridges now being converted to Electronic Toll and Traffic Management systems (ETTM).

Texas Instruments is scheduled to produce a final prototype of its new RFID transponder by the middle of this year, with production volume planned for the second quarter of 1994.

"The TIRIS transponder is at the center of an array of technologies that will increase highway efficiency, unsnarl congested traffic, and offer motorists new information services," explained Kevin Moersch, president of MFS Network Technologies. "RFID tags link car and driver effortlessly with systems that automatically pay tolls and will eventually provide traffic updates and even information on alternate routes."

"Within two years, people will carry these portable RFID transponders the same way they carry car keys," said David Slinger, general manager of the TIRIS North American operation. "TIRIS offers a simple, convenient, and foolproof way to tie into the new smart highway services evolving this decade."

And once again, there's that word! We not only have *smart cards,* now we have *smart highways.*

Well, that's southern California—what do you expect? But what about nice traditional Boston, Massachusetts? Fear not! Technology has not passed them by. *Boston Globe* reporters Wong and Palmer wrote an article with the banner: "Camera would catch state's driving cheats." They examine this automation from the perspective of both the driver and the state. Here are some excerpts:

> In a move that might have surprised even George Orwell, the Legislature's latest solution for dealing with traffic offenders is a high-tech monitoring system that would snap photographs of speeding cars and red-light runners.
>
> Cameras installed beside an intersection would photograph an offending car that trips an electronic sensor embedded in the roadway if the motorist runs a red light.
>
> Roadside cameras hooked up to radar guns would begin shooting pictures when a car is traveling more than 15 m.p.h. over the speed limit. Photographs would be sent along with the traffic tickets to the car owners. The law makes no allowances for someone else driving your car, but no points would be charged against your insurance.
>
> The idea of an automated ticketing system brought mixed reactions from drivers in Boston yesterday.
>
> Some had visions of $50 fines mounting up in their heads, along with images of "1984."
>
> Others said it's about time—the law is the law, and too many people consider red lights merely signals to put the pedal to the metal.
>
> The demonstrations showed that an average of 40 drivers a day in Somerville ignored the traffic signal on Mystic Avenue by the Fellsway, which has been designated the most dangerous intersection in the state. And an average of 80 motorists ran red lights each day at an intersection on Boston Road in Springfield.
>
> The legislation includes provisions intended to safeguard against violation of civil liberties. For example, the photographs could be taken only of the rear of the car and not the front, to

protect the identities of occupants.

Wayne A. Jefferson, who conducts tours of Boston for Beantown Trolley. . . . said, "In Boston, when the red light goes on, three cars go through it."

And I thought they only drove like that in Los Angeles. . . or was it Dallas?

International Highways magazine, November, 1993, carried an article concerning highway control on a global scale. This new "666" highway system tracks and controls vehicle movement electronically via transponders and networked satellites. The article is entitled, "More Traffic but Less Congestion in Future."

> The simplest form of traffic management used to be the traffic cop on the corner, but now electronic, sophisticated lighting systems, computers, and satellites have replaced him.
>
> Radio signals transmitted from roadside beacons to various vehicles, or in fact from vehicle to vehicle, may be the way forward for traffic management.
>
> In many areas of the world cameras are already employed by the law enforcement agencies to counteract speeding vehicles and radio beacons are the next step.
>
> . . . there are many different systems. . . [including] the controversial road pricing systems used in the world's most congested areas, such as Hong Kong and Singapore.
>
> In the UK, an increasing number of motorists are installing the Trafficmaster....
>
> Carminant is another beacon-based system being developed by Renault in France with the assistance of Philips and both the French and Dutch governments. . . . Research is also underway into whether the existing network of cellular radio signals can be used in a traffic management setting. . . .
>
> Work is also in hand to investigate the possibilities of using today's satellite tracking technology to transmit details of the road ahead to drivers via some sort of antennae fitted to the car.

Permit me to introduce you to FasTrak. A slicker presentation folder you've never seen. It includes brochures about the reason for "The Corridors," maps, applications, sample cards, photographs, newspaper articles, operating diagrams, etc. FasTrak is handling operation of The Corridors, including collection of tolls, promotion of use of the new toll "corridors" (including a big sweepstakes), nabbing the toll violators, etc., etc. These are privately constructed highways, the payment for which is to be reimbursed by the tolls. They refer to these three highways as "The Corridors," and their slogan is "Because life's too short to sit in traffic." According to an article in the *Los Angeles Times,* this particular system will be built by Lockheed, using converted defense technology. (Other systems are by Hughes, Texas Instruments, *et al.*)

FasTrak literature says that this is the first toll road in California in 70 years. I'm guessing this is only the beginning. The transponder is affixed to your dashboard with velcro tape. When you are ready to enter the Corridor, you place your smart card into the transponder. The equipment reads your identification as you pass by it, then automatically deducts the amount of your toll from your prepaid account. Just like everything else in this cashless society for which we are headed, you can authorize the FasTrak people to automatically charge your credit card when your account gets down to a certain predetermined level—and you just keep on driving. If you still want to pay in advance by cash or check, the equipment will warn you when you are approaching the "refill" level by flashing a yellow light at you as it deducts your toll from your account when you pass by. Of course, as I reported above, cheaters will be caught. And it won't be cheap. The fines for driving without paying your toll *begin* at $76.00.

In *Government Technology* of September, 1994, an article appeared entitled, "Automated Highway Development Speeding Along." This article doesn't address the electronic collection of tolls or electronic maps to help you avoid a traffic jam. It deals with removing control of the vehicle from you, because you are not as fast or reliable as the automated controls. If you're the kind of passenger who pushes a hole in the floor where the brake pedal ought to be when you have to ride with someone else at the wheel, think how much fun you'll have in a car that thinks it knows how to drive better than you do. This is "cruise control" taken to the max.

> Engineering Research Associates. . . has been awarded a. . . contract to provide engineering support services to the Federal Highway Administration for [its] Advanced Vehicle Control Systems (AVCS) project.
> AVCS is one of five major functional areas of the IVHS program. . . .
> AVCS is designed to combine sensors, computers, and control systems in vehicles and the infrastructure to assist driver perception and reaction to impending danger. It might also provide *automated vehicle controls* such as braking, steering, and accelerating that are *more precise, reliable, and faster than the human driver* [emphasis added].

Well, that's Big Brother if I've ever heard it! As we've already learned, many people are referring to the new technology by that term . . . even those who are not particularly opposed to it, and certainly not opposed on the grounds that I am.

The October 26, 1993, edition of the *New York Post* had a headline reading, "Smile, Drivers! You're on Candid Camera." Reporter Rocco Parascandola began his article with, "Big Brother is here—and dangerous drivers are gonna pay the price." His story continues . . .

> The city yesterday set up the first of 15 cameras that snap photos of vehicles that run red lights at busy intersections.
>
> The Department of Transportation hopes the . . . program will reduce the 277 pedestrian fatalities that occurred on city streets last year.
>
> But the New York Civil Liberties Union said *the technology, if unchecked, can have dangerous implications.*
>
> The first camera was installed at East 86th Street and Third Avenue, where a half-dozen vehicles were seen running a red light during a 20-minute stretch yesterday.
>
> The other 14 cameras—plus five dummies, to keep drivers on their toes—will be installed, in bulletproof boxes, by December.

Of course, this action met with mixed reactions. Those in the habit of running lights weren't very happy for obvious reasons—either they have to slow down and stop running red lights, or they'll be paying heavy fines. On the other hand, they might live long enough to make it worthwhile. The NYCLU was skeptical because it might infringe on someone's rights and cautioned that we must be careful where all this new technology leads. Then there was the nice law-abiding John Q. Citizen who thought it was great because it would make the streets safer for him, from a traffic standpoint—I guess if it's a choice between safer streets and a camera, your privacy won't do you much good if you're dead at an intersection because someone ran the light. However, this may be the first and last time you hear me say this, but I'll have to side with the NYCLU on this one.

As early as 1991, these special highways were already past the "drawing board" stage and incorporated into George Bush's Transportation Bill. *USA Today* (Nov. 26, 1991) reported that, among other things, the Bill included "Smarter highways. The bill would finance high-tech systems to speed traffic flow, like computer-controlled monitoring and information networks."

You might learn to tolerate toll roads, if roads were built in such a manner that you could avoid the usual traffic jams. One of the articles referenced previously mentioned premium rates for peak hours in Hong Kong and Singapore. However, "congestion pricing," as it has come to be called, is a term which will become familiar to all driving commuters, as well as mass transit riders. "Economists have a better way: let drivers pay for the congestion they cause. Under 'congestion pricing,' people who take the expressway at 8 a.m. would be hit with a stiff charge, while those who drive at a less popular hour would pay little or nothing. If the fee is high enough, some might join a car pool or pick another time, speeding up the ride for everyone else —without widening the road. . . . Unless drivers are forced to face the costs of their motoring habits, those traffic jams are only going to get worse."

An article written by James Coates, of the *Chicago Tribune,* was picked up by *The Advocate,* in Baton Rouge, Louisiana, on October 29, 1993. It does an excellent job of reporting the various aspects of the smart highway which we have mentioned above, then carries it even further with an explanation of how the Global Positioning System (GPS) can affect our highway systems. I will address that in the next chapter.

Lawrence Yermack, Chief Financial Officer for New York's Triborough Bridge and Tunnel Authority, who has been involved in efforts to install electronic toll collection equipment on all of the region's toll roads and bridges, told reporter Guy T. Baehr, Newark, New Jersey's *The Sunday Star-Ledger* (March 13, 1994), that much of the technology was developed by large defense contractors for use by the Pentagon, and that part of the reason for the push to use it in the civilian transportation field is that the companies are seeking new markets now that the Cold War is over.

"Four major defense contractors—Westinghouse Electric, Hughes Aircraft, IBM, and Rockwell International—are in the midst of designing competing national IVHS systems for the Federal Highway Administration, with one system to be picked for the nation sometime in 1996, said Michael Schagrin, a systems engineer with the FHWA."

Here are a few excerpts from an article in *The New York Times* (May 3, 1995), written by Simson Garfinkel, entitled: "The Road Watches You."

> . . .these smart roads could lead to an Orwellian surveillance state if we aren't careful.
>
> . . .there is a dark side to this plan, a privacy problem that its boosters are trying to pave over. It offers unprecedented opportunities to monitor the movements of drivers. It would create a bank of personal information that the Government and private industry might have difficulty resisting.
>
> This data could also be sold illegally by insiders. . . .

> . . . Americans have always loved the freedom that their cars give them. Could that too become a thing of the past?

Vic Sussman wrote a very incisive article for the October 2, 1995, edition of the *U.S. News & World Report* magazine. He called it, "The Road Worriers: Can electronic tolls be a tool for Big Brother?" I'm going to close this chapter by quoting some of the very astute observations of Mr. Sussman.

> . . . The governors of Connecticut, Delaware, Maine, Maryland, Massachusetts, New Hampshire, New Jersey, New York, Pennsylvania, Rhode Island, and Vermont agreed this month to work toward setting up a multistate system of using ETC—electronic toll collection.
>
> . . . But privacy advocates say ETC could turn highways into massive surveillance systems.
>
> . . . The crucial issue, says Phil Agre, communications professor at the University of California at San Diego, "is whether the systems capture individually identifiable information"—that is, information that might identify drivers. Besides raking in tolls, transportation departments also can suck up tons of personal information about a traveler, including driver's license data, license plate number, destination, highway speed, vehicle identification, and time of day of travel.
>
> **Anonymous?** Who controls this information? Will it be sold or merged into other databases available to insurance companies, credit bureaus, marketers, and law-enforcement agencies? *The opportunities for mischief are enormous. . . .*
>
> . . . Another ETC company, Dallas-based Amtech, can install systems using **digital cash,** which would afford complete privacy.
>
> Electronic toll collection is clearly in its infancy, and state planners are only now confronting privacy issues. Their decisions will turn emerging intelligent highway systems into either models of privacy protection or invitations for Big Brother to hitch a ride. [Emphasis added.]

I think all that available information in one place is just too big a temptation for Big Brother and the New World Order crowd to resist, don't you?

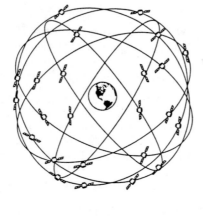

United States
GPS Satellite System

Russian GPS-type
GLONASS Satellite System

The U.S. has a 24-satellite GPS system (this is exclusive of the hundreds of other satellites in space serving other functions); Russia also will have 24 satellites when their system is complete. Work is currently in progress to merge the two systems. When fully linked, it will create a very tightly knit, extremely precise international navigation system which can be used for virtually any application, not the least of which is tracking you. Presently, individual tracking is limited to those carrying a receiver for the proper triangulation for calculation of location, however, they already have been reduced to "hand-held" size, so reducing it further to biochip size is not an unreasonable engineering expectation.

CHAPTER TEN

Global Positioning Systems

This chapter just as well could be called "The Crowded Skies." That's because without all those satellites up there, a Global Positioning System (GPS) would not be possible. But they are, indeed, up there—in abundance. In fact, they seem to be proliferating like little rabbits. Every big consortium with a big plan feels the need to have their very own satellites.

A simplified definition of GPS could be: The ability to locate and track people or things on a global scale, to know the almost exact position of anything, utilizing a battery-powered GPS receiver or other similar telecommunications device.

How does it operate and why is it needed? The answer to the first part of that question is very technical and the second part is very obvious. Simply stated, signals are sent from a series of satellites from space to earth. Receivers on earth triangulate the signals and calculate latitude/longitude position. The information then may be fed into a computer controlled by the entity or organization doing the "locating."

The possibilities for commercial use of this technology appear to be limitless. . .which means the possibilities for abuse of this technology likewise appear limited only to the imagination of the powers who control it. With Big Brother gaining more control and power every day, what do *you* think will be the eventual use of this kind of technology?

Winn Schwartau, in his book, *Information Warfare,* states:

> The question "Where are you?" will be answered at the push of a button. Global positioning satellites will know, to within a few feet, your exact location. Lives will be saved as personal digital assistants broadcast the location of lost or injured or kidnapped people. But what about employees? Will their every step be tracked to enhance security or to evaluate their performances

for promotions? To the dismay of the unions who say the practice is an invasion of privacy, we already track the routes and times of trucks to increase shipping efficiency. Computers already know almost everything about us; will we also decide to add our every location to this list?

The May 8, 1994, edition of *The Bulletin,* Bend, Oregon, carried an article by writer Ralph Vartabedian, entitled "Defense Satellite Technology Ready for Commercial Boom." According to Vartabedian, "The Pentagon is awash in obsolete nuclear bombs, mothballed battleships, and surplus military bases [Author's note: although FEMA apparently has plans to make use of these deserted bases], but out of the scrap heaps left by the Cold War has come a technology with a promising payoff." Below are some excerpts:

When the Defense Department laid plans in the 1970s for its Global Positioning System, a network of 24 satellites that broadcasts navigation signals to users on Earth, it was intended to help soldiers fight anywhere, from jungles to deserts.

Along the way, though, commercial interests saw a potentially lucrative concept that could revolutionize industries such as land surveying, trucking, environmental protection, and farming.

The technology [is] now poised to leap into virtually every facet of the American economy. . . .

With a special receiver that taps the satellite signals, civilian users can determine their position by latitude and longitude within 100 meters (328 feet) anywhere in the world. Once as big as a file cabinet, the receivers are now the size of a paperback book and still shrinking. Consumer models, used by wilderness backpackers, cost as little as $500.

Some visionaries anticipate the day when virtually everything that moves in U.S. society—every shipping container, aircraft, car, truck, train, bus, farm tractor, and bulldozer—will contain a microchip that will track and, in many cases, report its location. [Note: This is no longer just the dream of some visionaries—it's actually occurring now, and he forgot to mention they'll be tracking your garbage, as well. See chapter 15.] Massive computer systems, they say, will tie together the movement of assets in the economy, providing a sophisticated information system for the status and location of goods.

"Communications satellites were the first great success in space, but GPS is going to dwarf that," said . . . a former Hughes Aircraft chairman. . . ."GPS is going to pervade everything we do." [See chapter 9 re: Hughes participation in the control of the highway systems, via GPS technology.]

. . .eventually the price will drop below $50. . . . At that point,

> GPS would be inserted into a lot of other electronic gear. . .that could instantly alert police [or others!] to an individual's location. . . .
>
> Computerized maps are being used to track the spread of disease, pollution, and crime, based on data collected from GPS systems. Hamburger chains pore over these kinds of computer-generated maps to determine the best sites for new franchises.
>
> Interstate truckers use the system to keep tabs of their road taxes. . . .Cities use the satellite system to dispatch emergency vehicles and track the location of passenger buses. Railroads are finally able to figure out where their trains are.
>
> Orbiting 11,000 miles above Earth, the 24 satellites are the heart of the system. . . [emphasis added].

It's true, surveying and mapping are fast becoming a major function of the GPS, because of its incredible accuracy. An article appearing in *ENR* entitled "Surveying's Brave New Digital World," included the following preface:

> Surveying and mapping tools have progressed significantly from the days of meticulously entering transit readings in survey notebooks. From the latest in survey marker technology to the latest in computer-enhanced technologies, surveyors and engineers can do their jobs faster, better, and with more precision than ever before.
>
> Recent hardware advances, declining prices of hardware and software, and the greater availability of pre-packaged data are making geographic information system (GIS) technology an affordable and appealing technology for even the smallest firms. In some instances, state legislatures are funding new initiatives or enacting legislation requiring GIS use throughout the state, and Public Utility Commissions are mandating that utilities use GIS to ensure efficient and low-cost public services. Consultants hoping to contract services to these organizations will have to move into the "all digital" world or risk obsolescence. Many private sector clients—such as large engineering firms or developers—are also requesting surveying firms use computer-aided design (CAD) or GIS on projects and deliver digital products.
>
> In this year's special section on surveying and mapping, we'll look at what's new today and what lies just ahead in products and services—including some exciting trends for users of GIS technology, *global positioning systems (GPS),* and satellite imagery/ aerial photography [emphasis added].

This application of GPS technology can run from the mundane to the "Indiana Jones" adventure project. For example, one company was contracted to map a Caribbean island about 1,000 feet off the coast of St. Thomas. Since it was used for jungle warfare training during and following World War II, there was a real possibility of un-exploded ordinance remaining behind. "Lowe [the engineering firm] used the latest in both hazardous materials handling methods and surveying—including GPS, aerial photography, and GIS technology—to produce preliminary digital (CAD) maps in just 30 days." Gone are the "good old days" when two guys stood behind tripods and waved at each other. . . for the most part.

One of the major uses for all those satellites is telecommunications, in a myriad of forms. In *Informart* magazine, AT&T's Roy Weber, director of new business concepts, asks the question, "What's This World Coming To?" I'd be happy to tell him, but since he's the director for new business concepts, I'm sure he's one of those visionaries who is limited only by his imagination when it comes to what we can do with our technology in the future.

He is promoting a six-theme program which he calls, "Plan 2000." If that refers to the date (and I'm confident that it does), then his plans aren't too far in the future. These six steps run the gamut from visual communications and telephone automated voice recognition (in other words, it understands your words; you don't have to push a touchtone button) to "connecting the world" with a multimedia broadband network and numbering *you!* Of course, that's my favorite. It is Weber's Theme Five: ". . .we do everything wrong. We number telephones. You don't want to speak to the telephone. You want to speak to a person. . . .we're developing Global Personal Calling Services that will find you [anywhere]."

The Editor actually felt obliged—I'm sure because of the content of the article—to insert a somewhat tongue-in-cheek preface between the title and the start of the article. It begins:

> **Editor's note:** In the harsh light of the hospital nursery, the nurses are filling in the blanks on a birth certificate: name, weight, phone number. Phone number?
>
> The mere thought of assigning a number to a human being calls forth torrents of ethical and philosophical questions—questions about the relationship between man and machine, about individuality, about privacy. . . .
>
> For Weber, these questions are not simply a matter of intellectual curiosity, they are part of the exercise of inventing the future at AT&T. . . .

And may I remind you that AT&T is right up there with the big banks, MasterCard, and VISA when it comes to development and promotion of smart cards.

And for the future? Knowledge and technology are multiplying exponentially. All those cellular phones may not be obsolete as yet, but don't spend too much on one. They are about to go the way of all high-tech merchandise. They are being nudged out by the onset of wireless-telephone systems. Because they still have a much more powerful system, they will be good for awhile yet, especially in rural areas and small towns. However, in urban settings, they are being replaced by small pocket phones (about the size of a glasses case) that operate on three AAA batteries and offer a selection of services, depending on your needs, with fees charged accordingly.

They start with small phones just for walk-around use in downtown areas, convention centers, airports, shopping malls, etc. Subscribers can make—but not receive—calls on the tiny phones, through low-power relay stations strategically placed. And the price is right—$10.00 a month to access the system, $5.00 a month to rent the 7 oz. phone, and 13¢ a minute to talk.

The next level is the Urban Cellular (referred to as PTS), which is your regular two-way phone, but not as powerful as your car phone, which is still recommended for thinly populated suburban areas and smaller towns. However, your PTS only will cost you about half of your car cellular phone (they estimate that car phones average $85.00 a month).

Then we go from the sublime to the ridiculous. The problem with that assessment is that with advancing technology and decreasing cost, the ridiculous rapidly becomes the norm. According to *U.S. News & World Report* (February 3, 1992), "At the top of the market, satellite-based mobile services could be the Mercedes Benzes of telephony. Motorola is developing a $3.2 billion system called Iridium that promises to connect any two mobile phones in the world when commercial service begins in 1997 . . . . American Mobile Satellite, which already has an FCC license, plans a satellite service covering the United States by the end of 1994."

I haven't investigated current prices, but when this article was written in 1992 the initial cost of the Motorola Iridium handset was $3,000 and calls were to be $3.00 a minute (to anywhere in the world). Now, if you are a businessperson or missionary or anyone who is required to travel in areas where phone service is somewhere between terrible and nonexistent, even these prices begin to sound like a bargain. Of course, I'm sure they will arrange it so you can plug in your modem, computer, or fax to your phone and operate "high-tech," regardless of your location, which will make the expense even more justifiable.

Let's see what Schwartau has to say on the subject of satellite tele-communications.

> In under thirty years, satellite communications became an absolute necessity for international transactions. Today, the demand is such that hundreds of new satellite launches are being planned [Author's note: thus my opening comment about the crowded skies]. Motorola's Iridium Project, for example, will ring the planet with sixty-six satellites, permitting portable phone users to talk to anyone, anywhere, at any time. A true multi-national effort is under way, including Japanese money and manufacturing and Russian orbital launch capabilities. Two competing consortiums have also begun staging their own satellite-based competitive global communications efforts.

Now, if this wasn't going to be profitable, why would Motorola put $3.2 BILLION into it?

> . . .Charles Reich also noticed that technology and society were at odds. "What we have is technology, organization, and administration out of control, running for their own sake. . . .And we have turned over to this system the control and direction of everything —the natural environment, our minds, our lives."

It's hard to say it much better than that! But as the title of Schwartau's book implies, *Information Warfare,* he continues to issue warnings about the pitfalls involved.

> Not all of the switch connections are made through and across wires of copper and fiber optics. Communications increasingly use the airwaves, as we can see in the proliferation of cellular phones, Motorola's multi-billion dollar Iridium Project, and microwave and satellite transmissions. The electromagnetic ether represents a new battlefield for the Information Warrior.
>
> Cellular phone conversations, for example, are wide open to interception by $179 scanner devices that can be bought from Radio Shack, *Monitoring Times* magazine, or dozens of other sources. Courts have upheld that there is no reasonable expec-tation of privacy when one is talking on a cellular phone.

Then he proceeds to tell a number of different methods used in *tele-fraud,* and how much it costs the public. If you are convinced that your secrets (or any other information) are safe—even with encryption devices, because the government has the "backdoor key"—on the Internet, the superinformation highway, satellite telecommunications, your Smart Card, the social security computers. . .you're really just kidding yourself, probably because it's too scary to consider the alternatives. Before I conclude this chapter, I will mention just a few more situations involving the GPS.

The closer we get to the end of the century, the more we likely will see shows such as the one done by Oprah Winfrey on February 25, 1994. She called it, "Your Life in the Year 2000." And she covered much of what I have covered in this book but, of course, it was an "Oh, wow, will we really be able to do that?" kind of show. All the innovations were considered advantageous. They discussed having just one number that would "follow you everywhere . . .The satellite will just find you and beam you the signal." Then they showed the AT&T SmartCard, discussing all the potential advantages of a smart card, such as needing only one card—because everything there is to know about you would all be contained on the one card. And they told about the automatic toll payments on the electronic automated highways.

I have told you about the GPS tracking of commercial trucks, used for everything from keeping tabs of their time table, to accurate moment-by-moment location, to the amount of taxes they owe each state for their proportionate share of usage of their highways. But here's an interesting use that I have not as yet addressed. There was an article in the *Automatic I.D. News* entitled "Voice and location tracking systems alert riders of stops." The transit system in Scranton, Pennsylvania, is using a vehicle tracking and fleet management system based on the GPS that announces each stop via recorded voice. The in-vehicle tracking unit on 32 of their buses provides tracking information such as location, speed, direction, and status. Operators at the Fleetservice Control Center can view the entire fleet at any time. This "talking bus" system has over 400 announcements, "not just stops, but announcing the beginning and the end of the line, a welcome aboard, one that reminds people there's no smoking, eating, or drinking on the bus. . . ." Theoretically, this is to free the bus drivers from the distraction of having to make any announcements. So the next time you ride a bus (tracked by GPS), pay attention! It might just tell you where (or when) to get off.

The last article I will share with you on the subject of GPS appeared in *GIS World, Inc.,* June, 1994. The title was "Satellite Imagery to Track Agricultural Fraud."

> European agriculture will be monitored via satellite imagery. . . . [This] is the largest U.K. satellite monitoring project ever undertaken, *every European Community member state will be monitored. . . .*
> The satellite survey involved observing randomly selected

farms within undisclosed regions. . . . Digital multispectral images from SPOT and Landsat satellites will be used, as well as the European Space Agency ERS-1 satellite's Synthetic Aperture Radar instrument, which is capable of imaging through clouds and at night.

For each farm, individual field boundaries will be digitized. . . . The resulting information will be compared with farmers' claims, and MAFF will be notified of any irregularities.

"Satellite imagery is a highly cost effective and unobtrusive means to monitor large areas. . . . and is a strong deterrent to would-be fraudsters."

. . . which proved the success of satellite imagery to help identify ineligible claims of compensatory payments.

Not only is Big Brother watching you, he's watching from the big eye in the sky.

I'm glad that the Word of God says that God's eye is going to and fro across the earth. It's a comfort to know that He is still sovereign and in control of all things. . . with all that's going on around us in these last days, it's good to remind ourselves of that from time to time. We need to be prudent and be prepared, but we must never operate in fear, as that would give our enemy, Satan, an opening to gain a foothold in our lives. The New World Order government may be getting all their technology in place to number and track us, but we can be assured that it's all just the fulfillment of God's prophecies, foretold by His scribes in the Bible. It would be no problem for God to eliminate those satellites if He wanted to, but I suspect even they are part of His plan for the fulfillment of certain biblical prophecies, e.g., the gospel being preached to all nations, and every eye seeing Christ when He returns. Technically speaking, until these latest developments in telecommunications, it wouldn't have been physically possible for all the inhabitants of a globe that's round to view His return to one location at the "real time" that it occurred. At best, they could have seen it by tape-delay broadcasting.

Remember, God is the one who creates—technology or anything else. Satan either tries to destroy the creation, steal it for his own purposes, or counterfeit it and claim he created it, so he would get the credit.

Now, let's move right along to discuss the cashless society.

CHAPTER ELEVEN

The Cashless Society

Your bucks stop here! Having cash is freedom—and the worst night-mare of dictatorial regimes, since cash provides privacy and anonymity for one's transactions.

If you started at the very beginning of this book and read all the way to this point, you probably already have a pretty good idea of the significance of this subject and how it may work in the near future. However, keeping in mind that many people just check the Table of Contents and read the chapters that particularly interest them, I must be thorough with this subject because of its implications in scripture, Revelation 13, and its importance in relation to our future lifestyles. So, if you are one of those who faithfully read each page, please forgive any redundancy you find here. There must of necessity be considerable overlap. Yet, I still will strive for brevity, as much of this information will be discussed again in the chapters on identity cards (chapter 14) and biochips (chapter 15).

The New World Order economists are not ignorant of the importance of cash and its ability to inhibit their total control of the world. They are aware that in order to completely control, track, and monitor the global population, *they first must eliminate the use of cash.* With cash, there is no way to know how people are using their finances, whether for or against the government and its agenda. Because control of one's

finances typically equates with the control of one's entire life, the advocates of world government for decades have been promoting a move
toward totally cashless transactions, via a myriad of banking plans, ATM
machines, credit cards, debit cards, point-of-sale machines, credit data
—all funneled through massive computer systems. Eventually, the goal
is that all these computers will be controlled by them . . . the *Illuminists*
. . . Big Brother . . . the economic leaders of the New World Order system
of government.

In the non-banking part of the system, this will be a gradual transformation which will begin in random, innocent activities. Our fascina-
tion with the convenience of it all gradually will desensitize us to its
pervasiveness . . . until it is too late to reverse the process. I understand
that they held a most successful "cashless" Olympics event in Europe
recently. I want to quote four paragraphs by Don McAlvany, from the
August, 1994, edition of his newsletter, *the McAlvany Intelligence
Advisor.*

ELECTRONIC FASCISM: TOWARD A CASHLESS SOCIETY

In the high-tech era now emerging, government checks (i.e.,
Social Security benefits, government pensions, welfare checks,
etc.), physical food stamps, and other government benefits are
all to be delivered electronically as the Clintonistas implement
Electronic Benefits Transfer. Under the system, each recipient's
benefits will be credited to an account which can be accessed
with special debit cards and eventually via the all-purpose smart
(National ID) card.

Food stamp recipients will be able to use the cards to pay for
groceries at supermarket check-out terminals, just as many
consumers now use credit and debit cards to pay for purchases.
Those receiving Social Security, welfare, military pensions, and
other public benefits will use the cards to receive cash at automatic teller machines.

The EBT system is already in use in several cities throughout
the country and in the entire state of Maryland, and is now being
installed in many southern states (i.e., Florida, Alabama, Georgia,
North Carolina, South Carolina, Tennessee, Kentucky, Arkansas,
and Missouri). The Clintonistas predict that soon $111 billion a
year in benefits will be delivered electronically, and plan to spend
$83 million over the next three years to implement EBT. Health
and Human Services Secretary Donna Shalala [Author's Note:
Shalala is a member of both the CFR and the TLC.] brags that
"with EBT, we'll have an electronic audit trail for every transaction,
making fraud [**ED. NOTE:** or 'political incorrectness'] much
easier to detect and prosecute."

Similar debit/smart card/cashless systems are being installed throughout Europe and Asia where debit or smart cards are replacing cash (on a mandatory basis) for a host of transactions. *One of the essential elements of the New World Order is a cashless society, where all transactions are forced through the computerized banking and credit card system—eventually via the all-purpose National ID/smart card. One hundred percent monitoring and control of all personal activity is the goal and could become a fait accompli* over the next 5 to 10 years. And if you are "politically incorrect," Big Brother can pull your plug, and you will starve or be frozen out of the system.

I want to recommend a brochure by W. S. McBirnie, Ph.D., news analyst, entitled, "You're Already Using the New Money and May Not Know It!" This points out some of the steps we will encounter along the way to a cashless society, including the minimally publicized replacement of our currency with new money containing inconspicuous, but machine readable, coded information; an organization called FINCEN (Financial Crimes Enforcement Network); and others. This is Voice of Americanism Publication No. 1082, available by writing to: U.C.C.A., P. O. Box 90, Glendale, CA 91209. I suggest you obtain a copy of this and some of their other informative materials. Excerpts follow:

GOODBYE, CASH

According to financial advisor Lawrence Patterson, the number of new 20, 50, and 100s being issued is extremely limited and may, at some point, only be distributed—and rationed—upon presentation of your Social Security card and/or other national I.D. card. In other words, you may be allowed only a certain amount each month. This will force you to use checks or credit cards, which, in short, means you will be compelled to go cashless.

Laws requiring Cash Transaction Reporting forms (CTRs) to be filled out set the stage for tightly controlling the use of cash. They demand that banks (and many businesses) must report to the IRS any cash transaction involving more than $3,000, in which case, you would be put on a list of potential money launderers. Hundreds of U.S. businesses have been indicted and convicted by the feds for failing to report cash deals of over $3,000. Penalties incurred are sometimes worse than for drug dealing! Incidentally, non-cash bank instruments (money orders, cashier's checks) have now been subjected to these reporting requirements—but without an act of Congress!

Eventually, you may be issued some sort of "Americard," a biochip impregnated with your hand and/or retina prints to ensure foolproof identification. [Author's note: See chapter 13 on Biometric I.D. Methods.] All transactions would be recorded in a computer file and would be easy for the government to check. This would eliminate all financial privacy, smash the underground economy, and enable the government to collect hundreds of billions of dollars in new taxes.

Cashless experiments are taking place with increasing frequency. The 1992 Barcelona Olympic games were entirely cashless. Officials in Maryland, Oklahoma, New Mexico, and several other states no longer issue food stamps, but instead give recipients a plastic card to transfer funds electronically until the amount allowed for the month is spent. The giant U.S. Marine base on Paris Island, South Carolina, has gone cashless. Hillary's new health care plan could include a health card with a microchip containing all your medical information.

By 1995, the computer industry predicts that over half of the people in America, Europe, Japan, Australia, and through the free world will be using these "Smartcards." [Author's note: That's a prediction we've seen come to pass right before our eyes.]

All this is incredibly dangerous: If your only means of money exchange is through electronic funds transfer, then those with the power to cut off your access to electronic money can sever your very lifeline. The potential for totalitarian blackmail and control is immense. [Emphasis added.]

Can We Expect a Currency Call-in?

Without telling the public, the Federal Reserve gradually began calling in the old $100 notes on November 1, 1992. Only the 1990 magnetic ink bar-coded bills are to be distributed. Please take note: This is a **secret recall!** The public has not been notified. This proves malintent on the part of the government. The old cash notes will gradually disappear as a result of this call-in. Then, all denominations of the old money will be cancelled.

Eventually, however, we feel a major recall will occur (perhaps coming in stages, so as to avoid panicking the public): The absence of a watermark on our "interim" new money suggests that an entirely new currency will have to be issued—and all the old money recalled—so that U.S. currency will match the EC's, including have a blank area for a *world monetary unit overprint* (which can be stamped on by your local bank). (It's also possible that we may go directly to cashless, using Smartcards, without issuing new, EC-style money.) [Emphasis added.]

[Author's Note: Just prior to press time of this book, distribution of the new currency began, starting with $100 bills, containing the aforementioned watermark and blank area on the right side of the face of the bill.]

What might precipitate such a call-in? Perhaps an artificially created financial emergency. . . . but would our "benevolent" government really initiate a radical call-in with subsequent serious repercussions? Yes! It already has. After Pearl Harbor was bombed, the government issued a new currency for Hawaii (only usable there) and made it illegal for anyone to hold more than $200 in cash. The government confiscated stocks and bonds and imposed stiff penalties on those who broke the law. Military police opened all safety deposit boxes and confiscated all cash and investment securities.

Moreover, the same New World Order globalists that advise Mikhail Gorbachev are in control of the U.S. On Jan. 22, 1991, Gorbachev invalidated all 500 and 100-ruble notes—which comprised one-third of the total Soviet currency and amount to $96 billion! This was the largest single robbery in world history. Plus, Gorbachev froze bank savings accounts and permitted only a limited monthly withdrawal amount.

The Financial Crimes Enforcement Network (FINCEN)

The FINCEN is an insidious agency the U.S. public knows nothing about, and through which the financial records of banks, retailers, and individuals are being made available to foreign authorities, without public announcement or the permission of the people harmed. The Mutual Legal Assistance Treaty (MLAT), the main instrument of the FINCEN so far, is a written agreement between the U.S. and other nations (Switzerland, Mexico, and Canada are the first ones to sign one) to cooperate in collecting information on anything each government deems a financial crime in tracking money flows between countries and within each respective banking system.

The MLAT also guarantees mutual assistance in finding people, confiscating property, and taking cases of financial crime to court. Once all significant countries have MLATs with the U.S., the global planners will establish a world headquarters for tax investigation and prosecution, assisted by Interpol (the International Criminal Police Organization).

Conclusion

The real purpose for the "new" currency is to extinguish financial privacy, bring an end to the use of cash, and **usher in a cashless society, where every transaction is recorded and the amount of money you can have is strictly controlled** [emphasis added].

Don McAlvany is an excellent source of information on what the government is up to, regarding financial matters. In order to justify their meddling and monitoring of our activities, the transactions first must be deemed to be somehow illegal in nature. That lets them be perceived as the "good guys" trying to catch the "bad guys," and in that case, how could we possibly object to whatever means they consider necessary. Unfortunately, in their efforts to track the bad guys, they must have the authority to monitor all of us; therefore, former perfectly legal activities have been declared illegal so that banks, businesses, *et al,* can be forced to report your activities. They've even made a law to make it illegal to carefully follow the rules that they, themselves, have established . . .they are asking bankers and businessmen to be the judges of your **intent**—it's illegal to follow the "letter of the law" if your intent is wrong. Talk about Big Brother meddling in your life! The penalties for failure to comply consist of large fines and long jail terms, frequently higher than drug dealers. Sound confusing? Below I am reprinting a portion of the *McAlvany Intelligence Advisor* (July, 1991), because he has done such an excellent job of taking the confusion out of some of these new laws and their ultimate purpose, which undoubtedly is total control of global economics.

. . . Linking "smart cards" and the worldwide telecommunications network will open the door to universal electronic transactions in all walks of life. *The era of paper money and coinage is rapidly drawing to a close and the new age of a cashless society is dawning.*
The path to 100% electronic money, and total government financial control of citizens, as Harvey Wachsman explained in *The New York Times* article, is Americard—a "smart card" that does it all. Cash is freedom! A man without money is free to do very little. *If modern electronic credit and debit cards can be substituted for cash, then every financial transaction of your life can be catalogued and stored for future reference and those with the power to cut off your access to electronic money can strangle you in a heartbeat. The potential for totalitarian blackmail and control is incredible—but most Americans don't even seem to notice.*
1. CASH REPORT REQUIREMENTS —Starting about 1987, the US Treasury began enforcing the cash reporting requirements of Title 31 of the Bank Secrecy Act of 1986. These requirements, though not clearly or widely communicated to businesses or the public for over a year or so after the passage of the 1986 Act, called for banks, securities brokerage houses, coin dealers, car dealers, jewelers, and any other financial institution or business to report to the IRS (on a form 8300 for retail businesses and on a Cash Transaction Reporting form CTR for a financial institution) any customer spending, depositing, or withdrawing

cash over $10,000.

Since 1987, by regulatory edict, the IRS has greatly expanded the definition and scope of the cash reporting requirements and the kinds of transactions covered. *Often financial institutions or businesses do not find out the extent of these anti-cash regulations until after they have been victimized by an IRS "sting." Severe jail sentences and fines of up to $50,000 are then meted out to the unwitting businessman, banker, coin dealer, or one of their employees. In this pattern, the government destroys one or two victims from a targeted group or industry, to paralyze the rest of the group with fear.*

Former Congressman Ron Paul wrote recently in his newsletter, that with no new authority from Congress, the IRS made the following regulatory changes (recorded *quietly* in the Federal Register May 15, 1991, under "Notice of Proposed Rule Making"):

"Currency Transaction Reports (CTRs) have traditionally been required only for cash, but the new regulations make the CTRs rules applicable to *all* monetary instruments, including money orders, cashier's checks, bank drafts, and travelers checks. *By the simple method of redefining these instruments as cash, the government now requires that everyone who spends some combination of cash and non-cash monetary instruments in excess of $10,000 in one day (or over a period of 12 months) is required to fill out an 8300 form at retail outlets and a CTR at all financial institutions.*"

Cashier's checks, money orders, and the rest are *not* considered monetary instruments if their dollar denominations are in excess of $10,000, however. [Author's note: That's probably because the instrument was already reported to the IRS at the time you purchased it, if it exceeded the $10,000 limit.] What the IRS is trying to prevent is mixed transactions, like half cash and half money order, which are now considered an attempt to evade the law (called "structuring").

a. STRUCTURING—*In 1987, the "crime" of "structuring" was invented, which ruled that suggesting or thinking about ordering your transactions to avoid the reporting requirements was also a crime.* This was an historic first for American jurisprudence, to make an attempt to comply with the law, a crime. *If an investor or business "structures" a transaction with multiple payments (i.e., cash, personal check, cashier's or certified checks, or money orders) so that the sum is over $10,000, he is guilty of the money laundering crime of "structuring."*

As former Congressman Ron Paul has pointed out: **"The government loves vague laws. They are essential to tyranny and executive discretion."** Examples of such vague laws are the Hooliganism laws in the Soviet Union and the RICO laws in the US. If the US government can't find another criminal charge, it can charge you with "racketeering" or "conspiracy." The Bank Secrecy Act prohibits "structuring," which it defines as an attempt to evade the financial reporting requirements. But this law makes obeying the law against the law, a la Orwell's "double think."

Big Brother can now fine, convict, or jail *anyone* in the future, for "structuring" violations if he has deposited or withdrawn various amounts of cash (or other monetary instruments) *under the reporting requirements from his bank over a 12-month period. If an investor buys coins, antiques, art goods, or whatever several times in any 12-month period, paying in amounts of under $10,000 (but adding up to over $10,000 in toto), he can be accused and found guilty of "structuring." The banker, investment broker, or business selling that person the items will also be guilty of "structuring" if he/she/it doesn't report the customer on a CTR, or Form 8300, or if he or she gives the customer any advice or counsel whatsoever as to how to "structure" their transaction(s) to avoid the reporting requirements.*

Ron Paul wrote recently the IRS gives a number of examples of structuring: (1) "Under the first, the individual must fill out an 8300: 'D, an individual, purchases gold coins from M, a coin dealer, for $13,200. D tenders to M in payment US currency in the amount of $6,200 and a cashier's check in the face amount of $7,000 which D had purchased. Because the sale is a designated reporting transaction, the cashier's check is treated as cash for purposes of section 6050I and this section. Therefore, because M has received more than $10,000 in cash with respect to the transaction, M must make the report required by section 6050I and this section.'

(2) "Under this one, he is not: 'G, an individual, purchases a boat from T, a boat dealer, for $16,500. G pays T with a cashier's check payable to T in the amount of $16,500. The cashier's check is not treated as cash because the face amount of the check is more than $10,000. Thus, no report is required to be made.'

"There are three exceptions. First, the customer doesn't have to fill out a form if he can prove the money comes from a bank loan. Or if the money is received in payment on a promissory note or installment sales contract. Or if the money is part of a payment plan that requires one or more down payments.

"This is a highly significant step because it begins to bring non-cash bank instruments under reporting requirements. The next IRS goal is to make personal bank checks qualify as cash under the reporting rules.

"Another major change has to do with the way CTRs and 8300s are treated in tax audit. Beginning in a few months, IRS agents will have a complete file of all CTRs and 8300s filled out by the person being audited, and they will be scrutinized heavily."

[**Ed. Note:** One gets the feeling that a businessman, banker, securities, or coin broker will have to be a Ph.D. accountant or Philadelphia lawyer to accurately assess when the form 8300 or CTR must be filed. (Author's note: It's more like they have to be mind readers and fortune tellers, otherwise how are they supposed to know at the time you make your first transaction how many transactions you may make over the next 12-month period—and that's the time frame the IRS has established for cumulative transactions.) *The IRS has been extremely vague on these rapidly expanding reporting requirements over the past four years, but is still prosecuting and jailing businessmen, bank employees, financial brokers who through confusion or misunderstanding of the regulations have not fully complied.* The reporting requirements and the record keeping they generate are also very expensive for the businessman, banker, or financial broker to maintain.]

(b) **THE WAR AGAINST COIN DEALERS**—The IRS has been indicting coin dealers across the country who either don't understand its confusing cash reporting requirements or who have been entrapped into violating them by very clever "stings." Precious metals are one of the last loopholes of private, trackless investments in America, and the IRS and government bureaucrats would like to wipe out the industry. As the May '91 newsletter for members of the Industry Council for Tangible Assets pointed out: "That we (the precious metals/rare coin/tangibles industry) are a *targeted industry* is not just an IRS policy statement. It's a fact!"

As the *ICTA Washington Wire* described: "Several coin dealers have already been indicted for violations of these regulations. Others are awaiting sentencing or are already imprisoned. The penalties for non-compliance are very severe, ranging from staggering fines and jail time on up to actual forfeiture of your business. *IGNORANCE OF THESE REGULATIONS CAN COST YOU EVERYTHING YOU'VE WORKED FOR!*"

ICTA counsel Victoria Toensing made four points: (1) Cash is a "four letter word"; (2) Illegal cash is *not* just drug money; (3) The penalty for not filing required reports is serious; (4) The penalty for not reporting illegal cash is a mind-blower.

An IRS agent who addressed ICTA's recent dealer convention in Tampa, Florida, said: *"The IRS restrictions were aimed at creating a paper trail."* Another IRS agent said: "The goal of tightening the noose of illegal cash transactions is to make the profits from these illegal enterprises worthless. . . . If one knowingly takes *'cash generated illegally,' the first offense* is punishable by 4.5 to 5.5 years in prison. In conjunction, the new laws regarding forfeiture of assets *are more sweeping than the drug possession forfeiture laws."*

Coin dealers were also encouraged by the two IRS agents to report to them "any suspicious transactions or behavior"—just as bank employees are encouraged to spy on and report depositors who act suspiciously. Doesn't this remind you more of communist Russia or China than the America we have known and loved?

[**Ed. Note:** Think about the above statements: *Not reporting cash transactions is now considered by our government to be a more severe crime, and is more severely punished than drug dealing.* Note the term "cash generated illegally"—that's any cash not "fully taxed." In one IRS sting against a coin dealer, the agent "claimed" to have mentioned "untaxed money"—thereby making the transaction "illegal" because it involved "cash generated illegally."

MIA reader, do you see how serious the government is about pursuing unreported cash, about wiping out ultimately all cash transactions? Cash truly is a 4-letter word!]

2. **MONEY LAUNDERING ENFORCEMENT**—Joseph Battaglia wrote about the evolution of the money laundering juggernaut in the March '91 issue of *The American Advisor.*

"As with so many things the government does, the process of attacking the free economy has been a gradual one. It began with the introduction of so-called anti-money-laundering rules. These rules required banks and businesses to report to the IRS the name, address, and social security number of individuals who engage in cash transactions of $10,000 or more. This rule was established under the guise of attacking drug dealers.

"With the tremendous publicity given to the drug problem and so-called "money-laundering," the government was able to obtain this repressive, anti-freedom, money-laundering law.

"Subsequently, the government said that drug dealers were evading this money-laundering law and they needed a new tool. *Therefore, they added a provision to make it a crime for individuals to spend more than $10,000 in total cash transactions throughout a year without reporting it.* In today's inflated economy, $10,000 over the course of an entire year is not very much!

"The burden of enforcing this law was placed on private citizens. With this law the government turned businessmen and bankers into policemen. Banking personnel are instructed to report cash transactions of less than $10,000 if they think a customer look suspicious. *If a bank teller or businessman has reason to be suspicious and does not turn in the individual using cash, he could be guilty of a crime. This is the height of the "Big Brother" mentality made famous in George Orwell's 1984 and in Hitler's Germany.* [Author's note: The Bible tells of a time in the future when even the children will turn in their parents.]

"To effect compliance with these laws, the government began prosecuting business people across the country. Prosecutions began with the Florida and California drug money-laundering schemes. *In time, they prosecuted real estate brokers, car dealers, coin dealers, and a host of other business people who inadvertently or otherwise accepted cash from an ostensibly legitimate customer. Since this whole affair has been positioned as a part of the war on drugs, the American public has not objected to these repressive measures.* In fact, they have accepted them piecemeal, with hardly a second thought.

"*Now the real significance of these money-laundering rules is about to be felt. All individuals who hold large amounts of cash, but are not drug dealers, will soon find it's impossible to exchange their old currency for the soon-to-be-released new currency.*"

"On August 24, 1990, a Money Laundering Enforcement Conference was held in Washington, D.C., sponsored by the American Bankers Assn., the American Bar Assn., and attended by top officials of all Federal law enforcement agencies. Together, they comprise the financial enforcement arm of the New World Order. It was agreed that "a new domestic dollar was needed *to hamper private use of cash*" and "a new international dollar to make it more difficult to transfer cash in and out of the country."

The Financial Criminal Enforcement Network (FINCEN) said that "*we currently have nearly all financial information available on every US citizen.*" In the future, tax violations will be treated as *money laundering violations.* (Reread that last sentence!) This and other measures discussed at the meeting will wipe out virtually all vestiges of financial freedom and privacy for the American people.

As Ron Paul recently wrote:

> The IRS has virtually taken over enforcement of money laundering laws. (The 5/8/91 *Federal Register* stated that the Treasury Department was turning over its entire anti-money laundering operation to the IRS—which will have full control of investigations, seizures, and forfeitures in ML cases.) *Virtually all tax cases will be redefined as money laundering (ML) cases thanks to the vague definitions of ML the government uses.*

About ten years ago, someone at the Treasury had the bright idea that *ML laws provide a better means for enforcement of tax laws than tax laws themselves.* Why? First, Congress is much more willing to pass new ML legislation than tax enforcement legislation, which always leads to complaints from constituents. So far, *no* significant ML bill has been killed in Congress, although a few have been modified to please the banking industry.

Second, the enforcement of tax laws has a long and detailed court history behind it, and increasingly taxpayers are using that history to their own benefit, witness the number of successful suits against the IRS recently. When convicting on tax laws, the IRS risks getting itself tangled in complex legal webs. ML cases have much lower risks (for the feds). *Third, the penalties—both financial and jail—are twice to ten times higher under ML than under the old tax laws.*

In part, ML is the crime of using the banking system to wash undeclared income, and almost everyone convicted for tax law violations uses banks to some extent. *If a man is paid in cash for some service, deposits the cash, and doesn't report it, he is a money launderer.*

Another way to become a money launderer is to "attempt" to "structure" transactions to keep from filling out government forms. No one knows how widely the government plans to interpret the word "attempt." There will be court cases and fights over this during the coming years, but the IRS has *carte blanche* in the meantime.

Money laundering will be the term used more and more to identify simple tax violations. I predict that in the years ahead, we will witness an explosion of convictions on ML grounds. And with the administration's FINCEN apparatus —a detailed financial data base utilizing artificial intelligence—the fed will try to turn America into a Ceaucescu's Romania for finance, with the locus of control in the IRS Securitate.

On 6/11/91 the House passed a severe new piece of money laundering legislation (HR 26) that will expand the powers of the government over everyone's private bank account. The bill:

1. Enacts severe penalties, like revoking charters and removing deposit insurance, for banks that the Feds deem to be participating in money laundering. *This will greatly expand the banks' incentive to act like police instead of financial institutions.*

2. Gives state financial officials access to the federal government's enormous collection of currency transaction reports.

3. Grants the Treasury the ability to use state-level financial data on individuals, formerly a violation of the Right to Financial Privacy Act.

4. Calls on states to license and regulate non-bank financial institutions engaged in check-cashing and money transmittal. [Author's note: That would be like Western Union franchises and others.] They have previously been unregulated, so this eliminates a significant island of privacy.

5. Makes the operators of money-transmittal businesses subject to five years in prison for participation in money laundering.

6. Raises the maximum fine (to $50,000) that the Treasury can impose on financial institutions that display a "pattern of negligence" in policing money laundering.

7. Requires that banks report the names of customers required to file CTRs on their own behalf, like auto and boat dealers and jewelry stores.

8. *Prohibits* banks from telling customers when they've had a "suspicious transaction report" filed on them at the IRS.

9. Makes the penalty for "conspiracy" to commit money laundering the same as for actual money laundering. This gives the government a huge advantage in criminal prosecutions.

10. Gives "whistleblower" protection to any employee of a bank or other institution with cash dealings who turns in other employees.

The Senate nearly passed a similar bill last year, so this one's on the fast track. We have seen a dramatic shift toward prosecutions of money laundering since the definition is so broad, the powers of the government so strong during investigations, and the penalties so high.

Broadly defined, money laundering is the crime of using cash—even your own honestly earned and taxed cash—in ways that the government bureaucrats might disapprove of, without telling them first. In a free society, this ought to be no crime.

In addition, the bill would require the . . . Administration to expand negotiations with foreign nations on reporting suspected laundering transactions and give it authority to impose sanctions against countries that do not cooperate. The bill's primary author,

Rep. Frank Annunzio (D-IL) said in *The New York Times* 6/12/91, that giving regulators authority to revoke the charter of a Federal bank or lift the FDIC insurance of a state bank amounted to a "well-deserved death sentence for the bank—a way to execute a bank." He added: "Those who launder drug money are accomplices to every drug-related murder in this country." [**Ed. Note:** But what if all of us are ultimately labeled as money launderers.]

C. NEW INTERNATIONAL MONEY LAUNDERING INITIATIVES

The...Administration is making great headway in pushing money laundering enforcement on a global basis. First, there was the United Nations money laundering treaty, which attempts to outlaw bank secrecy. (The UN treaty, to which America is a signatory, criminalizes international money laundering, allows seizure of assets, attempts to destroy all bank secrecy laws, and weakens protections involved in the production of evidence, the taking of testimony, and the extradition of offenders.) Then the 12-nation tax treaty of the Organization for Economic Cooperation and Development was ratified to insure cooperation in harassing taxpayers.

Most recently we have a report from the Research Institute for the Study of Conflict and Terrorism (which works closely with the CIA) which argues that global money laundering is not just the $500 billion it is normally estimated to be, but 2 to 3 times that large. The report blames the lack of CTR regulations in most countries besides the US, and says that **Swiss, Austrian, Hong Kong, and Caribbean bank secrecy must be destroyed immediately** [emphasis added].

THE NEW WORLD ECONOMIC ORDER

The New World *Economic* Order is one of three aspects of the coming New World Order system of government. The other two are the political order and the religious order (called the New Age Movement). These two are discussed in other portions of this book. All three parts are working together energetically to bring forth the all-enslaving New World Order global government, however, such a system cannot be activated until there is a way to obtain total control over everyone, and that cannot be accomplished without first eliminating the use of cash worldwide. Their goal is to implement a cashless system as quickly as possible.

How will they do it? Above you have read some of the ways in which we are headed that direction. The laws are in place and the pressure has begun. Don't look for it to let up—from here on, things will heat up more and more and the pressure can't do anything but increase.

Let's consider some more cogs in the gears leading us to a cashless society.

I believe the primary method probably will be a downhill slide via the convenience factor, i.e., it's safer and easier not to have to deal with cash, then it's easier not to have to bother with the time or expense of writing checks, then it's so simple just to slide our little smart card through the slot to make our purchases, pay our utility bill, or our doctor, or the repairman. But what about having it lost or stolen? Well, since it will be tied to your physical person biometrically (via fingerprints, handprints, facial prints, voice prints, retina scans, or some combination of these), no one can use it but you (allegedly). But we can do better than that . . . just a tiny little RFID transponder (presently no bigger than a grain of rice, and maybe smaller in the future) implanted under the skin is perfect—it can't be lost or stolen, and it can do all that the smart card can do. Now you have arrived . . . welcome to Revelation 13!

Let me remind you before I go any further, that the reference to the mark of the Beast in the passage in Revelation has more than just a commercial application—it's true that you will not be able to buy or sell without it, but it is inextricably connected to a spiritual application, as well. No one is going to force you to take this mark— it will be your choice to accept or refuse, because those who accept the mark also will have to *worship* the Beast. Of course, there are severe consequences for refusing, once the Antichrist comes to power. Your refusal will cost you your head, according to another passage in Revelation.

Now for you diehards who believe it will take more than "convenience" to talk some people out of their cash . . . I agree with you, and there are financial plans already in the works to force the situation. (It is my opinion, though I'd like to believe I'm wrong, that the New World Order economists intend to activate these plans sometime in the near future.)

AN INTERNATIONAL EMERGENCY IS NEEDED

Those in control of the U.S. government, the globalists, the international bankers, the New World Order crowd, and the New World global religious believers (New Agers) all hate cash because it represents privacy, freedom, decentralization, and independence—all the things they are trying to abolish. I am firmly convinced that they presently are advancing their plan to create a series of global economic *emergencies* that will enable them to convince you that cash must be discarded immediately in favor of electronic money. They will insist that such a drastic course of action is necessary in order to eliminate crime and restore order to a world that appears to have crashed—accidentally, of course—into a state of international financial chaos!

THE COMING STOCK MARKET CRASH

Conservative analysts have been predicting a devastating crash for the stock market for quite some time, while at the same time holding their breath and hoping it won't happen. But history and experience, coupled with the facts available, convince them that our economy is artificially propped up, and it's only a matter of time before the establishment can no longer keep it propped up. I agree, but I believe there is something even more sinister going on.

I believe we are headed for a *planned* global stock market crash— and in the near future—unlike anything the world has ever suffered! Such a crash would permit the Illuminists and their cohorts to close thousands of banks in a matter of days, seize most personal assets, confiscate gold and silver, and *eliminate cash,* all under federally sanctioned "Declared Emergencies," activated by Presidential Executive Order. (Laws [Presidential Executive Orders formerly placed into law] are already on the books permitting the implementation of such controls, via FEMA and other departments. See the discussions on FEMA in earlier chapters.) After the crash, the worldwide financial system will be restructured into one that provides much more efficient methods of total enslavement—more so than any previous economic system in the history of the world. This will set the stage for the official establishment of the New World Economic Order.

It is expected that the *planned crash* will begin in Japan, then work its way around the globe, toppling the economies of nations like a string of dominoes, virtually simultaneously —*all completely by accident, of course.* Not true! This *accident* is being orchestrated carefully from behind the scenes by the power-hungry globalists.

If this sounds as though I'm on the radical fringe, I challenge you to check the facts for yourself. I'll give you some numbers and locations to help you get started. Go to any major library and ask the librarian to help you locate Presidential Executive Order No. 11490, as listed in the *Federal Register,* Vol. 34, No. 209. This order was signed into law by former President Richard Nixon on October 30, 1969. In particular, review the third page of this voluminous document (page 17569). Part 3, Department of the Treasury, specifies that in *any* national emergency that might *conceivably* confront the nation, the President is authorized to seize control over and regulate *arbitrarily* virtually all facets of the monetary system. In addition, the same Executive Order (page 17593) allows him to seize control over and regulate virtually all aspects of the stock market, as well. Are you beginning to get the picture?

Do you think it's possible that all this could be mere coincidence, or do you think, perhaps, there might be an evil master plan behind it? If you concluded the latter, then you have concluded correctly! These soon-coming cataclysmic events all have been strategically planned for the purpose of creating chaos and crisis. And don't rule out the natural disasters occurring around the globe, as we begin to witness more of what was predicted in the Bible for the end of the age, i.e., the unprecedented number of earthquakes and their increased magnitude; the awakening of volcanoes along the Pacific Rim known as the Ring of Fire, as well as in Europe and Asia—volcanoes which for centuries have been considered permanently dormant; the staggering number of devastating killer hurricanes—in this hurricane season alone they have nearly exhausted the entire alphabet in naming them, and they begin at "A" every season; the floods and the droughts—either too much water to grow food, or not enough. Need I go on? All of these natural disasters take their toll on the global economy, every bit as much as the man-made, manipulated crises and the national and ethnic wars going on somewhere in the world at all times.

ANY CHAOS WILL DO

Once these "problems" have been created, or a sufficiently large natural disaster or war has occurred, a number of prearranged solutions will be brought forth immediately. Such dictatorial "solutions" await only the golden moment of opportunity that will enable their implementation. This will be accomplished under a declared state of emergency during a time of horrible international chaos (of whatever nature) that will permit the New World Order Illuminists to do virtually anything they want, including eliminating all cash globally! But be alert! Watch out for the man who is able to bring order out of all this chaos and crisis. He is described in the prophetic books in the Old Testament, and in the book of Revelation he is called the Antichrist. It says because he is able to restore peace—albeit temporary—to the world, they will make him the unchallenged leader over all the earth. From this cashless economic system will evolve the New Political Order and the New Spiritual Order—the New Age occultic religion of satanism.

HOW OTHERS PROPOSE TO ELIMINATE CASH

In Don McAlvany's enlightening article printed above, he told us about Harvey Wachsman, *an attorney who advocates the total elimination of cash.* Let's examine some more of Wachsman's article, as it "says-it-all" regarding what's coming in the not-too-distant future. The strange and amazing thing is that—knowing all this—he still advocates it!

> First the government would change the color of the currency and require old money to be exchanged at the treasury. Then all the NEW currency would be returned by its owners to the bank of their choice. At that time all banks would be required to open accounts to all depositors free of charge. In place of this paper money, we would receive new plastic cards—called Americards —each *biometrically impregnated with the owner's hand and eye retina prints* to insure virtually **foolproof** identification.
>
> The government would supply all homes and businesses free of charge with scanner machines to read the new Americards, certify the holder's identity, and make instantaneous electronic debits and credits to their accounts. Think of the benefits to the average American. No more check writing would be necessary [Author's note: We're nearly there right now, only they're tapping our accounts automatically for whatever amount is due, based on a one-time authorization.] because bills would be paid electronically directly from their homes. In addition, individuals and businesses would no longer be able to conceal income. This would be great for the government. **All transactions would be recorded in a computerized bank file that would be easy for the IRS to check** [emphasis added].

Yes, but how "great" would it be for the law-abiding taxpayer? In chapter 14, I deal with the national identity crisis and the uprising demanding a national ID card. But since such a card is the preliminary basis for a cashless society, I will quote some recent articles concerning such a card. Even though the writers are in favor, it is interesting to note that even they recognize the potential for abuse and the probability of the loss of personal privacy.

Lawmakers Clash Over New Call for National ID Card

> . . .creation of a single, tamper-proof ID card. . .any such card would lead to an invasion of privacy. . .one can easily manufacture such cards. . .there is simply no way to enforce our existing laws without it. . .a social security card with a photo, fingerprint, or verifiable bar code. . .**a new ID card could lead to a national data bank with information about every American that would pose a threat to individual privacy** [emphasis added].
>   —*Los Angeles Times,* June 17, 1993

Another article in the *Los Angeles Times,* April 20, 1993, "L.A., the Cash Capital," stated the following about the merits of a cashless society: "...The idea is to eventually turn greenbacks into electronic blips...." In other words, let's eliminate cash and go to an electronic debit system.

The *San Diego Union-Tribune* (May 16, 1993) ran an article titled "Automated Teller Machines." The virtues of the cashless society were extolled as follows:

> ...Americans have heard about the cashless society for the past 20 years, but now the combination of technology and consumer demands for a highly convenient payment system have made the cashless society acceptable and visible on the horizon. ...Americans in the 1990s presumably are primed and ready for the next financial wonder: the cashless debit card and ATM machines....ATM debit cards subtract the amount of a purchase directly from a bank account....This will enable ATM cards to be used at vending machines, telephones, and parking meters. Such cards would be equipped with tiny computer chips....

Without coming right out and saying so, what they are describing is a smart card, because the other types of credit cards and ATM cards don't have computer chips. And we have been trained (conditioned) to use our ATM cards in this fashion for over ten years. In southern California supermarkets and self-serve gas stations for years have had point-of-sale debit machines where you just slide your card through and the purchase is automatically deducted from your checking account. Of course, you may just as easily charge your purchases by sliding your credit card through, instead of your debit card.

How convenient(!) it will be when there is only one card to slide through and push a button on the machine to tell it whether to charge your purchase or deduct it from your checking account. But what if I lose my one and only card?!? Well...you can see where I'm going with this—I've taken you down this road before.

CASHLESS SOCIETY LEADS TO 666 BIOCHIP IMPLANT

The combined push for a cashless society and a national ID card (a biometrically encoded smart card) will make it very easy for the coming New World Order Big Brother government to enslave us. Of course, the final step in this progression will be implanting your new ID/debit card (in the form of a biochip) just under the skin—it will contain all your data, both personal and financial. See chapter 15 for the complete story on biochip technology.

NO CASH EQUALS NO FREEDOM

Earlier in this chapter, I pointed out that having a cashless society equates with the total loss of freedom. I want to elaborate on that a bit. A person without cash is free to do very little.

If modern ID cards, credit, debit, smart cards, and ultimately biochip implants, can be substituted for cash, then *every financial transaction in your life easily could be stored, cataloged, analyzed, and accessed for future reference* by the New World Order bureaucrats. And if you think they have no interest in the mundane details of your life, think again! They would have at their fingertips the unparalleled, instantaneous power to cut off your electronic buying and selling "privileges" at will. It is a small matter to block your access to your funds. It is a simple entry to reprogram a computer to disallow any further transactions to your account. Thereafter, all future purchases would be declined. Such a fate will confront anyone who has somehow failed to "cooperate" with the coming New World Order's 666 system.

It is obvious that such arbitrary power in the hands of big government easily could strangle you in a heartbeat. The potential for comprehensive totalitarian blackmail and control would be incredible! And even though many Americans are beginning to see the "handwriting on the wall" and doing their best to slow the progress of this inevitable system, the majority still are slumbering blissfully where these matters are concerned. As obvious as it is, even when they hear, they refuse to believe. That's too bad.

ACCEPTANCE OF THE NEW 666 SYSTEM

Advocates of world government believe that the only efficient way to handle the complexity of a totally cashless society is to *let the government handle it!* (You expected something else?) However, they assure us that the development of such a system is just around the corner—a system capable of handling electronically the country's $300 billion annual currently-cash transactions. They want everyone to anxiously embrace their wonderful new system, so they must convince you of its flawless ability to handle all your needs, while at the same time being safe from tampering by hackers.

For the majority of people who have been using electronic banking for years—in the form of direct payroll deposits, direct-deposit of social security checks, use of the ATM (with its myriad of menu selections) to transfer your funds around, withdraw cash, etc., use of credit and debit cards (point-of-purchase machines), use of touch tone phones to access your account and move funds around, electronic automatic payment of your mortgage payment or utility bills—learning to use the new system will be a snap. You see, the New World Order planners are not stupid. You have been conditioned slowly for years to enjoy all these efficient, streamlined, and convenient forms of enticing electronic enslavement. And the infrastructure now is so firmly and smoothly in place that even those few who may be unfamiliar with electronic banking accounts will find them surprisingly easy to use.

Polls taken around the country overwhelmingly conclude that people approve and appreciate this convenient use of new technology, although many of them were not given a choice. The government instigated EBT payments of welfare benefits and food stamps, etc. It is the only way you can receive benefits—these recipients were mostly exclusively cash-users who indicated that they preferred the new debit-card system. A vast number of social security checks are electronically deposited, and the government would like to see it become *all* of them.

Remember, earlier in this chapter, I told you that the pressure was only going to get worse. The April 11, 1995, edition of the *New York Post* carried this article: "Companies are Hankering for Direct Deposit." Here are some excerpts:

> Corporate America is fuming that Washington is increasingly forcing direct deposit on government workers, while companies can't because of state laws.
> The Social Security Administration tomorrow is expected to announce its plans *to require* that all retirees who have a bank account accept getting paid by direct deposit rather than by check.
> This year, all 4.3 million federal government employees were strongly encouraged to take their weekly. . .paycheck by direct deposit instead of by check.
> The Department of Defense *won't even give an applicant a job unless he or she agrees to being paid by direct deposit.*
> The federal government's move to direct deposit, mandated under the 1994 Financial Management Act, is being watched closely by payroll managers and bankers across the country. Many have tried but failed over the past 20 years to get their workers to accept getting paid electronically.
> . . .a recent study. . .revealed that while fully 80% of all US companies offer direct deposit to their employees, only 20% of workers actually participate. [Very interesting!]
> [In] Japan, direct deposit is used by 99% of all workers, and Europe averages 90%.
> Even though Federal Reserve permits companies to mandate

direct deposit,. . . .36 states today specifically prohibit employers from making direct deposit mandatory.

The caption under the photo reads: "IN THE ARMY NOW:. . . Department of Defense employees are paid by direct deposit. . . ."

On December 20, 1993, an article picked up from AP was printed in the *Los Angeles Times*. It appeared in the "Your Money" section under the headline, "Road to Cashlessness Paved with Plastic" and a subtitle—Technology: A vast information network brings closer the day when money will blip, not jingle. It is a well-written article that tries to take some of the mystery out of what happens after a consumer hands their credit card over to the clerk and they slide it through that little machine hooked up to the telephone lines. I thought the following was very interesting. . . see if you can figure out what jumped out and caught my attention.

> Here's what happens after you hand your card over to the sales clerk:
>
> . . . [the information on your card is read and electronically transmitted over the phone line].
>
> Once the account information makes it to your bank, the computers ask several questions:
>
> • Is your card stolen?
> • Does the purchase exceed your credit limit?
> • Is the purchase unusual and way outside your normal buying habits?
>
> The computers answer this question by *instantly examining whether your purchase fits within your established record of buying behavior. Although some consumers might regard that as an invasion of privacy,* it is considered a useful way to help prevent unauthorized use of your card [emphasis added].

I told you they were keeping track of what you were buying! Of course, according to them, that's only for your own protection. . .*so far!* However, I don't truly believe that's all it's being used for, even now. I think it already is being sorted by categories of interest and sold on mailing lists to people who want to fill your box with unsolicited junk mail.

Then, there's the cashless phone calls. You just purchase a prepaid card for a predetermined amount and slide it through the slot, then talk till your card's all used up. According to an article in *The Denver Post* on August 22, 1993, it brings your rates down. "Whereas most credit cards have a surcharge of 75 cents or so per call, debit cards have none, which brings the calling rate down. The price of each call is automatically deducted from the prepaid amount you choose, which can be charged to your VISA or MasterCard. If the debit phone card gets lost or stolen, no one else can use it because it isn't imprinted with your personal code." See, you can go cashless all the way around here—and save on expenses, as well.

An article written by Phil Patton, entitled "E-Money," appeared in the July, 1995, edition of *Popular Science* magazine. It ran with the lead line: "If you thought e-mail changed your life, wait until you get a fistful of this." It reiterates mostly what I've already covered, but it is a comprehensive, well-written report, so I'm including some excerpts below.

> [You use your "stored value card" in telephones, vending machines, parking meters, or to board a bus, *et al.*] A text display above the slot where you once dropped quarters tells you how much is being deducted and the remaining value on the card. . . .You add value to the card by inserting it in an Automatic Teller Machine. . . .eliminating at last the major encumbrance of home banking: the inability to draw cash. Once e-money is accepted as universally as greenbacks, don't be surprised if a disheveled man on the street steps up to you and says, "Brother, can you spare a little stored value?"
>
> Such is the vision of smart card proponents, who push chip-embedded plastic both as a realistic alternative to cash and a tactile alternative to non-physical money that exists only as numbers on the Internet.
>
> "If we had our way, we'd implant a chip behind everyone's ear in the maternity ward," says Ronald Kane, a vice president of Cubic Corp.'s automatic revenue collection group. . .one of a number of companies and government agencies pushing the frontier of smart cards—the money of the future. . . .the next best thing is giving everyone a card—a high-tech pass with a memory that may, sooner than we imagine, *replace cash in our wallets.*
>
> . . .A true smart card contains a microprocessor. It is in effect a miniature computer, where a recorded balance can be added to or subtracted from. What makes a smart card like cash is that it is a debit card rather than a credit card: It already has value.
>
> . . .although we may not all end up with a chip implanted under our skin, the even smarter cards of the future may be validated "biomorphically" by fingerprints or retinal readers.
>
> Converting to smart cards will require massive, but gradual, refitting or replacement of equipment in stores. . . .*The transition will likely be a quiet, almost unnoticed process,* smart card pro-

ponents say. And it's already happening.

"This technology is sneaking into our lives from the back door, so to speak," says Bob Gilson, executive director of the Smart Card Forum. . . .the most powerful force behind the new cards.

Smart cards are moving us toward a cashless society [with] digital global transactions on the Internet. . . .

Smart card systems proven in Europe are likely to be the basis for our future systems. . . .The entire bank payment system in France, involving 22 million people, has been converted to smart card technology. Germany's health care system uses smart cards for patient information and billing.

. . .Fear about security remains the sticking point for the next step beyond the smart card: digital money that does not live in a computerized card but in a system of computers. Beyond smart cards *are no cards at all*—just numbers moving through computers and across phone lines.

. . .These transitional cards will gradually replace the driver's license, medical insurance cards, bank cards, and credit cards. . . .[Emphasis added.]

One final paragraph was of particular interest to me. Remember the lengthy section on money laundering earlier in this chapter? It was used to justify moving us forward toward a cashless society. Well, just as I suspected, as in the case of gun control or anything else, the crooks will always find a way around the laws or regulations, and the rest of the "good guys" (law-abiding citizens) get stuck under their oppression. Read this:

Then, there's a form of cybercash that cannot be linked to an owner or spender. One of the first forms of currency online is already international. DigiCash, based in the Netherlands, is the creation of David Chaum, a former computer science professor. With DigiCash, the user is anonymous—unlike with an RSA-type system. Banks and credit card companies are bypassed. DigiCash is untraceable cash and holds potential for money laundering and other fraud. Banks and financial institutions are likely to resist it for many years to come.

But that doesn't mean others (for sure, the bad guys) won't jump right on the Internet and take advantage of the privacy this service affords.

Space precludes me from including it here, but there is one other article that is very well written and comprehensive. I sincerely urge you to go to your nearest large library and borrow a copy and read it. In fact, it is the cover feature. . ."The Cashless Society: It's in the Cards" (*Information Week,* October 11, 1993).

PLAN FOR AN EARTH FINANCIAL CREDIT CORPORATION, AN "EARTH DOLLAR," AND A NEW WORLD ECONOMIC ORDER

The World Constitution and Parliament Association, Lakewood, Colorado, an affiliate of the United Nations and other globalist organizations, in 1987 prepared a rough outline for the New World Order financial system. (See "Main Features and Benefits" of the Earth Financial Credit Corp.)

Their 13-page booklet entitled, *Plan for an Earth Financial Credit Corporation and a New World Economic Order,* outlines the satanic plan to create a new, global, electronic "Earth Dollar" unit of exchange. They are planning to install an entirely new economic system, financed by a new global credit concept. It is highly recommended that you obtain your own copies of these documents so that you may personally examine them as to content. Only in this way will you, yourself, fully appreciate the degree to which such plans have advanced. Call the WCPA in Lakewood, CO, at (303) 233-3548 for information on acquiring these materials. These are also the people who have available the new *Constitution for the Federation of Earth,* designed to supplant all the constitutions of all sovereign nations on earth.

I think there are many places where scripture can be applied equally as well to earthly matters as to spiritual concepts, without any irreverence to the Word of God. One such scripture tells us to study to show ourselves approved unto God, workmen who do not need to be ashamed, because we are able to rightly divide (understand/interpret) the word of truth. I believe that this admonition applies to this subject matter; even though we are dealing with the physical realm, these are circumstances leading to the time of the fulfillment of biblical prophecy. Christians must not turn a deaf ear or put their heads in the proverbial sand, while many of us are crying the warning at the top of our voice. All signs indicate that the hour is late. . . I want you to be aware of just *how* late. Read on and learn how the noose is growing ever tighter.

CHAPTER TWELVE

ISO-9000

In this chapter, I'll probably be telling you more than you ever wanted to know about something called the European Intertek ISO-9000—no products can be sold in Europe without this "mark." Again, there is nothing inherently evil in the mark itself; it just serves to let you know that eventually **everything** will bear an identification mark, not just people and animals.

This mark is already widely in use in the European nations and many others. According to available information, this mark will be mandatory on all products entering EC nations (European Common Market) well before the year 2000.

Unlike some marks that identify the person or animal, and yet other marks which include anywhere from little to much information about that entity, the ISO-9000 mark is based upon the *quality* of products and their manufacturers. The EC is striving for and promoting zero defects from both their domestic and foreign manufacturers. It sounds like a lofty goal, and we certainly should not object to improving either our factories or our products (for years our electronics and automotive industries have been considered second rate when compared with Germany and Japan), but in the long run, it's just one more way to control or limit and track the movement of all goods.

Bert Moore, in *Automatic I.D. News,* August, 1994, said: "If you haven't at least heard about ISO 9000, you probably need to get out more; if you're at least a little confused about ISO 9000, you're definitely in the majority." Trying to avoid too much detail, I'm going to give you an overview of the ISO-9000 system. An article entitled, "ISO 9000 made simple . . .," appeared in the Fall 1992 edition of the *Lab Reporter.* Because it is written in the easy-to-understand question-and-answer format, I'm going to use excerpts to explain this subject. The photo caption reads: "Today large and small companies are coming to recognize ISO 9000 as the best route to worldwide markets—and improved efficiency. Routine calibration of your measuring instruments, such as the balance above, using certified weights for traceability, is part of the ISO 9000 picture." The article begins:

ISO 9000 is coming on us fast, yet not everybody in American industry knows what it is, much less what to do about it. And for good reason. It's not especially easy to explain, it isn't of equal importance to everyone here in the United States, yet, and it will not be simple—or inexpensive—to implement. It will, however, become very important to many American businesses and services in the coming years, and yours may well be among them.

Important does not, alas, mean *interesting*. If you're looking for an easy read, you might want to bypass our ISO 9000 discussion for the IRS longform, or last week's Congressional Record.

So, instead of attempting this as a lively "feature" story, let's cut right to the issues that will be important to your purchasing decisions. We'll try to hit on the key questions that you would ask the ISO 9000 experts if you had the chance.

Q: OK, let's take it from the top. What is ISO 9000?

A: It's a European-driven series of guidelines for a **global** quality system. It consists of five standards for quality management and quality assurance: ISO 9000 through 9004. These standards were first issued by the International Standards Organization (ISO) in 1987. They will become mandatory throughout the European Economic Community (EEC) [previously called the Common Market]. If a company wants to sell products or services in Europe after 1993, it will have to have ISO 9000 certification. [Emphasis added.]

Q: We don't sell in Europe, so why should I care?

A: Even if your organization doesn't sell its products overseas, many of your *customers* may. And that means they will likely only buy products that were made in a registered facility. So ultimately, ISO 9000 will end up dictating *who your customers buy from*. Furthermore, even if you are strictly a buyer of laboratory equipment for your *own* use, the ISO 9000 standards will help you make better product choices.

Q: Why do we need more governmental quality standards?

A: ISO 9000 is *not* governmental standards certification—registration, as ISO calls it, will be made and policed by the ISO and, in the United States, by the American National Standards Institute and the American Society for Quality Control. (ANSI/ASQC).

Why do we need them? Simply put, to grease the gears of the global economy—sort of a 1990s equivalent of standardizing the gauge of railroad tracks. To buy products wisely, you need to be sure you are comparing apples with apples. A purchasing agent in, say, England, knows English companies. He probably doesn't know their French or Portuguese competitors. With an ISO 9000 registration number on hand, however, those foreign companies are suddenly on a level playing field.

Q: What level of quality are we talking about here—just the highest?

A: Not at all. What is being measured here is *consistency.* Can a company maintain a specified level of quality—whatever that level might be—for its products or services throughout the manufacturing and processing cycle—*every time.* Even if you make the little paper umbrellas used in fancy tropical cocktails, your facility could still qualify for ISO 9000 certification—as long as you maintain the specified level of quality.

Q: Which products will need ISO 9000 certification?

A: *Products* don't get certified, *facilities* do. In that sense ISO 9000 is different from something like "UL," where the product itself is tested by Underwriters Laboratories.

Q: Okay, which PRODUCTS are most likely to need to come from ISO 9000 facilities?

A: Products used in your incoming inspection process or in your QC [quality control] lab should be the first to come from suppliers with ISO 9000 facilities. This includes anything used to measure the quality of products coming off your production line—measuring devices, balances and balance weights. Also glassware, particularly serialized glassware in the QC lab. And calibration kits, since ISO 9000 standards require you to demonstrate that you check your instrumentation regularly.

Q: We keep talking about ISO 9000 standards—plural. Why is there more than one?

A: The main reason is to allow companies to target what functions they want to have certified. ISO 9000 and 9004 can be considered. . ."bookends": 9000 defines the terms and concepts. . .and 9004 gives guidance for developing. . . .The three main standards—9001, 9002, and 9003—vary in comprehensiveness. These three are the ISO numbers you will begin to see your suppliers waving around. Incidentally, each of the European ISO 9000 standards has been duplicated word-for-word in the United States by ANSI and ASQC, and are known on this side of the ocean as the Q90 series.

Q: What are the differences between ISO 9001, 9002, and 9003?

A: ISO 9001 (or Q91) is the most comprehensive standard—it provides a model for a quality assurance system in design, development, production, inspection, installation, testing, and servicing. ISO 9002 (or Q92) covers production, inspection, testing, and installation. So it's less comprehensive than ISO 9001, but more comprehensive than ISO 9003 (Q93), which covers final inspection and testing.

Q: What's the No. 1 reason to try for ISO 9000 certification?

A: Back in 1987, when the International Standards Organization first issued the ISO 9000 standards, most companies looked at ISO 9000 certification as a competitive tool: a "we-have-it-and-they-don't-so-buy-from-us" advantage. Today, companies are beginning to view ISO 9000 facility registration as necessary for survival in the global marketplace. It seems inevitable that one day soon companies without registration will not be able to do business with the mega-billion-dollar European Community.

Already more than 40 countries have adopted ISO 9000 standards as national standards. And countries elsewhere around the world are expected to follow suit. But ISO 9000 is also about improving the way you do business. It can help you learn a lot about your own manufacturing setup. Just going through the process can help you see where you can integrate or automate various functions, making you more efficient.

Q: Will companies have to be re-certified?

A: Part of the certification process includes what's called "surveillance." This means the registrars who granted you certification will come in at their discretion to ensure continued compliance....at least annually.

Q: How does a company actually get certified?

A: After an assessment and periodic audit of a company's quality system by a third party, known as a "registrar."

Q: Any final words of wisdom about becoming registered under ISO 9000?

A: Document what you do, and do what you document! ISO 9000 is really as simple —and as hard—as that.

Well, Big Brother has graduated from your personal life and financial matters right into your business. And since the Bible predicts the future Antichrist will rise up from the conjoined European nations, it is interesting that the control and surveillance of all businesses internationally originated and is centered in the EC.

The October, 1993, edition of *Export Today* covered these regulations and the penalties for noncompliance. The subhead reads: "New standards dictate performance levels rather than specific designs." The penalties for failure to include the mark or compliance with the regulations the mark indicates are very stiff. "If the product does not comply with the declaration or the CE [ISO 9000] mark has not been affixed, then the manufacturer or his agent will be in breech of the law. In the UK, for instance, this may have significant legal implications and result in a fine of up to 5,000 Pounds and a period of three months in jail . . . . Surveillance of the manufacturer is required to ensure he fulfills his obligations."

We will discuss the subject fully in chapter 15 on biochips, but it is interesting to note that this article selects randomly for an example a heart pacemaker "which must meet the Active Implantable Medical Devices directive . . . . "

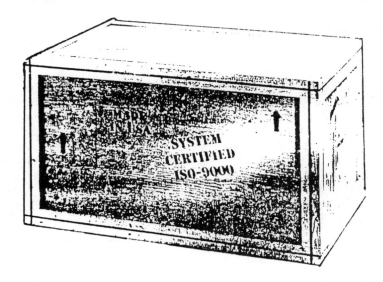

The headline on a flier from Intertek boldy states: **With INTERTEK, You Won't Be Rejected on Seven Continents.** In their company slogan, they refer to themselves as "The Quality People® ." The copy on the flier reads:

> INTERTEK is one of the first U.S. companies with ISO-9000 accreditation traceable to an EC member-state. That makes our certification mark immediately recognizable throughout the world. And more and more countries are enforcing these rigorous standards for Quality Management Systems. So our ISO-9000 Certification will be increasingly essential for anyone who sells abroad.
>
> With the INTERTEK mark, your company name will have the respect and opportunities accorded to an ISO-9000-certified

organization. Without it you could risk rejection . . . on seven continents.

You will want to read the *USA Today* article entitled, "U.S. companies push for perfection." It reports about Motorola, *et al,* striving for perfection in the quality of their technical products. Defects in Motorola's products are less than 3.4 defects per million parts produced. That is truly amazing, but not willing to stop short of perfection, their new target—to be reached within six years, according to their spokesman— is 3.4 defects *per billion* parts. Eastman Kodak produces Kodacolor film containing less than 1 defect per million parts produced. L. L. Bean catalog company last spring shipped 500,000 packages without an error, but their overall error-free rate is still only 99.92%—considerably behind Motorola's impressive 99.99966% (3.4 defects per million).

American Papermaker, June, 1992, says, " . . . it has become the minimum standard required to do business in the worldwide marketplace of the 1990s and beyond . . . . The U.S. Department of Defense, NATO, and the FDA have all announced their intention to adopt ISO 9000 . . . . if two suppliers are trying to land the same contract in Europe, the one that has achieved ISO 9000 registration of its quality system may have a clear competitive edge . . . . North American companies that either want to continue or are looking to start exporting goods to the EC will need ISO 9000 certification as their calling card. Moreover, in a growing number of areas of the U.S. and Canada, ISO 9000 certification is becoming or, in some instances, has become, a minimum standard for doing business."

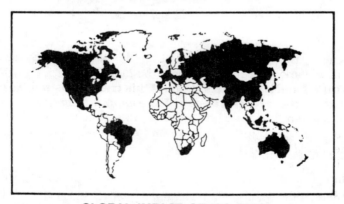

GLOBAL IMPACT OF ISO 9000

There is a worldwide political and trade policy trend toward quality system registration. Tens of thousands of companies have been registered and at least 30 nations are applying the standards (Sue Jackson of DuPont reports 51 countries, as of 1992).

Let me offer you one more question and answer.

Q: What is the global impact of ISO 9000?

A: Within five years quality system registration will be basic to doing business on a global basis.

The Twenty Elements of ISO 9001

1. Management Responsibility
2. Quality System
3. Contract Review
4. Document Control
5. Design Control
6. Purchasing
7. Purchaser Supplied Product
8. Product Identification Traceability
9. Process Control
10. Inspection and Testing
11. Inspection, Measuring, and Test Equipment
12. Inspection and Test Status
13. Control of Nonconforming Product
14. Corrective Action
15. Handling, Storage, Packaging, and Delivery
16. Quality Records
17. Internal Quality Audits
18. Training
19. Statistical Techniques
20. Servicing

Copies of ISO 9000 and Q90 standards can be purchased from the American National Standards Institute, 11 West 42nd Street, 13th Floor, New York, NY, 10036. Phone (212) 642-4900.

As I mentioned at the beginning of this chapter, as well as earlier in this book, the day is coming when everything on the planet will be identified in some way. If it walks, talks, meows, barks, or none of the above . . . if it just lies there and gets transported from place to place, *it will have a number!* And somebody will know where it is, where it has been, and where it's going. Unfortunately, by the time everything is in the system somewhere, the "somebody" who will have access to all that information will also have total dictatorial power, which means that freedom, as we know it, will be a thing of the past.

Now, let's move on to the next chapter where the identification **really** gets personal. . . Biometrics!

The only thing I want to do before I close this chapter is to remind you of the scripture that says to *comfort* one another with these words. . .when you see these things begin to come to pass, look up, for your redemption draweth nigh.

CHAPTER THIRTEEN

Biometric I.D. Methods

There are all kinds of technical descriptions and definitions for biometrics, but in a nutshell, it is *combining* some part of your *physical anatomy* with some *card* (or other form of identification) to make a *positive identification* of a person, one which is difficult—if not impossible—to forge or falsify.

The *Automatic I.D. News,* in June, 1995, defined it as follows:

Biometric ID
Typically used for security and access control applications, biometric identification techniques digitally store some physiological trait as a means of personnel identification. In a fingerprint ID system, for example, a person gains access to a secured area after placing his or her finger on a reader that matches the fingerprint to one digitally stored in a database. Identification is made in less than two seconds.

Other personal characteristics being digitized and stored in computers include blood-vessel arrangements in the hand or wrist [and now in the face, as well], blood vessels in the eye's retina or iris, voice patterns, hand geometry, facial features, typing patterns, and signature patterns. The most widely used of these techniques is the fingerprint scanner. Most widely implemented in high-security areas at banks and government installations, the systems are being tested in applications ranging from prisoner identification, to security for truck drivers transporting loads of dangerous gas, to health spa member identification.

I feel that the majority of these methods are in compliance with the requirements of the prophecy in Revelation 13:16-18 which calls for the location of the identification mark to be in the forehead (the face) or the right hand (biometrics of the hand usually specify the right hand).

However, there are more microscopic parts of the anatomy that are exclusively unique to a particular individual, and therefore, make an excellent method of identification. Of course, I'm referring to the genetic material, DNA. As yet, the testing for DNA comparisons is too complex and costly to make it a viable alternative for regular biometric use, although thanks to your tax dollars, that may not be the case in the near future. The government is spending millions of dollars developing a convenient method of DNA identification, and they already have begun collecting a database from military personnel. Read the following article which appeared December 6, 1992, in the *Tribune Newspapers (Newsday)*. The title is "Military IDs found in genes: DNA database being established."

FORT DRUM, N.Y.—When Sgt. Robert Hopkins stuck cotton swabs into the mouths of hundreds of servicemen in an Army gym here Saturday, he was helping create a new genetic database that could end the need for more tombs to unknown soldiers.

In an *unprecedented move*, the Pentagon is obtaining blood and saliva samples from all soldiers who may be deployed to Somalia from this Army base in upstate New York near Watertown. The samples will be placed in a *DNA database*, which would be used to identify remains of soldiers destroyed beyond recognition. [Author's note: Or those who weren't, at some point down the road, well after they have left military service. Are they going to purge their files of that information when you depart? I think not! It will remain there to come back and haunt you in the future.]

The Department of Defense announced in January that it intended to obtain DNA specimens from all 1.5 million armed forces members over the next five years, but Fort Drum soldiers were the first active duty forces to give the samples before leaving on a potential combat mission.

Civil libertarians have expressed concern that such a massive database could lead to discrimination based on genetic predispositions to certain physical or mental conditions.

But Jim Canik, who heads the DNA identification laboratory at the Armed Forces Institute of Pathology, which oversees the program, said the samples would be used exclusively to identify a soldier and would not be converted into testing material unless identification was required. [Emphasis added.]

The implications of this technology are self-evident. I know it sounds like what you see weekly on *Star Trek, Babylon 5,* or some other futuristic sci-fi show but it's not something that far into the future . . . it is very prevalent now, all around us. Depending upon where you are employed, you may have encountered biometrics already; or if you are a frequent international traveler, you may have an INSPASS card, which requires scanning your right hand for comparison with the digitized identity information embedded in the computer chip in your INSPASS card; or a bank has made you put your fingerprint on a check you wanted to cash.

Or you may do business at a bank which very recently has *generously* offered to trade your *old-fashioned ATM card*—free of charge—for a nice new one with your picture and signature on the front. . . for your protection, of course. That's just a precursor of biometrics. . . as well as a way to get the old cards out of circulation and replace them with smart cards that will hold all the information they want to store on you in the card's microprocessor chip.

Now that I have told you this much, there is not much more to tell you about biometrics, other than to reference the many uses that are surfacing for biometric identification, and point out that they are emphasizing the "right" hand for their readers, which is consistent with Revelation 13.

In an article about using biometrics (right hand images) to detect welfare fraud in the state of California, we read: "A California county has begun taking 'hand images' of General Assistance recipients in an effort to reduce the chances that a person will apply for more benefits under an assumed identity. . . .There is no way to tell how much duplicate aid is going on."

In the April, 1994, edition of *Security Management,* Donald R. Richards, CPP, wrote an article entitled, "ID Technology Faces the Future," which is a play on words, since this article deals with biometric identification relying upon various characteristics in the face.

> Identification system operators have long sought a device that works effectively without human involvement or intervention in either the data reading or decision-making processes. The system that operates without further direct human input after the enrollment process is the ultimate biometric product. Such a system is limited to identification verification based on discriminators that can be seen or measured from a distance. Since users are likely to be clothed from head to toe, *the identification decision must be based on the hands or head*. . . [emphasis added].

Automatic I.D. News, August, 1994, carried an article about biometric identification of organization members to gain access to facilities. "Local YMCA replaces membership cards with high-tech handshake.

The October, 1994, edition of *Popular Science* magazine carried an article on computers that match faces in a video camera with a stored (digitized) image on their electronic ID card. This is an excellent method, although it is a visual process to a certain degree. The next step in facial identification is more advanced and reliable—thermal faceprints.

Automatic I.D. News, July, 1995, ran an interesting article on the new thermal faceprinting, "A defaced face can't beat the heat: Thermal faceprints are hot new ID method/Thermal faceprints provide new kind of secure automatic ID."

Captions under the two photos (one of the visual face and the other of the thermal scan) read: "System displays unique thermal facial characteristics which it uses to identify a face in six seconds."

John Burnell, News Director for *Automatic I.D. News,* writes:

> A "hot" new technology that never forgets a face is the newest form of personal automatic identification. If you're one in a million, there are 5,000 people in the world just like you—except that your face releases heat in a pattern as unique as your finger-print. . . .
>
> The system uses an infrared video camera to take a thermal picture, called a thermogram, of a face. Software processes the image and makes the recognition based on analysis of the vascular system, facial tissue, and skin heat emissions. . . . Perspiration, bruises, swelling, and *even plastic surgery or disguises* won't change an individual's heat emission pattern.
>
> "The applications for this technology are endless. We envision a day when consumers won't need cards at ATMs, high-level telephone communications can be fully secured, and *newborns can be protected before leaving the hospital* through the creation of private family records. . . . Ear and nose temperatures aren't included in the analysis because they are highly sensitive to temperature changes. The infrared camera is insensitive to light and produces accurate images in total darkness from up to four feet away, although the range could be extended. . . . the technology is more accurate than other biometric identification techniques. . . and is more user friendly because it only requires looking into a camera. . . .
>
> . . . TRS will pursue eight applications during the next five years: access control, computer security, identification credentials, credit card security, communications security, private records, and law enforcement support. [Emphasis added.]

Benjamin Miller, of *Personal Identification News (PIN),* wrote an article for *IEEE SPECTRUM* (February, 1994), entitled "Vital Signs of Identity," a special report on biometrics. He advises that before examining biometric approaches, it is useful to understand the concepts of identification, in general.

> . . . A straightforward model of the process postulates three

building blocks: something a person knows (a code), or possesses (a card), or has (a characteristic). From this static model can be derived a much more dynamic model for an identification scheme that balances such variables as types of threat, value being protected, user reaction, and of course cost.

The most dramatic evidence of the evolution is the falling price of biometric verifiers, according to the *1995 Advanced Card and Identification Technology Sourcebook.* In 1994, the average price per access point protected was approximately $2,000, compared with over $6,000 five years ago.

As early as 1988, the *Ocala Star-Banner* ran an article by Suzanne Cassidy of *The New York Times,* entitled "Vein readings make abuse of credit: Using Vein Patterns to Prevent Fraud." This article was written about an event that occurred in London—the Europeans have been on the fast track all along, where this positive identification issue was concerned. The first illustration (there are five total) shows a drawing of the *right* hand and the veins on the back of the hand. The caption reads: "The vein pattern in a person's hand or wrists is digitized and the data stored on a credit card magnetic stripe. As proof of identity, a card user's hand is inserted into a device that matches the vein pattern of the hand with the digital pattern of the card." The other captions read: "COMPUTER ACCESS: The card could provide access to such things as data bases and corporate information." "MONETARY ACCESS: The card could be used instead of signatures for access to check cashing facilities." "PHYSICAL ACCESS: Vein pattern recognition could replace the use of keys and other physical security devices." "VEHICLE ACCESS: Instead of door and ignition keys, cars might read veins before doors would open and engines start." Below are some excerpts from the article.

> LONDON—After a fellow worker at the Eastman Kodak plant in Nottingham, England, stole Joe Rice's credit cards and forged his name to buy hundreds of dollars worth of merchandise, Rice decided to invent a credit-card security system.
>
> Working in his kitchen, the Kodak electronics engineer invented a system that uses the veins in the back of the hand or the wrist to certify that the person presenting a credit card is authorized to use it.
>
> *As a result, future shoppers may be asked to hold out their hands for a "vein reading" rather than signing for a credit card purchase.*
>
> An electronic camera scans the subcutaneous veins and converts their pattern into digital information that can be stored in the magnetic stripe on the back of a credit card. The vein pattern could also be programmed into a "Smartcard," a credit card-like

device that would have a wide variety of information stored in a computer chip on the card.

"There may be a time when you leave your video camera on a park bench and when you come back for it, it will still be there because it won't work for anyone else.

Remember, in an earlier chapter we discussed the fact that the IRS and other agencies were turning bank and business employees into their own personal police force, by making it illegal *not* to assist them by reporting suspected offenders. It is suggested in this article, as well. They want clerks who are given a card for a purchase that doesn't match the hand scan of the purchaser to switch the camera quickly to record the person's scan so they can catch potential thieves. Read this:

> If someone tried to make a purchase with somebody else's Smartcard and the presenter's vein pattern did not match the pattern stored on the card, the store employee could simply adjust the electronic camera from its usual mode and photograph the person's actual vein pattern. The vein patterns of suspected retail thieves could be stored.

On July 3, 1995, *USA Today* ran an article by Lisa Green and Cheryl Phillips entitled: "Strategy against check fraud: Fingerprinting." PriMerit Bank in Las Vegas had six-figure losses from check fraud in 1993 and 1994. Since they started fingerprinting in February, 1995, they have had only two forgeries. However, it is my belief that this is merely an excuse to move us forward even further toward a national ID card. Below are excerpts.

> More banks are requiring non-customers to provide a fingerprint before cashing checks.
>
> The Arizona Bankers Association announced a program last week involving Bank of America, Bank One, First Interstate, and Norwest Bank.
>
> It will roll out this summer at banks primarily in the Phoenix and Tucson areas. . . . Bank of America started fingerprinting at Las Vegas branches last year. . . .
>
> Because many criminals use fake IDs, it's nearly impossible to trace them.
>
> People who cash a check where they don't bank will be asked to press their index finger on an inkless pad and then on the lower center of the check. The print is invisible to the eye, but not to the check-reading equipment. If a check bounces or is forged, a fingerprint can be given to police.
>
> Robert Ellis Smith, publisher of *Privacy Journal*, objects to fingerprinting. "Fingerprints are thought of in a criminal con-

text...."

"Our philosophy is, if you don't have anything to hide, (finger-printing) shouldn't be a problem," PriMerit spokeswoman Kristin Schultz says.

Yeah, right! I'm curious to know where the computer stores the finger-prints of the people whose checks *don't* bounce. I'm not gullible enough to believe that they are just discarded. The majority of checks are put on microfiche, then destroyed (a few people still pay to get theirs returned) within a few days of the transaction. (I'm sure you've seen the kind of document you get if you request a *copy* of the micro-fiche for proof of some payment.) If the fingerprints aren't stored on that microfiche, then how are they going to give them to the police for law enforcement purposes? Perhaps I'm wrong about this, but given all the other things they're doing, it seems a logical assumption.

In the News Briefs section of *Personal Identification News (PIN)*, January, 1994, it was announced that "Sprint Goes National with Voice Activated Foncard." The article reports that "Voice Activated Foncard [is] a service that should quickly become the world's largest applica-tion of biometric identification technology." The Foncard system is based on Texas Instruments' MultiServe Telecommunications (MST). "According to Sprint, the use of biometrics is a major selling point with customers who are increasingly aware of long-distance toll fraud."

A newspaper article by Martin Peers—about the same announce-ment—gives you the easy-to-understand version. Here are the high points.

> Worried about someone stealing your telephone calling card and bankrupting you with calls all over the world?
>
> Worry no more. Long-distance telephone company Sprint is introducing a phone card which relies on a voice imprint as its security protection.
>
> The card will also have a memory capacity to carry 10 numbers, allowing a user to tell the phone to call someone.
>
> All you'll have to do is say "phone mother" to prompt the tele-phone to dial your mother's telephone number, for instance.
>
> Major long-distance carriers are now quick to spot a suspicious pattern of calling,. . . . [Author's note: Would you like to guess how they know that it's suspicious? They wouldn't—if they weren't already keeping track of who and where you were calling.]
>
> . . .a spokesman later added that the card would work even if the customer was tired or ill and the voice was slightly different than normal.

Well, by now you should have a pretty good working knowledge of biometrics used in conjunction with computer-stored data for positive identification of a person. I am going to conclude this chapter by incorporating a portion of my October, 1995, newsletter, *Pressing Toward the Mark*. The section is called "Biometrics and Biochips in the New World Order."

Biometrics and Biochips in the New World Order

In February of this year, VISA International announced that it would introduce the first chip-based credit card in July. This has now occurred and you will be seeing major promotions which are already appearing. VISA is accepted at 11 million retail outlets worldwide and is affiliated with more than 20,000 financial institutions. There are 357 million VISA cardholders and the company gains almost 15% new cardholders annually. VISA is huge and, not surprisingly, a board member of the Smart Card Forum advancing worldwide acceptance of microchips. Seventeen manufacturers of smart cards, reading devices, and network services finally have signed agreements with VISA to develop products conforming to VISA's new chip-based credit card.

Joining VISA in this venture was MasterCard International, Schlumberger Smart Cards systems, and Europay International. A Schlumberger spokesman commented that "smart cards could become part of daily life in every country in the world within a decade because of this pioneering work." Indeed, says John Burnell, News Director for *Automatic I.D. News,* "Including a chip on a credit card will enable credit card companies to provide more services and security for their cardholders. VISA initially plans to use the chip to increase card security because the cards will be very difficult to counterfeit and could be combined with biometric technology for secure transaction authorization." Folks, there is no **could** about integrating biometric technology into your VISA card—they **will** do it, and soon. All chip-reading terminals will be ready by late 1996.

Biometrics is the ultimate in positive ID because it identifies your unique characteristics, such as retinal scan, voice, fingerprint, signature, thermal faceprints, etc. Regarding bank cards, Sensar, Inc. in Princeton, NJ, has just teamed up with IriScan for the exclusive rights to provide retinal scan technology to all Automatic Teller Machines (ATM). This device will work from two to four feet in order to accommodate people standing at the ATM machine or in a car at a drive-thru machine. "The 256 byte iris template would likely be stored on a magnetic stripe or in future smart bank card chips" *(Personal Identification News,* July/Aug., 1995). Technology will be rolled out by July, 1996.

One of the more innovative uses of biometrics to come on the scene is the thermal faceprint, or thermogram. Introduced by Technology

Recognition Systems (TRS), a thermogram uses an infrared (IR) camera and computer database to record the unique heat patterns in your face. Veins and arteries flow with blood warmed deep within your body and are hotter than surrounding facial tissue. An analysis of your face takes only 6 seconds (perhaps 6.66 seconds!) and **no** two faces are the same. David Evans, CEO of TRS, insists that this technology is more accurate than any other biometric identification technique.

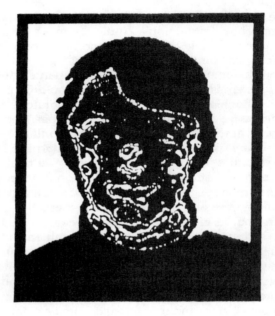

"We envision a day when consumers won't need cards at ATM's" *(Automatic I.D. News,* July, 1995). According to company literature, this system works passively, "Thus even uncooperative subjects can be easily imaged at a distance." Commercial applications are scheduled for release by Spring, 1996.

Biochip transponders (which are about the size of a grain of rice) are finding their way into some very interesting uses—everything from beer barrels to bicycles, literally! In Germany, the beer capital of the world, manufacturers are using Radio Frequency Identification (RFID) to track wooden barrels of beer in the brewery and in transit. Biochip transponders are "embedded in each barrel's collar." In Copenhagen, Denmark, 500 public bicycles are located at 120 different sites in the city to promote environmentally friendly tourism. Bikes can be used by inserting a 20-kroner coin in the lock, the same way travelers get luggage carts at airports. Bicyclists get the coin back when they return the bike. This idea has proven more successful than a similar campaign in The Netherlands in which **all** the bicycles were stolen! What's the catch? Riders are informed that "an electronic chip is hidden in the frame to help trace and identify lost bikes" *(The Denver Post,* 6-1-95).

Biochips also have moved into the area of sports. For the first time, this summer athletic runners in Europe were tagged with "velcro wrist-bands" containing RFID transponders in order to keep runners honest and accurate. Some transponders were worn on the tip of the lace on the athlete's shoe. Containing a 20-digit number, the transponder passes an antenna and is then fed to the host computer system. Remember, you can run, but you can't hide!

And for you ski enthusiasts, the Texas Instruments SKIPPO hands-free ticketing system is now in action at the Foppolo/Carona ski resort in Milan, Italy. Biochip transponders are incorporated right into the ski passes and waved over the readers on the slopes. Here in the U.S., they have something called "Ski Key" which contains a microchip worn on a velcro wristband. "It's in use at California's Northstar at Tahoe, where scanners on chairlifts keep track of vertical miles skied. Like members of airline frequent-flier clubs, Ski Keyers win prizes for accumulated mileage. Skiers can charge lift fees and meals directly to the Key, and it even alerts them to phone messages, so the office is never more than a mogul away" *(Newsweek,* 1-16-95).

On a more serious note, it appears that government authorities are moving closer to implanting humans with biochip transponders— the ultimate in biometrics. In a preliminary step, the Pima County Jail in Tucson, Arizona, uses a barcoded, riveted wristband on inmates in order to promote a cashless jail. "The wristband is keyed into the central computer system and contains each inmate's physical descrip-tion, name, picture, and number, and is used to keep track of inmate location, visitation, library, and medical use" *(Government Technology,* Aug., 1995). By monitoring the flow of cash, the Pima County jail has eliminated contraband problems. Nearby in New Mexico, Gov. Gary Johnson recently suggested that prison inmates be implanted with biochips. "We can insert the microchips into people's brains and control their behavior that way," said Johnson *(The Albuquerque Journal,* 9-1-95). He added, "With the technology advancing all the time, who knows what technologies we're going to have in the future to . . . be able to implement innovative ways of parole and work release." Gov. Johnson faced considerable opposition for proposing this idea, but others are quite serious. One individual is controversial New York criminologist Dr. Wayne Varnys.

Dr. Varnys points out: "The operation is very simple—by implanting computer chips into the cerebral cortex—the part of the brain that thinks and reasons. . . .This procedure will not only wipe out the convict's power to think for himself, it will also let employers order him to do various preprogrammed tasks by touching a remote control device." Dr. Varnys notes that surgery already has been successful on wild chimps. He stresses that the operation only be used on "habitual criminals convicted of vile and violent crimes." Naturally, groups are protesting this idea. Cheryl Jirvo, head of the New York-based organization Let's Ensure Prisoner's Rights (LEPR) argues, "Regardless of what they've done, these people are human beings." "America is sick of that crybaby liberal tack," said Dr. Varnys. "What kind of dignity and respect did these rapists, murderers, and child molesters show their victims?" *(Weekly World News,* 7-11-95). Dr. Varnys currently has 200,000 signatures of New Yorkers who favor the plan. He hopes to get the New York State Legislature to pass a Bill that will legalize the surgery by late 1996.

Unfortunately, it appears that the U.S. Intelligence Community has not waited for "legalization." According to Dr. Antony C. Sutton, Editor of *Future Technology Intelligence Report,* September, 1995, there are a "limited number of agents" who are utilizing Remote Neural Monitoring (RNM) on federal prisoners at Fort Meade, Maryland. In a copy of an original document supplied to Dr. Sutton, the case of John St. Clair Akwei v. NSA at Fort Meade (Civil Action 92-0449) cites the misuse of intelligence operations by experimenting and harassing the plaintiff for 12 years by means of RNM. RNM is not the same as biochip implants, but just as effective. The frequency to which the various brain areas respond varies from 3 Hz to 50 Hz. According to this document, "only NSA Signals Intelligence modulates signals in this frequency band." Information can be subliminal to perceptible, based on each individual's unique set of bioelectric resonance/entrainment frequencies. Dr. Sutton notes the fact that Mr. Akwei's case was dismissed in U.S. District Court by Judge Stanley Sporkin. Judge Sporkin was previously Chief Counsel for the Central Intelligence Agency (CIA). So much for "equal justice under law" in the New World Order. The spectre of Big Brother draws closer with each passing day.

By now it should be obvious to even the most naive that there will be no escape from the global electronic web in the evil, all-enslaving New World Order—with one exception . . . belief in Jesus Christ. The world is being sucked in little by little, and they soon will become inextricably trapped in the quagmire of the New World Order *convenient* system of electronic bondage. Accepting Jesus Christ as one's Savior is the only way to avoid being here when the Antichrist rises to complete and total power, with both the political ability and the technical capability to mandate the mark in the right hand or forehead in order to buy or sell. If you do find yourself still here at that time, it is not too late to be saved if you will call upon the Lord, but Revelation and other books of prophecy are clear. . .unfortunately, it will cost you your head to reject the Beast and his mark. I hope none of you who read this book will be in that position, because I have extended both the warnings and the invitation to accept Jesus in nearly every chapter, but remember this one thing above all else, even if your choice to accept Jesus and reject the Beast costs your physical life here on earth, that is still preferable to accepting the mark and losing your soul for eternity.

Much has occurred to move us toward electronic enslavement, but it seems evident that the next step on the horizon toward gaining complete control of our lives is the matter of identifying each person; in this country we will be issued a national ID card. Eventually, this identification will be the ultimate in biometrics—an implantable bio-chip (see chapter 15), but first let's take a detailed look at the interim methods, smart cards, MARC cards, and others.

America's Identity Crisis And the Emerging National I.D. Card

The 1960's search for *identity* has returned but this time it is not an idle search for some intangible "self." This time it is for a verifiable *electronic* identity, confirmed by some method of biometrics (as discussed in the previous chapter). Indeed, the word for tomorrow is your *digital identity*. Commercial entities of every variety and government agencies from the IRS to the DMV—and all the others in between— are making plans to computerize and identify you electronically.

The term *identity crisis* was coined by German-American psycho-analyst Erik Erikson, a term which he popularized in his theories on identity/identity crisis. Erikson holds that people grow through experiencing a series of crises, from which they must achieve their own identity. In researching *identity crisis,* I ran across an even more interesting concept put forth by one of Erikson's predecessors, psycho-analyst and social philosopher Erich Fromm, who argued that *freedom* was stressful, claiming that in some societies the populace actually followed a dictator in order to be relieved of the stress of having to make decisions themselves. Frankly, I prefer the stress of making my own decisions to the even greater stress of having someone else make them for me! However, I am addressing another type of crisis in this chapter. . . read on.

America—indeed, the entire world—is experiencing a crisis, but rather than an *identity* crisis, it could be described more accurately as an *identification* crisis. Globalist leaders assert that an *identification crisis* exists worldwide, whereby soon everyone on earth must possess a national ID card of some kind. Why? Because Big Brother and his global government, the New World Order, cannot rise to complete dictatorial power until it can accurately make positive identification of everyone on the face of the earth (beginning with the modern industrialized nations, I'm sure, followed by the third-world countries). In order to enslave you, which is their goal, they first must be able to keep track of you and all your transactions. Positive biometric identification permits surveillance, which leads to control!

The target date for achieving this goal is the year 2000. By then, government and/or globalist leaders hope to have issued all of us a unique, biometrically confirmed, digitized ID card that will incorporate a microprocessor, the technologically advanced "smart" card with an integrated circuit chip (IC chip). This smart chip will be capable of storing an immense amount of personal data on everyone. It will result in an unparalleled, illegal invasion of our privacy, and an unprecedented violation of our constitutional rights. This technology will enable the digital profiling and tracking of everyone in a worldwide electronic, all-enslaving cashless society, using a myriad of linked/networked data bases sharing information—until they decide to put all the information in *one place,* the hardware for which is already in design.

Your first reaction may well be that, "I'm not important enough for anyone to care—all that spying and surveillance will be reserved for those with access to sensitive data." Don't you believe it—they want to control *you.* It doesn't matter if you work for the CIA, or IRS, or what your job is, or if you are a drug dealer or money launderer. The ultimate goal is to control your *buying and selling,* as described in Revelation 13—and that isn't limited to certain people, it refers to *everyone.*

Information as to what you purchase, and where, and how much, has been collected secretly for some time. And even though no one has publicly confessed that they are accumulating such information on us, they have admitted it in a "backhanded" sort of fashion, in fact, they are so proud of how well it's working they now are advertising some of the side benefits generated by the collection and sorting of such details. I will give you three examples.

You may have seen a television commercial recently by a major credit card company, bragging on themselves for their terrific efficiency in their efforts to *protect you* and your card from misuse. It was a clever little scenario showing a guy you could loosely call a "slob," who never purchased anything but "slob" stuff. Then one day he went out and bought a tuxedo in which to get married. This terrific, efficient credit card computer determined that this was outside the "norm" for this customer and went "tilt." So someone called to assure that it really was him charging on his card, and not some imposter. Wasn't that a considerate thing to do? As I have pointed out numerous times, it's always for our convenience. But did anyone stop to think *how they knew it was outside the norm?* Of course, they avoid mention of this in their commercials, but there is only one way. . .the computer has been collecting information about your private transactions long enough to establish a profile on you, and it now knows what is the "norm" for you.

The IRS announced several months ago that it was tying in all kinds of data bases so they could tell if your spending was outside the "norm," i.e., the amount of your reported income. They readily admit they are doing this to eliminate the underground economy, as well as trap illegal banking activities, crime, etc. For example, if you are a waiter who reports income based on minimum wage and meager tips, but the DMV reports you own a Jaguar, and Bank of America's computers show you have a big checking and savings account, and VISA or American Express shows you're a big spender and pay your hefty bills on time, and the state property tax data base shows you own a million-dollar home in Malibu, and TRW gives you an unlimited credit rating. . .stand back and watch the IRS computer go tilt. All these networked or shared data bases will *automatically* sound the alarm when something doesn't fit well within the established profile.

Then there's Sprint telecommunications. They proudly profess that they will get in touch with you if they think someone has stolen your phone card, or watched over your shoulder as you punched in your secret PIN, and just issue you another number, cancelling the card and number in question. Again, this is because someone has started charging excessive calls to your account—calls that don't fall within the range that has been established as your "norm" for calling. Same convenience. . .same problem. There's only one way they could know what the "norm" is. . .tracking your calls! *But you won't find that in the commercials.*

Once the cashless society has been attained, no one will be able to buy or sell anything without the approval of some computer somewhere. And like overextended credit cards right now, you will hear the term "declined" when someone wants to deny you the privilege of buying or selling. The goal is to control *all* money and *all* information, because those who control the money and information *control the world.* Technically speaking, of course, it won't really be money as we know it (i.e., currency or coins), but probably will be called money, for lack of a better term (although we presently are being conditioned to the terms *debit* and *credit*). Actually, it will just be a bunch of numbers being pushed around somewhere out there in cyberspace. But that's the goal for the New World Order. Control and surveillance is the name of their game—it's how they will achieve total global electronic enslavement.

Whatever you call it—a national health card, a tamper-proof social security card, a state or national driver's license, an electronic benefits transfer card, or some other universal card—what we really are getting is a *de facto* NATIONAL IDENTITY CARD.

Instead of "your papers," as Adolf Hitler demanded, you will be required to produce your electronically digitized ID card. Upon insertion into the proper automated readers, all there is to know about you may be accessed from the terminal and pop up on the screen . . . your complete electronic profile from *hundreds* of networked data bases.

Just exactly what will these new cards divulge? Virtually everything about you that's stored presently on over 910 data bases in America alone—your driving history, digitized photos, arrest and warrant records, bank account balances, social security number, marital status, children, divorce records, health records, home ownership and personal property records, car ownership and DMV driving records, various consumer profiles, credit history and profile, employment records, religious affiliation, and even statements from any enemies you may have—all this now is accessible easily on any personal computer via modem connections. All could be instantly displayed on a computer screen at the touch of a button! The more high-tech we become, the more privacy we lose.

What is the excuse being given as the need for a national ID card? There are several, but two of the major concerns are the illegal immigration that has become out of control and the call for health care reform. The New World Order powers in control have deemed the best solution to be the unalterable positive identification of everyone, in order to limit abuse in both areas. A card, linked with some form of biometric confirmation, is likely to be the ID of choice. And since it would only make sense to make the most of the technology at hand, the card of choice would be one which contains the microprocessor chip, allowing the constant updating of information every time a transaction is made or service provided. This kind of technology is referred to as a *smart card.*

It is just beginning to be widely accepted in America, but has been in use in Europe for quite some time. It is being promoted on this side of the Atlantic by an organization called the Smart Card Forum. *World Card Technology,* February, 1995, carried an article written by Catherine Allen, a Vice President at Citibank and Chair of the Smart Card Forum, titled "Influencing Infrastructure Development in the US." Here are some excerpts.

As evidence of the anticipated growth and interest in smart

card technology in the United States, more than 170 companies, as well as the U.S. Treasury, U.S. Department of Health and Human Services, and the U.S. Department of Defense, joined forces in 1993 to create the Smart Card Forum, a consortium charged with developing business specifications and recommending standards for a North American smart card infrastructure.

The Forum's members include American Express, AT&T, Bellcore, IBM, Hewlett Packard, MCI, Microsoft, MasterCard, Visa International, numerous smart card technology vendors, and several large banks, including Citibank, Chase Manhattan Bank, Chemical Bank, Bank of America, Wells Fargo Bank, Nations-Bank, Corestates Bank, and National Westminster Bank. . . .

Citibank has taken a leadership position in helping to establish the Smart Card Forum because it is in the Bank's interest. . . .

You will note that the majority of the above-mentioned organizations are either backed by Rothschild or Rockefeller, or members of the CFR or TLC . . . or any combination of the above.

According to their literature: "Smart Card Forum, with over 190 corporate and government members, provides an arena for the private and public sectors to foster the development of multiple use/multiple application smart cards in the North American market. Its objective is to promote communication resulting in market trials of smart card-based payments and information services within the next two years. Membership is open to organizations with a use or business applications focus. Work groups are active in the areas of electronic purse, health care, government, education, technology, legal and regulatory issues, and telephony."

The Smart Card Forum answers the question "What is a Smart Card?" this way:

Similar to a credit card, a smart card stores information on an integrated microprocessor chip located within it.

There are two basic kinds of smart cards. An "intelligent" smart card contains a central processing unit—a CPU—that actually has the ability to store and secure information, and "make decisions," as required by the card issuer's specific applications needs. Because intelligent cards offer a "read/write" capability, new information can be added and processed. For example, monetary value can be added and decremented as a particular application might require.

The second type of card is often called a memory card. Memory cards are primarily information storage cards that contain stored value which the user can "spend" in a pay phone, retail, vending, or related transaction.

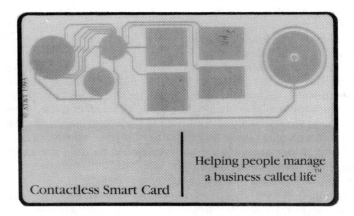

A letter from Catherine Allen accompanied the literature on the Smart Card Forum. It read, in part:

> We invite you to be part of a *cross-industry effort to accelerate the wide-spread acceptance of smart card technology in the United States*. . . .
> The Forum's mission is to accelerate the widespread acceptance of smart card technologies that support multiple applications by bringing together, in an open forum, leading users and technologists from both the public and private sectors. Our goals are to promote interoperability across appropriate business applications of technology, as well as to facilitate market trials.
> . . .The Forum members think there are some compelling reasons to relook at smart card technology as well as to participate in development of the infrastructure in the United States.
> • The convergence of information technologies. . . .
> • New, non-traditional players are entering the businesses of financial services, computing, and information services. . . .
> • The cost of smart card and computer technology continues to decrease rapidly.
> • Fraud is rising and firms are searching for more secure technologies.
> • Most importantly, consumers are demanding convenience....

Right! But what about the immigration problem and the health care concerns? Do they justify issuing identification cards to everyone? Let's address them one at a time and find out.

Immigration Time Bomb:
The Call for a National ID Card

Perhaps nothing poses a greater threat to our civil liberties and personal privacy than the national debate over immigration reform. This topic is *vitally* important, and you must know the implications of new legislation and how it will affect you and your family. This administration, current presidential candidates, and a majority of the states all are calling for some form of positive ID for worker verification. Recent proposals all include use of the smart card in combination with some form of biometric data. So how serious is this immigration problem? Not surprisingly, hardest hit are California, Texas, and Florida, as well as New York and Illinois. In six of our largest cities, 20% of all arrests are of illegal aliens, while one out of four inmates in federal prisons is an illegal immigrant.

In Los Angeles, 40% of all illegals released from jail are re-arrested for new crimes. Unpaid medical bills cost taxpayers over a billion dollars a year, and each year $24 billion in fraudulent claims are made to collect government benefits. Presidential candidate Pat Buchanan points out: "It is outrageous that American taxpayers . . . have to provide social welfare benefits for those whose accomplishments are to break the laws to get into the United States and to get on welfare." "Outrageous" seems a conservative term for it! But is the solution to make *everyone* register for a national ID card? The call is no longer just for immigrants, but for everyone to have the card, so employers would know who it was safe to hire.

People woke up just in time and raised such a furor about the proposed National Health Card that the idea seems to have been tabled . . . but I'm sure it's only temporary. Watch closely, as I'm sure it will rear its ugly head again, and probably sooner than later . . . perhaps under a new name.

I now have acquired so much documentation on this subject that it is difficult to decide what to omit and what to include. I still have to cover some of the more important functions of smart card technology (in addition to its commercial uses, such as banking and purchases, etc.), for example, INSPASS, EBT cards, health cards, motor-voter cards, new-style pilot's license, and perhaps most important of all—the MARC card.

As more and more people gain access to more and more information about you, your privacy diminishes in direct proportion. I am sure these ID cards are nothing more than a predecessor to the implantable biochip (described in the next chapter); in any event, they are establishing the beachhead for the positive identification of every person. In the July 15, 1994, edition of *USA Today,* the following article ran under the heading, "Today's debate: PROVING CITIZENSHIP." The article was titled, "National ID cards let Uncle Sam spy on you," and was followed with—"OUR VIEW: The idea is hot in Washington and carries a heavy price both financially and in loss of privacy." The writers are extremely astute. Here are some eye-opening excerpts:

> Think the federal government already knows too much about your private life? Hang on. The granddaddy of all privacy invasions —a national ID card—is marching onto Capitol Hill.
>
> Startling numbers of Democrats and Republicans, liberals and conservatives, are embracing variations of the identity card — all in the name of immigration reform. They contend the cards could keep illegal immigrants out of American jobs by requiring potential bosses to use the cards and accompanying national data base to verify citizenship.
>
> Sound like a cheap and harmless fix? Wrong. The cards present gargantuan potential for abuse with enormous costs.
>
> . . . Fear of constant harassment is wrong. Having to carry a card to guarantee your freedom is not what the Founding Fathers had in mind.
>
> Then there's the price tag. Most plans on Capitol Hill—and there are dozens in various bills—require all U.S. citizens, not just recent immigrants, to get cards.
>
> . . . proponents believe the means justify the end—closing the jobs door to illegals. They believe "tamper-proof" IDs, verifiable through the national data base, will stop the use of fraudulent documents. . . .
>
> National ID cards are an old idea and a bad idea. The last thing the federal government needs is another peephole on personal privacy that ends up costing U.S. taxpayers more money than it saves.

In the October 17, 1994, issue of *Forbes 400,* Presidential Candidate and Editor-in-Chief Malcom S. Forbes, Jr., included the following on his editorial page:

1984 **UPDATED?**

> A cry for a national identification card is rising again. The catalyst is the desire to get a tool that will cut illegal immigration. We should resist the temptation. Such a card will rapidly be used for far more than employment. The loss of privacy outweighs any gains.
>
> It is disconcerting enough to know that computer snoops can dig up a lot of supposedly confidential information about our lives. The IRS recently admitted that thousands of its employees

> routinely, without authority, examined tax returns of friends, enemies, and the famous.
>
> Assurances that laws would protect our privacy rightly ring hollow. With a national ID card your whole life could end up on a government central computer file. All tax returns, all banking transactions including cash taken from ATMs, all medical records including individual prescriptions, every hotel stay, every store purchase, every moving and parking violation, etc., would be centrally accessible.
>
> Do we as a nation of individualists really want that? Do not be fooled by the idea that a Social Security or national ID card can be made counterfeit-proof by having our photos and fingerprints on it. Warped technological wizards will find a way to beat any government-designed system.

It's hard to say it any better or more concisely than that! Unfortunately, many people can't see the handwriting on the wall . . . or they are part of the Big Brother New World Order crowd who will gain more control over us . . . or they are just naive and capitulating for a modicum of convenience.

Mike Hale, executive administrator for Florida's Information Resource Commission, said: "One of the biggest forthcoming issues in government is going to be on the development of a universal card for citizen identification." He believes states need to take a close look at issuing everybody one card for identification and for the delivery of services, from health care and human services to libraries and special events. "The card can become a way to standardize service to the citizens," says Hale. *Government Technology,* January, 1994, says such a card might be one way for government to consolidate the delivery of many services with one universal system.

To expedite the "telling of this story," and to condense much of the documentation, I am going to put many newspaper and magazine articles in chronological sequence and just take excerpts from them below. Source, date, and title of article will be given on each for verification purposes.

As early as April 21, 1992, an article appeared in both the *Los Angeles Times* and the *Las Vegas Review-Journal* announcing the unveiling of credit cards with the cardholder's photo right on the card. This is where the infrastructure began to be laid for the full-blown smart card technology to follow. In trying to combat fraudulent use, these new cards were issued by Citibank, who reportedly sustained a $1 billion loss from credit card fraud in 1991.

By the next month, the term "smart cards" was being used widely. The following, written by Jeffrey Blair of the Associated Press, appeared in an article entitled: "Smart cards: Convenience and market data rolled into one," in the May 31, 1992, edition of the *Las Vegas Review-Journal.*

> It looks and acts like your average bank card, but it knows a lot more about you than you may think.
>
> The smart card—a piece of plastic with a computer chip on its face—is slipping into the United States with uses from defense and health care to retailing and transportation.
>
> The cards have replaced food stamps for some Ohio shoppers and meal tickets for students in college. Marines and peanut farmers are whipping them out for boot polish and crop reports.
>
> Someday they may also pay highway tolls, or unscramble satellite TV signals, as they're used in Europe today. . . .
>
> "The average American who has a dozen pieces of plastic in their pocket probably doesn't even know what a smart card is...."
>
> So first, an introduction to these data dynamos:
>
> —Unlike today's financial cards, the smart card doesn't need a magnetic stripe on the back.
>
> —Instead, it's equipped with a wiry silicon chip, often displayed at left center but sometimes hidden in the plastic. (Smart cards may also have embossed account numbers, holograms, graphics, and photos on the front or back.)
>
> —Like a bank card, the smart card is slipped into a computer. Then the owner enters a four- or five-digit ID number and uses the card to make purchases, convey information, or both.
>
> —The card can hold three pages worth of typewritten data, compared to one line of type for a magnetic-stripe card. That means several accounts could be loaded onto one smart card....
>
> —Smart cards cost from about $1 each for a disposable card to $4 for the most common cards to about 10 times that for security cards that hold complex information such as voice patterns or retina scans [linked to biometric identification].

Since newspaper articles generally are written for the laymen, rather than the scientist or technician, this is very clear and concise. But as with all computer technology, three years can make a great deal of difference in capabilities. For example, as I covered in detail earlier in this book, EBT (electronic benefit transfers) is no longer available only in Ohio; it is being used in many states and the federal government presently is laying the infrastructure to use it in all federal benefits programs, from welfare, to social security and health care. And the highway tolls already are being collected in several places by smart card technology, and the governors of all the states in the northeast have joined together to install such systems on their interstate freeways.

Probably the greatest improvement in the technology is that "three pages" of data is now obsolete; in certain types of cards well over a thousand pages of data can be stored about you on your smart card (some can store nearly 2000 pages).

June 17, 1993, *Los Angeles Times*, "Lawmakers Clash Over New Call for National ID Card."

> Creation of a single, tamper-resistant identification card to verify employment eligibility—a controversial proposal designed to reduce illegal immigration—received a largely sympathetic hearing Wednesday from members of a House subcommittee.
>
> . . . Rep. Anthony C. Beilenson (D-Woodland Hills), has introduced a bill to establish a national identification card for all eligible workers. "There is simply no way to enforce our existing law without it."
>
> Civil liberties groups contend that a new identification card could lead to a national data bank with information about every American that would pose a threat to individual privacy.

The following are excerpts from an article that appeared in the July, 1993, edition of *Monetary & Economic Review*.

Smart Cards: They Make Our Enslavement So Convenient

Last month in *MER* we briefly touched the subject of the "smart card" and its important role in the New World Order. It is these little pieces of plastic and metal that will control the everyday happenings of the individual. Your purchases can be tracked, your bank account observed, and your entire history can be stored on these cards. They are capable of containing information from blood type to background, all in a package no bigger than a regular credit card. But just how close are these new threats to personal freedom? Right around the corner, and closer than anyone ever thought. [Author's note: Keep in mind, this was written in 1993.]

You may be familiar with the latest commercials from AT&T. Views of a world of ease based upon new technological breakthroughs. The first picture is the portable fax machine, followed by the video phone, and finally we observe a card capable of containing your personal history and medical records. It would seem that AT&T has taken the lead in the smart card industry and is now implementing the cards into daily life. According to AT&T, the smart cards are small, 8-bit microcomputers with their own operating systems, capable of storing 3 kilobytes of information. The cards are contactless, meaning that the microchips are fully enclosed, reducing wear while making it possible to scan the cards like a normal credit card. [Author's note: The new ones linked with biometric data are designed to scan from a distance, without even putting it into a reader/machine.] The information on the card can be read through either a special card reader or through a regular hook-up to a personal computer.

We can already see the beginnings of the smart card in our everyday life. Many banks offer debit cards that replace check-books for their customers. Virtually every phone company has a card with your account number on it for access to long distance calling without the hassle of finding change. Your credit card is an instrument of trade that has in many cases become easier for people to use than cash. These are but a small taste compared to the newest advances of smart card technology.

In Italy, the Olivetti company, along with AT&T, installed a new pension management system using smart cards to keep infor-mation on pensioners and their accounts within their pension fund. The pensioners must have their card in order to withdraw any of their money and the card keeps a record of all transactions.

Also in Italy, the government has installed systems on toll roads that require smart cards to pay the toll. . . .

In many corporations around the world the cards have been implemented for building security. . . .The company can literally track the location of individuals at any time. . . .

It all sounds so nice and easy, but consider the ramifications. Your assets can be frozen in the blink of an eye; anyone with the authority could bring up all of your history and background. Every single one of your records could be accessed by the Internal Revenue Service, the FBI, or any other government agency in an effort to control the actions of the people. It all reminds me of those futuristic movies where the people become a number rather than individuals, whose efforts are put toward the goals of the state. All privacy, whether it be personal history or financial, would be gone forever.

If this sounds far off, consider this: the cards are being set up for use in the United States as they are in the rest of the world. In southern California the smart card is being used on new toll roads. . . . AT&T Smart Cards has openly stated, "equipped with smart cards, commercial vehicles could be located, classified, weighed, and identified for taxation and other purposes while in motion." [Author's note: Again, this is another technology that has been implemented in several states since this article was written.]

If it is possible to be used in commercial trucks, could it not be used in an individual's car? National Cash Register has teamed up with AT&T to produce a dual smart card and voice print identification system, for use on automated teller machines. The voice print on the card must match your voice while making the transaction in order to be validated. Even the United States government uses smart cards in the form of employee identification. When I worked at the White House, it was necessary to wave my card with a microchip to pass the gate and go to my office.

It is easy to see the advantages and sheer ease this allows the New World Order crew in the supplying of information on governments, corporations, and individuals. Though the beginnings of the smart card in society are scattered, it is very simple to take all information from several smart cards and move all files to a single card. It is just a matter of time before the people of this nation and others allow the full use of smart cards in their businesses and private lives. **Remember, the goal of the New World Order crowd is to control the economic and social behavior of everyone. Many people will succumb to this financial slavery out of mere convenience** [emphasis added].

After those last two articles, almost anything else I add will be redundant, but I will make brief reference to the other articles just so you can see the sheer *weight* of the evidence.

September 10, 1993, *Los Angeles Times,* "Wilson Expands on Plan for ID Card."

> **Immigration:** Governor wants the state to be a testing ground for the tamper-proof documents. But he admits that it would probably be impossible to come up with a foolproof system. . . .
>
> There have been periodic proposals for a national ID card, but they have always run up against strong opposition on civil liberties grounds. . . .
>
> Wilson said an identification card is the key to the enforcement of any of the sanctions written into federal law. . . .

December 24, 1993, *Los Angeles Times,* "Orange County to Test Medi-Cal 'Credit Cards.'"

> **Welfare:** Program is designed to speed reimbursements and to cut down on fraud. It should be in effect statewide by June.
>
> The new California Benefits Identification Cards will be mailed to most of the 230,000 people in Orange County who are eligible for Medi-Cal health insurance and the almost 42,000 elderly, blind, or disabled residents who receive benefits under the federal Supplemental Security Income program. Four other counties also will participate in the pilot program; all of the state's 5 million Medi-Cal recipients are expected to have the new cards by June.
>
> A magnetic strip on the back of the card—similar to automated

teller machine cards—will be run through a machine to link doctors with computer information in Sacramento. The computer also will show if the card has been lost or stolen.

. . . in addition to controlling fraud and abuse, the computerized system will give the state access to new information such as "improper or potentially deadly prescription usage."

"This puts the technology foot in the door for future benefit issuances, such as food stamps, and [welfare] payments.". . . A similar pilot program for food stamps will begin late next year in San Bernardino and San Diego counties, and possibly expand to other counties by early 1995.

January, 1994, *Government Technology*, "Health Care: It's in the Cards."

As Congress prepares to hammer out a national health care plan, state and local government experience with swipe-card and smart-card technology may help provide some answers.

January 25, 1994, By Paul Samyn, *Legislature Reporter*, "New card to track drug use." [In Manitoba, Canada.]

A new Pharmacare tracking system to start April 1. . . .The arrival of the computerized Pharmacare system—which will use the new purple Manitoba Health Services Commission card—is likely the first step toward the so-called "smart health cards" that would allow health professionals to tap into a person's entire medical history. "It will be like a little travelling medical file. . . .It will go further than protecting our system (from abuse), it will also protect our health.". . .With a push of a button, druggists will know what medication a customer is on—and if he or she is abusing the system . . . .the new system would immediately alert a druggist if a prescription for any drug had been recently filled elsewhere.

March 14, 1994, *New York Post,* "Village Hails Cop Crackdown on IDs."

Greenwich Village merchants and residents yesterday applaud-ed a newly launched police crackdown on nuisance crimes, but civil-liberties advocates said the focus should be on violent crime.

Cops in the Village's 6th Precinct have been ordered to accept only government-issued photo identification . . . .

During a 90-day trial run, those who don't produce acceptable photo-ID will be arrested and brought to the stationhouse to be photographed and fingerprinted, a police spokesman said.

The program . . . is expected to be expanded city wide by the summer.

March 25, 1994, *American Banker,* "AT&T's Smart Card Chief Plans Two-Front Push."

The president of a new AT&T business unit sees 1994 as a crucial year in the development of a U.S. market for smart card services . . . .

Smarter Smart Cards

The chips in AT&T smart cards currently [1994] have about 3 kilobytes of memory. By the end of the year. . .the standard AT&T card will boast 8K, and plans call for a 100K card in the next few years.

With the larger memory, cards could carry personal information, such as medical records, in addition to the financial and identifi-cation data that banks would likely put on the cards.

Experts say that expanding the smart card's utility beyond financial transactions will hasten consumer acceptance . . . ."I think 1995 is the year that the consumer is going to become acclimated to having one card for debit, for credit, and for a host of other things," said Mr. Bermingham [President, AT&T Smart Card Division].

April, 1994, *Security Management,* "TVs to Toll Booths: Smart Card Capabilities."

Organizers of the 1992 World Expo in Seville, Spain, needed a way to allow holders of season passes to enter the expo area quickly while preventing them from granting others access on the same ticket. They solved the problem with smart cards and biometrics. A fingerprint biometric terminal controlling each season ticket holder turnstile was installed. More than 100 turnstiles were implemented—52 for the 110,000 season pass holders, and an additional 48 for the 30,000 expo workers. The season passes and the workers' passes were personalized at more than 60 fingerprint digitizing and recording stations. The system was capable of passing one person through a turnstile every 8 seconds, with complete confidence in the validity of the pass and of the holder.

A smart card is a credit card-sized piece of plastic with an integrated circuit (IC) chip embedded in it. It is visually indistinguishable from an ordinary plastic credit card, except for the small circular button on the left side, with six or eight gold-plated contacts inscribed if the card is the contact type. There are also non-contact types where the only clue of the presence of the chip is the more rigid feel of the plastic.

July 13, 1994, *USA Today,* "National citizen ID is proposed."

All U.S. citizens and legal immigrants would get the equivalent of a national ID card under an expected proposal to Congress by the Commission on Immigration Reform.

Similar proposals have been embraced by Congress but vehemently opposed by some immigrant and privacy advocates as costly and prone to abuse.

The new Social Security-type cards, including photo and fingerprints, would allow employers to verify work eligibility *through a national data base* [emphasis added].

July 13, 1994, *The Orange County Register,* "U.S. may issue ID cards to citizens."

IMMIGRATION: Gov. Pete Wilson wants California to be the test state for "Employee Verification Registration," a TV report says.

The federal government, in a response to its inability to control illegal immigration, may soon ask every American to carry a national identity card. . . .

"Rather than wait for the development of a nationwide system, I strongly recommend you designate California as the first state in which a working system can be implemented on a fast track," said Wilson.

[A national identity card] "will create a neo-Nazi state in the United States where we will be required to tell on each other. . . next thing you know, we'll have tattoos on our bodies," [said Enriqueta Ramos, vice president of Rancho Santiago Community College's board of trustees].

...other lawmakers expressed concern that the program would be ineffective, costly, and an incursion into personal privacy.

"Will government really be able to do the job it is claiming? And if not, we've just spent billions of dollars and just given up some major, some severe privacy rights for nothing," Rep. Xavier Becerra, D-Los Angeles, told CBS.

August, 1994, *The McAlvany Intelligence Advisor,* "The Emerging National ID Card."

In all communist countries, the citizens (or slaves) must carry identification papers on their person at all times and must be ready to present their papers to communist authorities at *all* times—at border check points, at train or bus stations, airports, road blocks, etc. Every such citizen fears the ominous words "show me your papers." *But those papers were not computerized.* The new National Identification Card being pushed by the Clintonistas will ultimately be a computerized smartcard that can carry hundreds of pages of data (up to 2000 pages) on each American citizen.

The Establishment/New World Order crowd and their Clintonista employees are very close to locking the chains on all Americans via a high-tech National Identification Card linked to government databases that will destroy 100% of all Americans' privacy and enable the government to control virtually all aspects of our lives.

The All-Purpose National ID (Smart Card)

The government has proposed three separate ID cards, but all are likely to be ultimately merged into one all-purpose card: the INS ID card, the National Health Care card, and the U.S. Postal Service all-purpose U.S. Card. [**ED. NOTE:** Good salesmen always give their target several choices—all of which the salesman can live with—and the Clintonistas are doing the same.]

The INS National ID Card—The...liberal establishment types...are pushing hard for a single, tamper-resistant INS card for all Americans (including your Social Security number, photo, fingerprint, and bar code)....linked to a nationwide government database....

Marc Rotenberg, director of the Electronic Privacy Information Center, said in *USA Today* (7-14-95) that "It will become a way to monitor people, like an internal passport." This Orwellian nightmare will, like the government's privacy/bank/cash reporting laws, allow the government to monitor 260 million Americans who are *not* illegal aliens, just as they monitor the cash transactions of 260 million Americans who are *not* drug dealers.

Lucas Guttentage, of the ACLU (with whom this writer seldom agrees) said in the same *USA Today* article, "It won't work, it will cost billions, it won't solve the problems, and it will cause new forms of discrimination."

And Steve Moore of the Cato Institute points out that just as the government has abused the once-private Social Security number and now uses it as a national ID number which ties together dozens of U.S. databases on each U.S. citizen, so it will abuse this card. Moore observed: "Look at history and see the abuses—they used Social Security numbers to round up and incarcerate the Japanese-Americans during World War II."

The National Health Care Card—One of the major side benefits for the Clintonistas, of their socialized medicine program . . . is forcing a national ID card down the throats of every American.

This high-tech ID card is designed to keep permanent, accessible records of all aspects of your health care, including the details of every doctor visit, every drug store prescription, and every hospital treatment. This card could well be used to crack down on welfare fraud, trace deadbeat dads who refuse to pay child support, supplement our Social Security cards, our draft card, maybe our passports, and even to register voters and control voting fraud. *The uses will be limited, not by technology (which is awesome and ever-expanding) but only by the imagination of government officials and their respect for our privacy.* [Or lack of it!]

To make this tracking system work, everyone of us must have a number that can be fed into the national computer banks.

The Postal Service All-Purpose "U.S. Card"—This general purpose smartcard is most likely to emerge as America's new national ID card—incorporating all the functions of [the two described above] and much more. The Clinton administration is no longer debating **if**, but **how** they can create and introduce this smartcard (which will interact with any and all government agencies) to **all** Americans.

At the recent April Card Tech/Secure Tech Conference, the *Postal Service (which was directed by the Department of Defense a couple of years ago to develop a people-monitoring electronic card system)* unveiled its general purpose U.S. services smartcard . . . .

Postal Service representative Chuck Chamberlain outlined how *an individual's U.S. Card would be automatically connected with the Department of Health and Human Services, the U.S. Treasury, the I.R.S., the Veterans Administration, and all other government agencies (i.e., ATF, FBI, CIA, OSHA, EPA, FDA, etc.), the banking system, and a central database of digital signatures* for use in authenticating electronic mail and transactions.

The Postal Service has acknowledged that it is prepared to put more than 100 million of the cards in citizens' pockets within months of Administration approval. . . . And it is not being done with Congressional approval *but rather through a series of presidential executive orders.*

President Clinton is close to signing two executive orders that would greatly expand the government's access to personal records, including an order that would allow the IRS to monitor individual bank accounts and automatically collect taxes on the results. Chamberlain said the IRS is aggressively pursuing plans for an identity card for taxpayers. . . .

The U.S. Card is designed to mediate information about you (like a magic key) in every government database that contains information about you. But without your magic key, you will be out in the cold. You won't be able to file tax returns [**ED:** That might not be all bad.], collect your pension or Social Security, conduct bank or credit card transactions, or function in your business or personal life. . . .

It appears to this writer that the government databases are already far more integrated and the system far more developed (i.e., to the point of almost instant deployment) than most knowledgeable observers would have supposed. If the Postal Service could mail 100 million of these cards within months, it is very late indeed!

William Murray, an information system security consultant to Deloitte and Touche, said recently in the *Digital Media* article (5-94) entitled "Ever Feel You're Being Watched? You Will.": *"There won't be anything you do in business that won't be collected and analyzed by the government. This National Information infrastructure is a better surveillance mechanism than Orwell or the government could have imagined. This (blank blank) thing is so pervasive and the propensity to connect it is so great that it is unstoppable."*

Murray continued: "Most of this shift in privacy policy is apparently being done by executive order at the initiative of the bureaucracy and without any Congressional oversight or concurrence. They are not likely to fail. You know, Orwell said that bureaucrats, simply doing what bureaucrats do, without motive or intent, will use technology to enslave the people." [**ED. NOTE:** But, there is motivation and intent. It is called "people control"! It is called a "socialist police state"! It is called the "New World Order"!]

The government's proposed Health Care Card, Electronic Benefits Card (EBT), Social Security Card, Immigration Card, Postal "U.S. Card" are nothing less than disguised **National Identity Cards** for **all** Americans! They are ingenious devices for tracking and controlling the lives of everyone. *These new citizen ID cards will allow Big Brother and Big Sister (and their New World Order/Establishment controllers) to maintain computerized, electronically digitized, permanent, and accessible records on every man, woman, and child in America.*

The government wants us to believe that having such *Hitlerian cards* in our possession will benefit us by improving the overall efficiency, quality, or availability of government health care, welfare, retirement, and many other socialistic programs. But in reality, nothing could be further from the truth!

There is another piece of technology which would appear to be the ultimate in identity cards. . .at least for today. The **Lasercard** is an optical memory card produced by the Drexler Technology Corp. It is an updatable, credit-card-sized, multi-megabyte, data-storage card which can accommodate up to 1600 pages (i.e., 4.11 megabytes) of information on the carrier. It is based upon optical recording technology—the process of writing and reading with light.

The Lasercard has ample memory to store personal identification numbers (PINS), digital photos, signatures, voice prints, fingerprints, hand geometry, retina scans, and virtually any form of personal biometrics or biographical data on the cardholder, i.e. text, graphics, voice, pictures, software—virtually any form of information that can be digitized. In its literature, Drexler says that it can produce up to 40 million Lasercards a year.

August 18, 1994, *The Orange County Register,* "O.C. Mexicans have no voice in vote. . .CARDS: Underdog supporters protest plan."

The voices of about 600,000 Mexicans living in Orange County and an additional 4 - 5 million living in California will not be heard at the Mexican polls Sunday.

The reason: A tamper-proof voter-identification card, which was issued only to residents of Mexico, and has shut out millions of Mexican citizens living abroad. . . .

The government says the cards, with a photograph, fingerprint, hologram, invisible ultraviolet coating, bar code, and plastic laminate, are tamperproof and will guarantee the most honest elections in Mexico's history.

But not everyone agrees. . . ."People will always find a way to cheat, even with the cards. . . .The reason these cards were approved was to eliminate people from the process."

September, 1994, *Government Technology,* "MasterCard Moving to Chip Technology."

That magnetic stripe on the back of your credit cards is about to go the way of the Dodo. MasterCard International, the credit association owned by member banks, has begun a program to move toward chip-based "smart cards." The group's goal is to have all its payment systems including chip technology by the year 2000.

September 2, 1994, *Business Post/Bangkok Post,* "Drivers licenses with computer chip."

The National Police Agency is considering introduction of IC "smart card" drivers licenses that could be used as identity cards or even to start a car. . . .

Drivers will be able to customize their cards after inputting a personal code and use them as ignition or door keys or as membership cards to various clubs.

November 8, 1994, *The Orange County Register,* "Woman without ID denied hotel rooms."

There was no room at the inn for Linda Friedberg. No room at three inns, in fact, because she carried no ID showing that's her name.

The Econo Lodge, Howard Johnson, and the Queen City Motor Inn in Manchester, N.H., refused to rent the Chicago woman a room September 7, though she had $1,000 in cash.

All three companies said they only accept ID-carrying guests for safety reasons.

"It's to protect our business and also protect the people who are here," said Tracy Cole, assistant manager of the Econo Lodge.

A call to the state consumer protection bureau about the legality of the policy was not immediately returned Monday.

"We are the most livable state in the nation this year, but we didn't show that to you!" Gov. Steve Merrill wrote Friedberg last week. "I will do my best to see that no one is treated in such a manner."

December 15, 1994, *The Houston Post,* "High-tech ID: New Driver's License Debuts Jan. 2."

Magnetic and photogenic are the key words for Texas' new high-tech drivers' license, which the Texas Department of Public Safety will begin issuing on Jan. 2.

The new licenses will have a magnetic strip on the back containing basic information printed on the license. DPS squad cars will carry devices like credit card machines which can scan and verify data on the card.

The system also may be used by retailers scanning for hot-check artists.

January 10, 1995, *Los Angeles Times,* "Tough Rules, ID System Planned, INS Chief Says."

The Clinton Administration... is moving toward embracing a controversial national computer identification system.... a central registry or an even more controversial national identity card....

A proposal by the Administration for development of a central verification system would be strongly opposed by some immigration and civil rights groups on grounds that it would increase discrimination and violate privacy rights.

Meissner [Commissioner of the Immigration and Naturalization Service] called such concerns inevitable and legitimate....

February/March, 1995, *World Card Technology Magazine,* "Multi-Functioning Cards."

The buzz word in the smartcard market today is "multifunction cards." The concept behind these is to reduce the number of cards in the consumers' wallets by integrating many applications like banking, health, GSM SIM etc. all on one card....

...in this age of multifunction cards, the semiconductor manufacturer must find a way of cramming a greater number of memory cells into a smaller space. This is done by introducing smaller geometrys. Today, the standard transistor cell size is 1.2 um (a human hair is on average 40 um thick). Motorola is actively developing new, dense EEPROM cells to support multi application cards, which are significantly less than 1 um in length. *This will make smartcard devices with more than twice the EEPROM capacity a reality by the end of the century* [emphasis added].

March 21, 1995, *The Wall Street Journal,* "Three Banks, Visa Hope to Catapult 'Smart-Card' Use at Summer Olympics."

Three large Southeast banks in cooperation with Visa plan the most ambitious launch yet of a "smart card" in the U.S. in time for the Summer 1996 Olympics in Atlanta.

While the new cards look like credit cards, they're different in concept. A credit card represents a loan. A smart card, which is already popular in Europe, is an electronic purse that holds electronic cash. Each time it's used, the amount of the purchase price is automatically deducted by an electronic reader. When the "electronic purse" is empty, the card can't be used anymore.

Visa said the new cards, powered by a microchip, will come in two versions: a disposable one that will be discarded after the value has been spent; and a reusable or rechargeable card, that can have new buying power added by loading it into an automatic teller machine. The second type would be incorporated into a multiuse bank card that also functions as a debit card and bank-machine card.

"This will be the first rollout of the technology in the U.S.," said a Visa spokesman. . . .

Visa said the 1996 Atlanta Olympics makes for the perfect locale to trot out the smart card because of the large international audience it will bring, including many Europeans who are already comfortable with the technology.

April, 1995, *Automatic I.D. News,* "Technology adds funtionality to ID cards."

Get ready to replace that bulging purse or wallet-full of cards with a single, multi-function card. Now that's smart!. . .

The smart card population is going to increase its rate of growth. The increasing volumes of production and chip evolution prompted *Business Week* to forecast 1 billion smart cards to be produced in 1996. The United States market will mainly consist of pilots for prepaid cards, financial transactions, security access control, and portable databases. *The road-toll solutions are well established and growing rapidly. The military logistics and related applications are now proven. . .* [emphasis added].

April 10, 1995, *The Charlotte Observer,* "Social Security streamlining in the works/Changes in store for retirees."

The White House plans to streamline the Social Security Administration by changing the way future retirees receive their checks and apply for benefits. . . .

Officials also said they would seek to move all retirees with bank accounts into a direct deposit program, and may allow banks to issue a single debit card that would add Social Security benefits to other federal payments, such as welfare or food stamps, that are now paid via "smart cards."

April 21, 1995, *The Denver Post,* "Bombing may spark national identity cards," by Richard Reeves.

[The Oklahoma bombing] will change many things in the United States. . . .

Many of the changes in America were already well under way.

To cash a check in trusting California now, you have to show a photo-ID California driver license. If you do not drive, the Department of Motor Vehicles issues plastic identification cards so you can do the business of the day. So, in effect, California already has the kind of identity card—"Your papers, please?"—that Americans have always resisted as the internal passport of police states.

The California licenses have the usual magnetic strip across the back, and although officials swear that only relevant height and weight information is encoded in the strip, we all know that the things are capable of retaining every fact of a life, plus the Encyclopedia Britannica.

And soon they will, I am almost certain. One of the results of this crime against the American soul will be some form of national identity card. . . . I know there will be government and police abuses of such cards but. . .the information on each of us is already out there somewhere. . . .

And now—whoever did this—. . .the worst part of it will be restrictions we must put on our own freedoms.

May, 1995, *Government Technology,* "Students Like Cards & Kiosks."

> . . .Currently, 40,000 students, faculty, and staff use the FSU-Card, which serves as an ID, security card, library card, food and vending card, ATM and telephone calling card. John Carnaghi, Florida State vice president for finance and administration, calls the FSUCard "the most creative administrative tool I've ever encountered."
>
> FSU and MCI also introduced the FSU Connection Interactive Kiosk Network, which allows students to use their FSUCards to update local or permanent addresses, print transcripts and class schedules and apply for graduation. Eventually, the kiosks will allow students to pay tuition and register for courses.

June, 1995, *Automatic I.D. News,* "ID cards cut postage and fraud in food stamp programs." This article covers the use of ID cards in Los Angeles county and other California counties that are about to duplicate LA's successful efforts in the automation of their food stamp programs. Elimination of fraud, as well as savings due to the automation, are cited as the primary reasons for use of this new technology.

June 9, 1995, *San Francisco Chronicle,* "Rwandan ID Cards Same for Hutus and Tutsis."

> Rwanda will no longer distinguish between Hutus and Tutsis when it issues new identity cards, ending a practice that helped Hutu militiamen to select their victims in last year's genocide, officials said yesterday.

They said residency cards are being issued this week in Kigali and they will be distributed in the rest of Rwanda later.

During last year's genocide, Hutu militiamen demanded the identity cards of civilians they stopped. If they were listed as members of the Tutsi minority, they were hacked to death or shot.

June 12, 1995, *Los Angeles Times,* "Big Brother, Make Room for Big Sister." The following article by Ron K. Unz is one of the most astute and honest commentaries, as well as comprehensive analysis, that I have seen on the subject of identity cards and their potential for disaster in many different areas of our lives.

Immigration: Sen. Feinstein wants everyone to carry an encrypted, database-linked national identity card.

Timothy McVeigh, alleged perpetrator of the Oklahoma City bombing, is said to have believed that, while he was in the Army, the government implanted a microchip tracking device in his buttocks. Most of us would dismiss this as the ravings of an obvious madman. But to Sen. Dianne Feinstein, McVeigh is just a bit ahead of his time; she is a believer in "biometric" tracking of all of us. She proposes, as part of legislation for tougher control of illegal immigration, a national identity card for every man, woman, and child in America.

Captivated by advanced technology, Feinstein says that such a card could include a magnetic strip or microchip containing a digitized form of each citizen's vital statistics, photograph, fingerprint, voiceprint, and retina scan. The card would be linked to massive new federal computer databases, and would be presented whenever an American applied for employment or government benefits. The card would have to be renewed annually, presumably requiring refingerprinting to verify identity.

Now, subjecting every American to the humiliation of annual citizenship checks could hardly win popular support if presented purely as an employment program for tens of thousands of new federal document inspectors and file managers; an overriding justification must be found. In past decades, the magic words *national security* might have persuaded Americans to meekly sacrifice their traditional liberties. The Cold War is no more, but Feinstein has found an equivalent: the current "war" against illegal immigration. Once the 260 million legal inhabitants of America have been scanned, everyone caught with their fingerprints not on file might be presumed illegal and deported or imprisoned, solving the problem once and for all.

Whether Dianne Feinstein actually cares so deeply about the scourge of illegal immigration remains open to considerable doubt. Aside from happily placing her own home in the care of an illegal alien some years back, she strongly supported throughout the 1980s various San Francisco ordinances that declared the city a "safe haven" for all illegal immigrants and prohibited any local cooperation with immigration authorities. But politicians follow the polls, and if catching all those illegal nannies and gardeners now requires every American citizen to carry a microchip, so be it. Gov. Pete Wilson endorsed much the same approach just before the 1994 election when he said that actually Proposition 187 would probably require establishment of a national ID card.

Compared to Feinstein's proposal, Pat Buchanan's foolish idea of building a massive wall across the thousand miles of our southern border is far less harmful to American freedom.

A national ID database represents the slipperiest of all civil liberty slopes. A system employing tens of thousands of government clerks and administrators and costing tens of billions of dollars to build and operate would surely not remain limited to catching illegal nannies. Why not use it, at virtually no additional cost to track convicted child molesters, as well? Who would dare object? Why not then also track the movements of convicted murderers. And rapists. And drug dealers and felons in general. And fathers behind on child support. And tax-evaders. And "political extremists." Members of "religious cults." Drug addicts. AIDS carriers. Gun owners. With each turn of the political cycle, left and right would add their favorite batch of social enemies to the surveillance list.

Or consider employment issues. Since every private employer would have to obtain federal authorization before offering any individual a job, a database record of race, ethnicity, and gender could be used as an extraordinarily direct means of enforcing future affirmative action regulations. Imagine business owners receiving computerized responses such as "employment permission denied; you already employ too many white males."

Perhaps considerations such as these have persuaded the Clinton Administration, Sen. Edward M. Kennedy, and other leading liberal members of Congress to put aside any civil liberty concerns they might have and fully endorse legislation along the lines of Feinstein's "Big Sister" proposal. Some moderate Republicans such as Sen. Alan Simpson of Wyoming and Rep. Lamar Smith of Texas are also on board. However, leading conservative Republicans and libertarians—House Majority Leader Dick Armey of Texas, strategist Bill Kristol, the Cato Institute, the National Federation of Independent Business—are absolutely opposed, as are civil liberties groups such as the ACLU.

Requiring the law-abiding 98% of America's population to

carry a national ID card or undergo retinal scanning is un-American in the strongest sense of the word, and the only long-term beneficiaries of such federal policies would be the recruiting sergeants of the Michigan Militia. Our fractured society already contains large numbers of violent and paranoid individuals terrified of imaginary government plots against their freedom. [Author's note: I believe there is enough documented evidence in this book to convince anyone that these "plots" are no longer "imaginary."] Politicians who would give true substance to such fears by affixing microchips to every American's identity must be held accountable for the likely consequences. One Oklahoma City bombing is enough.

June 24, 1995, *Honolulu Star-Bulletin,* "Liberals, conservatives on immigration." This is another superb article by an excellent writer, Thomas Sowell, a senior fellow at the Hoover Institution.

Few things illustrate the difference between liberals and conservatives as clearly as the different approaches to the immigration issue by liberal Democratic Sen. Dianne Feinstein and conservative Republican presidential candidate Pat Buchanan.

Pat Buchanan would act directly against immigrants by a moratorium on even legal immigration and by fortifying the borders. Whatever the merits or demerits of this approach, it focuses directly on immigrants.

Dianne Feinstein advocates a national identity card that all Americans would be required to have and that all employers would be required to see to prevent hiring illegal aliens.

It is the classic liberal response of using a particular problem created by particular people to expand the government's power over other people. The same pattern is seen in liberal responses to crimes committed by people with firearms by cracking down on the far larger number of people with firearms who are committing no crimes.

Nothing polarizes the political left and right like the idea of a national identity card. Yet it is obvious why, in principle, this should be a liberal-versus-conservative issue.

Everyone should be against people escaping personal responsibility for their actions by pretending to be somebody else or by relocating to places where their sordid past is not known, thereby permitting them to victimize more innocent people.

Some hard-nosed conservatives have urged that sex offenders in particular be identified and not be allowed to escape their past and continue to prey on unsuspecting neighbors, or those neighbors' children, in the future.

Would not a national identity card also prevent other kinds of criminals, deadbeat dads, and other parasites from escaping their past and jeopardizing other people's futures?

Despite the many potential benefits of a national identity card, the painful fact is that battle lines are drawn over this issue for one reason: We cannot trust the government in general, and liberals in particular, to stop at a national identity card to be used to enforce immigration laws or to deter crime.

Control is the name of the game for liberals, even when they call it "compassion." A national identity card would not [be limited to merely] greater government snooping into people's private lives. The information gathered would lead to more laws forcing more people to do more things the way the politicians want them done. *It is a down payment on totalitarianism.*

Lack of trust is not some purely psychological reaction or paranoia bred by militias or talk show hosts. History is full of reasons to distrust governments in general and the political left in particular.

Most Americans probably have no more objection in principle to a national identity card than to some form of gun control. It is only in practice that we know that it will never stop there.

Put differently, many of the benefits that we could get from many policies must be forfeited because of the greater dangers created by the untrustworthiness of those who believe in big government as a means of imposing their own superior wisdom and virtue on others.

At the very moment when the liberal media are blaming "anti-government" feeling for such things as the Oklahoma City bombing and blaming conservative talk show hosts for promoting such feelings, the Supreme Court of the United States has given a free home demonstration of betrayal of trust by striking down term-limits legislation passed by overwhelming majorities of voters.

Nothing in the Constitution forbids the states to pass such legislation. Moreover, the 10th Amendment clearly sets forth the principle that the federal government *can do only* what it is specifically authorized to do, while the states and the people can do whatever they are *not* forbidden to do. [Author's note: It seems as if they are overlooking that Executive Order process which permits "end runs" around the framer's intent for the Constitution.]

But the learned justices decided to turn this principle upside down and claim that the states need specific authorization to act.

All this dishonesty served only to impose their preferences and prejudices on the rest of us. Instead of saying where in the Constitution such laws as term limits are forbidden, the Supreme Court majority quoted previous decisions by their predecessors, who also made it up as they went along [emphasis added].

June 29, 1995, *San Francisco Chronicle*, "Clinton Orders Tighter Federal Security."

> The president said the new steps, ordered in the wake of the Oklahoma City blast, would help protect federal agencies.
> . . .The report also called for the installation of shatter-proof glass and better alarm systems, locating new buildings farther from the street, and *tougher standards for employee and visitor identification* [emphasis added].

In addition to the immigration problems, terrorist threats have been used as one of the primary reasons for implementing stronger security measures, including positive identity methods and expanded surveillance of groups with an agenda not considered "politically correct." The threat can be genuine or imagined. . .and achieve the same result. It can be domestic or foreign in origin; the work of a group or a disturbed individual.

The following article deals with the 17-year ongoing mail bombings by the single person dubbed the "Unabomber," who has created massive confusion in airports on the west coast by announcing he had planted a bomb on an aircraft. Extra security measures were implemented immediately and caused not only added time and inconvenience to passengers, but created delays in mail delivery because all large letters and packages were being subjected to extra scrutiny at every airport.

June 29, 1995, *San Francisco Chronicle*, "Unabomb Security Clampdown/All airline passengers must show ID."

> Responding to the Unabomber's threat to blow up a jetliner, authorities yesterday took unprecedented security precautions at airports around the state and temporarily shut down California's air mail system.
> "Further examination has confirmed that this letter originates from the Unabomber subject. It is a credible threat."
> . . .Yesterday, in what aviation experts said is the strictest case of domestic airport security in U.S. history, airport officials required all passengers to show photo identification that matched the name on the passenger's ticket. Luggage belonging to people who failed that test was opened and searched for bombs.

July 13, 1995, *USA Today*, "Cracking Down on Fake IDs." This was the front-page feature, continuing on the whole of page two. Even though it focuses on fake ID's, the estimated cost of all that fraud, the ease with which they can be obtained, and the changes being made to the drivers' licenses in an effort to eliminate the fakes, one portion deals with the high-tech aspects of future ID methods by various concerns—both businesses and agencies.

The growing crisis costs the living billions of dollars—and the dead their identities. Photo caption: Wanda Jones died at age five in 1944. Her identity has been assumed by the unknown woman in the ID card above.

Experts say fraudulent identities are epidemic, and its victims are the living as well as the dead.

Voiceprints, hand geometry, bar cards, magnetic stripes, and fingerprints—they're all soldiers in the war on fake IDs.

"Big Brother is here," says Jim Gaughrin, a fraud investigator for the U.S. Secret Service. "If somebody gets your name and Social Security number and applies for credit, you're screwed. Wouldn't it be better if nobody could get credit unless they matched your fingerprint?" [Author's note: Is that supposed to be a rhetorical question?!?]

That attitude is behind the push by government agencies, the credit and banking industry, and security businesses for counterfeit-proof IDs:

►At Kennedy, Newark, and Toronto airports some international travelers put their hands on a *Star Trek*-like computer that scans various shapes and distances—their hand's geometry—as part of an Immigration and Naturalization Service test program.

►The INS also is testing voiceprints for legal immigrant work cards. If the process works, a worker could call a computer and say a phrase into the phone, and the computer would verify that person's identity. Now, a person who is not eligible to work can counterfeit a work card and get a job illegally.

►Even fingerprinting's going high-tech. Banks are using barely visible inkless methods to fingerprint non-customers who cash checks.

►Drivers' licenses now come with a credit-card look and holographic images to make tampering difficult.

Vital statistics—name, height, weight, hair color—are printed over ghost images of photos or state seals, making it tough to replace accurate information with false. License bureaus are using digital photography so a picture can be filed in a computer and called up on the screen with the touch of a button. Some states require a thumbprint.

Increased security doesn't stop with driver's licenses.

Credit-card companies—which, depending on who is counting,

lose between millions and billions of dollars annually because of fake IDs—are stepping up their efforts, too.

Visa has slowed fraud through a computer system that watches for the same address or phone number used on multiple credit applications, often a sign of fraud.

"Let's face it—if 350 applications are coming from a P.O. box in the Bronx, we've got a problem," says Allan Trosclair, vice president of fraud control for Visa USA. Trosclair credits the new computer system with helping Visa push its rate of fraudulent credit cards from 6% to 3% since 1993.

Even the Social Security Administration, *in the past extremely secretive with its information, is verifying records for driver's license bureaus.*

But crackdowns come at a price, privacy advocates say [emphasis added].

July, 1995, *Popular Science,* "E-Money."

If you thought E-mail changed your life, wait until you get a fistful of this.

Just imagine: no jangly coins in your pants, no crinkled bills in your wallet. To buy a soda you simply insert something called a stored value card into the vending machine. . . .Once E-money is accepted as universally as greenbacks, don't be surprised if a disheveled man on the street steps up to you and says, "Brother, can you spare a little stored value?"

Such is the vision of smart card proponents who push chip-embedded plastic both as a realistic alternative to cash and a tactile alternative to non-physical digital money that exists only as numbers on the Internet. Smart cards are also referred to as chip cards and electronic purses.

"If we had our way, we'd implant a chip behind everyone's ear in the maternity ward," says Ronald Kane, a vice president of Cubic Corp.'s automatic revenue collection group. Cubic is the leading maker of smart card systems for mass transit systems, highway tolls, parking, and other applications and one of a number of companies and government agencies pushing for the frontier of smart cards—the money of the future. For Kane and his colleagues, the next best thing is giving everyone a [smart] card—a high-tech pass with a memory that may, sooner than we imagine, replace cash in our wallets.

. . .smart card is like cash. . . .Smart cards are moving us toward a cashless society. . . .

Two articles appeared side by side in the August, 1995, edition of *Government Technology:*

Privacy Group Warns Congress

Congress should keep a cool head in the wake of the Oklahoma City tragedy, the Electronic Privacy Information Center (EPIC) wrote in a letter to Sen. Orrin Hatch (R-Utah), chairman of the Senate Judiciary Committee. The Clinton administration has been using the bombing to renew its request for encryption controls and other ways to prevent what it says is terrorist activity using the Internet for communications.

EPIC, a Washington group pushing computer privacy, urged Congress to take "careful and deliberate consideration of any proposal that would alter current guidelines for government investigation and monitoring of domestic political activity or the collection and use of personal information."

UK Opens National ID Card Debate

After months of rumors and press reports, the British Government announced plans for the introduction of a national ID card system. According to Prime Minister John Major, however, the plans are far from rigid, and the idea is still very much at a discussion state.

The UK has not had a national ID card system since 1952, when the wartime ID card system was scrapped. In a recent report, the government steered clear of a firm decision in favor of any one ID card proposal and, if anything, only serves to cloud the issue in the UK still further.

British opinion polls show that most people—up to 75% in one survey—now back the idea of national ID cards.

It never ceases to amaze me how people can become so deluded about something when all the current evidence is so readily available, in addition to the historical evidence in the case of the British.

October 2, 1995, *U.S. News & World Report,* "The Road Worriers: Can Electronic Tolls Be a Tool for Big Brother?"

Imagine driving from Maine to Maryland virtually nonstop, breezing through hundreds of miles of turnpikes and bridges, never stopping at a tollbooth. This traveler's dream is actually a step closer to reality. The governors of Connecticut, Delaware, Maine, Maryland, Massachusetts, New Hampshire, New Jersey, New York, Pennsylvania, Rhode Island, and Vermont agreed this month to work toward setting up a multistate system of using ETC—electronic toll collection.

. . .The crucial issue, says Phil Agre, communications professor at the University of California at San Diego, "is whether the systems capture individually identifiable information"—that is, information that might identify drivers. Besides raking in tolls, transportation departments also can suck up tons of personal information about a traveler, including driver's license data, license plate number, destination, highway speed, vehicle identification, and time of day of travel.

Anonymous? Who controls this information? Will it be sold or merged into other databases available to insurance companies, credit bureaus, marketers and law-enforcement agencies? [Author's note: There's another one of those rhetorical questions.] The opportunities for mischief are enormous. . . .

November 2, 1995, *The Kansas City Star,* "FBI seeks extensive wiretap plan: Submitted proposal calls for upgraded monitoring system." (This article originated in *The New York Times.*) *Look out. . . Big Brother is getting bigger!*

The FBI has proposed a wiretapping system that would give law enforcement officials the capacity to monitor simultaneously as many as one out of every 100 phone lines in some high crime areas of the country.

Such a surveillance ability would *vastly exceed the needs* of law enforcement officials around the country, who in recent years have conducted an annual average of fewer than 850 *court-authorized* wiretaps—or fewer than one in every 174,000 phone lines. [Author's note: "court-authorized" is the key phrase here . . . there is no way of knowing how many *unauthorized* taps are conducted by the ATF, IRS, FBI, CIA, Secret Service, *et al ad nauseum.*]

The plan, which needs congressional approval for financing, would still require a court warrant to conduct wiretaps.

Generally, FBI officials contend that an advanced, high-capacity monitoring system will be necessary as more of modern life— and crime—takes place as voice or computer conversations over digital phone lines.

On digital lines, communications are transmitted in electronic pulses represented by the 1s and 0s of computer code. Such communications are harder to monitor than with the old-fashioned analog lines in which conversations are transmitted as electronic signals corresponding to audible sound waves.

An FBI spokesman declined to elaborate on the need for such an expansion of its wiretapping abilities.

"The full implementation is absolutely essential for law enforcement and public saftey," said Mike Kortan, an FBI spokesman in Washington. "We are in ongoing discussions with the communications industry. Therefore, it would be inappropriate to comment further at this point."

The plan was published in the *Federal Register* on Oct. 16 but has not drawn much attention yet outside law enforcement and industry circles. It is the first comprehensive outline by the FBI of the surveillance capabilities it will require under the Digital Telephony Act that President Clinton signed in 1994. [Emphasis added.]

Do you recall our discussion earlier in this book about Big Brother wanting a key to the "back door," so they could override any encryption you might use on your communications and Internet use to ensure privacy as you conduct your business transactions? Remember the Clipper Chip. . .and the big bill they tried to stick on the telephone companies (which ultimately got stuck on the taxpayers) to develop a way they could quickly and with great ease eavesdrop on conversations on the new fiber optic systems? Well, there has been no announcement as yet, but I give you my guarantee. . .*this is all wrapped up together somehow!*

And a last-minute article has appeared entitled: "Automated FAA Certifications?"

The Federal Aviation Administration is exploring the possibility of using an automated system to collect and validate the information needed before issuing pilot certificates and ratings. The new Airman Certification and Rating Application (ACRA) system would use a DataCard with an *embedded computer chip* [smart card] to record the applicant's information. . .and transmit it, along with the applicant's digital signature, to the Oklahoma City Airman Certification Branch for processing. The DataCards, more impressive than the current flimsy paper certificates, resemble thick credit cards and feature a color photograph and bit-mapped signature of the applicant. According to FAA officials demonstrating the application process at the EAA Fly-In at Oshkosh, the data chip on the card has the capacity to store a variety of additional information about the cardholder [emphasis added].

November 14, 1995, *USA Today,* "Smart cards teach about easier travel."

Betsy Barclay no longer dreads being told to drop everything to catch the next flight.

Barclay simply goes to the airport, walks to the Delta Shuttle gate, swipes her AT&T Smart Card through an electronic reader, and boards the plane. She doesn't need a ticket, and she doesn't waste time checking in at the gate.

This may be how most travelers get on planes as smart-card technology expands over the next two to three years.

. . . In the 5 seconds it takes to swipe the card through an electronic reader, a computer chip in the card records the reservation,
the flier's credit-card number for billing purposes, and credits
the frequent-flier miles to the flier's account. The traveler gets
a receipt, but never sees a ticket.

The next generation of smart cards may even have sensors that
can be picked up by machines at the airport. "The traveler may
not even have to take the card out of his jacket. The sensor would
tell the machines that the passenger is ready to board the
flight. . . ."

Americans and Europeans are not alone. . . the whole world is
going cashless (just like Revelation 13 says it will). Two more newspaper articles tell of smart card activity in the orient and other parts
of Asia. The system is expected to be available in Thailand, Hong
Kong, China, India, Indonesia, Macao, Philippines, Singapore, Sri
Lanka, Taiwan, and Malaysia. The service will be launched in 1995.

This documentation could go on indefinitely, but I will end it here
and make brief mention at this point of each of the special subjects
to which I referred early in this chapter.

EBT (Electronic Benefits Transfers)

As the title implies, these are some form of government benefits
which are now, or soon will be, dispensed by electronically transferring
the funds, food stamps, social security checks, welfare assistance, *et al*,
directly into an account in your name, which you may access by way

of a smart card to be issued to you. At the moment, individual programs are handled separately, but studies are well underway to determine how they may be combined onto only one card. Many states
and a number of federal programs currently use this system, and many
more soon will follow. (This subject is covered in detail in Chapter
7, Computerizing People.) Here are excerpts from just a couple of the
articles.

May, 1994, *Personal Identification News,* "Vice President Announces
National EBT Strategy."

Eight-point Plan and Nine-state Prototype Outlined in Official Ceremony.

Vice President Gore officially embraced a national strategy for
the widespread adoption of Electronic Benefits Transfer. . . saying,
"I am firmly committed to making this happen."

EBT, the card-based delivery of a wide range of benefits in
social service programs, may eventually encompass over 31
million cardholders and $120 billion of payments. The program
has become one of the hottest initiatives in the Federal government's efforts to reinvent itself. . . .

April, 1995, *Automatic I.D. News,* "N.J. grocer installs online debit
card reader for food stamp transactions."

Twin County Grocers became the first grocery store chain to
install integrated card readers that can process food stamps,
credit, and debit card transactions for the Families First electronic
benefits transfer (EBT) system.

June, 1995, *Personal Identification News,* "Ohio Awards Smart Food
Stamp Project to Citibank."

On May 10, after six months of delays, the state of Ohio
announced its intent to award a contract for a statewide Smart
Card Food Stamp program to Citibank. The state's bold move
to broad roll out the smart card technology follows a successful
pilot program involving 12,000 households conducted in 1993.
Ohio hopes to have Citibank under contract by August 1 and
expects the first of 545,000 microprocessor cards to be issued
about a year later. Citibank's Chicago-based EBT Group will
develop the system using 1K EEPROM microprocessor cards
supplied by Gemplus.

Motor-Voter-Worker

Not to be outdone by the Postal Service, which claims it can issue 100,000 ID cards on very short notice, the directors of the state departments of motor vehicles are meeting with each other and representatives of the federal agencies to discuss the feasibility of tying your driving, voting, and working privileges all together on one identification card—your driver's license (managed by the state DMVs), since the driver's license currently is recognized as the ID of choice in all states. In fact, if you don't drive, the DMV will issue you an official "ID card" so you can cash checks, check into hotels, rent things, etc. This proposed system is referred to as "Motor-Voter-Worker," which is really just another way of saying "National ID Card."

You may be familiar with the term "Motor-Voter." It is a phrase that was coined to describe the process of registering a person to vote at the same time they are issued a driver's license. Now it is proposed to link the system with the Social Security Administration (SSA), as well, using the SSA as a clearing house for the comprehensive driver's license, to verify that all the information is correct. Like I said, no matter who ends up issuing it, it is still nothing more than a National ID card.

As early as 1991 the state of California DMV issued information to its offices statewide about the new style of license that would be issued in the future. It would be plasticized and "similar to a credit card in size, thickness, and consistency." The important thing to note from this memo is that the "new process involves capturing and storing the applicant's photo, fingerprint, and signature in digitized form, along with the application data, on a cassette." The cassette then will be used to produce the card/license and to create a centralized data base containing all this information for future retrieval, display, or exchange.

The importance in this information lies in the fact that everything is digitized, which is a prerequisite for later moving us into syringe-implantable biochip technology. Eventually, this information will be linked together in one giant database; at present 12 states already are in it.

INS PASS

INS PASS ostensibly was developed for the convenience and expediency of the frequent international traveler. It is a combination of a smart card and biometrics (hand geometry). *Business Week* (May 1, 1994) describes it this way:

A Better Passport: The Human Hand

Fed up with waiting in long passport lines when you get back from an overseas flight? If you're one of the nearly 10 million passengers who returned home last year through John F. Kennedy or Newark International Airports, the U.S. Immigration & Naturalization Service is offering a way to zip you through. You won't even have to show your passport.

The INS Passenger Accelerated Service System (INS PASS) allows you to use an electronic hand reader to verify that you are who you say you are. The key to the quick ID review is the human hand. Like fingerprints, every hand pattern is unique. The INS digitally captures the design of a participant's hand and embeds it on a wallet-size white plastic card, which the traveler carries. Readers located in INS PASS kiosks at arrival terminals then can identify the person by matching the print on the card against his or her hand placed palm-down on the machine. [Author's note: This is the *right* hand you must insert into the reader.]

The program is open to all U.S. citizens and most Canadians, Japanese, and Western Europeans. Expansion to more international airports is anticipated.

Pressing Toward the "MARC"

The prototype for the national ID card already is being used by the U.S. military. The MARC card (**M**ulti-technology **A**utomated **R**eader **C**ard) is a smart card now being issued by the Department of Defense (DOD) to military personnel. This is not just one of those "rumors";

it has been occurring for quite some time and is fully documented in this chapter. I have samples of the actual cards in my possession (see sample below).

MARC

CHARLES R. WESTINGHOUSE
20/123456789   TAMC

RANK	SERVICE	STATUS	DATE OF BIRTH	BLOOD TYPE
1LT	USA	AD	19690615	O-POS

This smart card uses several information-storage media: a standard 3 of 9 bar code, magnetic stripe, embossed data, printed information (including a digital photograph), and an Integrated Circuit (IC) computer chip.

The combination of several media on one device gives the MARC its unique versatility—it can interface with a variety of technologies and systems, from rudimentary imprinting machines to computer systems that use IC chips as data carriers.

The DOD initiated the MARC project several years ago to provide itself with the ability to instantly track and control all U.S. military personnel worldwide. It is a prototype for the national ID card which probably will be issued to every U.S. civilian as we slide ever closer toward biochip implantation.

The MARC card's IC will be used by the DOD to store and manage all your personal data, both prior to and during your military service. It will be used to manage all medical information on all military personnel worldwide, first individual records on an individual's own card, then downloaded into the mainframe computer's enormous database. It will store (and update as needed) all personal data about the card-holder, i.e. legal information, family information, educational background, police record, religious background—everything you would expect to find on a highly detailed job resumé, *and then some!*

Think of the MARC as your ever-so-enhanced dog tags. The DOD considers one of its most important functions to be the ability to continually identify and track the location of the holder—worldwide— at all times. On certain bases, the MARC already has replaced the meal card. It is keeping track of meals eaten, and without it you don't eat on base!. . .or buy food or other goods at the base exchange. Without the card, you are denied access to treatment in military medical facilities.

The DOD and civilian project coordinators presently are evaluating the MARC card for use in paying personnel (just like the EBT cards). The MARC will be linked to the electronic banking system and the military person can kiss his cash goodbye—all financial transactions will go through a computerized banking system. Using their "captive audience" as guinea pigs, the government will work out the bugs, then move to issuing the MARC to **all** military personnel. From there, it is just a short hop to issuing them for all U.S. civilians. In the August, 1994, edition of *The McAlvany Intelligence Advisor,* Don McAlvany says: "This writer has seen and closely examined one of these MARC Cards. It is real, it is high, high-tech, and *its implications for people control of the American civilian population in the near future are most frightening indeed."*

An Information Paper has been prepared by Lt. Cmdr. Michael D. Sashin at The Pentagon, reporting the results and personnel responses concerning use of the MARC. Hawaii's Channel 4 TV News (January 5, 1995) did an interview with military personnel espousing the great convenience of the MARC, the reduction in paperwork, etc.

The 1995 Advanced Card and Identification Technology Sourcebook had this to say about the MARC:

> The first 20,000 of over 300,000 MARC cards were issued to soldiers and their dependents in Hawaii in late 1994. . . .The cards are truly multipurpose cards used in force readiness, cafeteria, logistics, and personnel applications. . . .The cards are truly multifunction cards used for health insurance, medical records, small purchases from PXs and cafeterias, skills inventories, equipment sign-out, and an increasing number of related uses.

April 11, 1995, Gemplus issued a press release (excerpted below):

Gemplus Receives a 60,000-Microprocessor Card Order
> Gemplus Card International Corp. announced today the receipt of a 60,000-microprocessor card order to supply cards to the Department of Defense. The Gemplus MCOS16K EEPROM cards are being supplied as a part of the Department of Defense's AIT contract. . . . MARC. . .cards will be issued to military personnel in Oahu, Hawaii, to test the concept of multiple applications and technologies on a single card.

> "We are optimistic that the MARC card concept will be rolled out DOD-wide. . . .Gemplus is also providing the Gemplus Pocket Reader to the MARC program." The goal of the test is to develop a joint military services multimedia tool. . .and to demonstrate the feasibility of *complete DOD implementation* [emphasis added].

They also were issued to the troops dispatched to Haiti, with similar success.

In the January 25, 1994, edition of *Current News,* (published from the Pentagon) there appeared an article titled "National Health Plan is Tracked," in support of smart cards worldwide, the MARC in particular.

> The use of MARC as the DOD's "smart card" for patient care and tracking follows closely with National efforts to define universal health benefits and access to health care using smart card technologies. The National Smart Card Forum [Author's note: described fully early in this chapter]. . .was attended by several DOD representatives. A significant interaction. . .created an extremely worthwhile alliance between commercial and government interests.

Whether or not that could be considered a truly "worthwhile alliance" probably would depend upon just whom you asked! I don't much believe in coincidences, so I surely find it amazing that when the implantable biochip technology replaces the DOD's present MARC/smart card technology, the name of the device still will be the **MARC**. Could the military's new MARC be used as the final sales gimmick to condition society into readily accepting the evil "MARC of the Beast" when it finally arrives?

In the book *Revolution* (Harcourt Brace Jovanovich, 1988), by Martin Anderson, whose newspaper articles we have referenced much throughout this book, he relates an experience that occurred during the Reagan administration. It was another immigration problem, and the proposed solution was the same—a national ID card. Here is how Anderson describes the incident.

> . . .one day in 1981, the attorney general came to present his border-control plan—for reasons he thought were good—to the president and his cabinet. Attorney General Smith was a patrician lawyer from Los Angeles who was smart and able, and he had done his homework very well with other members of the cabinet. Smith was Reagan's former personal lawyer and held his trust and confidence. He was seated, in accordance with long tradition, almost directly across the table from President Reagan, speaking

directly to him.

I was seated a couple of feet behind the attorney general, in one of the soft leather seats along the back wall that were reserved for senior White House staff, again in accordance with long tradition. I could see the back of Smith's head, nodding slowly up and down, as his agile brain directed the flow of a flawless, brilliant presentation. It was working. As he moved on from point to point, the members of the cabinet were becoming persuaded. The national identification system was described simply as up-grading the social security cards to make them counterfeit-proof. Not a single objection. It all went down smoothly. A few minutes later Smith was through. He stopped and I knew he was smiling. The president looked up and around the room to see if anyone had any comments. I knew there weren't going to be any. The subject was complex. Nobody else in the cabinet had spent much time on it. And Smith's presentation was very, very good.

So I raised my hand.

I knew I was breaking an unwritten rule, the rule that says senior staff members may sit in on cabinet meetings but they are not to speak unless spoken to. But in the second or two I had to think about it I reasoned that I did not want to be part of the administration that foisted a national identity card on Americans, especially when most of the cabinet seemed to be quite unaware of what they were doing. The worst that could happen to me was to be fired, and if I were fired I would have to go back to sunny California, which didn't seem like a bad prospect at the time.

After a few seconds went by there were no comments coming from the cabinet and the president noticed me. I guess it was pretty obvious, my hand was raised directly over the back of the attorney general's head. He simply said, "Yes, Marty."

And I began to speak. One reason I loved Reagan was his casual neglect of unnecessary protocol and formality. He liked to do things that worked. I assume he figured I had something worth-while to say or I wouldn't have raised my hand. Anyway, the room grew quiet and a lot of eyes, some topped by slightly raised eye-brows, focused on me. I knew this wasn't the time for a longwinded, theoretical critique of national identity cards, so I decided to try humor, leavened with a little shock.

"Mr. President," I said, "one of my concerns about the national identity card is that the Office of Management and Budget has estimated that it could cost several billions of dollars to produce a counterfeit-proof social security card for everyone." That state-ment didn't seem to make much of an impact. By that time a billion dollars or two didn't bother anyone in the cabinet.

"I would like to suggest another way that I think is a lot better.

It's a lot cheaper. It can't be counterfeited. It's very lightweight, and impossible to lose. It's even waterproof.

"All we have to do is tattoo an identification number on the inside of everybody's arm."

There were several gasps around the table. A couple of the cabinet members looked as if they had been slapped. No one said anything for a long time.

The first person to speak was James Watt, the secretary of the interior. . . .

His thick eyeglasses sparkled as his booming voice rolled across the table, "Why, it sounds to me that you are talking about the mark of the Beast. That's terrible."

Most of the people seated around the cabinet table looked puzzled. Except for the president, few of them knew that the mark of the Beast was a biblical reference to Revelation 13:16-18. But now they were alert. Watt was an astute politician, especially knowledgeable about the political thicket populated by right-wing Republicans. You could see the questioning looks come over their faces, each one crinkling and moving in his or her own special way. Nobody seemed to know quite what to say. First the image of Nazi concentration camps and now the mark of the Beast. What next?

The attorney general started to shift back and forth in his chair, getting ready to quell the incipient mutiny. But President Reagan cut him off. The president spread his hands forward across the polished surface of the table, leaned back and looked directly at the attorney general. Smiling broadly he joked, "Maybe we should just brand all the babies."

For about ten seconds everybody laughed and smiled, and that was the end of the national identification card for 1981.

Somehow, I don't think we will be so lucky with the Clinton administration; remember, his advisors are the ones who want to put a chip behind the ear in the maternity ward. . .and, trust me, they aren't making a joke!

There's another "coincidence" of which I'm not too fond—Chapter 666 of Public Law, dated August 10, 1939 (it's a matter of public record—just look it up), was called the "Social Security Act Amendments of 1939." Since all this national identity business was spawned and implemented by the Social Security Act, somehow I seriously doubt the "coincidence" theory.

And when it comes to conditioning us (or as I prefer, desensitizing us), the government doesn't have a corner on the market. The New World Order crowd has permeated every avenue of our daily lives, not the least of which is the media and entertainment business. I have quoted enough newspaper and magazine articles throughout this book that the liberal bias of the media has been more than proven to my satisfaction. But the entertainment industry is at the same time covert and blatantly overt in their messages. Whenever they present a Christian or other devout religious person, they are always represented as anything from just a weird kook and "nerdy" all the way to downright evil; and their evil acts are done, of course, because God wants them to be a serial killer, or He told them to commit some awful act. Usually the most heinous individuals are portrayed as "Christians" or "born again." This type of conditioning affects people . . . it's sort of like advertising: they say it has no real effect on people, but if they really believe that, why are they wasting all those millions of dollars every day to convince us to buy their pet product or service?

It used to be that the message was very subtle, but no longer. Science fiction used to be "good clean fun" and a way just to let your imagination run toward how technology might be in the future. If you live just a few years longer, you usually find out that what was science fiction technology in the past is sitting on your kitchen counter today, for example, microwave ovens. Well, if you have checked out any of the late releases from the Hollywood studios you will find movies like *The Fortress* and *The Demolition Man*. And there is a television program called *Babylon 5*, on which they all have their communicators implanted in their right hands. This is the same communicator they use when they want to access some of their "credits" (cyberspace money), identify themselves, make phone calls to earth (or Mars colony or wherever), be tracked/located by "the bridge," and a myriad of other functions. And I wonder how they came up with the name of "Babylon" for their new station in space. I'm sure that most of you are familiar with the connotation of that name. Coincidence? I doubt it, but maybe I'm just suspicious.

Whether or not they conspired in the physical realm to desensitize the public in this way, that is what they are accomplishing. And if it is not an intentional conspiracy, I see only one other alternative . . . it must be a spiritual conspiracy. Now, doesn't that sound just like the devil . . . by the time the technology (which is already here) is developed to the stage of becoming the Mark of the Beast, the teenagers who have grown up on this stuff will be adults, and they won't even blink, much less resist, when they are offered this "wonderful new technology."

The only answer for a spiritual problem is a spiritual solution. We must be diligent now, even as we watch programs of this nature with our youngsters, to be careful to point out these things and acquaint them with biblical prophecy, especially Revelation 13. We must introduce them to Jesus Christ . . . being a born-again believer in Jesus is the only escape from what is to come.

But we still have a little legislative ground to cover before we can move on to the chapter on syringe-implantable biochips.

Statement of U.S. Representative Stephen Horn

Stephen Horn (R-CA) testified before the Subcommittee on Immigration, Senate Committee on the Judiciary, on May 10, 1995. Since this is a matter of public record, and you may obtain copies if you desire, I will be selecting only a few excerpts for this chapter (as I will with the Marshall Rickert testimony, reported further below).

> . . . America is the only industrialized country without a national identification system, it is time we looked seriously at the "functional equivalent" of such a system [Author's note: I wonder if he ever considered the possibility that this is why America is number one in the world, that the majority of the other nations are referred to as "third world countries," and that so many people want to immigrate here, even if they have to do it illegally.] . . . . bold measures had to be taken. . . . The House Subcommittee on Government Management focused its March hearing on the Jordan Commission's most debated recommendation—setting up a nationwide employment verification registry. . . . The Commission's national computer registry makes sense . . . We already have, in state motor vehicle databases, substantial information which could be linked together. . . . shared with Federal agencies . . . linking together the various databases. . . . I would propose standards for counterfeit- and tamper-resistant cards and for a positive link between documents and their bearers [biometrics]. . . . for positive personal identification.

On the same date, verbal and written testimony was presented by Marshall Rickert, Motor Vehicle Administrator, State of Maryland, on behalf of The American Association of Motor Vehicle Administrators (AAMVA).

> The AAMVA represents state and provincial officials in the United States and Canada. . . . The Association's programs encourage uniformity and reciprocity among the states and provinces, and liaison with other levels of government and the private sector [Author's note: "Liaison with the private sector" means they sell for commercial purposes anything in their files on you or anyone else that anybody wants to buy!].
> There has been much talk of a national identification card. The Oklahoma disaster supports such a concept and I would submit

that such a system is already in place. . . . the driver's license.

. . . the final program draft should be adopted by. . . August. Once approved, the working group will begin developing training materials and procedures to assist members in implementing the model program.

A key element of the program is the development of a unique identifier which *will allow a person to be tracked throughout North America [biometrics]*. AAMVA is recommending that the social security number serve as the unique identifier and that the number be verified through the Social Security Administration prior to issuance.

The Social Security Administration published a notice in the March 29, 1995, *Federal Register,* of their *intent to allow the motor vehicle administrators (MVAs) access to their computer system (SSA's) for the purpose of verifying the identity of drivers license / ID card applicants.*

The Association is also taking steps to obtain electronic access to the Immigration and Naturalization Services computer system. . . . INS has been mandated by Congress to share information. . . in its computer files with criminal justice agencies for enforcement of criminal laws. *Such access should be extended to MVAs.*

. . . the Association developed a Drivers License Reciprocity (DLR) program. . . to electronically transfer information regarding automobile, motorcycle, and light-weight truck operators. . . . The Association is developing standards for the transmission of digitized images and use of bar codes and magnetic stripes.

. . . [Presently] Nothing requires a person to provide his/her social security number.... To ensure state compliance with many of these issues, federal requirements/sanctions must be effected. . . . Sanctions should be severe enough to discourage fraud. . . [emphasis added].

L.U.C.I.D.© 2000

As I have pointed out previously, prior to this time in history a system of computerized global control was not technically possible. *All that has changed!* Such a system is presently being installed right before our eyes, as it were, though few are aware of it. Its secular designers have named it "L.U.C.I.D.© 2000." In my opinion, L.U.C.I.D.© 2000, in concert with the Internet, will be the means by which we ultimately will lose control over both our privacy and our finances, completing the final link in our electronic enslavement.

Although you may not have heard of it, L.U.C.I.D.© Net (as it is frequently called) is a new, extremely complex and sophisticated international system of networked, computerized identification databases that will transfer information on us digitally and instantaneously any-where in the world. The worldwide Internet will serve as the electronic medium through which future local, national, and international cyber-bartering must pass. This global cashless society is being encouraged by business, government, and the media. You will be spending "E-Money," that is, if you have the proper "mark" to do any buying or selling.

It is very early in my research into this new system. For example, no matter who I have contacted, I have yet to locate anyone who can tell me what the letters in the acronym L.U.C.I.D.© actually represent. I am pursuing this diligently and will publish a book on the subject in the near future, exposing as much as I am able to uncover.

World Citizenship?

To conclude this chapter on our identity crisis, I want to include some evidence that it doesn't stop at our own borders. . .they want us to be good citizens of the world. And if you think that's just a figure of speech, think again. There is an organization called the World Service Authority, based in Washington, DC, who is ready to "sign you up" right now. . .in writing. . .on paper! And they've been around for awhile—they were founded in 1954. When I made inquiry about their organization, they promptly mailed me an application form "for registration as a citizen of the World Government of World Citizens."

Apparently, joining entitles you to all kinds of documents. "All World Service Authority documents—including the WSA passport, *World Identity Card,* World Citizen Card, and World Birth Certificate are in seven languages: Arabic, Chinese, English, Esperanto, French, Russian, and Spanish." They also issue "International Exit Visas and International Residence Permits." In the case of the latter, "only regis-tered World Citizens may apply."

Here is some of what they have to say:

> You are already a World Citizen by birth and in fact. By register-ing as a citizen of the World Government of World Citizens— which does not require renouncing any lesser allegiances [Author's note: Referring to my patriotism for America as "lesser alle-giances" makes me very hot under the collar, as by now you may have concluded about me on your own.]—you are joining a fast-growing, sovereign constituency which has committed itself to establishing social, economic, political, and ecological justice throughout the world in accordance with the fundamental moral codes of all major religions [Author's note: Can you say *New Age?*], with basic human rights and with scientific techniques

of organization.

As a registered World Citizen, you have the opportunity to help evolve just and democratic World Laws through the World Syntegrity Project, launched July, 1993, a unique, ongoing strategy to evolve a democratic world constitutional process valid for the next millennium. [Author's note: I don't know about you, but I plan to spend my next millennium under the thousand-year reign of peace of Jesus Christ! And as rapidly as things are progressing, I don't think it will be too many more years.]

The World Government of World Citizens in fact is already functioning in representing you and your needs on a global level. It issues World Passports, World Citizen Cards, World Identity Cards, World Birth Certificates, World Marriage Certificates (all in seven languages), and World Postal Stamps. These represent your human rights and are mandated by the Universal Declaration of Human Rights, proclaimed by the General Assembly of the United Nations 10 December 1948.

I should have seen it coming. . .there's the tie to the UN. Sometimes it pays to just skip to the bottom line—but don't do that yet. All the groundwork has been laid, and it's time to move on to the most important chapter in the book, biochip technology and where it's leading us. So, save "The Bottom Line—A World in Disorder" (my summary) until you have learned all about biochip implantation. . .present and future.

Prepress Update

Just prior to press time there was a major news release announcing that all recipients of government payments (i.e., social security, welfare benefits, et al) must have a bank account to receive benefits via direct deposit (EBT), as in the near future the government will cease issuing checks for these benefits. Further, nonprofit organizations have been notified that—depending on their gross income—all future tax deposits must be made by direct transfer, as well. Watch carefully for full implementation in the near future.

CHAPTER FIFTEEN

Biochip Implants & RFID Technology: The Mark of The New World Order?

666
MARK

We are not part of a military program to implant tags in humans. In fact, we are not part of any plan to implant tags in humans, but a glass encapsulated animal tag only begs the question of the definition of what type of animal, and if that definition is "a mammal," certainly it would include man. Are humans running around somewhere on the globe with tags— RFID tags—implanted in them? Yes! Absolutely, conclusively so.
—Donald G. Small, Hughes Identification Devices
Excerpted from the video *Mark of the New World Order*

Let me begin this chapter with a categorical disclaimer and a warning to those action-oriented individuals who might choose to react radically toward any of the companies mentioned in this book, and in this chapter on biochips and other RFID technology in particular.

I wish to make it *very clear* at this point that *nowhere in this book* am I accusing any manufacturer of radio frequency identification devices (RFID) of working directly for the devil in helping him bring about biochip ID implants! Such accusations are absurd!

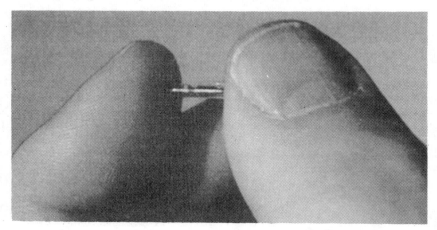

Most officers and employees of biochip transponder-producing companies are very fine people who simply believe that they are helping to advance identification technology that one day will benefit society. Most are completely unaware of the New World Order crowd's ulterior plan eventually to use this technology for identifying, numbering, and controlling people.

Therefore, I wish to state clearly that this book was written to expose *Satan's SPIRITUAL PLAN* to fulfill the Bible's "last days" or "end times" prophecies, rather than to accuse any particular RFID manufacturing company, officer, or employee of being involved in a diabolical plan to harm or enslave anyone. I hope I have made myself clear in this regard. Now, let's get on with some very important information.

The Mark of the New World Order: Mark of the Beast—666

For centuries Christians have speculated about the concept of the Mark of the Beast as described in Revelation 13:16-18. A few liberal theologians have suggested that the Mark of the Beast in the hand or forehead is not a literal concept at all. They have said—and some still say—that the Mark is an allegorical, or perhaps even mythological concept. Other Christians have said the Mark is nothing more than a spiritual concept revolving around Catholicism and the Pope. And for the past decade or so, Christian fundamentalists have pondered over whether or not bar code technology eventually would be used as the *literal* Mark of the Beast in the right hand or forehead, since interpreting scripture literally always is the best first approach. This subject seems to confuse many people when it really should not. It is quite easy to understand, given modern technology and proper interpretation of the original language of the text.

Allow me to put to rest all further speculation by making the following statement: It is my well-researched opinion that the Mark of the Beast, as related in scripture, is *absolutely literal.* Soon, all people on earth will be coerced into accepting a Mark in their right hand or forehead. I am convinced that it will be an injectable passive RFID transponder with a computer chip—a *literal* injection with a *literal* electronic biochip "mark." Exactly as scripture says, without the mark, people will not be able to buy or sell anything anywhere in the world. I believe that such an implanted identification mark *literally* will become Satan's Mark of the Beast, as we will discuss further in this chapter.

However, before proceeding further into microchip implant technology, we first need to spend a few moments analyzing the scriptural basis for my position.

"And he [the Antichrist beast] causeth all, both small and great, rich and poor, free and bond, to receive *a mark in their right hand,* or in their forehead: And that no man might buy or sell, save he that had *the mark, ...* count the number of the beast: for it is the number of *a man* [the Antichrist]; and his number is *Six hundred threescore and six* [**666**] [emphasis added]." Revelation 13:16-18 (KJV)

The King James Version

Pay particular attention to the above scripture that says the mark will go **in**—not on—the right hand. This is the key to correct understanding of the technology that must be used to carry out its implementation. Over nineteen hundred years ago, John, The Revelator, received a vision from God that no one on earth would be able to buy or sell in the "last days" without the devil's mark **in** their hand. To help you grasp an accurate understanding of this concept, let's examine the definition of the words that appeared in the *original Greek manuscripts* of the Bible, in addition to secular dictionary sources.

The English word *mark* (*Strong's Exhaustive Concordance of the Bible,* No. 5480) is from the Greek word *charagma* (pronounced Khar'-ag-mah). *Charagma* is connected by *The Expanded Vine's Expository*

Dictionary of New Testament Words to *stigma, Strong's* No. 4742, in which *Strong's* references *stigma* back to the Greek word *stizo,* then defines *stizo* as follows:

> ...**to prick, stick, incise, or punch for recognition of ownership**. . . .Scar of service: **a mark** [emphasis added].

This is perhaps the best definition of HOW the Mark of the Beast will be given to everyone. I think it is a clear picture of the identifier being placed into and under the skin. . .and for now, the technology that fills the bill is the biochip RFID transponder.

The secular *American College Dictionary* defines *mark* as:

> ...an impression upon anything, such as a line, cut, dent, stain, bruise, brand,. . .an affixed or impressed device. . .a sign or token. . .a distinguishing feature. . .to put *a mark on for identification*. . . .

It also defines *stigma* as:

> A mark of disgrace or infamy; a stain or mark of reproach; a mark or sign of defect or degeneration; a mark on the skin; *a mark made* by a branding iron *on the skin of a criminal or slave* [emphasis added].

Another secular reference, *Rodale's Synonym Finder,* lists the following synonyms for *mark:*

> ...cut, gash, scratch, slash, scar, pock, notch, chip, nick, pit, dent, impressions, bruise, sign, symbol, indication, *brand, identification; marking,* token. . . [emphasis added].

By this time it ought to be obvious to anyone with an open, unbiased mind that the Mark of the Beast of the Antichrist will be used to *identify* those who are owned by him during the seven-year period known as the Great Tribulation. Without his mark of ownership in the skin of the right hand or forehead, no one on earth will be permitted to buy or sell anything. Remember, the Greek word *stizo* indicates that the Mark will be *"pricked, stuck, incised, or punched"* into the skin "as recognition of ownership." Doesn't this sound incredibly close to having an ID microchip/biochip transponder the size of a grain of rice injected with a twelve-gauge hypodermic needle through and under the skin? Could this be merely a scientific coincidence. . .or could it be an exact fulfillment of "end times" scriptures, such as Revelation 13:16-18?

Think about it for a moment! Does this leave any room for other methods, such as bar codes or tattoos? You know what I think, but is there any evidence from secular sources within the media or identification industry that supports my convictions? The answer is a resounding, "Yes!" (probably the most profound of which is the quotation with which I began this chapter). In fact, there is such a deluge of evidence in the media and in industry brochures and news releases that I have had to omit the preponderance of the documentation because of space constraints.

Technological advances are pushing us rapidly toward this method of global identification, and it is my goal through the rest of this chapter to present you with overwhelming evidence from all possible sources that this event is not only on the horizon, but probably will occur during our lifetime.

In our previous chapter on the emerging national ID card, we quoted an extensive passage from Don McAlvany's *The McAlvany Intelligence Advisor* (August, 1994). He concludes that report by asking a question for which we all know the answer: "Is the National ID (Smart) Card the first step to an implanted biochip?" Then he presented some of my research on the subject and arrived at the following conclusion:

> . . . Ah, the wonders of high technology! *Several years ago the DOD [Department of Defense] began to experiment with tiny microchip implants in GI's fillings in lieu of dog tags.*
> So the observations of Cook and [Martin] Anderson . . . are *not* so far-fetched, or off the wall. *They reflect the present state of high technology in America (and globally) and the desires of the New World Order to track and control us all from the cradle to the grave.*
> The government's proposed Health Care Card, Electronic Benefits Card (EBT), Social Security Card, Immigration Card, Postal "U.S. Card" are nothing less than disguised NATIONAL IDENTITY CARDS for *all* Americans! They are ingenious devices for tracking and controlling the lives of everyone. *These new citizen ID cards will allow Big Brother and Big Sister (and their New World Order/Establishment controllers) to maintain computerized, electronically digitized, permanent and accessible records on every man, woman, and child in America.*

Computer Chips in People

Computer chips/biochips already are in use widely in animals and inanimate tracking protocols, and I will cover that more thoroughly later in this chapter, but the question on everyone's mind is, "Can they do it in humans . . . or more important, *will they?"*

Popular Science (October, 1994), in its "Computers & Software" column, printed an article titled, "Future Watch: The Body Binary."

Within the next ten years, we'll have miniature computers inside us to monitor and perhaps even control our blood pressure, heart rate, and cholesterol. Within 20 years, such computers will correct visual and hearing signals, making glasses and hearing aids obsolete.

At least that's how Bertrand Cambou sees it. As director of technology for Motorola's Semiconductor Products in Phoenix, Cambou has been a part of the miniaturization of microprocessors and the development of wireless communication technologies. Both would have central roles in putting computers inside the human body.

It's now possible, notes Cambou, to put the sensors, processors, and wireless radio frequency (RF) devices for an internal computer onto a single, tiny chip. The RF signalling would permit accurate readouts of vital statistics without attaching anything to—or drawing anything from—the body. Even more amazing, internal computers might enable the deaf to hear and the blind to see. A chip implanted on the optic nerve, for example, could correct defective images or simply transmit entire images to the nerve.

The notion of putting computers inside the body may be more realistic than it sounds. "We are not aware of any current obstacles to the encapsulation and implanting of electronic devices within the body, and the transmission characteristics [of radio frequencies] through the body are well known," says Cambou.

The illustration caption reads: "Tiny computer chips implanted in the body may one day monitor and correct our most vital functions." Now if that doesn't qualify for an Oscar in the category of "We're only doing it for your own good," nothing will! And there is no question that technology will bring with it many benefits—we never have denied that point. Our concern is over the excess baggage the benefits bring with them, not the least of which is the loss of privacy, as all these new medical marvels will be tracked and monitored. And failure to do so brings hefty penalties and fines (read about the Safe Medical Devices Act described a few pages later.)

Helping you see and hear better is only the beginning. The February 1, 1994, edition of *The Wall Street Journal* carried a frightening article headlined: "Nervy Scientists Move Toward Union of Living Brain Cells with Microchips." Below are excerpts.

Researchers said they took a key first step toward creating electronic microchips that use living brain cells.

The researchers said they had learned how to place embryonic brain cells in desired spots on silicon or glass chips and then induce the brain cells to grow along desired paths. The scientists hope to be able within the next six to 12 months to get the brain cells, or neurons, to grow connections to each other that will crudely mimic the circuitry that neurons form in the brain.

"I want to emphasize this is fundamental research," said biophysicist David L. Stenger of the Naval Research Laboratory in Washington, worried that the research might be misinterpreted as a fledgling effort to make an artificial brain.

And with good reason, I suspect. Their alleged purpose is for the development of better computer networks of artificial neurons. "It also may be possible to eventually make 'biochips' that drug makers could use to see if new compounds might interfere with, or perhaps enhance, functions like memory or learning." Your name doesn't have to be Frankenstein to see where that research is headed!

By March, the research was reported in a comprehensive article in the *Defense News*. The headline read, "Naval Research Lab Attempts to Meld Neurons and Chips: Studies May Produce Army of 'Zombies'." Before you read on, I think it would be appropriate to ask you to keep in mind, this *isn't* one of those "the aliens have landed" articles in the *National Inquirer.* Here are some excerpts.

> Battles of the future could be waged with genetically engineered organisms, such as rodents, whose minds are controlled by computer chips engineered with living brain cells. . . .
>
> Such a scenario could become reality within the next 15 years if research conducted at the Washington-based Naval Research Laboratory pays off, they said.
>
> The research. . .grows live neurons on computer chips, ...
>
> "This technology that alters neurons could potentially be used on people to create zombie armies," Lawrence Korb, a senior fellow at the Brookings Institution, said March 16. [Author's note: In my opinion, Brookings is a New World Order think tank, therefore, this is quite an admission by Korb.]
>
> "It sounds like science fiction, but science fiction is only 10 to 15 years ahead of [these kinds of] novel technologies," said Kyle Olson, vice president of the Chemical and Biological Arms Control Institute. . . .
>
> The research has captured the attention of the U.S. intelligence community. [Author's Note: No surprise there! Can you just imagine what the CIA, Armed Forces, FBI, NSA, etc., etc., could do with perfected research of this nature?]
>
> "Once this technology is proved, you could control a living species,". . . .

> . . . For all the desirable applications, it may have horrific
> application,". . . .
> In the near future, Navy scientists hope to create living
> neural computer networks that can learn. . . .
> "This opens up whole new applications in bioelectronics,
> where you could use the memory on a [biological] chip, pop
> it into your head and learn French,". . . .
> "This is a class case of military [research and development].
> The door swings in two directions. You've got this Frankenstein-
> type weapon on one hand, and it can deal with problems of
> the human condition on the other," Olson added.
> However, experts say it is unlikely that Pentagon officials
> would ever unleash genetically engineered soldiers on adver-
> saries.

Now, doesn't that give you a sense of safety and assurance. When has
the Pentagon ever given us cause for concern? Well, just ask the people
who lived near the nuclear power plants who were intentionally subjected to released hazardous waste without their knowledge (because
the researchers wanted to know what effect it would have on people)
. . . and of whom more than half have died of cancer or other related
diseases. Or ask the farmers near Rocky Mountain Arsenal in Colorado,
after they finally found out why all their sheep were dropping dead.
After all these years, the government has admitted being guilty of
a limited number of such incidents, and even has made financial resti-
tution in some cases. I am confident, however, that this is only the
tip of the iceberg, and that we don't even have a clue as to the extent
to which innocent Americans have been used as guinea pigs in some
government experiment. . . not to mention military personnel who
are guinea pigs in just about everything the government wants to try
out before it foists it off on the masses.

In Winn Schwartau's book, *Information Warfare,* he addresses this
subject (p. 360).

> Futurists in the bioelectronic industry are looking at ways of
> merging conventional electronics with *living systems* to increase
> speed and density, and reduce power and heat in a new generation
> of information systems. Widespread commercial applications are
> not likely to come about for twenty years, but we inch towards
> such goals with pacemakers and remote triggered electrical
> stimulation for behavior control. [Author's note: Read further in
> this chapter, as well as the article, "Walking Prisons," by Max
> Winkler (*The Futurist,* July-August, 1993), about proposed

methods for monitoring released sex offenders and child molesters.] This is about as personal as an information system can get.
As information systems are embedded within the human body,
the ethical and legal perplexities are only compounded. Will they
make us think better and remember more? Or perhaps they will
help postpone the aging process by optimizing the body's functions. . . .Or can they be used to manipulate and control the
unwilling? Both.

While bio-chips are on the horizon, direct man-computer
communications is here now. The military calls them SQUIDs,
or Super Quantum Interference Devices. SQUIDs are placed on
or near a subject's head to detect brainwave pattern activity. The
SQUID and the subject learn from each other, so that when, say
the pilot of a jet fighter thinks about arming and firing an air-
to-air missile, it arms and fires. In the coming years SQUIDs will
evolve and will be able to electronically read minds as Hollywood
imagined in the Natalie Wood movie *Brainstorm*. When SQUIDs
become reversible and can communicate thoughts and information right into the brain, that's when we really have to watch out.

In the future, the ultimate form of Information Warfare may
prove to be the direct insertion of information into an adversary's
brain from afar. . . .Can minds be forced to act in one manner
or another or even to shut down by remote devices targeted at
specific individuals? We're already examining the possibilities
in research on nonlethal weaponry [emphasis added].

So, you see, RFID biochips to track vehicle and people movement
seem to be "small potatoes" when compared with some of the other
research and development on the drawing boards of some of our
nation's leading labs and engineering departments (primarily military
or government funded).

In the July 24, 1994, issue of *The New American,* William F. Jasper
tells us about the kind of advice the Clintons are receiving from the
people with whom they choose to surround themselves. The article
is titled, "High-Tech Nightmare." Below are some excerpts.

The "smart card" is also a central feature of the Clinton "health
care reform" program. However, some "Friends of Hillary" have
even grander visions. Mary Jane England, MD, a member of the
executive committee of the White House Health Project and
president of the Washington Business Group on Health, a national
outfit comprised of some of the nation's leading corporate welfare
statists, is especially excited about the potential for implanting
smart chips in your body. Addressing the 1994 IBM Health Care
Executive Conference last March in Palm Springs, California, Dr.

England said: "The Smart Card is a wonderful idea, but even better would be the capacity not to have a card, and I call it 'a chip in your ear,' that would actually access your medical records, so that no matter where you were. . .we would have some capacity to access that medical record. We need to go beyond the narrow conceptualization of the Smart Card and really use some of the technology that's out there. The worst thing we could do is put in place a technology that's already outdated, because all of you are in the process of building these systems. Now is the time to really think ahead. . . .I don't think that computerized, integrated medical records with a capacity to access through a chip in your ear is so far off and I think we need to think of these things."

Martin Anderson wrote a priceless article that appeared in *The Washington Times,* October 11, 1993, under the headline: "High-tech national tattoo." Of course, he immediately recognizes the Clinton proposed health security card as the *national identity card it truly is,* and after telling of the dangers inherent in such a system of tracking individuals and their daily activities, he gets right to the bottom line . . .what if you should lose it?

> . . .Can anyone who finds the card or who steals it get access to the information?
> There is another solution, although I hesitate to mention the idea because one of Mr. Clinton's White House aides may take it seriously.
> You see, there is an identification system made by the Hughes Aircraft Company that you can't lose. It's the syringe implantable transponder. According to promotional literature it is an "ingenious, safe, inexpensive, foolproof and permanent method of. . . identification using radio waves. A tiny microchip, the size of a grain of rice, is simply placed under the skin. It is so designed as to be injected simultaneously with a vaccination or alone."
> How does it work? Well, the "chip contains a 10 character alphanumeric identification code that is never duplicated. When a scanner is passed over the chip, the scanner emits a 'beep' and your. . .number flashes in the scanner's digital display."
> Sort of like a technological tattoo. . . .Of course, most Americans will find a surgically implanted government microchip repugnant. At least for the foreseeable future, the use of this ingenious device will be confined to its current use: the tracking of dogs, cats, horses, and cattle.
> But there is no difference in principle between being forced to carry a microchip in a plastic card in your wallet or in a little pellet in your arm. The principle that Big Brother has the right

to track you is inherent in both. The only thing that differentiates the two techniques is a layer of skin.

Once you denigrate the idea of privacy, all kinds of innovative government controls are possible, things that didn't even occur to Aldous Huxley when he wrote his chilling novel, *Brave New World.*

What a difference only two years can make. The Bible tells us that in the last days knowledge will increase, meaning that it will increase exponentially. Anderson's article was written only two years ago, and at this writing I can list a number of ways in which biochips are now used in humans, some in bracelets and anklets (early parole prisoners, Altzheimer's patients, 50,000+ refugees housed at Guantanamo Bay Naval Station, and others) and some inside the body (mandatory in body parts implants effective 8-29-93), and allegedly in some military personnel used as guinea pigs in testing the technology. We've come a long way, Baby!

Although the Bible states the implant will be in the right hand or forehead, and even though most of the biometric technology is using "right hand" verification, a number of people still seem to like the spot behind the ear. The July, 1995, edition of *Popular Science* carried an article called "E-Money." Even though it was primarily about smart cards, digital cash, and the electronic cashless society, Ronald Kane, vice president of Cubic Corp., stated: "If we had our way, we'd implant a chip behind everyone's ear in the maternity ward." In lieu of being able to do that, "the next best thing is giving everyone a card."

As early as April 2, 1989, the *Marin Independent Journal* (Marin County, California) carried an indepth article titled, "Future shocker: 'Biochip—Science fiction technology here.' " Writer Teresa Allen carefully outlined the whole plan, including scanning your hand (with the biochip) after you scan your purchases, and the strong aversion people have to being implanted. And even though written five years prior to the revelation of the experiments on living brain tissue, it alludes to such technology by stating: "Within 15 to 20 years, the regular microchip will be outclassed by a biochip made out of living protein."

The Safe Medical Devices Act

Legislation has been enacted, effective August 29, 1993, known as the Safe Medical Devices Act, for the express purpose of tracking and identifying medical implant devices. Failure to comply can bring severe civil penalties and heavy fines on manufacturers ($15,000 to $1 million). The Safe Medical Devices Act (Public Law 101-629) was signed into law by President Bush on November 18, 1990. It was published in the *Federal Register* dated Monday, August 16, 1993, Part IV Department of Health and Human Services, 21 CFR Part 821.

Manufacturers must adopt a method of tracking devices that are permanently implanted in a human, and they are required to conduct postmarket surveillance for certain devices, including permanent implants. The tracking device of choice seems to be the Hughes RFID biochip, which will contain information about the implanted device, its manufacturer, date, model, name of patient, patient's doctor doing the procedure, etc., etc.

Below are excerpts from a Medical Device Bulletin that was published October, 1993.

FDA Issues Final Rule on Manufacturer Tracking of Certain Medical Devices

The Food and Drug Administration has issued a final rule designed to protect patients with critical medical implants and life-supporting devices if malfunctions arise.

The rule . . . requires manufacturers of 17 implants and 5 other medical devices to keep track of patients who receive the devices so they can be contacted if problems develop that would threaten patients.

Manufacturers will be required to have systems to track certain products from the manufacturer through the distribution chain to the patient . . . .

. . . Manufacturers will be required to update the information in the tracking system and to audit the system twice a year for the first three years and once a year thereafter.

No specific method of tracking is required . . . .

Medical devices to be tracked are:

Vascular graft implants
Ventricular bypass devices
Implantable pacemaker pulse generators
Cardiovascular permanent pacemaker electrodes
Annulopasty rings
Replacement heart valves
Automatic implantable cardioverter/defibrillators
Tracheal implants
Implanted cerebellar stimulators
Implanted diaphragmatic/phrenic nerve stimulators
Implantable infusion pumps
Breathing frequency monitors
Continuous ventilators
DC-defibrillators and paddles

> Silicone inflatable breast implants
> Silicone gel-filled breast implants
> Silicone gel-filled testicular implants
> Silicone gel-filled chin implants
> Silicone gel-filled angel chik reflux valves
> Electromechanical infusion pumps
> Jaw implants
> Inflatable penile implants

Other devices will be subject to tracking in the future, as necessary to protect the public health.

It is my understanding that future devices may be added to this list simply by publishing that intent in the *Federal Register.*

Here are some other pertinent questions.

> Who has primary responsibility for the tracking of a medical device? The manufacturer. Does the regulation require a specific method of tracking? No. Is a manufacturer's tracking method subject to FDA inspection and audit? Yes. Routine inspections will include a review and audit of tracking systems. FDA will inspect tracking systems at any other time that it feels necessary. Does a patient have the right to refuse to participate in tracking? Yes. A patient may refuse to have their device(s) tracked. Such refusals should be documented and be provided to the manufacturer by the product, model, and serial number. The manufacturer must maintain these records for the useful life of the products. Must a final distributor *obtain written consent from a patient in order for the patient's tracking information to be released* to the manufacturer? **No.** The regulation does not require that a patient give written consent to have a device tracked or to release their identity to the manufacturer [emphasis added].

In the August 17, 1994, edition of the *Los Angeles Times,* an article by Kathleen Wiegner appeared under the headline, "Giving Surgical Implants IDs." Here is what it had to say:

> At least 6 million medical devices a year worldwide are surgically implanted in people—everything from breast implants to chin implants, vascular grafts and penile implants. Years later, if a patient visits a doctor because of problems, medical information such as the manufacturer of the implant or the name of the surgeon may not be available.
>
> No problem, if the patient's implant carries an implant of its own—a microchip on which all relevant information has been encoded. Called SmartDevice, the chip, which is about the size of a grain of rice, is manufactured by Hughes Identification

Devices, a subsidiary of Hughes Aircraft Co. In the event of complications with an implant, a doctor could retrieve the information from the chip using a "gun" that emits a radio beam. The gun operates in much the same way that decoders in supermarkets decipher bar coding. The information on the chip would also be recorded on a computer-linked global registry.

LipoMatrix Inc., 33% owned by the biotechnology company Collagen Corp. of Palo Alto, has been issued a patent for the use of SmartDevice in medical devices and has begun putting them into its soybean oil breast implants. SmartDevices are already in . . . LipoMatrix breast implants tested since October on women in Britain, Italy, and Germany.

Stanford University Medical Center will conduct a study on the breast implant chips starting in September.

There you have it! Biochips implanted in the medical implants headed for human bodies for the express purpose of tracking you. And they will be aided by a "global registry" (just another tentacle of the octupus network of databases linked together so the New World Order crowd can keep tabs on everyone). These body parts, containing the same biochip currently being implanted in pets and livestock, will be tracked globally, as the FDA mandates that the manufacturer must be able to reach the implant carrier in ten days or less, or pay the consequences of violation of the Safe Medical Devices Act.

Even Oprah Winfrey is considering the ramifications of biochip implants on her popular talk show. In a program on February 25, 1994, in a show titled, "Your Life in the Year 2000," Winfrey and her guests had been discussing futuristic technology, including virtual reality games, smart cards and the cashless society, never being lost anymore because of the automatic highways, and other subjects, when one guest announced, "We're going to have little chips implanted. You'll be able to track a child that disappears and get them back globally . . . because we'll all have our little memory chip." To which the other guest promptly responded, "I hope not . . . I don't want a chip in me."

To that I say a big "Amen!" I wholeheartedly concur.

Miniaturization of Computer Chip Technology

Smaller and mightier is the goal of the producers of computer chips and other electronics. Make it hold more, make it do more, and make it fit on the head of a pin? Not as farfetched as you might think. In July, 1993, *Popular Science* carried an article titled: "Integrated Circuits: Chips Reach the Atomic Level." We tend to think that something has gotten as small as it possibly can get . . . then someone announces that they have shrunk it again. I'm not sure when we will be "maxed out" when it comes to downsizing the hardware. I suppose it will be when it gets so small they can no longer create tools small enough to manufacture it, but then they will just change directions and figure out how to make the present size hold more capability and operate more efficiently (see above reference to merging living brain cells with man-made chips).

Sematech Corp. announced in 1993 that they had developed a device 1/200th the size of a hair (0.35 micron), and they are working on smaller chips—only 0.10 micron in size. Sematech is a consortium of prominent developers and producers of computer chips and other electronics. Fourteen large electronics corporations have joined forces—their research and development teams are working together to further advance and miniaturize computer chip technology. One of their goals was to bring dominance in the industry back to the United States, and they believe they now have accomplished that.

Although Sematech does not make biochip implants, Texas Instruments does, and they are one of the partner corporations in Sematech. Obviously, this advanced technology will spill over into transponder implant biochips, allowing them eventually to get smaller, as well. Of course, biochips contain no batteries and are passively energized from external forces. They are in the range of 125 kHz RF.

No one can tell their own story better than Sematech, so below is a reprint of a Sematech press release dated January 21, 1993.

0.35 Micron: Gateway to Talking Computers, Home Medicine & More

Sematech's ability to make semiconductors containing devices as small as 0.35 micron on all-American equipment helps pave the way for U.S. production of 64-megabit and 256-megabit computer chips.

According to industry observers, these high-density chips—in the form of microprocessors and dynamic random access memories—will usher in a high-tech future of talking computers, lifetime telephone numbers, and sophisticated in-home medical tests.

"As transistors get smaller. . .they allow more things to be done inside a single electronic package," author David Gabel writes in a recent technology forecast in *Electronic Buyers' News*. "Thus, higher device density doesn't just get more bits per square micron, but it also allows designers to put processors, memory, and I/O (input/output) control on the same chip."

This capability, writes Gabel, could translate into real-world improvements like:

- A personal communicator—smaller than a cellular phone and more powerful—that fits in your pocket. Keyed to your personal phone number and linked to a global network, it lets you take calls virtually anywhere in the world. [Author's note: This was covered at length in a previous chapter; it is accomplished in conjunction with many strategically placed satellites.]
- A "medical module" linked to your home computer that lets you do your own blood test and then alerts you and your doctor to any real or potential health problems.
- Office and home computers which carry on intelligent conversations with you and can also recognize and respond to the voices of your spouse, children, and co-workers.

Similarly, a 1989 speculative piece in *Electronic Business* envisions mind-stretching potentials from chips with internal devices of 0.35 micron and below. These include:

- Workstations as powerful as today's supercomputers and supercomputers able to process billions of instructions per second.
- Intelligent automobiles equipped with chips that monitor and control everything from fuel mixture to the suspension system.
- Medical imaging equipment with higher resolution and improved high-definition television.

More forward leaps from semiconductor technology are predicted by *Business Week* in a Sept. 7 cover story. The article, "Your Digital Future," does not specifically discuss semiconductor technology, but it does forecast digital applications that can be achieved only through denser chips. Some of these applications include:

- Interactive TV that lets you watch a lion hunting game from the lion's point of view.
- Flat-panel wall displays that show you a Van Gogh painting one day, a soothing nature video the next.
- Stereos with "surround sound" that mimic the acoustics of your favorite concert hall.
- Videophones that give clear images, take messages, and handle faxes.

Whether all these technically feasible advances actually happen depends on outside factors such as investment, marketing, and public acceptance. But there's little doubt in the semiconductor world that "denser," "more powerful," and "more advanced" will be the passwords to the next century of electronics.

And the Sematech consortium plans to be leading the way! As Walt Disney envisioned—ahead of his time—"It's a small world after all, it's a small, small world." The time of clichés, such as "the bigger the better," seem to have outlived their usefulness, in favor of other clichés, such as "good things come in small packages."

The History and Advance of Implantable
Biochip Technology and Manufacture

First, let's get a brief explanation of RFID and how it works. RFID is an acronym for a **R**adio **F**requency **I**dentification **D**evice, which uses radio signals to "read" identification codes and other data stored in an RFID transponder and is a reliable way to electronically detect, control, and track a variety of items, information, animals, and people.

The core of the technology is a small, low frequency transponder attached to an object. A reader sends a radio signal to the passive, or battery-free, transponder. The signal charges the transponder, allowing it to return a signal carrying a unique ID code. Lasting less than one-tenth of a second, the process can take place within a "read range" of up to 15 feet. The data collected from the transponder either can be sent directly to a host computer through standard interfaces or stored in a portable reader and later uploaded to the computer for data processing. RFID transponders are designed for long life— up to 175-250 years according to Donald Small, Hughes Identification Devices.

It all began so innocently. During the late 1980's, pet owners and animal shelters around the country became increasingly aware of the need to identify or track animals in order to return lost pets to their owners and decrease the growing number of animals euthanized. This seemingly harmless and beneficial idea gave rise to an entire industry now devoted to this very purpose; however, this technology has ominous overtones for anyone concerned about the potential for human application. Although I cannot yet document its occurrence, this is precisely what some futurists and intellectuals are both predicting and suggesting, and it *is* thoroughly documented that the RFID technology is being used on humans today; we just can't prove injection of an implantable biochip at this time.

The basic prototype for the microchip used in the biochip transponder first was introduced in 1979 by California inventor Mike Beigel. AVID, Inc. (American Veterinary Identification Devices) was incorporated in Norco, California, in 1985, and spent the next six years in research and development. Implantable microchips were tested first in 1987 when International InfoPet Systems, based in Agoura Hills, California, started marketing a microchip made by Destron IDI. By 1991, the market began to heat up and Destron IDI sold its identification card technology to Hughes Aircraft, converted its Boulder, Colorado,

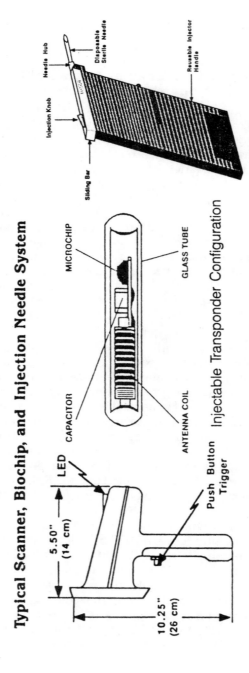

Typical Scanner, Biochip, and Injection Needle System

Injectable Transponder Configuration

location to a research facility, and merged with a Minnesota-based firm.

Destron-Fearing Corporation now offers a wide selection of implantable biochips. Also in 1991, InfoPet changed hands and became InfoPet Identification Systems, which markets a microchip developed by Trovan. Trovan is a German-based subsidiary of AEG/Telefunken, which is the major supplier of this technology in Europe. Countries using this technology include Austria, France, Germany, Holland, Ireland, Spain, Italy, Switzerland, and the Scandinavian countries, as well as Australia, the United Kingdom, and the United States. At this same time, AVID, Inc. introduced a third type of microchip, and Texas Instruments has gotten into this growing market. By 1993, one industry observer described the implantable ID market as a "mosaic of technology."

Various animal shelters, clinics, and human societies have begun calling for a unified ID system. "Last spring, the National Animal Control Association, members of which include animal shelters and humane societies, suggested a boycott of microchips until the companies agree to share enough information so any chip could be read by any scanner" (*The Orange County Register*, 3-7-93). AVID and Destron agreed on the need to develop a standard system, while InfoPet was not so willing.

Lindy Harton, an InfoPet Senior Account Executive, says her chips and scanners are better because they work from a farther distance and don't have to be used as closely. In the end, she argues, "The best technology will win." Currently, AVID has the most popular technology because its scanner can read at least four microchips used in the United States. In 1992, Destron entered negotiations with Texas Instruments Corporation to develop jointly a worldwide operating standard for animal ID. Daryl Yurek, Chairman of Destron, says, "Developing and implementing a worldwide standard paves the way for governments and government agencies to adopt electronic identification without worrying about being locked into a single proprietary technology."

Doesn't a worldwide operating standard for electronic identification sound like a great idea? Just think of all the happy pets and pet owners who will benefit from this wonderful technology! Try to imagine a future world dictator getting hold of this technology and you will have some idea what the New World Order is all about. Better yet, try to imagine this kind of power for surveillance and control falling into the hands of a dictator, and him *not* using it to his own advantage. I believe the latter is the bigger challenge!

Regardless of manufacturers' claims, even the best of existing low-frequency passive transponder technology is limited in its read-range capability. In other words, existing technology generally is limited in its transmission range to within less than two feet from the animals into which transponders have been injected. In fact, the majority are limited to a 2" - 12" read-range. However, though little information currently is available, I will be reporting to you later in this chapter about fish in Europe being tracked with some type of new long-range radio frequency transponder technology. Transponders are being inserted into the stomachs of these fish, which apparently are being tracked by some means of long-range satellite or GPS (see chapter ten, Global Positioning Systems). I presently am investigating this new development.

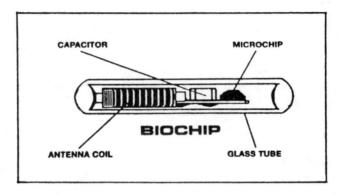

The technical description is given above, but here is a good layman's version of how implantable biochip technology actually works. The basic system consists of an implantable biochip transponder and an external scanning device. The transponders come in various sizes, the smallest of which (at this time—but remember, everything is getting smaller) is about the size of an uncooked grain of rice (11 mm). The transponder is a glass tube made of soda lime glass which is known for biocompatibility. During manufacture, this glass tube is hermetically sealed so it is not possible for any body fluids to reach the internal electronics (or vice versa). There are only three components inside (see illustration). The first is a computer microchip (a custom integrated circuit) which contains the unique ID number which has been etched onto the surface of the microchip. Once the microchip has been encoded, or encrypted, by the manufacturer, it is impossible to alter. The second component is a coil of copper wire wound around a ferrite (iron) core. This coil functions as a tiny radio antenna to pick up the radio signal from the external scanner and to send back the encoded ID number. The third component is a capacitor which tunes or facilitates the signal to and from the microchip.

This type of transponder is a passive device, meaning it has no batteries and never can wear out. It is energized by a low-frequency radio wave from the scanner. Most scanners use a frequency of 125 kHz, the signal used in AM medium-wave broadcasting. These low-frequency radio waves can penetrate all solid objects except those made of metal. Electronic ID based on these radio signals is referred to as RFID (Radio Frequency Identification Device). Once the scanner is activated, it digitally displays the decoded ID number on a liquid crystal screen. Destron can encode up to ten digits on their smallest biochip. Texas Instruments has a brand new chip which will allow the encoding of up to nineteen digits. By combining the digits in a variety of combinations, the smallest biochips can be programmed with up to 34 billion code numbers. A spokesman from Trovan says that with the latest technology "the number of possible code combinations is close to one trillion." That's a lot of identification capability!

One of the more interesting features of implant technology is the injection system. The trademark name for Destron's injection system is called "LifeChip." It would be hard to imagine a more deceptive title than this, especially as this technology moves closer and closer to human applications (implanted). "There is a way which seemeth right unto a man, but the end thereof are the ways of death" (Proverbs 14:12).

Each transponder comes prepacked inside a sterilized needle, which is discarded after use. Because of the sharpness of the needle, "there is minimum discomfort." Special injectors are necessary because most transponders come with an "antimigration tip." In order to prevent the biochip from moving around, one end is sheathed in a polypropylene shell. This coating offers a surface with which fibrous connective tissue begins to bond within 24 hours after injection. In other words, once the biochip is implanted, it becomes part of you with an "unlimited lifespan" (Trovan). "Once implanted, the identity tag (RFID) is virtually impossible to retrieve. Surgical removal, using the most advanced radiograph techniques available is extremely difficult" (AVID).

The final stage in the biochip technology is the ability of the scanner to transfer ID codes to a variety of external computers and printers. InfoPet has a "Recovery Network" with a 24-hour Hotline. Government animal regulation and control agencies, shelters, and clinics participate in this network. InfoPet can identify any of its registrants through the microchip number. . . pet's name, owner's name, social security number, zip code, or telephone number. AVID is participating with the PETtrac, which is a national computer network. The average cost for pet identification is $40.00.

Though other applications are covered in detail elsewhere in this chapter, it still should be noted here that this technology definitely is not limited to pets, livestock, fish, or wildlife. The developers at Trovan envision a day when transponders will replace the bar code system. Possible applications include coded automobile chassis numbers, automatic tolls, parking, copyright protection for video and computer software, documents, passports, ID cards, credit cards, badges, warehouse/stock handling, valuable items registration, insurance, shipping containers, luggage tags, cargo pallets, ammunition, arms, spare parts, aviation parts, body parts, customs, seals, blood samples, and laboratory applications. It is not surprising to see European firms way ahead of everyone else when it comes to advanced identification technologies. Scripture clearly indicates that the Antichrist will rise out of the European theatre and use the technology which already is available (Daniel 2:1-45; 7:19-27; 9:27; Revelation 17:8-18).

The Canadian Kennel Club, as well as nearly 500 humane societies, has endorsed the Destron chip. Destron President Jim Seiler is enjoying his firm's success, but he also is aware of concerns which trouble the public and assures us that Destron "is not considering human application." Mr. Seiler may not be considering human application, but others certainly are—in fact, in their considered opinions, the sooner the better.

One such individual is Tim Willard, Executive Officer of the World Future Society. In a disturbing article appearing in *The Marin Independent Journal* (4-2-89), Willard openly suggested using biochip technology on humans. "The technology behind such a microchip is fairly uncomplicated and with a little refinement could be used in a variety of human applications. Conceivably, a number could be assigned at birth and go with a person throughout life." Most likely the biochip would be implanted on the back of the right hand so that it would be easy to scan. Willard says it would be like a universal ID card, replacing all other forms of ID. "At the checkout stand at the supermarket, you would simply pass your hand over a scanner and your bank account would automatically be debited." Sounds so convenient, doesn't it?

Remarkably, Willard goes on to suggest that a human microchip identification system "would work best with a highly centralized computer system." Willard comments, "While people over the years may have grown accustomed to artificial body parts, there is definitely a strong aversion to things being implanted. It's the 'Big Brother is watching' concept. People would be afraid that all of their thoughts and movements were being monitored." And rightfully so, I might add! Willard adds, "People tend to be romantic about their independence and privacy." Mr. Willard, and others like him in the New World Order crowd, always display their arrogance when it comes to sentimental notions like freedom, independence, national sovereignty, and privacy. After all, this is a New Age, isn't it? And we have to think globally, don't we? Wake up, folks! This is not *Peter Pan*—if we let our freedoms be taken from us, we will not be able to resurrect them just by "believing and clapping our hands," in Tinker Bell-fashion.

To reiterate the quotation given earlier from Martin Anderson: "The principle that Big Brother has the right to track you is inherent in both [smart card and biochip]. The only thing that differentiates the two techniques is a layer of skin."

I think by now you have more than sufficient information on how the biochip system works and why we are escalating so rapidly to its extensive use on a global scale. Now let's see the extent to which it already has been implemented, and future uses currently on the drawing boards.

The Trend Toward Electronic Tracking of Everything

The trend toward tracking everything from packages to garbage to freight to animals to people is expanding at a staggering rate. The newspaper and magazine articles and technical brochures are coming in faster now than I am able to keep current on them. This is truly a burgeoning business, and furthermore, it is a global business.

Even though freight lines (truck, train, and ship), parcel handlers (UPS, FedEx, etc.), and retailers (merchandise identification) are still using bar codes, the trend is moving away from bar codes to RFID transponders, some of which are "read only" and others "read/write," which allows all shipping details to be placed in the microchip and updated at each stage of the shipment. And the bar codes that remain are becoming much more sophisticated. In chapter eight of this book, "Bar Codes," I described 2-D bar codes and other more advanced models coming into use. Yet, even with these advances, it seems that RFID is becoming the preferred technology of the future.

In order to keep this extra long chapter somewhat organized, it is necessary to segregate the remaining information into specific categories. . . knowing in advance that there necessarily will be some overlap involved. By now, most of you have a pretty good working knowledge of how a biochip/microchip operates, so for now, let's just consider these categories for existing and proposed usage: tracking of inanimate objects; tracking of pets, livestock, fish, and wildlife;

tracking of humans; and some highly unusual proposed usage, some of it merging biometric identification with the implanted biochip in conjunction with inanimate objects.

Examples cited for the aforementioned categories will be brief, as most have been described in length in previous chapters herein.

Tracking Inanimate Objects

Texas Instruments (TIRIS) and Hughes are heavily involved in providing passive transponder microchip systems for inanimate objects. Hughes (as well as a number of others) produce much of the technology for the automated highway systems.

In addition to its U.S. activities, in its international report, Texas Instruments has announced much activity abroad by its TIRIS division. TIRIS has RFID tags buried in the roadway for tracking of trams (public transportation) in Helsinki. They can do everything from report the location of the tram to changing the signals ahead to make traffic flow smoother to changing the signs on the tram about the stops ahead, and even make audible announcements about the shopping in the area. TIRIS RFID's are used in supermarket carts in England to prevent theft. The readers are stationed throughout the store and carts are tracked as a customer shops. If someone attempts to walk out with the cart before paying for the groceries, an alarm is sounded. Carts are checked in and out by the system when a person comes in to shop. TIRIS is supplying a high-frequency RFID system for electronic toll collection in the U.K. TIRIS supplied a unique hands-free total security system installed at a new Derby hospital carpark in England.

Sensormatic Electronics (Florida) has announced an alliance with TIRIS to co-develop a series of security "smart tags" for companies to automatically identify and track their valuable assets. They also announced that they will provide a security system for the 1996 Olympic Games in Atlanta based on TIRIS.

"Luxurious Italian Hotel Gets Hi-Tech Parking Garage." This was the headline on the article announcing installation of the TIRIS tags to handle the financial transactions of the parking charges and the raising and lowering of barriers without operators at the new multistory parking garage of the Ergift Palace Hotel in Rome. It will accommodate over 1200 vehicles and 50 buses.

An RFID AVI (Automatic Vehicle Identification) system to track buses, based on TIRIS technology, is scheduled for implementation in Sao Paulo, Brazil, involving more than 11,000 buses, operated by 82 private companies, servicing 1200 routes throughout the city. TIRIS has joined with MFS Network Technologies to replace AT&T as developer for automatic toll collections on the new Foothills Corridor toll freeways in southern California. TIRIS transponders were worn on the running shoes of many who participated in the Berlin Marathon in the fall of 1995. Custom antennas mounted along the route for the first time kept truly accurate records of running times through the course, as well as at the finish line.

In Hannover, Germany, Continental AG has begun field testing its TIRIS-based truck tire management system. A read/write transponder is attached to the inside of each truck tire manufactured. A TIRIS ID card is provided to a tour guide at the Visitor Exhibits at the BMW plant. As the guide approaches with the transponder, the RFID is signaled and automatically starts up the action—signs switch on, films begin to run, music starts up, models turn on, and PC's are activated.

In Munich a TIRIS-based positioning system will be used with line-controlled vehicles, such as forklift trucks, for efficiency in logistics management. In Dusseldorf, wooden beer barrels and kegs are tagged with a read/write transponder. There are aftermarket-theft-prevention systems based on TIRIS. The car won't start unless the dashboard-mounted transceiver detects the correct code from the transponder mounted inside a tag attached to the keyring. TIRIS is targeting rental cars and truck fleets. (Many variations on this system are produced by TIRIS for a number of different functions.) To eliminate the *necessity* for aftermarket-theft-prevention devices, just buy a vehicle that comes with the immobilizer built in and the TIRIS transponder fitted into the ignition key (on Ford cars in the U.K., and soon to be introduced into the U.S., according to TIRIS). RFID has been installed to identify and track production line and quality control for a pharmaceutical company in Italy, as well as tracking the transport containers. TIRIS transponders are used in automatic pallet identification for inventory control in the Netherlands. Automated Pallet Transport System was set up based on TIRIS RFID in Copenhagen. In Vancouver, B.C., a TIRIS system is used to weigh the garbage as it is collected and charge the household accordingly. The TIRIS RFID system is used in fuel dispensing management. Goodyear's "Smarttire" is the result of a recent breakthrough to create a method to mold TIRIS transponders into tires.

Not all activity involves TIRIS, though they certainly seem to be the most anxious to announce and promote their projects. The American Railroads have adopted the AAR system by Amtech Corp. of Dallas, Texas, for the RFID tagging of rail cars. For exporters, the most significant aspect of the AAR tracking system may be its rapid acceptance as a worldwide standard. European railroads have decided to adopt the same RFID technology. And Liberty Mutual Insurance is now offering as part of its coverage tracking devices with an alleged 95% success rate in recovering stolen vehicles and capturing the car thief.

Tracking Pets, Livestock, Fish, and Wildlife

Biochips in pets and livestock is old news, and their use now is being extended into tracking of fish and wildlife to determine their numbers and ability to survive when their species becomes endangered. There are now so many articles that I have tried to select only one or two telling about each type of use. Here are some excerpts.

The Valley Sun, (South Central Alaska), January 5, 1993:

Computer Chips Identify Iditadogs

Organizers of this year's Iditarod Trail Sled Dog Race will use computer chips instead of paint to identify dogs taking part in the 1,000-mile trek across Alaska.

Tiny chips the size of a grain of rice will permit officials to use portable hand-held scanners to check every dog in the race—hundreds of animals—and help prevent illegal attempts to substitute dogs along the route from Anchorage or Nome.

Chief veterinarian for the 1993 race, Dr. James Leach III, said the chips have been injected in animals ranging in girth from birds and puppies to llamas.

So far, he said, there've been no bad reactions.

St. Louis Post-Dispatch, January 8, 1995:

Dog Bytes: Technology Finds Lost Pets—Computer Chips Implanted Beneath Skin Provide IDs

Dr. Dan Knox, the head veterinarian for St. Louis County's division of animal control, said he hopes pet owners throughout the area will consider having their cats and dogs "chipped". . . .This is a great technology, Knox said. . . . Ideally, Knox said, the agencies and local veterinarians all would use the same brand of microchip and the same brand of scanner—"AVID" is the one commonly used here. . . . Knox said the county also implants chips in animals offered for adoption. For two months, the Humane Society has implanted chips in animals offered for adoption. . . .

There is an abundance of similar articles appearing nationwide and around the world. I'll just reference a few of them here, quoting anything of exceptional interest that has not been reported as yet.

November 9, 1991, *The Daily Breeze:* "A novel ID: Implant plan for pets OK'd." Computer-compatible cats and canines are about to be unleashed in Los Angeles.

November 9, 1991, the same article appeared in *The San Diego Union.*

December 3, 1992, *The San Diego Union-Tribune.* "Vets chip in for pets: Tiny implants can provide foolproof ID."

> Your precious pet iguana has turned up missing, and the guy down the street is suddenly showing off a new reptile that looks suspiciously familiar.
>
> Now, how would you be able to positively ID an iguana?
>
> With a microchip, of course.
>
> Dr. Bob Stonebreaker, a Del Mar veterinarian, reports that the microchipping of all ostriches and emus in San Diego County is virtually complete.
>
> "It was a big job; must have been a couple thousand or more to do," said Stonebreaker, who breeds the giant birds as a sideline.
>
> The veterinarian said "a lot of ostrich rustling occurs in this county. These birds are worth a lot of money, and this is a surefire way people can ensure their birds are permanently ID'd."
>
> Dr. Jenkins, meanwhile, has been targeting pot-bellied pigs.
>
> "You can't tattoo 'em—their skin is black," noted Jenkins, a Mission Valley vet who specializes in birds and exotic pets, including reptiles and the popular pigs.
>
> "Besides, tattoos can be altered. The microchip solves the problem."

January 7, 1993, *The Sun* (San Bernardino, California). "High Tech Tags: Animal control officials introduce microchip implants for pets."

January 8, 1993, *The Orange County Register.* "Microchip implants aren't the perfect pet ID." The gist of this article is that there are a number of different systems on the market and not yet a single standard to enable any scanner to read all implants.

March 7, 1993, *The Orange County Register.* The following letter to the editor by Linda Stearns of Tustin, California, appeared under the heading, "The ramifications of microchip pet implants," and begins to recognize some of the implications of this technology when projected further into the future.

> Often things begun with the best intentions are easily transformed into procedures that are less than desirable.
>
> Implanting microchips in our animals sounds reasonable enough. We own our pets. If they are lost, we have a better chance of finding them if they are picked up by animal shelters that are equipped with scanners.
>
> However, it seems to me that we are in the beginning stages of a larger experiment. Suppose these chips could be enhanced

to emit radio waves that are readable at greater distances? We would then have a tracking device. Suppose we implanted microchips in our littlest children in case they are lost or stolen. We already have programs to fingerprint them, why not implant them? But in the process of protecting them, aren't we, in effect, declaring ownership of them? At what age would we declare that person sovereign? Perhaps it would be decided to leave the chips in place to aid in census taking or some other benign purpose. [Author's note: She apparently was not aware that the chips are virtually impossible to remove—even by high-tech surgery.]

We could conceivably have the beginnings of a whole society of people registered by some agency and traceable anywhere in the world. Perhaps we could find dead-beat fathers; perhaps we could all be monitored for our movements and associations.

Suppose those chips were further enhanced to receive? What kind of messages might be programmed into an individual? And from whom? [Author's note: Sounds like she's been reading Schwartau's book...except he didn't write it till 1994!]

This may sound like paranoia or science fiction, but the technology isn't that far away. Implanting sounds like a good idea when we're talking about dogs. What will we say when it's suggested for humans?

Congratulations! That's very astute of you, Ms. Stearns!

March 15, 1993, *Anchorage Daily News.* "Microchips identify lost dogs."

> ...The AVID system is one of four available nationwide, Schenck said, but it can read the microchips of the other systems.
>
> The SPCA put more than 5,000 dogs and cats under euthanasia last year, more than half the total that turned up at the shelter. ...most animals they deal with are pets, not strays. Eventually, he would like to see chips implanted in all animals before they are adopted.
>
> Schenck foresees "chipping" pets as a standard procedure performed when vaccinations are done....

August 8, 1993, *The Honolulu Advertiser.* "Injected microchips help reunite pets with owners."

August, 1993, *Dog Fancy* Magazine. "Beyond Dog Tags: Identification methods combine tradition with technology" is a four-page article exploring the latest in ID methods, again emphasizing the need for compatability in the scanning systems.

September 18, 1993, *The San Diego Union-Tribune.* "Pet technology finds a home: County's 3 shelters adopt injected tags to ID lost animals."

In 1994, the *Weekly Reader* children's magazine featured two articles in language at their level explaining, first, what they call the "pet microchip," followed by an explanation of its purpose and operation.

May 22, 1994, *The Charlotte Observer* (North Carolina). "Gaston pound gets chip ID system: New scanner will help find owners of pets with microchips."

You see the pattern here—universal usage—by county and city animal control departments and local humane societies, in addition to use on a personal level by local vets and pet owners. In a matter of just a couple of years, usage has escalated from some strange experimental process to worldwide and nationwide acceptance by the mainstream in animal control (as you will read a little further on, Europe has been much quicker at implementing this technology than we have).

April 14, 1995, *Current Science.* "Computer Chips Identify Lost Pets."

Now the companies who produce these systems have gone into *direct* advertising "big time!" With a full-color, full-page ad on the inside back cover of the *TV Guide* one week and the inside front cover the next week (July, 1995), the "New Home Again Companion Animal Retrieval System" tugged at our heartstrings with a photo of a sad, drenched dog lost out in the rain. The lead line read: "Until now. . . good friends *were* hard to find," and the text was prefaced by "Your Best Chance to Find Your Missing Pet." After giving the basic explanation of how the biochip implant system works, they continued:

> **HomeAgain** also taps you into a *national, 24-hour year-round recovery program* managed expertly by the American Kennel Club, Inc. (AKC). When a lost pet's **HomeAgain** identification code is read, the AKC recovery program's 800 number is contacted and every possible step is taken to reunite owner and pet.

Trust me—that's a three-hankie photo. Who wouldn't want to provide something so wonderful for their beloved pet? However, until now, all this love was expressed primarily on a voluntary basis, but you soon can say goodbye to that concept. In fact, in certain places animal implants are already *mandated* by local authorities, and there is no doubt that the number will grow rapidly with the reports of success of such programs.

April 27, 1995, *San Francisco Chronicle.* "Novato [a suburb of the north San Francisco Bay area] Orders Microchip IDs for Cats."

> Overriding objections that their actions had Orwellian overtones, Novato City Council members mandated early yesterday

that cats have identifying microchips implanted between their shoulder blades.

July 11, 1993, *Sunday Advocate,* Baton Rouge, Louisiana. "Spaniards supplant pet ID tags with microchips." (Michael M. Phillips, Associated Press Writer, reporting from Madrid, Spain.)

Spaniards are teaching their dogs a very new trick.
Dogs and cats in Spain's largest cities must now undergo microchip implants....

Four of Spain's 17 regions now require dog and cat owners to identify their pets with chips or tattoos—apparently the only such laws in western Europe or North America....

"The whole object is not only to make it nationwide, but also Europe-wide and then universal," said Dr. William Hutchinson....

The original purpose of the Madrid law—like statutes covering such cities as Barcelona, San Sebastian, Bilbao, and Pamplona—was to monitor rabies vaccination rates and keep tabs on the pet population.

The Madrid law went into effect six months ago, and 50,000 cats and dogs have already been "chipped".....Officials expect 100,000...by year's end....

...the chips do not infect or otherwise irritate the animal and will outlast even the most durable dog or cat....

Ranchers already use them to identify livestock in many countries, and European zoo keepers implant them in some animals.

The system is used on pets on a voluntary basis in Norway, Portugal, Great Britain, Belgium, Ireland, and the Netherlands.

In the United States, a few community groups, shelters, and vets have started small voluntary programs in New York City and northern Califoria.

Organizers of this year's Iditarod Trail Sled Dog Race implanted chips in the hundreds of dogs....

But unlike in Spain, there are several brands of chips in the United States and scanners don't read all of them, slowing the system's growth.

The Humane Society of the United States has held off endorsing microchipping of animals in hopes that American companies will develop a universal microchipping system.

Well, that should adequately cover the subject of household pets, whether common or exotic. Now, let's take a brief look at the livestock of the ranchers mentioned above, and some really wild wildlife tracking.

Amelita F. Donald founded the International Equine Recovery Net in 1990 after researching the problems and solutions of horse theft as it touched her life. She sees electronic identification technology (RFID) as the "battle in defense of honesty."

June 15, 1993, the *San Francisco Chronicle* ran an article headlined: "High-Tech Horse Branding: Microchip implant may replace traditional way to track livestock." So you thought the rustlers went the way of the old TV westerns? Wrong! In this article, by Dan Turner, *Chronicle* Correspondent, Ms. Donald is quoted as claiming, "The problem shifts, and right now the problem is in California." Below are some excerpts from that article.

> Stealing horses might seem like a rather old-fashioned way to make a living, but a rash of California horse thefts in recent years has led to a very modern solution.
>
> Veterinarians are beginning to implant microchips beneath the skin of horses, which provides a way to identify the animals if they are stolen. The method, which has been used to identify pets since the late 1980s, is just starting to replace the brand as the best way to track livestock.
>
> Horse theft is a lucrative business that seems to be just taking off in California. Although horse meat is not sold in the United States, it is popular in parts of Europe and Japan and prices have risen markedly in the past two years.
>
> There are 13 slaughterhouses for horses in the U.S., four of them in Texas. They will pay up to $1 a pound for a grade A horse, said. . .Great Western Meat Co. in Morton, Texas, the biggest horse slaughterhouse in the country.
>
> With a well-fed animal, that could mean as much as $1,000 for the horse thief.

Theft is not the only reason horses are being "chipped." Quarantine and preventing the spread of disease is high on the list of priorities for positive identification of animals. The Louisiana Department of Agriculture & Forestry is dealing with an outbreak of Equine Infectious Anemia (EIA) which is spread by the horse fly and is usually fatal. Sellers must produce a clean bill of health for animals before they can sell them. "Beginning February 1, 1993, horses tested for EIA must be individually and permanently identified. The department is recommending the new microchip implants for identification."

And TIRIS is getting into livestock identification abroad, as well as its involvement in inanimate object RFID. In Australia unbreakable, reusable RFID pellets are being injected into the rumen of cattle for purposes of identification and tracking of the history of the animal. The pellet settles in the rumen, stays with the animal for life, is removed at the time of slaughter, and available for use again—the perfect definition of recycling.

In Alberta, Canada, TIRIS is participating in the development of a feed-monitoring system for ostrich growers.

And earlier in this book we described the biochip, linked to the computer, that recognized old Betsy's RFID, directed her to her own personal stall, and by the time she arrived there, had her own custom diet (both amount and content) already on hand and waiting for her.

Earlier in this chapter we mentioned the fish that caught the fisherman (sort of a takeoff on the old cliché that "dog bites man" is not news, but "man bites dog" is news). Well, here's the article I promised you: "RF-tagged salmon catches poacher." It appeared in the August, 1994, edition of the *Automatic I.D. News.*

> A poacher was tracked to his home after netting RF-tagged salmon from the river Hirnant, near Bala, Gwynedd, U.K.
>
> The tags transmitted radio signals to bailiffs at the National Rivers Authority as the poacher walked home with his illicit catch. Able to pinpoint exactly where he lived, bailiffs arrived at the poacher's home to find four prime salmon lying on his kitchen table.
>
> Tagged salmon transmit data over great distances to icthyologists tracking migratory habits, allowing them to estimate numbers entering the river each season.
>
> "This case should act as a warning to other poachers," the National Rivers Authority said. "Although the microchip usually tracks migrating habits, it can also track poachers."

As I said before, I am investigating this, because—at the moment—I am not aware of any technology this advanced. I can assume only that it is based upon some type of GPS (Global Positioning System) technology, or triangulation, or a combination of both. If this is a *passive* RFID system, the readers are more powerful than anything I have yet encountered. However, the way technology is advancing exponentially, it would take more than this to surprise me.

Then there is the tracking of the *really* wild wildlife. October 13, 1992, *Los Angeles Times.* "Call of the Wild: Electronic Signals from Collars Track Welfare of Cougar Population—Big cats cope with a shrinking habitat."

And I'll close this section by referencing an article in the *Orange County Register* which advances the tracking systems from animals to humans, which is our next section. "Keeping track: Electronic device can monitor people and pets—Tracer: Several devices have been donated to people afflicted with Alzheimer's disease.

Whether you need to track an endangered species or an errant grandparent, Spence Porter can help.

Porter, president of Communications Specialists, Inc. in Orange, is one of a handful of manufacturers in the nation who design devices to monitor the movement of birds and other animals.

He has developed transmitters worn by the creme de la creme of endangered species: bald eagles; California condors *[et al]*. . . .

. . . people will see stories about transmitters on condors and bald eagles "and call the zoo and ask if they could put one on grandpa or their dog." He is experimenting with the new system and has donated several devices to people with Alzheimer's disease.

Tracking Humans

In this section it is difficult to know even where to begin. I think I'll begin by telling you where many people (scientists and laymen, alike) think we are headed, then tell you how far we've progressed . . . in other words, where we are now, technically speaking.

The June 6, 1995, edition of *USA Today* carried an excellent article entitled, "Embedded electronics, a chip off sci-fi," written by Mike Snider. It carefully points out how biochip technology—the implanted computer chip—is not-so-gradually becoming embedded in our popular culture.

►In the new movie *Johnny Mnemonic*, Keanu Reeves plays a 21st-century courier with an overloaded data chip embedded in his head.

►Robert Ludlum tosses a chip into his latest mega-selling espionage novel *The Apocalypse Watch* (No. 2 last week on *USA TODAY's* Best-Selling Books list). Nazis brainwash a secret agent and implant a mind-control chip.

►In the news, Timothy McVeigh, charged in conjunction with the Oklahoma City bombing, told acquaintances that the U.S. Army implanted a computer ship in his buttocks to monitor his whereabouts.

►And, in an outside-of-court conference earlier this year, Colin Ferguson, the man found guilty of the Long Island Rail Road murders in 1993, accused the CIA of implanting a computer chip in his brain.

Other recent chip-ins include the 1994 MTV series *Dead at 21,* in which the main character carried a chip implanted at birth, set to self-destruct at age 21. And in ABC's 1993 miniseries *Wild Palms,* a cult leader tried fusing a chip into his brain to gain immortality.

Believe it or not, science isn't so far behind science fiction.

Then he tells about pet implants, including the system managed by the AKC (the one I described above which appeared in the *TV Guide*). Next, he proceeds to the medical uses, starting with pacemakers, implants, and prostheses. Then he moves ahead to future medical uses for the technology, speculating about helping the deaf to hear and the blind to see and the paralyzed to stand. To me, this sounds more like a miracle (or maybe sci-fi) than technology. But then he settles down to some future uses that actually are in the realm of possibility in the foreseeable future, such as implants that contain personal information on you, including your medical records, X-rays, MRI images (not to mention your positive identification, with biometrics, and your financial info, etc., etc.). Then they extrapolate this data out to some *really* wild projections. I strongly recommend that you read the whole article.

Now for some of the uses presently in practice in the tracking of humans: these use RFID technology—they just aren't *implanted* as yet (that we know of). They are attached to the body in some way—actually, in a variety of different ways.

Athletics is turning to RFID technology because of the accuracy of both identification and timing. I told you earlier about the running shoes with the RFID tags. In Europe entrants in a triathlon are issued an RFID wristband (which, by the way, must be worn on the *right arm*). Here is how it works:

> The beauty of the IPTA system is its simplicity. Each athlete wears an IPTA wristband which has a built-in [TIRIS] transponder. . . .Special antenna are installed in timing boxes for reading these. . . .boxes are located at the beginning and end of each transition zone and at the finish line. The athletes slap the box [with their *right* hand] as they pass each zone and their exact time is recorded. As the times are recorded, they are sent via cable to individual computers at each zone and then via radio frequency to the host computer. In order to be absolutely sure that no data has been lost during the radio transmission, the data from the individual computers at each zone is loaded into the host at the end of the event for figuring the final results.

This same technology usage was discussed in the July, 1995, edition of *Automatic I.D. News* in an article titled, "Chip chipping in to run honest race." This article by James E. Guyette discussed a number of different kinds of races and RFID technology being used to make them more accurate, and to keep them honest. Runners and swimmers have the transponders in a velcro bracelet. Bike racers have them mounted on the bikes. "The new system prevents participants from taking shortcuts in an effort to win. Checkpoints play a crucial role in these types of events." This is especially true in marathons, where one person got caught trying to better his running time by taking a three-mile shortcut.

A number of articles have appeared about prisoners being fitted with home-monitoring devices and confined to their homes to alleviate the overcrowding of jails and prisons. February 17, 1992, *The Orange County Register* carried an article, "More prisoners serving their time out of jail," with a photo of the monitoring device. On July 31, 1994, the *North Jersey Herald News* carried another such article, "Anklet is put back on parole."

Without a doubt the most extensive use of RFID bracelets has been by the United States Department of Defense (DOD) for the processing and tracking of over 50,000 Cuban and Haitian refugees interned at Guantanamo Bay Naval Base in Cuba.

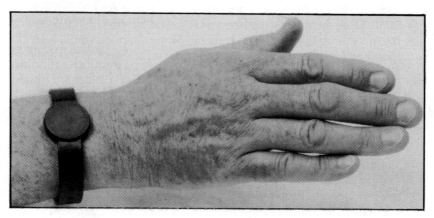

The *Automatic I.D. News* ran a front page (plus) article in its December 1994 issue, complete with photos, under the headline, "New DoD system tracks refugees: Navy deploys RFID-based human tracking system to cope with Haitian/Cuban exodus." Then they told the story of how our government was not only endorsing but implementing a program for identifying and tracking human beings by permanently riveting a bracelet transponder on their right wrist. Some of the refugees later devised ingenious methods to remove them, with great difficulty, I might add, but when this was discovered, the government took steps to stop it by embedding strips of metal in the bands to reinforce them and prevent their removal. Even the children got banded, however, even the smallest adjustment on the bracelet kept slipping off of their tiny wrists, so the Navy just turned them into "ankle bracelets." Here are some excerpts from that comprehensive article.

Banks of sophisticated computer workstations are connected... to CCD photo cameras, fingerprint scanning terminals and... RFID transponder readers.... The entire 2,000-square-foot interior of this former base restaurant has been converted into a state-of-the-art computer processing center to identify and track the more than 50,000 Cuban and Haitian refugees who flooded into this 45-square-mile base between June and September of this year [1994].

Last June, the United States Atlantic Command (USACOM) ... implemented the Deployable Mass Population Identification and Tracking System (DMPITS).... Now, having performed beyond its designers' greatest expectations, the DMPITS system has also been purchased by the U.S. Department of Immigration and Naturalization Service (INS) and installed October 1, 1994, in border patrol stations in the San Diego area. A new era of tracking illegal aliens and immigrants with automatic identification technology has begun.

At its peak, the 81-person DMPITS unit was processing 400 to 500 people an hour, 24 hours a day. A total of 22,000 Creole-speaking Haitians and 32,000 Spanish-speaking Cubans passed through the system.... Approximately 8,000 Cubans volunteered to be moved to more comfortable refugee camps in Panama. (Another complete DMPITS system was ordered for the Panama operation.) The transfer of so much humanity taxed the capabilities of the DMPITS unit to the max.

[FingerPrint USA] received emergency orders for three more complete systems for the Navy and two complete systems for INS within three months....

How It Works

A new enrollee takes a seat facing a work station with an imposing array of technology: a Hewlett-Packard 715 or 735 UNIX workstation sporting a 2 gigabyte internal hard drive; a 19-inch color monitor, keyboard and mouse; an Identix

TV-555 Touchview Fingerprint Scanner; an AVID ID Tag Scanner; and a Panasonic CCD color video camera. The system's server configuration includes an HP-735 workstation with 80M of RAM and a 525 GB external hard drive, a 9.6 kbps analog communications modem, a flatbed scanner, a Hewlett-Packard LaserJet IV laser printer with 6M of memory, and a V.42 high-speed modem. The DMPITS software is based on Cogent System's Automated Fingerprint Identification System (AFIS) software, "sailor-proofed" as Humphrey put it, to present a very user-friendly front end.

Military personnel place a black plastic wristband on the person's *right* wrist. The wristband contains a read-only AVID RF transponder containing a nine-digit identification number. It is secured using an aluminum metal pop riveter. Small children have the wristband attached to an ankle. Infants are identified with a wristband placed on their mother's left arm.

Since the pop riveter resembles a large metal drill, Paschall was concerned that it would frighten some refugees, especially children. After some dress rehearsals with marines, it was decided that the crew would wear civilian clothing, and the job of fastening on the wristbands would go to women soldiers. However, it soon became clear that the problem was not as big as expected. Said Paschall, "Once the first individual did not scream in agony, it tended to be much easier after that."

The enrollee places the right index finger on the glowing red surface of the Touchprint scanner. A reproduction of the fingerprint appears in a window on the DMPITS enrollment screen. The system searches the entire database to see if that fingerprint has already been recorded. If not, the left index finger is scanned. The individual's picture is recorded by the Panasonic CCD camera and also appears on the screen. The name is key-entered into the proper field. Finally, the processor interrogates the individual's wristband with the RFID reader, recording the unique identification number. With the aid of interpreters, some demographic information is obtained: name, sex, date of birth, age, place of birth, nationality, names of family relations, point of origin, whether the individual is the head of a family, any perceivable handicaps, and whether the individual is an unaccompanied minor. Finally, the individual's camp number, tent number, and cot number are recorded . . . .

When refugees are transferred between camps, or transferred off the base, their ID bracelets are read. The system
updates the camps' population census and creates a manifest
for departing ships and flights. Couriers accompanying Cubans
who have chosen to move to the Panama camp carry DAT
tapes with the DMPITS records of the people on each flight.
Upon arrival, those records are downloaded into the Panama
camp's database and verified.

In this same issue, Mark David, Editor-in-Chief of *Automatic I.D.
News,* wrote of the DMPITS operation: "It is an incredible application—
one of the first to cross a controversial line and tag humans with RFID
transponders." They failed to mention, however, why people were
trying to rid themselves of the offensive bracelets by trying to chew
them off, or cut them off with crude knives. In a previous chapter I
gave you the full story, but let me remind you that one of the refugees
was unhappy with the technology because it reminded him of the
mark that people would be forced to receive in the Book of Revelation
. . . that was a pretty sharp refugee!

Also the same issue of *Automatic I.D. News* contained an article
titled: "RFID products hold fingerprints." Dateline: Vancouver, BC.

> Infotag's latest products improve RFID system range and pro-
> vide a secure, biometric ID card.
> The company's new Multi Function Transponder RFID tag is
> active (battery powered) and *can be read from 300 feet away.*
> It holds up to four kilobytes of data and is reprogrammable.
> The new identification card offers the security of fingerprint
> biometrics *without the need for an external database for verifica-
> tion.* User fingerprints are scanned and stored in a 64 byte code
> on a chip on the card. The person uses the card by placing the
> card and fingertip on a special reading device. The fingerprint
> is scanned and compared to the file stored on the card. The only
> record of the fingerprint is stored on the card.

Just how big a leap can it be to progress from *wearing* your RFID
transponder on your right wrist to *implanting* your RFID transponder
in your right hand? Not nearly as big as I would like. In fact, as far
back as July 20, 1989, *The Arizona Republic* carried an article suggesting a program of implantable biochips to find lost or kidnapped
children and runaway teens. Jack Dunlap envisioned a program called
KIDSCAN, where parents would have their children "chipped" and
assigned an identification number. A veteran of the missing-persons
division of the Phoenix Police Department admitted that some parents

would be nervous of the "Big Brother" aspects of KIDSCAN, but still thought the concept attractive. "Any technology that can be used to detect missing children and children that are in danger would be welcomed." At that time Dunlap was not aware that passive biochips have to be scanned at short range . . . in fact, since he expected "signals" to be picked up on satellites to provide the location of the subject, it sounds like he had a battery-powered unit in mind. But 1989 was still very early in this technology, and things are progressing!

In his editorial in the August, 1994, *Automatic I.D. News*, Mark David raised the question: "If 'chips' are for pets, why not for kids?" Their cover story that month discussed the advantages of "chipping" animals, then continues:

> A recent newsletter from tag maker Destron/IDI picks up a report from the *Sydney Morning Herald* about a 2½-year-old boy who was found wandering in Blacktown, Australia, with his dog, neither of them with any idea of where they lived. The dog, however, wore a tag indicating it had been chipped. Officials took the dog to a nearby vet clinic, where it was scanned. A quick call to the national chip registry identified the dog's owners—the boy's worried parents. . . .
>
> This happy tale got me thinking about the possible advantages of "chipping" children. After all, not all 2½-year-olds found wandering the streets are lucky enough to be with their dogs, whether tagged electronically or not.
>
> [Author's note: Mr. David seems suddenly to find himself in a dilemma when he considers the possible impact of what he is proposing. Read on.] Now, the idea of electronically tagging humans is not one that I could easily embrace. Numbering humans is tainted with the air of jails, concentration camps, and people-as-numerals totalitarianism. For as long as I've been sitting in this editor's chair, I've been railing against the oft-repeated notion that humans will soon be branded with bar codes. . . .
>
> I'm also well aware of the Big Brotherly potential for database abuse and invasion of privacy that grows with every scan of every item in our grocery carts.
>
> [Now, here's that dilemma I mentioned.] But as the father of three small children, I can't help but feel there could be some legitimate arguments made for the voluntary "chipping" of kids. [Author's note: Voluntary for whom? The parents or the child? And when the child grows up, he is still going to be carrying around the chip . . . as an adult who *did not* volunteer to get the implant and who has no choice in the matter now. It's like the lady mentioned above in her letter to the editor, about *owning*

a child, at what point does a child become a sovereign individual, and after he does, what—if anything—can you do about the existing implant?] After all, just yesterday, my senseless 18-month-old, Joe, made his way out the front door (which we thought was locked), down the steps, and out onto the sidewalk before we realized he was missing from the house. And any parent who has ever had the experience of losing a child in a crowded store or theme park would quickly wish that every mall and park had a lost-child patrol equipped with RF scanners.

Mr. David goes on to extrapolate this concept to include more sinister disappearances, health benefits, and even making a "net" by installing RFID "portals" at the entrance of such "kid magnets" as zoos, theme parks, and McDonald's to catch children listed as missing. The biochip would give their true identity, no matter what name was given by the adult with them. He supposes that the ultimate finder system would combine elements of infrared personnel tracking systems with the wide-area anti-theft systems which allow police to locate and track stolen cars via RF tags. However, after carefully weighing all the factors, Mr. David gives a hearty "thumbs down" to this use of the new technology.

> Despite these potential advantages, I can't sign off as an advocate of such a concept: The idea of chipping children just doesn't fit comfortably under my skin. And if chips are for kids, why not adults too? No thanks. The potential for abuse seems too great and the sacrifice of personal freedom too high.

Unfortunately, a lot of people disagree with him. In the November, 1994, edition of *Automatic I.D. News,* the following letter to the editor was submitted by a reader from Mountain View, California:

> I was compelled to write to you after reading your editorial in the August issue of *Automatic I.D. News.* The title of the editorial was, "If 'chips' are for pets, why not for kids?" While I can understand your reservations over using RFID technology for tracking people, I am troubled by your firm lack of support of this application.
>
> While our forefathers wrote the Declaration of Independence and formulated a guideline for civil rights, I don't think they had in mind that there would be a time when repeat criminals are allowed to roam free. Conversely, if they did envision this time, they certainly never offered a plan that would enable families to recover their children safely after an abduction, from the home no less.
>
> Privacy issues appear to be a matter of subjected interpretation

of the law that makes no distinction between when or whose privacy should be protected. Therefore, we must ask ourselves whose privacy should be protected in a variety of circumstances. In cases where a child has been abducted, I would think the privacy issue would be clearly defined. Certainly, the child would want to have his or her privacy unprotected if it meant a speedy rescue from the prospect of being brutally raped and/or murdered. Maybe the criminal would want his or her privacy protected in the midst of a crime, but does society as a whole?

Instead of worrying about the abuses of this application, we should explore the benefits. I believe that if we look closer at the number of child abductions, we may find an age group that may benefit from using this technology. I also believe that "chipping" inmates would be a good idea if it meant that the inmate could be quickly located after an escape. Furthermore, chipping repeat offenders that are out on parole could also prove beneficial in cases where the parolee chooses to "skip town."

In a final note, I want to say that I applaud the RFID industry and the technological advancements industry participants have made. I will continue to applaud and support this industry and I look forward to the day when a child is safely recovered just minutes after an abduction. I ask you to reconsider your opinion of this application and put it into the perspective of how you might feel just minutes after you realized one of your own children was abducted.

This person probably will be at the head of the line when the national identity cards are passed out and later on when the Mark of the Beast is implanted.

There are many other newspapers and magazines I could quote, including a very thorough article by Lisa Crosby in the June 15, 1994, edition of *The Tucson Weekly* titled, "Electronic Leash: The Implantable Biochip is Already Here. Is Big Brother Just Around the Corner?" and one by Wayne Laugesen in the October 19, 1995, edition of the *Boulder Weekly* titled, "Under Your Skin: Biochip implants could find missing children or end personal freedom." The latter is a well-written article which contains much of my personal research. I believe there is a mountain of evidence to support my conclusion that some form of the syringe implantable biochip based on RFID technology will become the Mark of the Beast described in Revelation 13.

Unusual Usage of RFID Systems

Some people with very creative minds are developing some very innovative ways to use RFID technology in commercial situations.

Some of these ideas are quite unique and probably will make somebody quite wealthy. For example, the following article appeared in
Newsweek magazine, January 16, 1995. The headline read: "High-
Tech Skiing—Trends: Microchips and other slope-smoothers—For
frequent skiers: The wrist microchip."

> With their spandex bodysuits, oversize goggles, and neon skis,
> skiers already look high-tech, ready made for the millennium.
> But fashion isn't all that's futuristic on the slopes this season.
> Here's some of the new stuff you'll see:
> The "Ski Key" is a watch-size black box (worn on a Velcro wrist-
> band) that contains a microchip. It's in use at California's North-
> star at Tahoe, where scanners on chairlifts keep track of vertical
> miles skied. Like members of airline frequent-flier clubs, Ski
> Keyers win prizes for accumulated mileage. Skiers can charge
> lift fees and meals directly to the Key, and it even alerts them
> to phone messages so the office is never more than a mogul away.

Please don't think I'm promoting what I'm about to say, because
I'm adamantly opposed to it. But those who advocate biochip implants
in children for safety reasons, at least should consider the possibility of
using DMPITS-type external chips so the child could have it removed
when he grows up, if he chooses. Of course, it would have to be something small and not readily visible or an abductor would just cut it off.

Another clever use of RFID is the merging of the human with the
inanimate in order to enable function. One example is the "smart
gun," which would employ user-recognizing devices to eliminate the
possibility of firing (accidental or otherwise) by an unauthorized user
of the firearm. Guess what? The safety can be released only when
it "recognizes" the proper biochip implanted in the gun hand of the
holder of the weapon. An article called "Future Firearms" in *Omni
'95* explained all this and more. A similar article called, "Gun Control
is Bad Medicine," appeared in the February, 1994, edition of *American
Rifleman.*" They included a futuristic projection of what it might be
like to purchase a firearm in the year 1999. It was humorous, but too
close to the truth really to be very funny.

Similar technology is now proposed so that in the future your vehicle
ignition won't start the car unless the biochip in your hand is compatible with it. At the present time, this system is already in effect,
only it must match the RFID in your key or on your keyring instead
of the biochip in your *right* hand (ignitions in vehicles are always on
the right side, of course). And since the majority of people are right
handed, most of the implants to operate a firearm, naturally, will be
in the right hand, as well.

"RFID tags: please phone home" is the headline in the January, 1995, issue of *Automatic I.D. News*. It explains that "radio computer tags (RFID) combine an onboard processor with satellite/Internet communications to call in their whereabouts." This one is really on the cutting edge. Here is how the article began:

> An RFID tag that can initiate communications to the Internet and report its own whereabouts? A system that simultaneously locates and identifies thousands of assets over a wide area? True quantum leaps in technology read like a magical kids' story. . . .

They refer to this as finding assets, which can be defined as just about anything that moves, though for the moment they seem to be targeting trucking and freightlines. Not to be left out of anything new, of course, the military has jumped on the bandwagon with the following uses: tracking of hazardous materials and munitions between Europe and the U.S.; tracking equipment and material in and out of Somalia, Bosnia, Haiti, and Korea; and tracking jet engine parts.

Other Events of Importance

A number of other recent events have come to my attention, and even though they are not directly related to biochips, I wanted to be sure they were included in this book . . . and eventually, I'm sure, they either will work in conjunction with or be superceded by biochip technology.

The first is the announcement that Interlink has launched a smart card banking system in Russia. *World Card Technology*, August, 1995, described them as "hybrid" cards, containing both a magnetic stripe and a smart card chip. The cards are manufactured by Gemplus (manufacturers of the military's MARC card) and contain two "electronic wallets" on each card—an unprotected wallet for low value transactions and a PIN protected wallet for larger amounts. It seems the Russians are well on their way to a cashless society, just as the rest of the world.

The *London Times*, September 17, 1995, announced that by the summer of 1996 all British drivers will get new licenses . . . with bar codes. They wanted one that could contain lots of personal information, so the bar code selected was PDF 417. But the article repeatedly refers to the license as "an identity card," which obviously is its ultimate intended purpose. This is not unexpected, as I have pointed out before, since Europe, and the EC in general, are considerably ahead of the United States in such matters.

I consider the following to be a post script to, or an extension of

information contained earlier in this book about FEMA and its transformation of deserted military bases into regional "holding facilities"
for the transfer of masses of humanity. The following article appeared
in the November, 1995, issue of a publication by The Present Truth
Ministry, Uniontown, Arkansas. The sign in front of the facility in a
photo reads: "Texas Department of Criminal Justice—Institutional
Division, 550 Bed General Psychiatric Facility, Lubbock, Texas."

Prisons & Mental Hospitals Grow Like Cancer Across U.S.

There isn't a week that goes by that patriots don't see a new
prison being built in America. Those who publish patriot newsletters and magazines receive countless phone calls, faxes, and
letters with photos of new prisons under construction.

During the past few months, another type of prison has been
seen in our nation which is reminiscent of Soviet mental hospitals.
They are called "Psychiatric Facilities." One such installation has
been discovered near Lubbock, Texas. The huge complex is surrounded by fences topped with razor wire, and is serviced by rail
with ramps that unload directly into the buildings. Another
virtually identical facility has been located by patriots in
Northern Florida.

One diabolical tactic of the communists [during their rise to
power] was to have an enemy of the State declared insane and
transport them to a mental hospital for evaluation. This same
tactic may be used in America. We find evidence of this in a book
called, Brainwashing: A Synthesis of the Russian Textbook on
Psychopolitics:

"With the institutions for the insane, you have in your country
prisons which can hold a million persons and can hold them without civil rights or any hope of freedom. And upon these people
can be practiced shock and surgery so that never again will they
draw a sane breath. You must make these treatments common
and accepted" (page 3).

"Psychopolitics is a solemn charge. With it you can erase our
enemies as insects. You can cripple the efficiency of leaders by
striking insanity into their families through the use of drugs. You
can wipe them away with testimony as to their insanity. By our
technologies you can even bring about insanity itself when they
seem too resistive" (page 3, 4).

"Use the courts, use the judges, use the Constitution of the
country, use its medical societies and its laws to further our ends.
By psychopolitics create chaos. Leave a nation leaderless. Kill
our enemies. And bring to Earth through Communism, the
greatest peace Man has ever known. Thank you" (page 4).

"An insane person has no rights under law. No person who is insane may hold property. No person who is insane may testify. Thus, we have an excellent road along which we can travel toward our certain goal and destiny. One of the first and foremost missions of the psychopolitician is to make an attack upon Communism and insanity synonymous. It should become the definition of insanity, of the paranoid variety, that 'A paranoid believes he is being attacked by Communists.' Thus, at once the support of the individual so attacking Communism will fall away and wither" (page 25).

It is obvious that the politicians are preparing to imprison and control American citizens in the future. The question remains as to what events they are expecting to take place which will require the arrest of so many people. The same kind of rulers that were master minds behind the communist takeover of Russia are plotting the takeover of America. The same strategies used there will be used here. The same excuses to arrest citizens there will be used here.

As the Scripture admonishes, don't let those days take you unaware.

Secular "Big Brother" or Biblical Antichrist? Will the REAL Son of Satan Please Stand Up!

Author George Orwell popularized the expression "Big Brother" in his 1949 novel, *1984*. This famous novel is set in an allegedly imaginary future where freedom of thought and action utterly have disappeared. In Orwell's scenario, humans are under the constant scrutiny of an all-powerful, all-enslaving global government symbolized by *Big Brother*, a male dictator whom the world must worship and follow. Posters everywhere warn citizens that "Big Brother is watching you." Children are taken from their parents and love relationships are strictly forbidden. The Secret Police control and monitor all individual thought and movement by continuous surveillance. Personal privacy is both nonexistent and illegal.

Orwellian "Newspeak" Propaganda

The term *newspeak* is another concept popularized by this novel. In *1984*, the world is enslaved by totalitarianism, wherein the thoughts and actions of each individual are controlled and manipulated by carefully designed "brainwashing" propaganda. All truth is replaced with redefined language called *reverse-speak, doublethink, doublespeak, or "newspeak."* An attribute of newspeak is the ability to hold two *contradictory* opinions simultaneously, whenever the government so dictates. The purpose of newspeak is to condition the mind to the ideology of the Big-Brother police state and to make it impossible to find words to express any other "heretical" thought—which, of course, was any thought contrary to Big Brother's. In newspeak, words like *justice* and *democracy* no longer exist, and the word *free* never can be used to convey the thought of *political* freedom. Such circumstances seem to resemble more closely the present day New World Order than some fictional tale from the 1940's, do they not?

The cover of Orwell's book contains the following quotation:

> *I do not believe that the kind of society I describe [in 1984] necessarily WILL arrive, but I believe. . . . that something resembling it COULD arrive. I believe also that totalitarian ideas have taken root in the minds of intellectuals everywhere.*

> —George Orwell

Grolier's 1994 Multimedia Encyclopedia has some very interesting things to say about Orwell's *1984*: ". . . Although *1984* is sometimes thought of as *science fiction,* it is actually a notable work of *Utopian literature* that emphasizes what Orwell believed were the *dangers inherent in modern, bureaucratic society* [emphasis added]."

What does this encyclopedic "doublespeak" really mean? Obviously, *Grolier's* is saying that *1984* really isn't a *novel* at all—rather, it is a *forecast of things to come* in our modern world!

Grolier's Encyclopedia also has some very interesting things to say about George Orwell, himself. It indicates clearly that "Orwell was a socialist." Then it defines socialism as: "A comprehensive set of beliefs or ideas about the nature of human society and its *future desirable state.*" It continues the link, by way of Marx and Engels, right down to the Communist Manifesto; the only logical conclusion of which is that socialism is the initial stage of communism. When the New World Order achieves ultimate power and authority, what we will have, in reality, is global communism. Can you see this progression in world affairs today?

The only important thing missing from Orwell's *1984* vision of global control by Big Brother was the biochip implanted under the skin of everyone's right hand—and if the technology had been available at the time, I'm sure Orwell would not have overlooked such an efficient device of tracking and spying on everyone. It probably would have been called the "Mark of Big Brother," but the result would have been the same, without a doubt.

The New World Order, National ID Cards, and Syringe-Implantable Biochips

If space permitted, I would go into a lengthy dissertation on socialism and communism, because the history of these two philosophies is important to understanding the basis of the New World Order philosophy. Of course, we are being told otherwise by our socialist, leftist, liberal media, as well as by our socialist, leftist, liberal government leaders who have sold their souls to the New World Order crowd, in exchange for prestigious, powerful, high-level political positions, money, and worldly glory. That's right! We are being told lies on a daily basis by our media and politicians. Even the ones claiming to be conservative constitutionalists are coming into question now. Many are turning out to be wolves in sheep's clothing—don't accept any at face value; verify everything! That's why I have used so many pages of this book documenting my statements and allegations.

They are plying us with Orwellian *Newspeak* (read that "double-crossing, double-talk") to mentally prepare us for the final transition from capitalism to communism. The New World Order means exactly that!

Accordingly, the governmental concept of hard-core communism is now being *repackaged and remarketed as global democracy.* You may ask, "How does all this tie into the subject of this chapter, biochips?" Well, I'm about ready to tie it all together for you . . . read on.

"Global democracy," and other such deceptive terms, is just a *newspeak* lie. This "new thinking" is being sold to us by means of the most sophisticated, satanically-inspired, effective propaganda campaign the world ever has witnessed. As a result, most of us are so brain-dead and asleep from years of having been exposed to such mind-control conditioning, that we're not even aware how close we actually are to being conquered and enslaved.

Here's that connection I promised you . . . before we can be enslaved and controlled completely, we first must be **positively identified.** *Without a sophisticated, computerized system of positive biometrically verifiable electronic identification, we cannot be surveilled. Here is where the New World Order ID cards and biochip implants emerge.*

In 1933, Americans were assigned their first national ID cards in the form of a newly inaugurated Social Security system. That same year, all Russian citizens received their mandatory national ID cards, as well. The Russian cards allowed communist leaders totally to enslave, control, and surveil their population. Americans didn't suffer the same consequences concurrent with the issuance of their Social Security cards, but now everything is nearly in place to allow this to happen.

In 1986, author Joseph W. Eaton published a very informative book on national ID cards, entitled *Card-Carrying Americans: Privacy, Security, and the National I.D. Card Debate.* On page 102 of his book he makes some very interesting observations about the Russian National ID card system, as it pertains to control and surveillance of the populace:

> The Soviet control system relies heavily upon personal identification documents. Each resident is issued an I.D. document at age sixteen. The document includes the bearer's picture, name, and date of birth. The document provides officials with basic personal data which can be used to enforce existing travel restrictions. In Russia, no one can visit anywhere for more than seventy-two hours without police permission. The secret police (the KGB) can insert restrictions in the I.D. document, effectively preventing a holder from traveling, and risking arrest if he does so.

On page 100, Eaton says this about Americans' opposition to a national ID card system: "Opponents of an American national identity program fear that it could lead to *a universal card and totalitarianism.* No one can dismiss such a concern lightly [emphasis added]."

On pages one through three, Eaton says:

> Computers have woven a net of information about nearly every adult American. A growing number of personal information files, under public as well as business management, utilize the Social Security number to facilitate the process of matching and comparing information about any given individual in different files. However, it is difficult for the average person to access his own records and monitor what they contain and make corrections to erroneous data. . . .
>
> A thoughtful minority of Americans are concerned about America's transformation into an "instant information" society. They fear that traditions of individual freedom and privacy are in grave danger. They often refer to George Orwell's classic novel, *1984.* Years ago, Orwell envisioned people being manipulated to serve the whims of a computerized "Big Brother." At the time *1984* was written, the technology of such computerized surveillance was not yet developed, but it now approaches perfection.

I believe that Joseph Eaton's observations above express all I need to say about this.

It should be obvious to all by now what is happening in this regard. First, Americans will be forced into a new computerized, international identification system (infrastructure) with instantly accessible digitized personal data. New sophisticated ID cards will be issued to everyone in order to make the system work. Shortly thereafter, all existing ID cards, debit cards, drivers' licenses, and credit cards will be consolidated into a single, technologically advanced *multiple-use smart card* with an embedded integrated circuit chip capable of storing both electronic money and personal identity information. It probably will be called the **MARC Card**, meaning **M**ultitechnology **A**utomated **R**eader **C**ard.

Almost simultaneously with this, the world will have been taken cashless, and all currency and coin will have been illegalized so that we must all buy and sell via computerized exchange . . . just a bunch of numbers floating around out in cyberspace. Then, we'll be informed that our new cards easily can be lost or stolen, and if they are, we'll not be able to function in the New World Order. In the final step, Big Brother will tell us he has a solution to these problems. He will cause us all to receive an injectable ID biochip transponder under the skin of our hands that will replace our ID cards. Upon taking the chip implant, we all will have been properly identified or MARKED in the new system of global communism called the New World Order. No one will be permitted to buy or sell anything without it. It will be the *Mark of the New World Order!* And it will enslave us for eternity.

> And he causeth all, both small and great, rich and poor, free and bond, to receive a *mark in their right hand* or in their foreheads. And that no man might buy or sell, save he that had *the mark,* or the name of *the Beast,* or the number of his name. Here is wisdom. Let him that hath understanding count the number of the *Beast:* for it is the number of a man; and **his number is 666** [emphasis added]. (Rev. 13:16-18.)

Shakespeare said "a rose is still a rose by any other name." In the same line of logic, "the Antichrist is still the Antichrist by any other name." And, "totalitarianism is still authoritarianism by any other name!" Whether the coming global dictator is called Big Brother or Antichrist, or the New World Order is called global democracy, socialism, communism, totalitarianism, authoritarianism, Nazism, or *whateverism,* is really unimportant.

What is important is this: the Mark of Big Brother, the Mark of the Beast, and the Mark of the New World Order **are all synonymous terms.** They mean exactly the same thing . . . they are interchangeable. They all are describing the mark revealed in Revelation, Chapter 13. If you choose to accept this mark, the consequences you may expect are described in Revelation, Chapter 14: "If any man worship the beast . . . and receive his mark in his forehead or in his hand, the same shall drink of the wine of the wrath of God . . . and he shall be tormented with fire and brimstone."

Some Christians are reluctant to give up the idea that a tattooed bar code will be the mark described. I don't believe the facts support that conclusion. Personally, I am convinced that the syringe-implantable biochip (or some advanced form of the same technology) will be that mark. All the ramifications are spelled out clearly in the concluding section that follows: "The Bottom Line—A World in Disorder." Please consider it carefully.

1996 Summer Olympics Update

A plethora of futuristic ID technology was unveilled and implemented at the 1996 Summer Olympics in Atlanta, Georgia, USA. Bill Rathburn, Director of Security is ". . .counting on bar codes, radio frequency (RF/ID), biometric security to get the job done. . . . [however,] An RF/ID chip embedded in the ID badge is the primary means of identification and access control" (*Automatic I.D. News,* July, 1996).

How much longer will it be before they decide the chip will be better placed beneath the skin, instead of in a badge? Furthermore, all this elaborate security still was not adequate to prevent acts of terrorism, with loss of lives and many injuries. Of course, all this provides the perfect excuse to add even more stringent security measures. . . *spell that "surveillance and control!"*

CHAPTER SIXTEEN

The Bottom Line—
A World in Disorder

Public speakers—and in particular, preachers—are taught to "tell them what you are going to tell them, then tell them, then tell them what you told them." In book parlance, that could be interpreted "The Introduction," "The Chapters," and "The Summation." It is a proven technique that helps the listener or reader comprehend and remember a larger portion of the material being presented to them. Being a firm believer in a couple more clichés, i.e. "don't mess with success" and "if it ain't broke, don't fix it," I make it a practice to follow that time-proven formula in my books. Therefore, in wrapping up this book, it seems fitting to quote again Revelation 13:15-18; 14:9-11:

> . . .and cause that as many as would not **worship** the image of the beast should be killed. And he [Antichrist] **causeth** all, both small and great, rich and poor, free and bond, to receive a mark **in** their **right hand**, or **in** their foreheads: And that no man might buy or sell, save he that had the **mark**, or the name of the beast, or the number of his name. Here is wisdom. Let him that hath understanding count the number of the beast: for it is the number of a man; and his number is Six hundred threescore and six [**666**] . . . . If any man **worship** the beast and his image, and receive his mark **in** his forehead, or **in** his **hand**, The same shall drink of the wine of the wrath of God, which is poured out without mixture into the cup of his indignation; and he shall be tormented with fire and brimstone in the presence of the holy angels, and in the presence of the Lamb; And the smoke of their torment ascendeth up for ever and ever: and they have no rest day nor night, who **worship** the beast and his image, and who-soever receiveth the **mark** of his name [emphasis added].

In Chapters 14 and 15, I have gone to great lengths to explain to you how the ID system and biochip technology work (including extensive documentation), as well as the ramifications of the use of this technology to electronically enslave us on a global scale.

I am convinced firmly that these things are leading us down the broad path of "convenience" toward the ultimate identification. . .the **mark** spoken of in the Book of Revelation in the Bible. And because the New World Order propagators don't want to "kick the sleeping dog," as it were, and create a rebellion to these methods, they are lulling us into a state of complacency about the long-term implications of what they are doing by giving us one little "convenience" after the next, each progressively more advanced than the previous one. . .desensitizing us, if you will.

But these things are merely "technologies," they are not spiritual, nor can they send you to hell. As described in the scriptures quoted above, receiving the mark of the beast *is not* something one will do unconsciously. With all their dire implications, neither the MARC card, the national ID card, nor the biochip are, in fact, **THE** mark (of the beast) referred to in scripture, even though biochip implants seem to be the technology available which most closely matches that described in Revelation 13 (**in** the hand or forehead). Receiving the mark of the beast is going to be a matter of worship, not merely of economics. Notice, it does not say you will be *forced* to receive the mark, but you will be *caused* to receive it. . .in other words, by coercion you will *choose* to receive it because of the pressure brought to bear upon you, both economic pressure and peer pressure. Rev. 13:16 clearly specifies that those who reject the mark will be excluded from the world economic order the Antichrist is creating. No one will buy, or sell, or work, or eat, or receive government benefits (i.e., social security, medicare, welfare/food stamps, unemployment, etc.), or transact any business in a global cashless society without his mark.

No one will knock you out and inject an implant (mark) in your body (although you will remember the recommendation I quoted calling for all babies to have an implant behind their ear before they left the maternity ward). . .that would defeat their purpose, namely, getting everyone to worship the Antichrist (beast), and as indicated in the first scripture above, those who refuse to worship and take the mark will be killed. How this will be done is described in Revelation 20:4:

> . . .and I saw the souls of them that were **beheaded** for the witness of Jesus, and for the word of God, and which **had not worshipped** the beast, neither his image, **neither had received his** [Antichrist's] **mark upon their foreheads, or in their hands**;. . .[emphasis added].

So the punishment for rejecting the Antichrist is the loss of one's head—not a very pleasant thought! But as with all things prophesied in the Bible . . . it will come to pass! This is a matter of your eternal destiny, and God created man with a free will—the ability and privilege of making the choice of whom he will serve. Therefore, you can't go to hell by accident, nor can anyone else send you there (by forcibly injecting you with the mark—you still would have to choose to *worship* the beast). But it is a decision I strongly advise that you **not** postpone; it is *late* and the time for choices is *now*, before it is *too* late. At the end of this chapter, I have given you full instructions on how to make this choice and seal your eternal destiny with the Lord in heaven, rather than in hell with Satan and his demons. Accept Christ today.

Many places in the Bible we find the phrase, "I would not have you ignorant." My sentiments, exactly! And many other places in scriptures, especially in the words of Jesus Christ, we find the admonition, "Take heed that ye be not deceived." That is why this ministry exists—I want to warn you about deceptions lurking out there just waiting to ensnare us. We find that warning from Jesus in Matthew 24, Mark 13, and Luke 21, *et al.* In Matthew 24, Jesus is educating his disciples about the end times. They were curious: "Tell us, when shall these things be? and what shall be the sign of thy coming, and of the end of the world?" (Matthew 24:3). Since Jesus didn't want them "ignorant," He spent nearly the entire chapter of Matthew 24 (and many other places in scripture) telling them (and us) what could be expected to be seen by the generation that was alive upon earth when the "end" arrived. He began his reply by saying, ". . .Take heed that no man deceive you*, For many shall come in my name, saying, I am Christ; and shall deceive many" (24:4,5). Then He tells about all the terrible events leading up to the end. But right in the middle of the chapter He returns to the warning not to be deceived. "For there shall arise false Christs, and false prophets, and shall shew great signs and wonders; insomuch

---

* Because the Church—the body as a whole—is so trusting, they are extremely susceptible to being deceived by smooth-talkers using all the right Christian "buzzwords." In fact, in many cases, they are trusting to the point of being gullible. We are admonished by the Lord to be as wise as serpents and harmless as doves; we are to use our (hopefully, well-honed) gift of discernment to recognize the wolves who come among is in the proverbial sheep's clothing to render havoc among the flock. I'm sure there are many, but let me warn you of one in particular who is circulating among certain prominent denominations representing himself to be a credentialed scientist and developer/inventor of the biochip technology. However, upon investigation, the alleged credentials of Carl Sanders have proven to be forged or nonexistent. When confronted, he acknowledged this and agreed to cease misrepresenting himself to the Church. Unfortunately, he abstained only temporarily, and it is my understanding that he again is up to his old tricks. Pastors, please take the time at least to verify the credentials of those you allow to occupy your pulpit and teach/preach to the flock over whom God has given you responsibility.

that, if it were possible, they shall deceive the very elect. Behold, I have told you before" (24:24,25).

Then Jesus continues with other terrible events that will occur and tells us that even though we won't know the day nor hour (24:36), we can know the season (24:32), by recognizing that it is scripture being fulfilled when we see these events happening all around us. "So likewise ye, when ye shall see all these things, know that it is near, even at the doors" (24:33). Then Jesus tells us that ". . .This generation [the one that witnesses these events] shall not pass, till **all** these things be fulfilled" (24:34) [emphasis added].

Even though He tells us (24:36) that no man can know the day nor hour, He does indicate (24:32) that we can know the season, if we are careful to observe the signs occurring about us (24:33).

You may ask how this all ties in to our study of the New World Order and identification technology. . . read on.

The Real Origin of the New World Order

It is my opinion that we are that generation of which Christ spoke, and that all things found in Matthew 24 (and other related prophetic books, i.e., Daniel, Ezekiel, Revelation, *et al*) will be fulfilled in our lifetime. Ever since the Tower of Babel (in the book of Genesis), Satan has been attempting to create a New World Order where people would worship him as the God of this world. Scripture indicates that God, indeed, will permit this to occur at the end of the age. For the past 200 years, specifically subsequent to May 1, 1776, the Luciferians, New Agers, witches, Satanists, socialists/communists, fascists/nazis, liberals, *et al* , all have been using a new term to describe this final form of global enslavement under the Antichrist. The term they have been using is the New World Order.

It should be obvious by now that there is ample evidence to support my conclusion that this final New World Order is about to occur. Scripture says that the devil will divide the world into 10 kingdoms, and, indeed, that has occurred under the Treaty of Rome, which divided the world into exactly 10 regions, the United States and Canada being region number 1 of this New World Order occultic world government.

Jesus warned us that deception would be rampant during this time —so much so, He specifically warned us that even the elect of God would be deceived and believe the lie of this New World Order under the devil, if it were possible. He implied that only the elect *could not* be fooled, and this is why so few today are able to discern the truth of what's occurring. Most people—unfortunately, even most Christians— are blind to what's happening in terms of the prophetic scriptures, as they apply to the times in which we live. I Thessalonians 5 warns us to beware when people speak of peace and safety, and indeed George Bush promised us peace and "security" (safety) when he announced the beginning of the New World Order, then committed the U.S. to fight in the Iraqi war. The Lord tells Christians that they should not be asleep like the rest of the world; rather we should be awake, aware, and watchful regarding these end times events. Unfortunately, most *are* dead asleep or blind to what's happening. The signs of the Lord's second coming—the end of the age, the New World Order under the Antichrist and his 666 economic mark system, and Armageddon—all are apparent so visibly, even in our secular news media, that no one should miss the signs of His soon return.

Pentagon Calls for Armageddon in the Year 2001

Even *The New York Times* indicated in a 1992 article that the Pentagon is planning for a total mobilization for global war in the year 2001.

Many top fundamentalist/evangelicals subscribe to the dispensational belief that there will be a total of 6000 years from Adam until the end of the age, when Christ returns with His believers to fight and win the battle of Armageddon, ushering in the millennium—the 1000-year reign of peace. I, too, subscribe to this belief. Numerous chronological studies have been done throughout the years and are available for your perusal at most Christian bookstores and libraries. These studies indicate that the years 2001-2004 may conclude this 6000-year period.

The Epistle of Barnabas and the 6000-Year Plan

To the best of our ability to calculate and taking into consideration all known calendar errors and changes, etc.—somewhere around the year 2004 this age should end. There is a little-known book called the *The Epistle of Barnabas,* included in a respected work by Lightfoot entitled *The Apostolic Fathers.* Although no one can attest for certain that this is the same Barnabas who accompanied Paul in the book of Acts, it is believed to be true. In chapter 15 of the Epistle of Barnabas, this 6000-year plan is mentioned specifically as God's total plan from beginning to end. It says that at the conclusion of 6000, the sabbath millennium will begin.

Please understand that I am not setting dates for either the end of the age or the return of Christ (although the Bible definitely indicates, in Jesus' own words, that we should be able to see these events and know that the end is near), nor am I implying that the Epistle of Barnabas is some missing part of the Bible. As a matter of fact, there are many other extrabiblical historical books that indicate that

"6000 years" holds some special significance, and may indeed witness the conclusion of all human history. Revelation 20 implies this, because it mentions six times that there will be a thousand-year millennium of true peace, under the true God of this world, Jesus Christ, in a true New World Order, of which this present New World Order is merely an evil counterfeit—just as Satan counterfeits other manifestations of God's power.

Matthew 24:36 only restricts us from knowing "that day and hour" of the end, but other scriptures (Matthew 24:33, *et al*) say we will know when it is very "near, even at the doors," because we will witness the events outlined in Matthew and other prophetic books. Therefore, be very clear—I am NOT saying that I know the day nor the hour nor the specific year. . .but I believe that the 6000-year plan may hold prophetic significance; all signs seem to indicate that things are about to wrap up soon. . .and we were told to *watch the signs.* It appears that Lucifer's final hour is at hand and the Great Tribulation period is about to begin, being ushered in by the current New World Order. It is not overly significant whether this period begins on or around the year 2000, 2004, or even a little later; the fact of the matter is, we were told to be watchful and aware so that the Day of the Lord should not overtake us as a thief in the night.

It is also interesting to note if you go into any New Age bookstore or acquire any occultic literature, that the New Agers, the Satanists, the Freemasons, the occultists, and the witches (in other words, all of Satan's representatives in whatever form, shape, or title), all are talking about something very significant they are expecting to happen about the year 2000—a harmonic convergence for a New Age which will bring about a global transformation. They indicate in their books and other literature that the old age under Christ ends, and the new age under Lucifer begins around that time. This is why New Agers call themselves "New Agers." They are looking forward to the New Age under Lucifer in the year 2000.

Again, I would remind you it is very interesting that the Pentagon is planning a global war in the year 2001, and scripture says that Armageddon will wrap up the age and inaugurate Christ's millennial reign about that same time.

One of the signs pointed out by Christ that would signal the advent of the end of the age is worldwide famine. A *Los Angeles Times* article dated January 1, 1993, says: ". . .global food shortage looms by the year 2000." There are just too many "coincidences" occurring during this generation to warn us that some type of major transformation is in the works for the end of this century. All but the blind (especially the willfully blind) can see it clearly.

Pat Buchanan's Denouncement of the New World Order

Reference to the New World Order is turning up in literature of all types, but most significantly in articles and books dealing with politics, the military, and the United Nations. In a January 10, 1995, article in *The Charlotte Observer*, Patrick J. Buchanan liberally refers to the New World Order, though mostly in a derogatory context. No surprise, he says:

> . . . Dr. Kissinger is often invoked as our most insightful guide to The New World Order. . . .

Of course, this article is addressing, in particular, the situation of the U.S. bailout of the Mexican economy, of which Buchanan was in staunch opposition. He continues:

> As Wall Street is taken off the hook, U.S. taxpayers are put on. That's what the game is all about. The U.S. branch of The New World Order conscripts America to bail out its Enchilada Chapter in Mexico City. . . . Take away the smoke and mirrors, and what the "New World Order" comes down to is capturing America's wealth and squandering it all to prop up the dreams and designs of the globalists, until the last dollar runs down the gutter. . . .
>
> Either America jumps ship from this doomed vessel, The New World Order, or one day, we go down with it. . . .

Mr. Buchanan is not just your ordinary newspaper reporter, he is a former presidential advisor, a former presidential candidate, a 1996 presidential contender, a syndicated columnist, and host of *Crossfire* on CNN. He keeps tabs on the activities of the New World Order, to which he adamantly is opposed, as you can see. His colleagues and other politicians would do well to heed his advice.

Bush's Disarmament Plan for the New World Order

Buchanan has addressed the New World Order from the economic viewpoint, but George Bush carries the implications of the New World Order much further, into every area of our lives, but in particular the military, defense, and "police action" portion of our nation. In the September 28, 1991, edition of *The Honolulu Advertiser*, in an article titled, "New (safer) world order," Bush's plan for the disarmament of the U.S., following the end of Desert Storm, is announced.

> . . . the plan outlined by Bush yesterday calls for such weapons to be dismantled and destroyed after they are withdrawn.

Then he states that he hopes this will encourage the Soviets to do likewise. He calls for the elimination of ground-launched, short-range nuclear weapons; removal of all short-range nuclear arms from submarines and ships worldwide; removal of all U.S. strategic bombers from day-to-day alert status and the return of their weapons to storage area; withdrawal from alert of all intercontinental ballistic missiles scheduled for deactivation under the yet-unratified strategic arms reduction treaty (START); abandonment of the controversial rail-based system for the MX missile. All the while, our military forces are becoming increasingly subjugated to U.N. control.

Then there is the matter of our Air Force. Are you interested in how a B-52 meets its end? I'm more interested in *why* it meets its end! In the July, 1995, edition of the Smithsonian publication, *Air & Space,* there is an article entitled, "Death of the Beast." By the way, in this edition there is an unusual number of biblical terms used throughout the publication, e.g., their Viewport column is titled "Tower of Babel," this article refers to "the Beast," using a "guillotine" to "decapitate" the tails of the aircraft, and actually quotes the scripture found at Revelation 13:18, then the acronym AMARC [a mark of the beast? a MARC card?] is used for the name of the place where the aircraft came to be retired. Very curious!!

Anyway, about the loss of our B-52s...a veteran of 157 combat missions and recipient of a Distinguished Flying Cross referred to this as an "execution." AMARC is the facility where the U.S. military stores aircraft and Titan II missiles it has removed from service. The article points out that AMARC also has the responsibility for destroying aircraft—often perfectly good ones. Our tax dollars at work!! In 1993, the center began carrying out the terms of the START treaty mentioned above, which called for the deactivation of so much of our military apparatus.

> ...To disable the bombers visibly and permanently, as the treaty requires, AMARC personnel use a six-and-a-half-ton steel blade deployed from a crane to chop them up. Afterwards, the remains are left in place for 90 days so that the treaty signatories can use satellite overflights to verify the destructions.

It must be like a big graveyard for the bombers that have served us so well. AMARC was to have destroyed 217 B-52s by December 15, 1994.

> ...Today the guillotine would descend on tail number 666. Nicknamed "the Beast" because of the Biblical reference to that number ("Let him that hath understanding count the number of the beast...and his number is six hundred sixty-six," *Revelations* 13:18)....

The guillotine chops the B-52 in four places: the tail, each wing, and the fuselage section aft of the wings. This was an emotional time for all concerned, especially the former pilots who had come to witness the destruction of the planes that once had accomplished the mission and brought them home safely.

> *Rolling Thunder,* its back broken and its wings severed, lay on its side like a dead fish. A junk dealer had paid 18 cents a pound for it. Nearby, an older bomber painted Air Force gray bore a blue stripe and the sun-bleached words, "Peace Is Our Profession"— the motto of the Strategic Air Command, the now-defunct division then in charge of the Air Force's bombers and missiles.

Small wonder they referred to this as an execution. Even the caption under the photos tell of "the bombers' crudely broken bodies [that] give the desert landscape at AMARC a post-apocalyptic look," but they stress that this signifies a more peaceful era of international relations. Ooops. . .don't forget about that "peace and safety" scripture.

Of course, the end of the cold war is the excuse that was used for the elimination of our protection.

The headline on the Bush article is "New (safer) world order." If anything expresses the intent of the scripture, this does. "When men cry peace and safety, sudden destruction comes upon them."

However, as the well-known saying goes, men who forget their history are doomed to repeat it. See if some of the following quotations sound familiar—this is not a trick, I'll tell you in advance this was not written by or about George Bush. It is one of those things we should have learned from history, so we won't have to repeat it. But as with so many other things we should have learned from history, we obviously didn't learn this lesson either, because we currently are in the very midst of repeating it!

"Another" New World Order

> . . .with amazing rapidity the whole standard of living fell throughout Europe to a level which had not been known for centuries. In less than a year, it seemed as if one hundred and fifty years of civilization had been wiped out. Near-famine in certain regions, want and scarcity everywhere became the norm. Culture receded. Only a few books were published. . . .The freedom of the Press disappeared. . . .Seldom had Europe as a whole been subjected to such physical and spiritual degradation. Seldom had a whole form of civilization been so quickly and radically menaced by the destructiveness of tyranny.
>
> But no echo of this disaster can be found in [his] speeches. Quite the contrary; and if future historians had nothing to base

their judgment on except these speeches, their conclusion would be that Europe had never been so close to the millennium nor so anxious to hasten the final triumph of its new Messiah. . . . the messianic conception he had of himself is what enabled him so consistently to disregard the ruins and misery which his conquests spread and to assert that out of these ruins and sufferings, in spite of all evidence to the contrary, a New European Order was being born.

The *leit-motiv* of the New Order was not new. . . . the purpose of [it] was to transform radically the political, social, and spiritual complexion of Europe. The fundamental idea of the New Order was that all European nations should be integrated into one vast economic and political unit. . . . On the contrary, the picture offered an increasingly sharper contrast between [his] dream of a regenerated and peaceful world and the frightful reality. [Author note: remember what the Bible has to say about the "peace and safety" promises.] Europe was changed indeed, but what that change meant was a tragic regression, an accumulation of ruins and untold suffering.

. . . The plundering of these borderlands and the enslavement of the conquered nations were the basis of [his] New Order. And what this New Order actually meant in practice could now be seen: it was nothing but the system by which [his] armies could be maintained at the expense of the conquered.

The New Order in fact was only an attractive word to designate the rule of military occupation [emphasis added].

. . . [this] New Order was indistinguishable from domination supported by force and that as long as other powerful groups of nations such as the Anglo-American bloc refused to recognize [his] rule, there could be no New Order and no peace.

See how important it is for the citizens of a nation to stand their ground—tyrants recognize that as long as they continue to do so, there can be no New (World) Order. Now, listen to this direct quote of some of his promises:

. . ."The world shall open up for every one. Privileges for individuals, the tyranny of certain nations and their financial rulers shall fall. And last of all, this year will help to provide the foundations of a real understanding among peoples, and with it the certainty of conciliation among nations."

Sounds like he is just about to build the organization that will supercede the United Nations, doesn't it? But in the midst of (realistically) chaos, he talks like we're all headed for Utopia.

. . . [he] had to prophesy, as he had always done, that the end was near and that peace, order, and happiness would reign on earth . . . [words] intended to deceive . . . .

There is little new in [this] strategy . . . . One finds the same persistent effort to exonerate himself from all responsibility . . . [even casting a] morbid spell produced by his oratory. His appeals for peace fall on deaf ears . . . .

Although most of the similarities end here, there is one other to point out. Think back to the Oklahoma City bombing and President Clinton's remarks about purging the "forces of darkness," then compare them with the following:

The third motive was the hope of spreading confusion all over the world . . . . [They presented their] propaganda as the crusade of civilization and Christianity *against the forces of darkness.* . . . [He], in his new role of champion of Christianity, was to lead the whole of Europe against Moscow and destroy Communism once and for all. This was a new war aim and a new and convenient ideological basis for the European New Order.

Well, by now you undoubtedly have determined that the above excerpts refer to Hitler and the Nazis. The quotations are from the book, *Adolf Hitler, My New Order,* Edited with Commentary by Raoul de Roussy de Sales, Angus and Robertson, Ltd., Sydney/London, 1942. Long out of print, this rare copy was located just this year. Coincidence? I think not. Isn't it amazing how well it fits with the New World Order being thrust upon us today? Even the terminology is similar—not just the philosophy.

In Ecclesiastes we learn that "there is nothing new under the sun," and this certainly proves the point. As I have explained before, the New World Order is really just an Old World Order that Satan unsuccessfully has been trying to foist on mankind since the Tower of Babel, and before. I'm sure he is dancing with glee to realize that it finally will come into existence in the near future; I'm also sure he is painfully aware that his time is short and this New World Order is the final stages of his death grip on this earth. As I mentioned at the beginning of this chapter, when God's New World Order arrives, Jesus will be the King of kings and Lord of lords over this earth and its inhabitants. As I also warned you, if you are not prepared for that event, I recommend you get prepared at once—time is short. If you don't know how, continue reading . . . I'll give you full directions later in this chapter.

Ramsey Clark's Denouncement of Bush's New World Order

I want to recommend a book to you. It contains much heretofore undivulged information and is written by "an extremely reliable source," to quote a favorite line of news reporters. The only difference is, this is not "an unnamed" source—this source is a very prominent figure, having served as U.S. Attorney General under three presidents (two Democrats and one Republican) and having been a most vocal opponent of the United States' participation in the Gulf war activities. I am referring to Ramsey Clark and his latest book, *The Fire This Time: U.S. War Crimes in the Gulf,* Thunder's Mouth Press, New York, 1992, ISBN 1-56025-047-X. Let me make it clear that I don't necessarily agree with many of the notions espoused by Clark, as he is a liberal, pro-United Nations/world government man, and I am certainly the opposite (conservative, fundamentalist, anti-U.N., anti-world government, and anti-Antichrist), but the book is really interesting because it trashes George Bush, accusing him of being a dictator who trashed the U.S. Constitution, and accusing him of commiting high crimes, misdemeanors, and other gross international crimes in the pursuit of "George Bush's New World Order." However, the author must be somewhat confused, as he fails to recognize that the United Nations, which he supports, and the New World Order, to which he is opposed vehemently, are really one and the same, or, at best, the U.N. is the foundation upon which the New World Order will be established. The real point of this reference is to make you aware of the myriad of *major* things that were going on at the time which, because of a conspiracy, for the most part were concealed by the media, such as the formation of an International War Crimes Tribunal, to try those individuals and countries involved in the Gulf mission (almost totally ignored, except in the international press), and an actual resolution of impeachment brought against President Bush on January 16, 1991 by Congressman Henry Gonzalez of Texas (as reported by *The Texas Observer* on January 25, 1991), to name just two. Much of the content of this book is reminiscent of the terminology and phrasing that appeared in Hitler's book, *My New Order,* quoted above.

The conspiracy mentioned above is discussed much in Clark's book, but before I proceed, I want to give you a couple of dictionary definitions of the word *conspiracy,* as there is much confusion concerning its legal usage. In the *American College Dictionary,* published by Random House, conspiracy is defined as:

> 1. act of conspiring. 2. a combination of persons for an evil or unlawful purpose; a plot. *Law.* an agreement by two or more persons to commit a crime, fraud, or other wrongful act. . . .

Black's Law Dictionary, published by West Publishing Co., describes it this way:

CONSPIRACY. In criminal law. A combination, or confederacy, between **two or more persons** formed for the purpose of committing, by their joint efforts, some unlawful or criminal act, or some act which is innocent in itself, but becomes unlawful when done by the concerted action of the conspirators, or for the purpose of using criminal or unlawful means to the commission of an act not in itself unlawful. . . [emphasis added].

The reason it is so important to understand the definition of this term is because people are reluctant to believe you when you talk of conspiracies, yet conspiracy is going on all around us, and refusing to see it (the old "head-in-the-sand" approach) won't make it go away.

Based on everything I have covered in this book, it should be obvious to all but the most naive reader that there are at least two people involved in bringing about the unconstitutional/illegal New World Order.

Match some of the comments below, from Clark's book, with the quotations above, from Hitler's book. The similarities are mind boggling; the attitudes and actions of George Bush parallel Hitler's actions to an uncanny degree, and the naive have believed "the lie" and been deceived. I will address the matter of the deception further into this chapter.

. . .The most powerful capacity for propaganda and the most sophisticated technology for death in history acted in concert [Author's note: read that "conspiracy"] to slaughter an army, cripple a nation, name it liberty, and call for a celebration.

Almost exactly what Hitler did. And remember when Hitler practically proclaimed himself the Messiah and said he was waging that campaign to promote the Christian faith? Well, following Desert Storm, January 27, 1992, Bush spoke at the annual convention of the National Religious Broadcasters. His address included the following comments:

. . .we fought for good versus evil. . . .And today I want to thank you for helping America, as Christ ordained it to be a light unto the world.

They responded with an enthusiastic ovation. He promotes the occultic New World Order (and don't forget his Skull & Bones affiliation) and all it represents, then adds a few Christian "buzzwords," and everyone applauds! This was what Satan tried on Christ in the wilderness. . . quote a few scriptures (usually incorrectly) and many will be deceived.

Whereas Hitler, for the most part, ended the free press, ours just chose to play the game, using the "party line" to brainwash us when it came to reporting on what Clark alleges as the atrocities of the

Gulf war. Some of his stinging indictments follow:

> . . .The press rendered First Amendment protection meaning-
> less, because its wealthy owners uncritically supported the govern-
> ment as it destroyed Iraq. It barely reported dissent; when it did,
> it ridiculed, misrepresented, or marginalized those who criticized
> U.S. intervention in the Gulf. TV coverage of the Gulf crisis. . .was
> more a long-running commercial for war. . .than news reporting.
>   The media, owned by the wealthy, speaking for the plutocracy
> [Webster's definition: government by the wealthy/control by the
> wealthy], has the dual role of anesthetizing the public to prevent
> serious consideration or debate of such staggering human issues
> . . .and emotionalizing the people for aggression. . . .
>   . . .the American media, guardian of the First Amendment,
> has abandoned its ward in favor of Mammon. [Author's Note: the
> use of biblical terms is growing in popularity—I'm sure that is
> no accident.]
>   While receiving extensive coverage in the international press,
> the U.S. major media blackout of the Tribunal was almost com-
> plete. . . .

His allegations are not limited to the media; he has plenty to report
on George Bush, as well, including attempts to impeach him based
on a number of charges, not the least of which is conspiracy. (I will
paraphrase further below the speech Congressman Henry Gonzalez
from Texas made before the House of Repesentatives, calling for the
impeachment of President Bush.) First, I want you to read the letter
from Mr. Clark to President Bush, dated March 4, 1992.

Dear Mr. Bush:
    In May, 1991, you were sent an initial complaint by the Inter-
national Commission of Inquiry containing the 19 charges
against you and others of crimes against peace, war crimes, and
crimes against humanity. You were asked to submit any evidence
you wished in your own defense and invited personally or by
representative to attend any hearings and examine all evidence
against you. The Commission has since conducted hearings in
more than 20 countries with over 30 hearings in the United States
alone.
    On Saturday, February 29, 1992, in New York, the International
War Crimes Tribunal, having considered the evidence gathered
by the Commission, held the final hearing. At the conclusion of
the hearing, you were found guilty of all 19 charges. The other
defendants—Vice President Dan Quayle, Secretary of Defense

Richard Cheney, Joint Chiefs of Staff Chairman Colin Powell, former CIA director William Webster, and General H. Norman Schwarzkopf—were also found guilty of the charges against them. Enclosed is a copy of the Final Judgment of the Tribunal, a copy of the charges, and a printed list of the Tribunal Judges.

The consequences of your criminal acts include the deaths of more than 250,000 children, women, and men, mostly civilians, and the crippling of an entire country. You are held accountable by hundreds of millions of people around the world, as you will be by history. You have placed another bloody stain on the honor of your country and its people.

You must not engage in further violence, murder, and militarism. You must not let your arrogance, falsity, and hostility for the poor and the weak—all of which were aided by the silence of the media—lead you to commit further crimes.

If you have anything to say for yourself, the Commission and the Tribunal will hear you or your representative.

Sincerely,
Ramsey Clark

Here are some of the accusations he makes against Bush, most of which are valid and heretofore publicly ignored, which is why I am bothering to include Clark's efforts in my book.

. . .The people of the United States watched in general silence or outright approval as *President Bush seized absolute power* [Author's note: prior to any Congressional approval] to assault a defenseless people. . . . No dictator was ever less restrained [emphasis added].

Article I of the U.S. Constitution vests power over war and peace in the Congress. President Bush usurped these powers to wage his war. . . .

On January 9, President Bush reasserted his view that he needed no Congressional authorization to attack Iraq. He reinforced his earlier claims to presidential power with responsibilities created by UN Resolution 678. . . .

Remember, in an earlier chapter I warned you about the UN Resolution 666 (and following) which gave away our sovereignty to the control of the United Nations. That's what Bush used to take this unprecedented action of going to war without Congressional approval . . .he no longer needed it!—which he was quick to point out fervently in interviews covered on the national media when questioned about it. Clark is not the only one with this opinion of Bush's actions.

Congressman Calls for Impeachment of
President Bush—January 16, 1991

On January 16, 1991, the day President Bush ordered the bombing to begin, Congressman Henry Gonzalez of Texas spoke to the House of Representatives in a great act of individual courage, conscience, and vision:

Then he quotes the entire impeachment speech, as reported in *The Texas Observer* on January 25th. While corroborating this event, I spoke directly with personnel in the office of Congressman Gonzalez, who advised me that the facts are basically correct, but clarified one point: the Resolution as presented on January 16th contained some technical errors (primarily typos) which were corrected, whereupon the Resolution was re-submitted to the 102nd Congress in February. When I requested permission to duplicate the Resolution in my book, I was informed that there are no restrictions, as it is now a matter of public record. Their office was most helpful in this matter, and they agreed to answer any questions you may have. You may call the office of Congressman Henry Gonzalez, (202) 225-3236.

I have paraphrased the speech below, as it was reported by Ramsey Clark:

Mr. Speaker, it is with great sadness, yet with great conviction, that I introduce today a resolution of impeachment for President Bush. . . .

. . .The Iraqi people are as opposed to war as are the American people—the difference is that the Iraqi people have no choice but to support their country's leader, but the American people not only have the right to oppose and speak out in disagreement with their President, but they have the responsibility to do so if our democracy is to be preserved.

. . .I swore to uphold the Constitution. The President's oath was the same—to uphold the Constitution of the United States. We did not pledge an oath of allegiance to the President, but to the Constitution, which is the highest law of the land. The Constitution provides for removal of the President when he has committed high crimes and misdemeanors, including violation of the principles of the Constitution. President Bush has violated these principles.

My resolution has five articles of impeachment. First, the President has violated the equal protection clause of the Constitution. Our soldiers in the Middle East are overwhelmingly poor white, black, and Mexican-American.

Article II states that the President has violated the Constitution,

federal law, and the United Nations Charter by bribing, intimi-
dating, and threatening others, including the members of the
United Nations Security Council, to support belligerent acts
against Iraq. It is clear that the President paid off members of
the U.N. Security Council in return for their votes in support of
war against Iraq. [Author's Note: although two acts of conspiracy
are charged below, it seems to me that this would qualify as an
act of conspiracy, as well.]

Article III states that the President has **conspired** to engage
in a massive war against Iraq. . . .

Article IV states that the President has committed the United
States to acts of war without Congressional consent and contrary
to the United Nations Charter. . . .

Article V states that the President has **conspired** to commit
crimes against the peace by leading the United States into
aggressive war. . . in violation of. . . the Constitution of the United
States [emphasis added].

Do you remember seeing anywhere at that time that someone in
Congress was calling for the impeachment of the President? Talk
about your media blackouts!

I'm sure you all have heard the Marxist claim that religion is the
opiate of the people. Well, here is what Clark believes:

. . .The belief that governments will solve our problems may
be the *most dangerous* opiate of the people. . . [emphasis added].

As with most writers these days, Clark makes plenty of references
to Bush's New World Order.

. . .Orwell's doublespeak has become the official language of
the Pentagon. . . .

The apparent popular approval by the American people of the
destruction of Iraq is the greatest threat to the future.

Most dangerous of all, the United States in seeking a new
world. . . . Even those with short memories can see the cynicism
of this new world order, ...

. . .Millions foresaw more U.S. military actions as a principal
means to achieve the "new world order."

Yet only the morally blind will fail to see that U.S. political and
military leadership has proven itself totally untrustworthy to lead
the world to a new order.

. . .**But this is hardly a new order** [emphasis added].

Don't Be Deceived—Don't Believe the Lies
Of the New World Order

To reiterate—the Bible says if it were possible, even the elect of God would be deceived in the last days. Read Matthew 24:24-27; Mark 13:5,22; Luke 21:8—all the words of Jesus. He talks much about false Christs who would be coming in these final days, and when they do—don't follow after them, don't believe the signs and wonders they will perform, and other things. We must be on our guard; we need the renewed mind of Christ to avoid falling into the trap and believing the lie—even at that, Satan will attempt to ensnare us. Mr. Clark is a good example. He thinks he is right—he truly believes it—but he has been deceived. He has believed the lie. Study the following quotation, keeping in mind he has been firmly disavowing the New World Order (world government) throughout his book:

> . . . a brutal and deadly future is inescapable. The threat of a new world order based on technological violence and designed to control the poor for the benefit of the rich *has made organized and spontaneous worldwide effort absolutely essential for human fulfillment* [emphasis added].

In one sentence he both has decried the new world order and called for it as "absolutely essential for human fulfillment." Now, I am not talking about the "uneducated masses" here; Mr. Clark is a man of prominence, well educated, highly intelligent, and influential worldwide, yet he still does not recognize that he himself is confused and deceived. Jesus warns us multiplied times throughout the New Testament *not* to be deceived. Of course, such warnings would not be necessary if it were not possible for us actually to be deceived. I will deal more with Satan's deception as this chapter progresses, because the whole idea here is that the New World Order is a spiritual matter, and has been all along, but most have not yet recognized that fact.

Of course, there is a spiritual counterpart (or counterfeit) upon which the New World Order is founded—we call it the New Age movement. The New Age movement is the demonic world religion that ultimately will deceive the world into worshipping the leader of the New World Order as the Messiah (the Antichrist), which is specifically what Jesus warned us against in the scriptures referenced above. This book is designed to focus on the New World Order and the technological aspects that will be used to enslave us, therefore, I will not provide extensive discussion on the religion of the New Age. There presently is a wealth of material exposing the dangers of the New Age. Most Christian bookstores stock an abundance of books, videos, and cassettes/CD's by extremely knowledgeable people on the subject of the New Age, as well as other satanic deceptions. I recommend you become familiar with their content, if you currently are not aware of their infiltration into our day-to-day lives.

Will the United Nations Become The New World Order?

What about the United Nations? Is it going to evolve into the infrastructure of the New World Order? Only God knows for sure, but based on over six years of research into this matter, there is no doubt is my mind that it will. At present it couldn't accomplish that feat because it is still a collection of independently sovereign nations; whereas the New World Order eventually will relegate independent nations to the status of "world states" or "nation states," only operating under the auspices of the head of world government (Antichrist). But I believe that it is the forerunner that is laying the groundwork for the New World Order.

President Clinton Calls for a Reformed United Nations

Whether you are a Republican or a Democrat, it makes no difference to those pushing for a New World Order. We've heard a lot about George Bush, but he was not alone in his promotion of the New World Order. President Bill Clinton spoke at the 50th Anniversary Celebration of the United Nations, in San Francisco's War Memorial Opera House where President Truman signed the charter in 1946. President Clinton offered a number of telling and constructively critical remarks concerning the current status of the United Nations. He supports the organization, but believes a "reformed" U.N. would do more for the world. He urged reform of what he called a "bloated organization." "The new United Nations must peel off what doesn't work and get behind what will," Clinton said.

Writer Steve Komarow, in a June 27, 1995, issue of *USA TODAY*, reported that Clinton said the U.N. too often appears to be spending money on meetings instead of results, and that this pattern fuels U.S. critics, including some who might be supportive if they felt U.N. money was better spent. However, Clinton made it clear that he was not among those who consider the U.N. useless. Clinton recommitted the U.S. to continue to pay "its fair share" (whatever that means) of the cost of the U.N. and its so-called peacekeeping missions, and attacked those to whom he referred as "new isolationists."

It is appropriate to remind you at this point that Bill Clinton is a member of the Council on Foreign Relations (CFR), Trilateral Commission (TC), and Bilderbergers, as is George Bush, who is also a member of the Skull & Bones "Brotherhood of Death" Society. So is there really any difference between the Democrats and Republicans? Not much, since most of the top leaders of our government have joined and sworn allegiance to these New World Order clubs, irrespective of their political party—there is really only one political party in America . . . the global government New World Order party. Contrary to what Rush Limbaugh says on national "conservative" talk radio, there is no difference between the Republicans and the Democrats—it's all for one and one for all in the New World Order.

Is there a conspiracy? You figure it out!

Our New Constitution?

As I write, there are numerous calls coming in nationally for a constitutional convention to rewrite our hard-won, time-honored guardian of freedom—the U.S. Constitution, which was purchased with the blood of the patriots from 1776 to 1996. One such recent call has been termed the "Philadelphia II Con-Con" (i.e., Constitutional Convention). Another effort to redraft the U.S. Constitution was called the "New States Constitution." There are others, as well. The unseen elite behind the scenes are pushing fervently to scrap our existing Constitution because they claim that it is outmoded, outdated, inefficient, and unable to deal with the demands of the New World Order. But their ulterior motive is clearly to eliminate the Constitution because it is our safeguard, a barrier to world government, and assures our nation's sovereignty, something they cannot tolerate.

In a previous chapter, I mentioned the Constitution for the Federation of Earth, which essentially relegates the U.S. to a position of statehood in the world society of nations. This particular constitutional draft is being acclaimed globally as a viable solution to fill the alleged need for a world constitution. They have called for a fourth parliamentary meeting to ratify this global constitution, the gross falacies of which I pointed out at length in the earlier chapter.

The World Constitution and Parliament Association happily concurs with Clinton regarding the reformation of the United Nations. In fact, they are the ones who believe the U.N. won't work because it consists of a collection of as-yet sovereign nations. In June and July, 1996, they will summon delegates from all over the world to the fourth session of the Provisional World Parliament. The stated purpose of the 1996 Parliament is to make "rapid progress towards the establishment of a functioning world federation and world government under the Constitution for the Federation of Earth."

This bunch would be laughable if it weren't for the fact that so many prominent people of influence take it seriously and actively are engaged in trying to bring about its program, including placing into effect the new World Constitution. Apparently they are feeling the heat from some of you out there, because they have included one rather paranoid paragraph in their letter of invitation. I quote:

> But, please, the...meeting is only for persons who sincerely want to help, and not for detractors. In a country where armed militia and ultra right groups are rampant, some of those receiving this letter may be unfriendly to our purposes. We recognize this hazard. That is why the enclosed reply form is drawn with a committment to support and assist the achievement of our defined objective. We must depend on your word of honor in this respect.

I feel compelled to quote some more of it here.

> The importance of our global campaign may be judged in the following light: We aim to accomplish—
> - What was not accomplished by World War One;
> - What was not accomplished by World War Two;
> - What was not accomplished by the League of Nations;
> - What has not and cannot be accomplished by the United Nations;
> - What has not been accomplished by 50 years of trying to amend or strengthen the U.N.;
> - What has not been accomplished by thousands of protest demonstrations against the military system.
> We aim to accomplish enduring world peace [Author's note: don't forget the advice that was derived from the compilation of the alleged Iron Mountain Report about how to deal with absolute peace.], total disarmament of war-making capabilities, a comprehensive program to save the environment and prevent impending catastrophes from climate changes, a new world economic order designed to give everybody equitable opportunities in life, and to establish those global institutions under federal world government by which the above mentioned problems and all problems which transcend national boundaries can be solved peacefully for the good of all by applied intelligence.
> Our aim is to begin World Government soon *with more than 70% of Earth included at the start...* [emphasis added]."
> What we are creating is an immediate and practical alternative to the present chaotic, destructive, unfair, life-threatening, and unsustainable course of human affairs on Earth, in which everybody is now trapped.

There is nothing covert about this organization—they openly promote one-world-government with all power over all nations controlled by one central enforcement agency. Will this be the "baby" that grows up to be the full-blown Antichrist-controlled New World Order? Maybe—at this point there is no way to determine that, but their goals certainly meet all the requirements. For more information or to purchase copies of their materials, write to: World Constitution and Parliament Association, Inc., 1480 Hoyt Street, Suite 31, Lakewood, CO 80215. Of course, I do not advocate becoming associated with them or supporting their new constitution, but it certainly is interesting to gain insight into their plans for us in their New World Order.

These aren't the only people who are meeting to form a "more perfect" world government. Remember, I told you earlier about a meeting in San Franciso in October of 1995, where Mikhail Gorbachev, George Bush, Margaret Thatcher, Al Gore, Bill Gates, *et al,* met to discuss "the fundamental principles the world should embrace in a New World Order," as well as to formulate an international braintrust and adoption of an "Earth Charter for An Environmental Bill of Rights" dedicated to the preservation of planet earth.

Still don't believe in conspiracies?

Information Warfare in the New World Order

In spite of the philosophical ideas being espoused by the globalists, all of the things I have discussed throughout this book are possible only in the new superinformation highway that is being pushed so strongly by Vice President Al Gore, Microsoft's Bill Gates, and other globalists, especially for third-world countries that currently are outside the system. You see, realistically, there can be no global government nor cashless economic system without a computerized information infrastructure in place that can handle the massive transfer of digitized information globally to make it viable.

In a book published in 1994, also by Thunder's Mouth Press, New York, author Winn Schwartau warns us about chaos on the electronic superhighway, which is somewhat ironic, considering he is a futurist and his book is distributed by the World Future Society, a New World Order think tank. The futurists are firm believers in one-world government and liberally promote the idea of global government. Mr. Schwartau, however, is intellectually honest enough to warn us about the disadvantages of the electronic control of the world in his book, *Information Warfare.* He addresses the assault on personal privacy, national economic security, industrial espionage, solutions in cyberspace, and much more.

Robert D. Steele, former deputy director, USMC Intelligence Center, says of this book: "Winn Schwartau is the most dangerous man in America—and the most valuable. His insights into our nation's vulnerabilities to information warfare, and his solutions, are the foundation for our survival. Computer sabotage will wipe out banks, and your savings, in two days, retailers in four, and factories in seven. Our national security is at risk, and the President has not acknowledged the problem. Winn Schwartau is the Nathan Hale of the 21st Century." These are more than just glowing accolades for Mr. Schwartau—these are alarming possible accidents going somewhere to happen.

Schwartau points out that currently information warfare costs the United States an estimated $100 to $300 billion a year through industrial espionage, hackers and "cyberpunks," malicious software and "viruses," data eavesdropping, code breaking and "chipping," attacks on personal privacy, and other causes.

In his introduction to the second edition, he states, " 'Information Warfare' was intended to be a prophetic warning of things to come... but...so soon?" Then continuing from his original introduction: "This book is about how we as citizens of both the United States and Cyberspace must come to terms with our electronic destiny,...the Information Age." Then he follows by referring to the "proposed National Information Infrastructure."

> As the specter of apocalyptic global warfare recedes into the history books (and stays there!), a collective sigh of complacency is replacing the bomb-shelter hysteria.... However, as equally dangerous international economic competition supplants megaton military intimidation, offensive pugnacity will be aimed at the informational and financial infrastructure upon which our Western economy depends.
>
> The Cold War is over and has been replaced by economic warfare,....
>
> The foundation of modern society is based on the availability of an access to information.... In today's electronically interconnected world, information moves at the speed of light, is intangible, and is of immense value. Today's information is the equivalent of yesterday's factories, yet it is considerably more vulnerable.
>
> Right now, the United States is leading the world into a globally networked society, a true Information Age where information and economic value become nearly synonymous. With over 125 million computers inextricably tying us all together through complex land- and satellite-based communications systems. ...Computers and other communications and information systems become attractive first-strike targets. "...an electronic

Pearl Harbor waiting to happen. As a result of inadequate security planning on the part of both the government and the private section, *the privacy of most Americans has virtually disappeared"* [emphasis added].

In a recent study, two-thirds of Americans polled said that computer usage should be curtailed if their personal privacy was at risk.

Information Warfare is an integral component of the new economic and political world order.

In other words, my friends, the New World Order. He goes on to inform us:

Cyberspace is a brave new world. . . . A world where the power of knowledge and information usurp the strength of military might. A world totally dependent upon new high-tech tools that make information available instantaneously to anyone, anywhere, at any time. *A world where he who controls the information, controls the people. A world where electronic privacy no longer exists.* . . . A conflict which turns computers into highly effective offensive weapons [on] the electronic financial highways. . . [emphasis added].

As with any profession, the computer industry has spawned numerous buzzwords, unique to the trade. Cyberspace is one such word. Schwartau defines it as: "that intangible place between computers where information momentarily exists on its route from one end of the global network to the other. If Cyberspace is 'that place in between' the phones or the computers, then there are no borders. As we electronically project our essences across the network, we become temporary citizens of Cyberspace, just like our fellow cybernauts."

Schwartau says that in Information Warfare, Information-Age weaponry (the age in which we now are living) will replace bombs and bullets. However, these "cyber" weapons are no longer restricted to the government or the CIA or KGB—they readily are available from computer catalogs, retail stores, and trade shows. Many can be built at home from hobby parts. He continues:

. . .of course, the military is developing its own arsenal of weapons with which to wage Information Warfare.

As I mentioned briefly before, in the coming New World Order, we will be living in a cashless society, so the world economy will depend upon the successful and reliable operation of the worldwide information highway. For a worldwide society to function, the individual must be a citizen of the world. . .which means all information about each person must be in a database which can be accessed by all who need information on you (and many who don't)—again, relying upon the dependability of the worldwide computer link (information highway). And any other type of control over all aspects of life in that era will be accomplished by way of electronics, even to the extent of sorting and recording the trash that you discard (see Chapter 14 describing the system already in use in Vancouver, B.C.).

Since our whole existence will depend upon the reliability of the hardware, software, and data input operators, you can imagine what kind of damage could be done to the world society if someone decided to intentionally (or even unintentionally) create havoc within the system. That's why Schwartau calls it *warfare*. He tells us in very specific terms what all this Information Warfare is about.

> *Information Warfare is about money.* It's about the acquisition of wealth, and the denial of wealth to competitors. It breeds Information Warriors who battle across the Global Network [Author's note: This is the global network which will support the infrastructure of the New World Order.] in a game of cyberrisk.
>
> *Information Warfare is about power.* He who controls the information controls the money.
>
> *Information Warfare is about fear.* He who controls the information can instill fear in those who want to keep their secrets a secret. It's the fear that the Bank of New York felt when it found itself $23 billion short of cash in only one day. [Author's note: Of course, this is the excuse businesses are using to promote use of the new I.D. system . . .e.g., you shouldn't mind giving them your fingerprint when you cash a check unless you have something to hide.]
>
> *Information Warfare is about arrogance,* the arrogance that comes from the belief that one is committing the perfect crime.
>
> *Information Warfare is about politics.* When the German government sponsors intelligence-agency hacking against U.S. computers, the concept of "ally" needs to be redefined. Or when Iran takes aim at the U.S. economy by state-sponsored counterfeiting, we should have a glimmer that *conflict* is not what it once was. [Author's note: It begins to appear that as much havoc and chaos can be inflicted using paper and electronics, as when you use the aforementioned bullets and bombs—without the blood-letting or the expense of the machinery and armies.]
>
> *Information Warfare is about survival.* France and Israel developed their respective economies and based entire industries on stealing American secrets. Japan and Korea purloin American technology as it comes off the drawing boards with the help of their governments.

Information Warfare is about defiance and disenfranchisement in both modern and Third World societies. From the inner cities of Cyberspace come fringe-element hackers with nothing to lose. Some will band together to form Cyberspace's gangs, Cyberspace's organized crime. They recognize the economic benefits of waging Information Warfare. [A New York bank recently lost $400,000 to a European team of hackers—who would have gotten away clean if they hadn't gotten greedy. They came back for another several million dollars and got caught in the act. They currently are fighting extradition to the U.S. for prosecution.]

Information Warfare is about the control of information. As a society we maintain less and less control as Cyberspace expands and *electronic anarchy reigns.* Given global conditions of the late 1980s and 1990s, *Information Warfare is inevitable.* Today's planet offers ripe conditions for Information Warfare, conditions which could not have been foreseen even a few short years ago.

The threat of a future computer Chernobyl is not an empty one. It is only a question of who and when. [Emphasis added.]

It is my opinion that such a "digital Chernobyl" is intentionally planned in order to create the necessary international "emergency" needed to force the reorganization required to initiate the new world economic order of electronic enslavement, or "cyberprison" under "cybersocialists."

Schwartau goes on to tell us that anyone with an agenda and an attitude can wage Information Warfare, at three distinct levels of intensity: personal, corporate, and global.

Can you guess what would happen if you suffered "Cyber-death"? "Electronic murder in Cyberspace, and you are *gone!* He has much to say about personal warfare, and *most of it is bad!* And he refers frequently to the "digital you," which is what we have become on the super information highway.

There is no such thing as electronic privacy. The essence of our very being is distributed across thousands of computers and data bases over which we have little or no control. From credit reports to health records, from Department of Motor Vehicles computers to court records to video rentals, from law enforcement computers to school transcripts to debit card purchases, from insurance profiles to travel histories to our personal bank finances, everything we do and have done is recorded somewhere in a digital repository.

The sad fact is that these very records which define us as an individual remain unprotected, subject to malicious modification, unauthorized disclosure, or out-and-out destruction. Social

Security Administration employees have sold our innermost secrets for twenty-five dollars per name. Worse yet, as of today, there is nothing you can do to protect the digital you. You are not given the option or the opportunity to keep yourself and your family protected from electronic invasions of your privacy.

Your life can be turned absolutely upside down if the digital you ceases to exist. Electronic murder in Cyberspace: You are just gone. Try proving you're alive; computers don't lie. Or if the picture of the digital you is electronically redrawn just the right way, a prince can become a pauper in microseconds. In Cyberspace, you are guilty until proven innocent.

The corporate information systems don't fare any better; in fact, they have much more at stake than individuals, on an economic level. Schwartau says:

... diligence in weighing the risks associated with placing our entire faith on a technical infrastructure remains in short supply.

As we shall see, the federal government must shoulder much of the blame for our current posture. In fact, it is often not in the government's best interest to assist us in *protecting* our computers and networks.

Now isn't that a surprise—I *wonder* why!?! They claim they will protect our privacy rights...they know what is best for us. I am reminded of that priceless classic line from the musical, *The King and I.* When faced with the possibility of Siam becoming a British protectorate, the king exclaimed, "Might they not protect me out of all I own?!" Without a doubt! Schwartau continues:

Their noncommittal attitudes have even harmed efforts now under way to enhance personal privacy and commercial national economic security.

Nonetheless, inane antique policies continue unabated, and in some cases, overt attempts on the part of the federal government have further undermined the electronic privacy of every American citizen. Even President Clinton's proposal to address personal privacy and protect American businesses was met with nearly universal derision, suspicion, and doubt. No matter how hard they try, politicians just don't get it.

Since the subject of this book is the one-world government theme, presently called the New World Order, we should be interested particularly in what Schwartau has to say about Information Warfare on a global scale. He says that all branches of our government are missing the point—they have not yet realized that " . . . [information] is a vital national asset." He continues:

> . . .they miss the fundamental concepts behind the New World Order, the National Information Infrastructure, and our place in the econotechnical Global Network.
> . . .Information. . .is intangible and does not have an immediately quantifiable monetary worth—unless you lose it. Then it costs a great deal more than you ever thought.
> . . .We must take off the blinders and accept—not deny—that *the New World Order is full of bad guys* as well as good guys. . . [emphasis added].

In much of his material, Schwartau refers to the "nation-states." It is very apparent that he believes we will be in a world-government situation. . .and soon, and since he refers to it frequently as the New World Order, I am inferring that he believes that's what it will be. He asks the questions: ". . .why will information warfare be fought?" and "Is it a foregone conclusion?" Then proceeds to tell us.

> The incredibly rapid proliferation of high-quality, high-performance electronic information systems have created the Global Network—Cyberspace—thus redefining how we conduct business. Not only did business and government buy into technology, but tens of millions of individuals were, within less than a decade, suddenly empowered with tools and capabilities previously limited to a select few. The comparatively simple technology required for Information Warfare is universally available. Technological anarchy is the result.
> The Global Network is a historically unprecedented highway system that defies nationalism and borders. *It places the keys to the kingdom, to our wealth, and our digital identity, within equal reach of everyone with a computer* [emphasis added].

Have I made my case?! Do you understand why in the banner above the title on the front of this book I announced: "The Cashless Economic System of **Global Electronic Enslavement** is Ready Now!"? Can you also envision how easily a global dictator could commandeer Cyberspace and control every aspect of our lives, including our "buying and selling," as described in Revelation 13:16-18?

When Jesus told us about all those signs for which we should watch, signaling that the end of the age was near, one of them was that "knowledge would increase." However, knowledge always has increased, as one generation passes on to the next what it has learned, creating cumulative knowledge, so how does that differ from the knowledge that will indicate the end of the age? I am told that taken in context, in the original Greek, it is implied that it really means *knowledge would increase exponentially*. In that case, this expansion of knowledge—just in the last decade—certainly would add to the other evidence of rapidly increasing knowledge in these days and fulfill at least that one prophecy.

I think by now you have grasped the importance of what is happening. . .everything about everything and everyone is in some computer, and the security stinks! Yet this is the infrastructure that will run the New World Order.

The book is by Winn Schwartau and is entitled *Information Warfare*, published by Thunder's Mouth Press, New York, ISBN 1-56025-088-7. Please keep in mind that I don't agree with much of Mr. Schwartau's philosophy, as he is a futurist who supports one-world government and all that goes with it, and his book is distributed by the World Future Society. But as I told you earlier, he is intellectually honest enough to point out what is inherently wrong with the system, as it pertains to the Information Age, and I certainly recommend you get this 432-page book and read it carefully. . .all the way through.

The Noahide Laws—Could These Be the Foundation for Capital Punishment in The New World Order?

Revelation 13:15-18 (quoted in the beginning of this chapter) calls for capital punishment for failure to **worship** the beast (Antichrist) or to accept his **mark**. Then in Revelation 20:4, we learned that the prescribed method of execution was decapitation/beheading.

I have spent this entire book laying the foundation for what I'm about to tell you, and giving you an overview of what the New World Order is politically, economically, and spiritually. I have attempted, hopefully successfully, to convey from a secular viewpoint (though I make no apology for the fact that I believe it fulfills prophecy in the Bible) how God's scripture is being fulfilled in our time. I have told you about electronic enslavement, biometrics, smart card identification on a global scale, which it appears ultimately will evolve into use of biochip technology *in our right hands* to totally enslave us. I have given you scriptures to tie it all to the fulfillment of Bible prophecy, i.e., you cannot participate in any of the world's activities without the **mark**, once the Antichrist takes command of the New World Order. And I have told you what will happen if you decline the offer of this Satanic **mark** (probably a biochip).

By now it should be apparent that this is all adding up to a spiritual choice—you will be required to *worship* this world dictator as god. The punishment for rejection will be swift and final—execution by decapitation. Now, in recent years, this has not been the form of capital punishment in practice, *but it will be*, if for no other reason than because the Bible says it will be. However, the Antichrist isn't likely to do anything recommended by the Bible—at least not intentionally. So we must have some foundation for switching back to this ancient form of execution, if the Bible prophecy is to be fulfilled as written. I believe we now may have such a foundation in place.

During Bush's administration, shortly before the Gulf war, an innocuous-sounding little piece of legislation was signed into law, allegedly to honor an old man on his ninetieth birthday. H.J. Res. 104 was signed into law as a proclamation to designate March 26, 1991, as "Education Day, U.S.A." Sounds innocent enough, doesn't it? Not so! Written into all the "WHEREAS's" were incorporated a number of references calling for the return to the ethical values of the Seven Noahide Laws. Now, you won't find any call for decapitation in this harmless appearing little document, but beware, that's just a smoke screen. When one begins to dig into the historical documents of the ancient Jewish Talmud with reference to the Noahide Laws, you will find the commandments they consider ethical values, and what they consider just punishment for breaking them . . . guess what, you lose your head!

Now, we don't want anyone to jump to any wild conclusions, because the law has no apparent "teeth" in it yet, as there is no prescribed punishment for violation of it—**the government did not call for the establishment of capital punishment by decapitation**, but by joint resolution of the House and the Senate it did establish Public Law No. 102-14 (published in the *United States Statutes at Large* containing the laws and concurrent resolutions enacted during the first session of the One Hundred Second Congress of the United States of America, 1991, and Proclamations, Vol. 105, Part 1, Public Laws 102-1 through 102-150), which calls for the return to the ethics of the Noahide Laws. I don't think it's too much of a stretch to extrapolate this into fulfillment of scripture, **once the Antichrist comes into power**. I believe the foundation has been placed into Law.

However, once the Antichrist comes to power, whether or not a foundation has been laid will become a moot point . . . he will be an absolute dictator, and if you don't worship him and take **his mark**, you'll lose your head! Because one of the Seven Noahide Laws concerns blasphemy, Christians who refuse to worship the beast likely could be executed under the violation of the blasphemy law, as they will not acknowledge the Antichrist as God.

I want to cite the Seven Noahide Laws, as defined in *The New Standard Jewish Encyclopedia,* Doubleday & Co., Inc., New York, 1977.

LAWS OF NOAH: Seven laws which the rabbis hold binding

upon all mankind, derived from early chapters of Gen. (e.g. 9:4-7). Six of these laws are negative, prohibiting idolatry, blasphemy, murder, adultery, robbery, and the eating of flesh cut from a living animal. The single positive commandment is that requiring the establishment of courts of justice. The "Noachian Laws" were much discussed by European scholars in the 17th cent. in connection with the Law of Nations.

These seven laws are again defined in *The Jewish Encyclopedia,* KTAV Publishing House, Inc., p. 648-9, followed by the prescribed punishment.

LAWS, NOACHIAN:

(1) not to worship idols; (2) not to blaspheme the name of God; (3) to establish courts of justice; (4) not to kill; (5) not to commit adultery; and (6) not to rob. . . .

. . .the prevalent opinion in the Talmud is that there are only seven laws which are binding upon all mankind. . . .

In the elaboration of these seven Noachian laws, and in assigning punishments for their transgression, the Rabbis are sometimes more lenient and sometimes more rigorous with Noachidae [non-Jews] than with Israelites. With but a few exceptions, the punishment meted out to a Noachid for the transgression of any of the seven laws is **decapitation**, the least painful of the four modes of execution of criminals. The many formalities of procedure essential when the accused is an Israelite *need not be observed in the case of the Noachid.* The latter may be convicted on the testimony of *one witness,* even on that of relatives, but not on that of a woman. He need have had no warning from the witnesses; and a *single judge* may pass sentence on him . . . [emphasis added].

There are numerous other references to both the seven laws and their prescribed punishment in other works.

Under these laws, would Christians be considered guilty of violating the blasphemy law, because they believe that Jesus, the Christ, is God manifest in the flesh? (You may recall that Jesus was tried for blasphemy because he claimed to be the Son of God.) Who knows at this time what the real ulterior motive of these laws might be.

As we make a cursory examination of the laws, we don't see anything blatantly objectionable. In fact, we encourage efforts to improve the ethical conduct in our nation. But I must tell you. . .there is more to this than can be seen from a cursory examination.

In the July-August, 1991, issue of *The Gap,* the newsletter published by the Noahide movement, the lead article revealed that there is pressure being applied for world-wide recognition of the seven laws. Professor of International Law Ernest Easterly, at Southern University Law Center, said: "With further recognition by other nations and international courts, **the Seven Noahide Laws should become the cornerstone of a truly civilized international legal order.**" *Read that: New World Order!*

My main goal here is to bring to your attention something about which few Americans are aware. I don't profess to have any supernatural insight as to what unseen forces may have propelled George Bush and the Congress to bring forth this kind of national law, but given my biblical insight regarding last days' prophetic events, I am extremely suspicious regarding why such a law may have been wanted in the first place. Could we now be seeing the beginning of the legal basis for future capital punishment by decapitation? There seems to be no apparent reason why such a law might be useful at this time, other than furthering the agenda of the New World Order advocates. However, since the Bible says that anyone who refuses to take the Antichrist's mark will be beheaded (decapitated), this very well could be the case. What do you think?

Postscript

I have some late-breaking news to share on this subject. Just prior to press deadline, I received information about some legislation before the State of Georgia proposing that execution by guillotine be offered as an alternative option for convicts sentenced to the death penalty. But the reason is strictly humanitarian, at least so they would have us believe. One article reads:

Guillotine Proposed as Means of Execution in Georgia
Georgia lawmaker Doug Teper (Democrat, 61st Dist.) has proposed a bill to replace the state's electric chair with the guillotine. Teper's reasoning? It would allow for death-row inmates as organ donors, he says, since the "blade makes a clean cut and leaves vital organs intact...."

The guillotine, invented by the French Dr. Guillotine, was mainly used in the 18th and 19th century and chops off a person's head. It hasn't been used for decades in any country in the world.

Excerpts from Georgia's legislation H.B. No. 1274 follow:

BE IT ENACTED BY THE GENERAL ASSEMBLY OF GEORGIA:
SECTION 1: The General Assembly finds that while prisoners condemned to death may wish to donate one or more of their organs for transplant, any such desire is thwarted by the fact that

electrocution makes all such organs unsuitable for transplant. The intent of the General Assembly in enacting this legislation is to provide for a method of execution which is compatible with the donation of organs by a condemned prisoner.

SECTION 2(a): All persons who have been convicted of a capital offense and have imposed upon them a sentence of death shall, at the election of the condemned, suffer such punishment either by electrocution or by guillotine. If the condemned fails to make an election by the thirtieth day preceding the date scheduled for execution, punishment shall be by electrocution.

SECTION 3: The Department of Corrections shall provide a death chamber and all necessary apparatus, machinery, and appliances for inflicting the penalty of death by electrocution or by guillotine.

SECTION 4: This Act shall be applicable to all executions occurring on or after August 31, 1996.

Of course, it contains all the necessary legalese to change and/or replace old laws and initiate the new policy, but the above gives you the "nuts and bolts" of the Act as proposed by "Doug 'Heads Will Roll' Teper," as he is called. Tabloids have had a field day with this Bill. The legislation failed to pass, but rest assured, you have not seen the last of such attempts. . .*The Bible says so!*.

Conspiracy Theories Grow

After the unfortunate 1995 Oklahoma City bombing tragedy, the government and liberal media began a barrage of propaganda against all fundamentalist Christians, conservatives, conservative talk-show hosts, patriots, *et al,* labeling them as extremists, ultra right-wing fanatics, "militia types," and/or armed and dangerous. It was as if they suddenly became "enemies of the state," as it were, for no other reason than their opposition to excessive government controls. Aren't you a little suspicious as to why one criminal (allegedly McVeigh) perpetrated an isolated event, and thereafter, the government began branding most conservatives and patriots as potential terrorists and/or fanatics who should be feared by the populace at large? Anyone (and anyone affiliated with them) who was opposed to the alleged conspiracy to subject the U.S. to a UN-controlled world government automatically was considered one of the above-mentioned radicals, and potentially dangerous. It almost seemed as though the government were waiting for such an opportunity so that it could castigate all opponents of the New World Order system. Suddenly, all who opposed global government became suspect in their minds. The dissenters were labeled as "anti-government" by President Bill Clinton.

The media joined right in with hundreds of articles maligning anyone who fit *their* description of **extremist!** One such media accusation on the front page of *The Detroit News and Free Press,* dated Saturday, April 29, 1995, conveys just such a message. This article reports the facts quite accurately, however, they inevitably put their own liberal spin on the material, apparently in an effort to defame or discredit anyone who believes the facts as stated. Unfortunately, even though McHugh's report technically was accurate, some of the people he quoted have made several incorrect assumptions regarding biochip technology. I have addressed this misinformation in Chapter 15 of this book.

Actually, this one article makes reference to George Bush's introduction of the term New World Order, which he subsequently used over 200 times in public addresses. But even the media in general has admitted that no one fully understood what he meant by the use of that term. His frequent use of the term is what awakened many conservatives and patriots to its imminent approach.

This newspaper article also discussed **Pat Robertson**'s 1991 book, *The New World Order.* In the article, reporter David McHugh accuses Robertson of "parroting the classic conspiracy theory, complete with Illuminati and Freemasons." McHugh says that Robertson claims the Gulf War was a ploy to get Americans to accept United Nations' rule. I fully agree with Pat Robertson and his view, and his book is excellent. I highly recommend you read it. Pat Robertson is no fool, and he is no religious extremist. In fact, he is a highly educated man with a law degree from Yale University, coincidentally Bush's alma mater. He is most articulate and an extremely reliable source of trustworthy research.

I will close my comments on conspiracies by pointing out that Clinton's remarks (above), labeling dissenters as "anti-government," are extremely hypocritical. Isn't it interesting that Bill Clinton, himself, started out as an anti-government "protester" of sorts in his youth. Rumor has it that he went to liberal/socialist colleges in England, avoiding participation in the Vietnam war, that he denounced the United States government, and that he visited Communist Russia for unknown reasons when it was still considered the "evil empire." He admittedly smoked marijuana (though he claimed he "never inhaled") —what a joke!), and now one of his ex-partners in adultery, Jennifer Flowers, has stated in a media interview that he used cocaine when they were together. Further, in 1994 (and following) the Clintons were under investigation for fraud and other crimes. And this man has the audacity to label Christians and conservatives as "anti-government dark forces which may need to be purged." What hypocrisy! Government propaganda has turned the tables on us now. . .where they used to accuse us of seeing everything as a conspiracy, now they see us as the conspirators.

Possible Scenario to Usher in the New World Order

Based on over seven years' of research, having read over 300 books, mountains of periodicals and technical product brochures, occultic newsletters, and various New Age and Masonic publications, I feel I have gained an incredibly good understanding into the mindset of Satan's people who wish to bring about this New World Order. I will attempt to convey to you a *possible* scenario that could occur in the next few years to bring about world government under the Antichrist. I want to make it absolutely clear that I am not prophesying—I do not consider myself a prophet in the biblical sense, however, the knowledge I have accrued during these seven years gives considerable credibility to my conjectures concerning these events.

The Luciferians, who desire a New World Order under the devil, often use a little-known Latin phrase that describes how they intend to bring it all about. That phrase is *ordo ab chao*. *Ordo ab chao* means "order from chaos." In other words, they purposely plan to create more than enough chaos in the world to convince us that we need a New World Order to fix it. The Book of Daniel says that the Antichrist will first come as a peacemaker, and "by peace he shall destroy many." So even though many wars and rumors of wars are occurring around the world presently, it's going to get worse, because the devil has to terrify the world into needing a worldwide peacemaker to bring order out of chaos. As this book goes to press, we are hearing the sabers rattle in Korea, Bosnia, and many other places. Frankly, I believe that in the not-too-distant future both Bosnia and Korea will present the Antichrist with the chaos he needs to pull this off. Both Bosnia and Korea could explode soon into "horrifying quagmires" that will call for a complete mobilization of U.S. Armed Forces to help quell the planned disorder. . .under the command of the United Nations, of course! There even could be a **limited** nuclear war, utilizing small atomic weapons. Such a nuclear conflagration—unheard of since World War II—would terrify the world into thinking that it was on the very precipice of Armageddon (even though *actual* Armageddon will be several years after the Antichrist comes to power). The world, then, would need a world government under a charismatic, global leader (the Antichrist) to restore order and create peace from chaos.

In addition to the war chaos scenario presented above, Satan's people also could create an international financial disaster—an economic cataclysm the likes of which the world never has seen—creating havoc around the globe that is unparalleled in history. Among other possibilities, additional chaos could be created as a result of an information "meltdown," created either by terrorists or others. As Winn Schwartau suggested in his book *Information Warfare,* quoted extensively above, an informational "Chernobyl" is inevitable—it's just a matter of where and when. As a result, virtually everyone's wealth will be wiped out over night—not difficult in a cashless society! Banks will close and circumstances will be desperate, even worse than the Great Depression of the 1930's, through which our parents lived. People will be reduced to poverty and will be dependent totally upon the government for subsistance. Money, food, medical assistance, and other benefits will be used to make people gratefully submit to the government's plan to resolve this and other global crises.

Dr. Henry Kissinger, a new world order "lieutenant," was quoted several years ago as saying that what the world really needed to make it realize that world government was necessary, was an outside threat of some kind. He postulated that a UFO alien invasion might be such a world-unifying threat (again, I hear echoes from Iron Mountain). He further stated that when confronted by this threat, the people of the world gladly would relinquish their national sovereignty and individual rights to receive protection from the UN-led world government against these "invaders." So, based on this insight from Mr. Kissinger, I surmise that in addition to war chaos, economic cataclysm, and other disastrous events, such as natural disasters, i.e. floods, hurricanes, earthquakes, volcanic eruptions, etc., we also may be confronted with a demonic manifestation in the form of a UFO invasion. New Agers contend that the "aliens" are poised and ready to make intervention into the affairs of mankind at just the right time to "save us from ourselves." And they widely believe that such events may occur near the year 2000.

By this time, advanced technology probably will have moved us forward to the point that our smart cards already have been replaced by a more positive, unalterable means of permanent identification (biochip implants—see Chapter 15). But until then, we are being preconditioned to accept such technology by means of routine use of biochip identification of animals, as well as an imminent national ID card—probably based on the current military MARC card. Keep in mind that I described the function of the MARC card in Chapter 14, and how it might possibly evolve first into a national citizen ID card, then eventually into a very personal, implantable ID biochip. Eventually, as citizens of the world, as well as members of nation-states, we will be required to accept a new system of international identification, the **MARK/MARC of the New World Order**, which likely will be the

mark of the beast described in the Book of Revelation. Since Revelation 13:16 calls for this **"mark"** to be placed either in the right **hand** or in the forehead, it is significant that we find the following in an article by Donald R. Richards, CPP, titled "ID Technology Faces the Future," which appeared in the April, 1994, edition of *Security Management* magazine, discussing biometric identification methods, which states:

> Since users are likely to be clothed from head to toe, the identification decision must be based on the **hands** or the **head**. . . .

This is specifically what the Bible calls for. . . now we know why! This is the first time in history that such ideas are being postulated and the technology is available to carry them out.

Ramifications of Accepting the Mark of The New World Order

Though I quoted it at the beginning of this chapter, it bears repeating here at the close of the chapter. In Revelation 14:9-11, we read:

> And the third angel followed them, saying with a loud voice, If any man worship the beast and his image, and receive his **mark** in his forehead, or in his **hand**, The same shall drink of the wine of the wrath of God, which is poured out without mixture into the cup of his indignation; and he shall be tormented with fire and brimstone in the presence of the holy angels, and in the presence of the Lamb: And the smoke of their torment ascendeth up for ever and ever: and they have no rest day nor night, who worship the beast and his image, and whosoever receiveth the **mark** of his name.

It is also important to repeat that neither the smart card, MARC card, national ID card, nor implantable biochip, in and of themselves, are in fact **THE mark** (of the beast), although some technically advanced form of the biochip seems the most likely contender to meet the requirements. You can't go to hell by accident, nor can someone send you there. Receiving this mark will be a conscious choice, as reiterated in the scripture above, because you must both **worship** the beast AND **receive his mark**. Acceptance or refusal of this economic mark of the beast will determine whether you may buy or sell (or receive government services and/or benefits) in the New World Order. It will be the economic coercion by which people will be forced to join Satan's Antichrist-led world system. In addition to preventing you from buying or selling, there will be severe punishment for refusing to worship the beast and rejecting his mark; as documented earlier, you will forfeit your head. (The foundation for such a method of capital punishment was laid earlier in this chapter.) The Antichrist will not physically force people to receive his mark, but he will "cause" them to receive the mark—because the consequences are extremely stringent—they will be excluded from transacting any business in his global, cashless, world economic order and ultimately be martyred if they continue to refuse to worship him. I know I've told you all this before, but it is so crucial I must tell it again.

Choosing the Right New World Order

The drive toward a New World Order continues. Jesus predicted a time of terrible judgment, so bad that if God did not intervene, there would be no flesh left on the earth (Matt. 24:22). Someday Jesus *will* return, and when He does, He *will* establish His reign on the earth for a thousand years (Rev. 20:6). This will be God's New World Order promised throughout the Bible. The time to choose which New World Order is for you is **now**, before the time for choices is past. Satan's counterfeit is near at hand and, according to Joel 3:9-12, millions will perish during his cruel reign; however, Jesus, the Savior, invites you to receive His grace and forgiveness instead, and rejoice in His New World Order forever.

No one can serve two masters; that is a biblical admonition, but you know it to be true from everyday experience. Two other scriptures warn us to "choose you this day whom you will serve" and that "today is the day of salvation." Those are easy to interpret. . .the choice is ours—don't wait until it is too late to make it; and today is the only day we have to accept the Lord's offer of salvation, since none of us have any guarantee of tomorrow.

In spite of New Age propaganda to the contrary, there are really only two choices: The Son of the one true God, The Lord Jesus Christ —or Satan, the fallen father of lies, the Antichrist, the false god, whose number (according to scripture) is 666! God said in the Old Testament: I set before you this day life and death—choose life! I also urge you to *choose life!* Not only are the rewards "out of this world," but you can escape God's judgment for rejecting his Son (described as taking the mark of the Antichrist in Rev. 14:11).

The Bible promises that all who have received Jesus Christ as their Savior and Lord will be saved from the coming wrath of God on a Christ-rejecting, God-hating world. Yes, you, too, can escape the coming New World Order horror by making Christ your Lord and Savior today. Don't procrastinate, do it now. Worship Jesus Christ, not the **Anti**christ. All it takes on your part is a sincere invitation (it's usually called a prayer), then Jesus does the part He promised. . .He washes you clean by His shed blood, welcomes you into God's family, and becomes your Savior. This is not *religion,* it's a *relationship.* Once you have established the relationship with Jesus by asking Him to become your Savior (an immediate transaction), then proceed to make Him the *Lord* of your life . . . seek to pattern your life after His example, described in the Bible, and seek His direction for your life. He has promised never to leave us nor forsake us. Then tell someone about this new relationship. The Bible says that you must believe in your heart and confess with your mouth—you can think of it as confirming the transaction.

Of course, being spiritually prepared is the most important thing, but you might give consideration to preparing in the natural, as well, i.e., store extra food, acquire some precious metals, etc., because some very precarious times lie ahead of us.

Jesus said, "Surely I come quickly." To which we respond, **"Even so, come, Lord Jesus."**

May God bless you and keep you in the days ahead.